Territorial Party Politics in Western Europe

Also by Wilfried Swenden

FEDERALISM AND SECOND CHAMBERS: Regional Representation in Parliamentary Federations: The Australian Senate and German Bundesrat Compared

FEDERALISM AND REGIONALISM IN WESTERN EUROPE: A Comparative and Thematic Analysis

90 0805420 6

7 Day

University of Plymouth Library
Subject to status this item may be renewed
via your Voyager account
http://voyager.plymouth.ac.uk
Tel: (01752) 232323

Territorial Party Politics in Western Europe

Edited by

Wilfried Swenden
Lecturer in Politics
University of Edinburgh, UK

and

Bart Maddens
Associate Professor of Political Science
Catholic University of Leuven, Belgium

First published 2009 by
PALGRAVE MACMILLAN

Palgrave Macmillan in the UK is an imprint of Macmillan Publishers Limited,
registered in England, company number 785998, of Houndmills, Basingstoke,
Hampshire RG21 6XS.

Palgrave Macmillan in the US is a division of St Martin's Press LLC,
175 Fifth Avenue, New York, NY 10010.

Palgrave Macmillan is the global academic imprint of the above companies
and has companies and representatives throughout the world.

Palgrave® and Macmillan® are registered trademarks in the United States,
the United Kingdom, Europe and other countries.

ISBN-13: 978-0-230-52162-9   hardback
ISBN-10: 0-230-52162-2   hardback

This book is printed on paper suitable for recycling and made from fully
managed and sustained forest sources. Logging, pulping and manufacturing
processes are expected to conform to the environmental regulations of the
country of origin.

A catalogue record for this book is available from the British Library.

Library of Congress Cataloging-in-Publication Data

Territorial party politics in Western Europe / [edited by] Wilfried
    Swenden and Bart Maddens.
      p. cm.
    Includes bibliographical references and index.
    ISBN 978-0-230-52162-9
    1. Political parties—Europe, Western. 2. Europe, Western—Politics
    and government. I. Swenden, Wilfried. II. Maddens, Bart.

    JN94.A979T44 2009
    324.2094—dc22   2008030662

10   9   8   7   6   5   4   3   2   1
18 17 16 15 14 13 12 11 10 09

Printed and bound in Great Britain by
CPI Antony Rowe, Chippenham and Eastbourne

Contents

Tables

Figures

Acknowledgements

The genesis of this book goes back to 2002, when its editors were successful in obtaining parallel research grants from the Flemish Fund of Scientific Research (Grant nr.G.0107.03) and the University of Leuven Research Council (Grant nr. OT/02/12). These grants allowed us to study the organizational and campaign strategies of statewide parties in the UK and Spain, and covered the full cost of two doctoral candidates, Elodie Fabre and Liselotte Libbrecht, who have been central to the success of this project. The grants also enabled us to organize two research workshops in which our findings could be tested against the expertise of some of the leading European scholars in the field. We wish to thank the Flemish Fund of Scientific Research and the University of Leuven Research Council for their support, without which much of what is presented here, and the organization of both workshops, would not have been possible.

In the autumn of 2004 Wilfried Swenden exchanged his (temporary) post-doctoral research fellowship in Leuven for a lectureship in Edinburgh. He became part of a dynamic territorial politics group, headed by Charlie Jeffery. A former director of the ESRC Program on Devolution and Constitutional Change, Charlie was instrumental in inviting some prominent scholars to Edinburgh for a first workshop in October 2005. Apart from those listed in this volume, the workshop was also attended by Daniele Caramani and Nicola McEwen. Without Charlie's contacts it may not have been possible to persuade everyone invited to attend, let alone to submit a chapter afterwards. A second authors' workshop took place in Leuven in February 2007 to fine-tune the chapters presented in Edinburgh. We wish to thank Elodie Fabre and Liselotte Libbrecht for assisting us in the organization of both workshops. Elodie has also been of much help during the final editing stages of the book (especially in carrying out some time-consuming and admittedly unpleasant jobs such as checking consistency in style, the accuracy of the bibliography, and compiling lists of tables, figures and abbreviations). We also thank Robertas Pogorelis, who worked on this project as a postdoctoral researcher during its first year.

The progress of this book had its usual ups and downs. Irina Ştefuriuc merits a special word of thanks for producing a high-quality chapter at relatively short notice. Yet, in the end, everyone delivered and all deserve our appreciation, all the more so since we are practising political science in an era when universities and research councils seem to downplay the added value of edited collections and put their faith in journals and impact factors instead. We thank commissioning editors Alison Howson and Gemma d'Arcy Hughes for their sustained patience, and hope it has been worth the wait.

Several contributors have acknowledged the financial support of research councils. Although this support is also acknowledged in separate endnotes to each chapter, it is worthy also of a mention here. Jonathan Hopkin acknowledges the support of the ESRC grant number L219252105 under the ESRC 'Devolution and Constitutional Change Programme'. Jonathan Bradbury acknowledges research conducted in the project 'Party Candidate Procedures and Characteristics at the 1999 Scottish Parliament and Welsh Assembly Elections' with the assistance of ESRC grant number L3227253004.

Last but not least, the editors wish to thank their life companions, who continue to show us their appreciation and dedication by putting up with our occasional absences in front of the home computer.

Edinburgh and Leuven,
21 April 2008

List of Contributors

Jonathan Bradbury is Senior Lecturer in Politics at the University of Swansea. His interests are territorial politics, devolution, multilevel politics, political parties, public policy and British politics. He recently edited *Devolution, Regionalism and Regional Development, the UK Experience* and has published articles in *Parliamentary Affairs, Regional and Federal Studies,* the *British Journal of Politics and International Relations* and *Publius*.

Klaus Detterbeck is Research Fellow at the Institut für Politikwissenschaft of the Otto-von-Guericke-Universität Magdeburg. He conducts research on political parties, federalism and multilevel politics, and has published in the *Jahrbuch Föderalismus, Party Politics* and *European Urban and Regional Studies*.

Kris Deschouwer is Professor of Political Science at the Vrije Universiteit Brussel. He has published widely on political parties, elections, consociational democracy and federalism. He has recently edited *Politics Beyond the State* (with M. Theo Jans) and *New Parties in Government*, and has published articles in *European Political Science, West European Politics, European Urban and Regional Studies* and *Regional and Federal Studies*. He is co-editor of the *European Journal of Political Research*.

Elodie Fabre is Research Fellow at the Centre for Political Research of the Katholieke Universiteit Leuven. Her research interests include comparative politics, party politics and British and Spanish politics. She has published in *West European Politics, Res Publica, Regional and Federal Studies* and the *European Journal of Political Research* (forthcoming).

Jonathan Hopkin is Senior Lecturer in Comparative Politics at the London School of Economics and Political Science and Associate Fellow at the Johns Hopkins Bologna Center. He has published articles on Spanish politics, political parties, political economy and corruption, in a number of journals, among which the *European Journal of Political Research, Party Politics, Political Studies* and *West European Politics*.

Dan Hough is Senior Lecturer in Politics at the University of Essex. His interests include German politics, post-communist politics, and political corruption. He has published monographs on German politics, most recently *The Left Party in Contemporary German Politics* (with Michael Koss and Jonathan Olsen). He co-edited *Devolution and Electoral Politics* with Charlie Jeffery and has published articles in *Party Politics, Regional and Federal Studies* and *German Politics*.

Charlie Jeffery is Professor of Politics at the University of Edinburgh. He was Director of the ESRC's research programme on Devolution and Constitutional Change. His main interests are German politics and electoral behaviour at the regional level. Recent publications include special issues on multilevel electoral competition in *European Urban and Regional Studies* (with Dan Hough), on the territorial finance in *Regional and Federal Studies* (with David Heald) and on devolution in the UK in *Publius*. He is managing editor of *Regional and Federal Studies*.

Michael Koß is Research Fellow at the Department of Politics and International Relations of the University of Oxford. His research interests include party finance, German politics and party politics. He co-authored *The Left Party in Contemporary German Politics*, wrote chapters on the Linkspartei and published articles in *Journal of Elections, Public Opinion and Parties, Zeitschrift für Politikwissenschaft* and *German Politics*.

Liselotte Libbrecht is Research Fellow at the Centre for Political Research of the Katholieke Universiteit Leuven. Her research interests are party politics, multilevel politics, electoral behaviour and Spanish politics. She is carrying out research on the manifestos of statewide parties in a multilevel context and has published in the *European Journal of Political Research* (forthcoming).

Bart Maddens is Associate Professor of Political Science at the Katholieke Universiteit Leuven, where he chairs the Centre for Political Research. He conducts research on elections, electoral behaviour, national identity and Belgian and Spanish politics. He regularly contributes to the debate on Belgian politics and regionalism in the media. His research has been published in *Electoral Studies, West European Politics*, the *European Journal of Political Research, Political Psychology* and the *Journal of Ethnic and Migration Studies*.

Enric Martínez-Herrera is a García-Pelayo Fellow at the Centro de Estudios Políticos y Constitucionales in Madrid. He has been a visiting scholar at the Katholieke Universiteit Leuven and a Fulbright postdoctoral fellow at the University of Maryland. He has contributed to edited volumes on nationalism and ethnic conflict, especially in Spain, and published articles in the *European Journal of Political Research* and the *International Journal on Multicultural Societies*.

Mónica Méndez Lago is Senior Lecturer of Political Science at the University of Murcia. She is currently on leave at the Centro de Investigaciones Sociológicas in Madrid, where she is Research Director. Her main research interests are party politics, electoral behaviour and federalism, which have been the main subjects of her publications.

Irina Ştefuriuc is a researcher in the Department of Political Science of the Vrije Universiteit Brussel. Her publications include book chapters and articles on government formation in *Party Politics*, and she has edited a special issue of *Regional and Federal Studies*.

Wilfried Swenden is Lecturer in Politics at the University of Edinburgh. He researches comparative federalism and territorial politics. He is the author of *Federalism and Regionalism in Western Europe: A Comparative and Thematic Analysis*. He co-edited a special issue of *West European Politics* on Belgium, and authored or co-authored publications in *Regional and Federal Studies, West European Politics,* the *Journal of Common Market Studies, Publius* and the *European Journal of Political Research* (forthcoming). He is co-editor of *Regional and Federal Studies*.

Pieter van Houten is Lecturer in the Department of Politics and a Teaching Fellow at Churchill College at the University of Cambridge. His research interests include party politics, regional politics and conflict management in Eastern Europe and the Balkans. His work has been published in *Archives Européennes de Sociologie* and *Regional and Federal Studies*. He co-edited a special issue of *Party Politics* on multilevel politics.

Frederik Verleden is Research Assistant at the Centre for Political Research of the Katholieke Universiteit Leuven. He has published book chapters on the political history of Belgium and Italian politics.

Abbreviations

AN	Alleanza Nazionale
AP	Alianza Popular
BAME	Black and minority ethnic
BNG	Bloque Nacionalista Galego
BSP-PSB	Belgische Socialistische Partij-Parti Socialiste Belge
CC	Coalición Canaria
CDh	Centre Démocrate Humaniste
CD&V	Christen-Democratisch en Vlaams
CDS	Centro Democrático y Social
CDU	Christlich Demokratische Union Deutschlands
CiU	Convergència i Unió
CMP	Comparative Manifesto Project
CSU	Christlich-Soziale Union in Bayern
CVP-PSC	Christelijke Volkspartij-Parti Social Chrétien
DC	Democrazia Cristiana
PD	Partito Democratico
DS	Democratici di Sinistra
DVU	Deutsche Volksunion
EA	Eusko Alkartasuna
EP	European Parliament
ERC	Esquerra Rupublicana de Catalunya
FDF	Front Démocratique des Francophones
FDP	Freie Demokratische Partei
FN	Front National
FNC	Federación Nacionalista Canaria
FRG	Federal Republic of Germany
GDR	German Democratic Republic
GRP	Gross Regional Product
HB	Herri Batasuna
IU	Izquierda Unida
KVV	Katholieke Vlaamse Volkpartij
LDD	Lijst Dedecker
MMP	Mixed Member Proportional electoral system
MR	Mouvement Réformateur
NPD	Nationaldemokratische Partei Deutschlands
NRW	North Rhine-Westphalia (Nordrhein-Westfalen)
NVA	Nieuw-Vlaamse Alliantie
OMOV	One member one vote
PAS	Partido Asturianista

PC	Plaid Cymru
PCI	Partito Comunista Italiano
PCS	Parti Catholique Social
PDS	Partei des Demokratischen Sozialismus
PDS	Partito Democratico della Sinistra
PNV	Partido Nacionalista Vasco
PP	Partido Popular
PVV-PLP	Partij voor Vrijheid en Vooruitgang-Parti de la Liberté et du Progrès
PR	Proportional representation
PRC	Partido Regionalista de Cantabria
PRC	Partito della Rifondazione Comunista
PRi	Partido Riojano
PRLW	Parti des Réformes et de la Liberté en Wallonie
PS	Parti Socialiste
PSC	Partit dels Socialistes de Catalunya
PSE-EE	Partido Socialista de Euskadi-Euskadiko Ezkerra
PSI	Partito Socialista Italiano
PSOE	Partido Socialista Obrero Español
RW	Rassemblement Wallon
SDP	Social Democratic Party
SNP	Scottish National Party
SP.a	Socialistische Partij – Anders
SPD	Sozialdemokratische Partei Deutschlands
UCD	Unión del Centro Democrático
UPCA	Unión para el Progreso de Cantabria
UPN	Unión del Pueblo Navarro
URAS	Unión Renovadora Asturiana
VLD	Vlaamse Liberalen en Democraten
VNV	Vlaamsch-Nationaal Verbond
WASG	Arbeit und soziale Gerechtigkeit – Die Wahlalternative

Introduction
Territorial Party Politics in Western Europe: A Framework For Analysis

Wilfried Swenden and Bart Maddens

Mind the gap: Bridging regionalization and party (system) literatures

In recent decades, social scientists have argued that in Western Europe government and governance should be increasingly understood from a multi-layered perspective. The EU has developed into an important supranational regulator, leading one American observer to label it as a 'regulatory' federation (Kelemen, 2004). Simultaneously authority has migrated to substate levels of government, strengthening regions in Western Europe in terms of their constitutional, legislative, administrative or fiscal capacities (Keating, 1998 and 2001a; Greer, 2006; Swenden, 2006; Hooghe, Marks and Schakel, 2008). Although this process has developed far from evenly across all member-states of the EU, it has affected most of its largest and/or multinational members (Belgium, France, Italy, United Kingdom and Spain). The strengthening of the regional tier is self-evident by studying recent constitutional developments in countries like Belgium (Deschouwer, 2005; Swenden and Jans, 2006), Spain (Aja, 2004; Moreno, 2001; Colino, forthcoming 2008), the UK (Hazell, 2000; Trench, 2004) or Italy (Gold, 2003; Palermo, 2005). Yet even Germany – sometimes portrayed as a 'unitary state in all but name' (Abromeit, 1992) – seems to be decentralizing, a development linked to growing socio-economic divisions between its regions, which dramatically intensified after unification (Sturm, 2001; Benz, 2006; Detterbeck and Jeffery in this volume). Several reasons have been put forward to account for this development: economists highlight that regions or small states are better placed to compete in a context where trade liberalization has made traditional state boundaries more porous and intensified competition for foreign investment or best innovation practices (Ohmae, 1995; Porter, 1998; Alesina and Spolaore, 2003). Policy analysts point at new modes of decision-making in which authority diffuses from hierarchical structures into non-hierarchical policy networks (Hooghe and Marks, 2001; Bomberg and Peterson, 1999; Peters and Pierre, 2005). Political sociologists point at the reawakening of territorial and linguistic cleavages in a more secular Western Europe from which Communism has largely disappeared.

The importance of regional or substate territory in Western Europe stands in apparent contradiction with the scholarly literature on party systems, party organizations and electoral campaigning. Much of the recent *party system literature* has focused on the extent to which such systems have become more or less *nationalized* (Caramani, 2004; Chhibber and Kollman, 2004; Jones and Mainwaring, 2003; Thorlakson, 2007). For instance, using an exhaustive database of electoral results at the constituency level from nearly all West European states, Caramani found that Lipset and Rokkan's 'frozen party system' thesis still holds today (Lipset and Rokkan, 1967). Despite several decades of regionalization and growing electoral volatility, party families built upon the cleavages generated by the National and Industrial Revolutions continue to dominate the contemporary West European party landscapes. Parties became *'catch-all-over-parties'* (that is, they sought to gain votes across the electoral constituencies of the state) before developing into mass or catch-all parties (Caramani, 2004).

Similarly, until recently, the *party organizational literature* largely ignored how parties organize at the regional level (even though analyses of the elite party, mass party, catch-all party or cartel party may describe how parties organize locally; Katz and Mair, 1993 and 1995; Krouwel, 2006). Processes of candidate selection have been studied primarily with statewide, less so with regional, electoral contests in mind (Gallagher and Marsh, 1988; Rahat and Hazan, 2001; Bille, 2001). Classifications like 'the party in public office' are concerned primarily with the party in central government or with MPs in the statewide legislatures in mind. How parties organize regionally is better known for those parties which self-evidently organize at *that* level in the first place, namely, the ethno-regionalist or autonomist parties of Western Europe (De Winter and Türsan, 1998; De Winter, Gomez-Reino and Lynch, 2006; Hepburn, 2008).

Finally, regions have been largely left out of the principal theories of *electoral competition* or campaigning. Most of these theories (like the proximity theory, directional theory or issue-ownership theory) make predictions with respect to campaign strategies at one level of policy-making, usually the statewide or federal policy level. Hence, they disregard the extent to which campaigns may be conditioned by campaign realities in different electoral arenas. Furthermore, although theories of electoral competition could be applied to the regional level of government, they are rarely tested at this level. For instance, expert surveys measuring policy positions of voters or party elites primarily do so with statewide elections or statewide politics in mind. Similarly, the Comparative Manifesto Project (CMP) maps the policy positions and issue salience of party programmes based on their *general* or statewide election manifestos (Budge et al., 2001). Recent efforts to broaden the scope of CMP data have focused on the new democracies of Central and

Eastern Europe, much less so on how the CMP could be meaningfully applied to regional or local elections (Klingemann et al., 2006; but Pogorelis et al., 2005).

One of the principal aims of this book is to narrow the gap between the regionalization and the party literatures on Western Europe. The latter have retained – notwithstanding several contributions in recent years, particularly in the field of party organizational studies – a strong 'national' focus (Jeffery and Hough, 2003; Hough and Jeffery, 2006a). We argue that, as a result of the process of regionalization described above, regional elections have gained in significance, regional political elites have become increasingly professionalized and parties are under increasing pressure to adapt their internal organization and campaign strategies to such new realities. In sum, regionalization has influenced the nature of the *party system* and the way in which parties *organize* and *campaign* in statewide and especially regional elections.

In this volume, we cannot possibly bring together a comprehensive analysis of the territorial aspects of all party systems or parties in all West European countries. Therefore, the focus of this book is limited in two respects: first, in the type of parties that are analysed and second, in the countries that are selected for in-depth or comparative analysis. With respect to the type of parties that are analysed, this book focuses on statewide parties alone. We define statewide parties as parties which participate in statewide and regional elections and are represented in at least three quarters of the regions in the state. We primarily focus on statewide parties because we believe that they face the most challenging coordination issues in terms of policy-making, organization and campaigning. This is so because they seek to maximize their following in statewide *and* regional elections, to participate in government or to influence policy in as many regions of the state as possible.

With respect to the selection of countries, the empirical evidence that is brought together in this volume relates to the territorial dimension of party politics in Belgium, Germany, Italy, Spain and the UK. As such it does not cover all West European states with a federal or regionalized character (for instance, Austria, Switzerland and also France are lacking from the analysis). Although this constrains the generalizability of our findings, our sample contains some of the leading West European states with an increasingly significant regional tier of government. For this reason, the analytical framework below uses only examples taken from the countries that are covered in this volume.

Before presenting an analytical framework that ties together the various contributions to this volume, we should briefly explain what we mean by 'region'. We see regions as the key meso-level of government in the state (sometimes called Land, Autonomous Community, Community or Region, province, 'nation' or canton). In general, we denote elections at that level as 'regional elections'. By comparison, we use the term 'state' to denote the highest level of governance within the state; elections which take place at that level are considered as 'statewide' (and not 'national' or 'general') elections.

Party systems in a multilayered context: From a 'national' to a 'multi-level' party system

The national bias in nationalization studies

In recent years, much of the party-system literature in Western Europe has focused on the so-called 'nationalization' of the West European party system. Caramani's influential study in this regard is based on an exhaustive collection and analysis of electoral data at the constituency or district level. His findings point at the overall nationalization of West European party systems, that is, an increasing homogenization of electoral competition across the regional units of the state (Caramani, 2004: 42). However, he mentions some exceptions. For instance, he acknowledges that in more recent times a tendency towards 'denationalization' can be observed, at least in multinational democracies such as the UK, Belgium and Italy. Using a broader variety of indicators to analyse party nationalization, Caramani finds a more denationalizing UK party system since the 1990s, at least compared with the average observed for the entire post-World War II period. This is consistent with Chhibber and Kollman, who, in a different study, observe a peak in the nationalization of the UK party system during the 1960s and 1970s, before they record a substantial decline (Chhibber and Kollman, 2004: 196–7). Denationalization is also observed for Belgium and – albeit to a much lesser extent – Italy (with relative stabilization *after* the implosion of the Christian Democrats and the rise of the Lega Nord in the early 1990s).

Importantly, Caramani records *no* significant overall changes in the nationalization of the Spanish party system since 1978. Similarly, the German party system did not become more 'denationalized' after unification (at least until 1999). In the league of West European party systems, Germany did not climb up the ladder of denationalization: in 1999 it still ranked behind Belgium, Switzerland, Finland, the UK, Spain and Italy. The cumulative standard deviation, that is, the extent to which constituency results for all German parties deviate from the overall mean, did not increase between 1990 and 1999. Thus, the German party system did not become more territorially fragmented in relative or absolute terms (Caramani, 2004: 92–3).

Caramani's observations on Spain sound counterintuitive given this country's 'federalization' in recent years (Moreno, 2001). Similarly, one would expect that the rising inter-regional socio-economic heterogeneity in Germany after unification would have coincided with a less 'nationalized' party system. Why do nationalization studies seem to contradict these expectations?

First, and most importantly, although not all nationalization studies use identical indicators, all of them are based on results for *statewide* elections *alone*. Yet regional elections in Belgium, Germany, Spain or Italy have been (or have become increasingly) relevant given that regional governments frequently control important aspects of capital-intensive policies such as education, industrial development, transport, infrastructure, health or social assistance. Therefore, to disregard regional election results is to leave out an increasingly important component of party system nationalization. Developments in the regional party systems must be considered as an essential component of party systemic developments in a federal or multilayered state.

Second, most nationalization studies are based on overall aggregate national patterns. As a result, they cannot fully account for the potential importance of limited or aberrant 'nationalization' in strong regions, such as Catalonia, Scotland, the Basque Country, Wales or even Bavaria, that represent relatively small sections of the population but play a key role in triggering the (further) decentralization of the state. Hence, Chhibber and Kollman make claims about the entire UK party system, but Scotland and Wales represent such a small share of the overall electorate that their findings cannot fully bear out the peculiarity of the Scottish and Welsh electorates. Until the 2001 statewide elections, only 10.9 percent of all UK constituencies were Scottish (and thus constituted a support base for the Scottish National Party) and only about 6.1 percent were Welsh. Similarly, many Spanish parties have a small statewide following but due to their regionally concentrated support can be significant forces within their regional party systems: most non-statewide parties cover less than nine percent of the Spanish constituencies (Caramani, 2004: 113; Montero, 2005). In Germany, the Bavarian CSU has had a more profound impact than the East German PDS in pushing the German nationalization index down. Yet it does not take an electoral specialist to realize that the East German party system is profoundly different from that which is found in the rest of the country. Related to this point, the 'nationalization' thesis cannot map – to borrow from Sartori and Bartolini – the regional 'blackmail potential' of autonomist parties (Sartori, 1976; Bartolini, 2004). Aggregated 'nationalization' indices do not express the relevance of these parties at the statewide level where they can wield significant political influence. For instance, the need of Spanish central minority governments to rely on the legislative support of one or several autonomist parties during most of the 1990s and again since 2004 has played a role in explaining more recent developments in the Spanish decentralization process (see further).

The party system as a multilevel party system

To remedy this deficiency in party system nationalization studies, Gibson and Suarez-Cao recently introduced the concept of a *federalized party system*, which they define as 'a party system in which more than one territorially delimited party system operates', that is, a national [statewide] and several subnational [regional] ones (Gibson and Suarez-Cao, 2007: 6). We suggest using the concept of a multilevel party system to denote what Gibson and Suarez-Cao perceive as a federalized party system. The multilevel party system brings together a *statewide* party system which emerges from statewide elections and a set of regional party systems reflecting the outcome for regional elections. Gibson and Suarez-Cao concur with our view that nationalization studies are incomplete so long as they do not take into account developments in the regional party system and incorporate their interaction with the statewide party system.

It is not difficult to see how re-conceptualizing a party system as a 'multilevel party system' can shed a different perspective on the nationalization studies reviewed above: using the framework of a multilevel party system we need to consider the properties of the regional party systems and analyse how they *interact* with each other and with the statewide party system. Similarly, we must take into account developments in the regional party systems when measuring *party-system change*. Party-system change is defined by Peter Mair as the transformation of a party system from one class or type of party system into another (Mair, 1997: 52). However, also in this regard change is primarily understood as change resulting from transformations of the statewide party system alone: for instance, to use Sartori's classification scheme, from a system of moderate into one of polarized pluralism (Sartori, 2005: 116–92). Yet multilevel party system change could also occur if party competition at the regional level transforms the direction of competition or produces a change of governing formula at that level. For instance, the election of an SNP minority government in Scotland in May 2007 certainly produced party-system change at the Scottish level since it forced Labour into joint opposition with the Conservatives and Liberal Democrats. This certainly generated a change in the direction of competition, notwithstanding the already distinctive character of the Scottish party system prior to such a change in the Scottish governing formula. Party competition is now structured around 'the regionalist issue', that is, the extent to which Scottish autonomy should be extended or Scottish independence contemplated.

The integration of a multilevel party system depends on the extent to which the same parties are represented at the various levels of the system and how evenly balanced their support is across the levels and regions of the state. A multilevel party system is fully integrated if the same parties are represented at the statewide and regional levels in about equal strength. A multilevel party system is loosely integrated if the support for statewide parties varies considerably across the regions and between the statewide and regional levels, for instance, due to the presence of regional parties. In the extreme case of a completely unintegrated system, each region has a specific party system with parties that differ from those in the other regions and those on the statewide level.

Patterns of interaction in a multilevel party system

The interaction between the component parts of a multilevel party system can take several forms. The simplest distinction relates to patterns of *vertical* interaction between the statewide and regional party systems (which may take a 'top-down' or a 'bottom-up' form) and patterns of *horizontal* interaction between regional party systems.

We start by considering the relevance of *vertical* interaction from a *top-down* perspective, pertaining to the extent to which developments in the statewide party system affect regional party systems. The notion that the outcome of a regional election is primary influenced by statewide politics is dealt with in the literature on regional elections under the heading of 'second-order elections'. For long, regional elections were seen to be *second order* relative to statewide elections because they generated lower turnout levels, boosted support for new or minor parties and, especially when held halfway through the statewide election cycle, harmed central-level incumbents and benefited central opposition parties (Reif and Schmitt, 1980; Hough and Jeffery, 2006a: 7–10). Recent empirical evidence demonstrates that regional elections in Western Europe still generate lower turnout levels and that, on the whole, this gap has not been narrowing (López Pintor and Gratschew, eds, 2002: 78–9; Font and Rico, 2003; Forschungsgruppe Wahlen, s.d.; UK Electoral Commission). However, evidence of 'second orderness' on the other indicators is less persuasive. For instance, since German unification, central incumbents still suffer setbacks in German regional elections when held halfway through the statewide election cycle, but the key central opposition parties may not benefit as much as the second-order model predicts (Lutz Kern and Hainmüller, 2006: 127–49; Hough and Jeffery, 2006b: 119–39). Furthermore, the proportion of the German electorate in regional elections that would have to change its vote to produce the same outcome as for federal elections has gone up. Similar observations have been made with respect to regional elections in Spain and Britain. In Spain, the share of voters who support autonomist parties is much higher in regional than in statewide elections (Pallarés and Keating, 2006). The same practice of 'dual voting' can be observed in Scotland and Wales, where SNP and Plaid Cymru (PC, the Welsh nationalists) score much better in regional elections, in part because larger shares of people who vote Labour or Conservative in statewide elections prefer to stay at home (Bromley, 2006: 197–9; Trystan, Scully and Wyn Jones, 2003). These examples attest that statewide and regional party systems do not necessarily respond to the logic of 'second orderness'. Indeed, it has been argued that voters in West European states increasingly perceive regional elections as electoral contests in their own right, instead of seeing them as 'popularity tests' for incumbent central governments (Hough and Jeffery, 2006a).

Second orderness focuses on the short-term spillover effects of developments in the statewide party system on regional party systems. Yet it is not difficult to see how some of these developments may generate more durable effects. For instance, if, as Caramani attests, parties develop a 'catch-all-over-strategy' first in statewide elections, then they are likely to pursue such a strategy in regional elections as well. For instance, no one ever questioned the theoretical possibility that the UK statewide parties would not participate in devolved elections in Scotland and Wales, whereas their absence from devolved elections for Northern Ireland was widely expected. Indeed, each of the three statewide parties (Labour, Liberal Democrats and Conservatives) had participated in statewide or Westminster elections in Scotland and Wales, but did not file candidates in UK elections in Northern Ireland. Conversely, parties which suffer badly or face extinction in statewide elections may ultimately also disappear from the regional party system.

Vertical interactions in the federal party system can also take a *bottom-up* direction; hence, developments in the regional party system can trigger changes in the statewide party system. For instance, notwithstanding the aforementioned practice of dual voting, some voters would not have supported autonomist parties in Spanish elections if they had not been successful already in regional elections also. As a result, Spanish minority governments felt compelled to negotiate with these parties, instead of signing coalition pacts with the (larger) statewide party competitor. This way, parties that appeared at the regional level acquired powerful brokerage (or, as alluded to above, 'blackmail') potential in the centre and extracted regional resources in exchange for supporting a statewide government (but see Montero, 2005, for a more critical analysis). Also, the collapse of the Spanish UCD at the national level at the beginning of the 1980s was due in part to the disastrous results of the party in the regional elections that preceded the 1982 national election (Hopkin, 1999: 221–5). To give another example, the input of the East German regions in the governance of the German federal centre is somehow disproportionate. The Bundesrat, the federal second chamber, provides the *East German regional executives* with an important co-decision right in approximately 50 percent of all federal legislation (a percentage that is expected to fall as a result of a recent federalism reform package (2006)). Through its participation in several regional governments (in coalition with the SPD), the PDS obtained important concessions from the SPD–Green-controlled federal government (1998–2005) in tax or health-care reform (Zohnlhöfer, 2003). More generally, the PDS could bring specific East German concerns to bear when in a position to co-decide on labour, health care, tax or fiscal equalization reforms at the federal policy level. Germany also illustrates that some parties (such as the Greens) may achieve electoral success and governmental representation at the regional level first, thereby paving the way for statewide electoral success and a role in federal government at a later stage.

Besides patterns of vertical interaction between statewide and regional party systems, we may consider the degree to which elections in one region influence elections in another. Again, support for autonomist parties in Spain became more widespread during the 1980s and early 1990s. Yet this was primarily a consequence of the rapid growth of such parties in the non-historic communities (such as the Canary Isles or Aragon) rather than of the further rise of such parties in the historic communities (Catalonia, the Basque Country, Galicia) (Pallarés and Keating, 2003 and 2006). Thus, the emergence of autonomist parties in the historic communities created a snowball effect, triggering their breakthrough in other regional elections as well.

Statewide parties as an element of linkage between the subsystems of the multilevel party system

Definition and typology of statewide parties

The subsystems of a multilevel party system (the statewide party system and the party systems within each of the regions of the state) interact with each other, vertically and horizontally. Parties are the most important elements of linkage between the statewide and regional party systems; other linkages may consist of 'communication flows, resource flows, [congruent or partially congruent] coalitions, electoral laws and so on' (Gibson and Suarez-Cao, 2007: 7).

However, not all parties provide an equally strong element of linkage between the statewide and regional systems of the multilevel party system. The linkage potential of a party is dependent on two factors: first, the territorial reach and depth of the party defined as the *territorial pervasiveness* of its electoral support and the *type* (*statewide and/or regional*) *of elections* in which it participates and second, the strength of the *organizational linkages* between the statewide and regional party branches.

Focusing on the first element alone, Kris Deschouwer (2006b: 292) suggest classifying parties along two dimensions: the *territorial pervasiveness* of the party (do parties gain political representation at one, several or all the regions of the state?), and the *presence* of a party at different levels of the political system (do parties participate exclusively in either regional or statewide elections, or do they take part in both?). The linkage potential is highest for parties with a high territorial pervasiveness and a presence at all levels of the political system. This is largely the case for statewide parties. Statewide parties can be distinguished from 'truncated' parties, which are parties that exist at only one level of government (Thorlakson, 2009). By contrast, although most autonomist parties take part in both statewide and regional elections (thus they are not truncated), their political representation is limited to one or at most a few regions of the state. Table 0.1 provides a summary overview and classifies those parties which will be discussed or mentioned in later chapters (therefore, it does not provide a summary overview of *all* West European parties).

A quick look at Table 0.1 reveals that, while most parties participate in both statewide and regional electoral contests, parties display a much broader

Table 0.1   Classification of West European parties on the basis of territorial pervasiveness and participation in elections

		Participation in elections		
		Regional elections only	Statewide elections only	Regional and statewide elections
Territorial Pervasiveness	One region	Partei Rechtsstaatlicher Offensive (Hamburg) PRC (Partido Regionalista de Cantabria) PRi (Partido Riojano)		CSU, SNP, PC, BNG, CiU, ERC, PNV, EA
	Some regions			PDS, Belgian parties
	Most regions			CDU, Conservatives, Labour, Liberal Democrats, PP, PSOE
	All regions			SPD, FDP, Die Linke, IU

Source: Own elaboration from Deschouwer (2006b: 292). The classification of the PRi and PRC is based exclusively on their participation in the most recent set of regional and statewide elections. The PRi participated in statewide elections, but not after 2000; the PRC did not participate in statewide elections after 1993. Also, the EA and PNV have participated in regional elections in Navarre (albeit under a different name). The PDS fielded candidates across all regions in statewide elections, but failed to gain representation in the Western *Länder*.

variety with respect to their territorial pervasiveness. For instance, the largest UK, German and Spanish parties compete in statewide and regional elections and are present across most regions of the state. In the UK, Labour, the Conservatives and Liberal Democrats do not compete in Northern Ireland (UK and devolved elections), but are present in Scotland, Wales and England. The German Christian Democrats do not compete in Bavaria (federal and regional elections) but participate in statewide and regional elections across the remaining 15 regions of the state. In Spain, the PSOE and PP compete across all regions of the state but the Catalan Social Democrats (PSC) and Naverrese Conservatives (UPN) nonetheless have a special status: they operate as autonomous parties in Catalan or Navarrese elections.

Conversely, a majority of the autonomist parties (for instance, the Catalan CiU and ERC, the Basque PNV and EA, the Galician BNG, the Scottish SNP or Welsh PC) participate in statewide elections and in one set of regional elections and gain representation at both levels. Parties such as the Italian Lega

Nord or Alleanza Nationale or the East German PDS are to be distinguished from the previous set of autonomist parties insofar as they pervade more than just one region, yet have a geographically concentrated support base (Northern or Southern Italy, East Germany). Similarly, Belgian parties participate in federal and regional elections but do not cover the entire territory of the state. Their electoral support is confined to Flanders and Brussels or to Wallonia and Brussels. Therefore, on the basis of territorial pervasiveness and presence *alone*, the 'Belgian' parties should be positioned with most of the West European autonomist parties (but see the contributions by Deschouwer and Verleden in this volume for why most parties lack some additional properties that are commonly associated with such autonomist or ethno-regionalist parties). If we leave aside Belgium, the multilevel party systems of Spain, the UK and Germany are still dominated by parties with a statewide character. This is the case even for most regional party systems. With the exception of Bavaria, the Basque Country and Navarre, statewide parties still capture a majority of votes in regional elections. The representation of autonomist parties is high in Catalonia, the Canary Islands, Scotland and Wales, but lower than that of the statewide parties.

Statewide parties provide a stronger link between the subsystems of the multilevel party system than autonomist parties or truncated parties, that is, parties which take part in elections at only one level. Yet not all statewide parties have equally strong linkage potential. Some statewide parties provide a more integrated organizational structure connecting the various branches or levels of the party. Therefore, we need a different set of terms to highlight variations in the *organizational* linkage potential of statewide parties. In theory, all parties which take part in statewide and one, several, most or all regional elections require some form of vertical integration. Even most autonomist parties have distinct ways of organizing as parliamentary parties at the statewide and regional levels, but tend to have only one party organizational core (executive, conference) to coordinate statewide and regional party matters. In contrast, statewide parties have distinct organizational branches at the statewide level and in each of the regions in which they contest elections. Therefore, statewide parties should provide the most extensive forms of vertical and horizontal (inter-regional) policy coordination.

Thorlakson (2009) classifies statewide parties on the basis of the extent to which they are vertically integrated and of the degree of autonomy of the regional party branches. Indicators of high levels of vertical integration include shared (as opposed to separate) membership structures, shared (as opposed to separate) finances and the participation of regional branches in the governance bodies (for instance, executive, conference) of the statewide party. Indicators of regional party branch autonomy include the extent to which regional branches can operate freely in policy-making, regional leadership and candidate selection (Thorlakson, 2009). Where appropriate, the freedom to sign regional coalition deals, or the autonomy to write the

Table 0.2   Typology of statewide parties based on levels of vertical integration and autonomy of the regional branches

	Typology of statewide parties				
	Split	Confederal	Federal	Regionalized	Unitary
Vertical integration	Very low to non-existent	Medium, regional branches retain veto	High	Medium	Not applicable
Regional autonomy	High	High	Medium or low, depending on type of federal structure	Low (statewide party in a position of hierarchical control)	None

regional party programme (manifesto), may be seen as complementary indicators of autonomy. Furthermore, the level at which membership dues are paid, the freedom of the regional branches to recruit personnel and raise revenue, and the right to organize and supervise subregional or local party matters are sometimes listed as additional indicators of autonomy (Deschouwer, 2006b: 294; Laffin, Shaw and Taylor, 2007). Table 0.2 distinguishes between types of multilevel parties on the basis of their levels of vertical integration and the autonomy of the regional party branches.

Applying vertical integration and autonomy to the aforementioned party organizational types, we find that in the parties of the *split* type the regional branches are completely independent from the central party, as a result of which vertical integration is weak to non-existent. At most, the two levels of party may form alliances (Thorlakson, 2009). Even in a *confederal* party, the locus of the party remains unequivocally with the regional party branches. The statewide party branch is subordinate to the regional branches and cannot function without their consent. The regional branches have a high degree of autonomy and the extent of vertical integration remains relatively low. Finally, in a *federal* party, the statewide party branch is more than the sum of its parts and each party level can make final decisions on certain matters. A federal party is a statewide party in which the regional branches participate in some decisions of the statewide party branch, yet retain sufficient autonomy to adapt their organizational structures to the territorial specificities of the electorates which they typically address. The higher the autonomy of the regional branches and the stronger their participation in the statewide party, the more decentralized is the federal party.

Beyond the three party organizational types which Thorlakson identifies, there may be scope for an additional type which nonetheless falls short of a *unitary* party. We could conceive of a *regionalized* party as a statewide party with regional party branches, but in which the statewide party branch retains the final say (at least formally) in all party organizational matters and has the right to overrule regional branches in case of statewide regional disagreement. The statewide party branch may 'involve' the regional branches in some of its decision-making bodies but not more so than some of the local branches or some functional associations (for instance, trade unions, young party members or female caucus). This further distinction between a federal party and a regionalized party may be useful, as it is possible that statewide parties in a federal system will give a limited form of autonomy to the regional branches while retaining the right to intervene in all party matters, thus falling somewhere between the federal and the unitary ideal-types. A unitary party would be a party without any regional party branches at all. In the remainder of this Introduction we focus on the federal and regionalized statewide parties alone.

Closing the circle: Party systems, party organization and party strategy

We can now see how party systems, party organizations and party strategy interact. Statewide parties, especially the federal, regionalized or unitary variants, provide a potentially very strong link between the various subsystems of the multilevel party system. Yet the extent to which they realize this potential depends on their ability to gather electoral support across all the regions of the state in statewide and regional elections. In turn, that ability hinges on their capacity to establish a cohesive party organization which is capable of coordinating the activities of the party across the various levels and regions of the state and of safeguarding some level of programmatic or ideological cohesiveness. However, statewide parties must also find an organizational structure which allows their regional branches sufficient freedom to take into account regional specificities (for instance, when filing candidates or devising an electoral programme for regional elections) *without* jeopardizing the overall programmatic unity of the party. Therefore, a statewide party which operates in a loosely integrated multilevel party system, that is, a system with substantial variation between the subsystems, is likely to harm its electoral fortunes if it adopts a unitary or at best regionalized party structure. A loosely integrated party system is thus likely to prompt statewide parties to organize as federal, possibly even confederal, parties.

The same observation applies to electoral strategy. In a loosely integrated party system, statewide parties will be able to obtain a strong position in the regional arena (and play their integrating role) only if they successfully accommodate the particularities of the regional electoral arena in which they compete. Still, while a regionally diversified campaign strategy is more likely in a federal party, we should not disregard the possibility that even a unitary party could decide to tailor its message in regional elections to regional sensibilities and to develop distinct regional strategies. Paradoxically, to the extent that the statewide party successfully adapts its organization and strategy to the multilevelled and loosely integrated nature of the multilevel party system, the overall integration of the system will increase. In other words, the more successful the statewide parties are in the various regions, for instance by beating the autonomist parties, the more integrated will the multilevel party system become.

The practice whereby statewide parties strike a balance between authorizing their regional branches to organize and strategize freely and safeguarding the organizational and programmatic unity of the party can be expressed by a few powerful metaphors. Carty, for instance, develops the notion of a 'franchise' party, in which the statewide party branch provides 'a product line, sets standards, manages marketing and advertising' while local regional units (individual franchise) 'deliver the product to a particular market, invest local resources, build an organization focused on the needs and resources of the local community' (Carty, 2004: 10; Fabre, 2008: 28). In this volume, Pieter van Houten introduces a '*principal–agent*' metaphor to express the same relationship between statewide and regional party branches. Arguably, this analogy may be appropriate for federal or regionalized parties in which the statewide party branch is the 'principal' that 'delegates' autonomy to the regional branches whenever such delegation is deemed to strengthen the party overall. In confederal parties, on the other hand, the roles are reversed and the statewide party branch operates as the 'agent' of the regional branches. For the purposes of this volume, we distinguish between three distinct ways in which a federal or regionalized party can strategize in response to the multilayered context in which it operates. First, how does the party adapt its *organization* to the multilayered context in which it operates? Second, does the party convey different *campaign messages* in the statewide and regional election campaigns in which it takes part? Finally, does the party support different policies when in office at the statewide and regional levels, and (where appropriate) does the party authorize the making of incongruent governing coalitions? On each of these questions parties can opt for different degrees of statewide–regional and inter-regional variation.

Explaining variations in the federal party system and the organization and electoral strategies of federal or regionalized parties

The multilevelled nature of the party system and of the organization of statewide parties, campaign strategies and policy preferences feature as the key dependent variables in the various contributions to this volume. The next logical step is to list hypotheses to explain variations in these variables. The explanatory variables can be broken down into four major clusters. A first cluster links territorial variations in party systems, party organization campaigning and policy to differences in *the type of federalism or decentralization of the state*. A second cluster links party systemic, organizational, campaign or policy features to the *territorial or social heterogeneity of the society* in which parties operate. A third cluster puts forward a series of *electoral variables*, in particular the simultaneity of statewide and/or regional elections and, in the case of non-simultaneity, the timing of regional relative to statewide elections. A fourth and final cluster is more *party-specific*: it accounts for variations in organizational decentralization, campaigning and party policy by proposing party ideology, party institutionalization and incumbency as explanatory factors. In the following section, each of these clusters is considered in greater detail. We only present a set of hypotheses; we do not predict the validity of any set of clusters or variables listed therein. Further chapters will highlight which variables have the strongest explanatory power when applied to one or a small group of relevant cases from Western Europe.

The territorial structure of the state

The first hypothesis investigates the correlation between the territorial structure of the state and our dependent variables. We can think of three important ways in which the distribution of competencies within a state matters: (1) competencies may be distributed according to a functional or a jurisdictional design; (2) regional competencies may differ in scope, that is, correspond with different policies or different levels of expenditure decentralization; (3) competencies may be distributed asymmetrically (see Hooghe and Marks, 2001; Watts, 1999; and Swenden, 2006, for comparative typologies).

A functional or jurisdictional federal design

The first variable relates to the difference between a functional (sometimes also called cooperative or integrative) and a jurisdictional (sometimes also called dual) design (Sawer, 1976; Watts, 1999). In a functional design, most legislation takes the form of framework or concurrent legislation, legislative and administrative tasks are typically attributed to different levels of government and the regions are financed primarily on the basis of shared tax revenues. In a jurisdictional design, the two levels of government are disentangled. Each level controls different legislative powers and is responsible for their administration, and also has sufficient tax revenue powers to finance the bulk of its expenditures. Functional federalism and jurisdictional federalism are ideal types, or rather two ends of a continuum. In reality, no federal state embodies a pure form of functional or jurisdictional federalism. Nonetheless, states clearly occupy different positions on this continuum. For instance, in Western Europe, Belgium, Scotland (and especially, but beyond the scope of this volume, Switzerland) come closest to the jurisdictional end of the continuum, while Germany and Wales are nearer to the functional end. Spain occupies an intermediary position.

If we hypothesize that the organizational structure of the state may bear some resemblance to the organizational structure of federal parties, then the autonomy of the regional branches should be highest in a jurisdictional design and lowest in a functional or cooperative design of federalism. For the same reason, we would expect the multilevel party system to be less integrated and the strategy of multilevel parties to diverge more in a jurisdictional design. Jurisdictional designs also reduce the pressure on the making of party-politically congruent coalitions across levels of government and are conducive to more multilevel variation in party policy. However, since a cooperative design gives rise to stronger interdependence between the two levels, the participation of the regional branches in statewide party affairs (for instance, via guaranteed rights of representation in the statewide party executive or conference) should be higher than in a jurisdictional setting.

Variations in the scope of decentralization

By itself, the distinction between jurisdictional federalism and cooperative federalism sheds light on just one aspect of federal design. The portfolio of competencies which regions control can vary substantially from one state to another. Policies such as health, education or transport are capital-intensive whereas monument conservation, vocational training or housing policies are not (or at least much less so). We define the 'scope' of federalism by measuring regional public expenditures as a share of all public expenditures: the higher the regional shares, the larger is the scope of decentralization. Accurate comparative data on this indicator are not always easy to obtain (yet easier than comparative revenue-raising data), and sometimes regional expenditures and local expenditures cannot be easily disaggregated (see Rodden, 2004 for some critical observations). Yet, if we consider available data from the late 1990s, it appears that regional expenditure levels are highest for Belgium (40.8 per cent) and Germany (38 per cent), followed by Spain (32.5 per cent), the UK (25 per cent) and Italy (Swenden, 2006: 112). The reported UK figure also lists local expenditures. Furthermore, an accurate UK reading would require us to separate data for Westminster expenditures benefiting Scotland or Wales from expenditures by the Scottish or Welsh governments. It may be assumed that, due to the legislative autonomy of Scotland in cost-intensive programmes such as health policy and education (but not in income-replacement schemes), Scottish expenditure levels stand at least on a par with the Belgian or German regional expenditure levels. Welsh expenditures levels may be lower but not by much, since the main difference between Scottish and Welsh devolution lies in to the extent of legislative autonomy, not the level of regional expenditure.

Linking the scope of regional competencies to the integration of the federal party system and federal party-organizational properties, we hypothesize that the larger the scope, the more disintegrated is the federal party system, the more autonomous are the regional branches and the stronger is their capacity to claim a participatory role in statewide party affairs. Higher levels of regional expenditure should increase the autonomy of the regional party branches since regional party elites control a potentially wider array of resources and will be held in higher esteem by the statewide party. For the same reason, a larger scope should also coincide with more territorially diversified campaign strategies and a stronger territorial variation in party policy.

Constitutional asymmetry

Finally, not all the regions of a state may have similar levels of *institutional or constitutional autonomy*. Among the sample of West European countries in this study, constitutional asymmetry applies to the three historic communities of Spain (the Basque Country, Catalonia and Galicia) and Navarre, Scotland and Wales. The highest level of constitutional asymmetry is found in the UK (where Scotland has the highest level of autonomy but England lacks any form of regional self-rule), followed by Spain (where after a period of levelling out asymmetries have increased again since 2006: Agranoff, 1999; Colino, 2008).

We hypothesize that, in regions with more constitutional autonomy, the party system is likely to be most distinct from the multilevel party system overall, and regional branches of federal or regionalized parties will have acquired a special status within the party. This should result in higher levels of regional autonomy or special participatory rights in statewide organizational affairs which other regional branches lack. For the same reason, the electoral strategies of statewide parties in electoral campaigns taking place within such regions or the proposed party policies are likely to be more distinct than in regions without such a special level of constitutional autonomy.

The state and the multilevel party system: From correlation to causality?

In the explanatory model presented above, the state structure is presented as an exogenous variable which affects the character of the multilevel party system, as well as the territorial organization and strategies of statewide parties. To take a more longitudinal perspective, it is assumed that changes in the party system, party organization or party strategy reflect changes in the state structure. Such a viewpoint is consistent with the analysis by Chhibber and Kollman, who argue that authority migration, that is, the shift of competencies from the centre to the regions or vice versa, triggers changes in the party system (and not the other way round). For Chhibber and Kollman, 'voters are more likely to support national political parties as the national government becomes more important in their lives' (Chhibber and Kollman, 2004: 222). Put differently, the (de)centralization of competencies normally 'precedes' the (de)nationalization of the party system. The authors identify four changes that have led to a centralization of the state and drive the nationalization of the party system: war or the threat of war (in particular World Wars I and II), economic depression (and, in the wake thereof, centralization of economic and fiscal powers, as was the case with the New Deal in the USA, for instance), nation-building and the development of the welfare state (Chhibber and Kollman, 2004: 227). True, they admit that in the UK, for instance, statewide parties responded to the threat of the Welsh and Scottish nationalism by extending the spending autonomy of the Welsh and Scottish offices. More generally, they acknowledge that 'reciprocal causation' cannot be ruled out, since governments devolve or centralize powers and public officers also function as party holders. By and large, however, important structural changes precipitate changes in the nationalization of the party system (Chhibber and Kollman, 2004: 227).

The views of Chhibber and Kollman are not universally shared. For instance, for Caramani decentralization or federalism in Western Europe did not lead to but rather *contained* the regionalization of voting behaviour (Caramani, 2004: 292). As a corollary, the regionalization of voting behaviour may have preceded decentralization. As an alternative explanation one could argue that the crucial issue is not who triggers change – the state (by migrating authority) or the voters (by precipitating changes in the party system) – but rather what are they *both* responding to. Changes in the party system and (de)centralization may both respond to new social cleavages. To the extent that such cleavages acquire a more regional or territorial character, the party system and the structure of the state in which they are embedded may both denationalize.

Some contributions to this volume shed light on the relationship between the state, the party system and the role of political agency. We take the view that authority migration may not be exogenous but can be determined by the dynamics of the multilevel party system. In other words, a disintegrating multilevel party system could result in demands for more regional autonomy and the emergence of dual federalism, whereas a more integrated multilevel party system may foster a centralizing federation with the adoption of a rather functional design. In some cases, the origins of the federal structure can be traced back to the transition to democracy (Germany, Spain), but in other cases the dynamics of the party system seem to have played a crucial role (Belgium). In Belgium for instance, the disintegration of the multilevel party system preceded the decentralization of the state structure. Hence, the state structure adapted to the territorial reorganization of the parties and the development of regional variations in the party system (Verleden in this volume).

The territorial heterogeneity of society

Territorial dimensions of socio-economic and cultural heterogeneity

Constitutional asymmetries do not arise out of the blue. They often reflect different social, economic or especially cultural (linguistic, religious) or historical (a shared common history pre-dating the emergence of the state) realities confined to one or several regions of the state. More generally, even federal or multilayered states without constitutional asymmetry (for example, Germany) display regional variations in economic development or in the extent to which their citizens identify with the state or a region. Such disparities can diminish or increase over time. Likewise, the extent to which citizens in a region experience regional as opposed to statewide identities is subject to continuous change and reinterpretation. The distinctiveness of a political community could also be assessed by analysing the specificities of its civil society and the media (Keating, Loughlin and Deschouwer, 2003; Greer, 2007; Erk, 2008). Regional economic disparities can be measured by comparing regional per capita GRP figures. For EU countries these have become widely available through EUROSTAT publications. Regional identity figures have been measured by using a variety of survey questions; the best known of these remains the Linz-Moreno question on regional identity. It asks citizens to position themselves on a five-point scale with exclusive identification with the state or region as the two outliers and equal identification with the state and region in the middle (Moreno, 2001). In Western Europe, levels of identification with the region (either exclusively or predominantly) are highest for the 'stateless' nations of the Basque Country, followed by Catalonia and Scotland. Galicia, Flanders and Wales generally display slightly lower levels of regional identity, but significantly higher than Wallonia or most of the other Spanish regions. Unfortunately, comparable data are missing for the federal states of Austria, Germany and Switzerland (at least as measured within each of the *Länder* or cantons of the state) and also for Italy. One may assume that, in Italy and Germany, the more important territorial cleavage respectively sets the northern regions apart from the South or the East from the West (Gold, 2003; Hough and Koß in this volume).

Linking inter-regional variations in identity and socio-economic development to party systemic and organizational features generates the expectation that a more territorially heterogeneous society coincides with a less integrated multilevel party system (Lipset and Rokkan, 1967). In turn, a territorially less integrated multilevel party system affects the organizational, electoral and policy strategies of statewide parties. There are two conditions under which statewide party organizations may be tempted to give their regional branches more autonomy: first, when support for statewide parties varies substantially across the regions of the state and second, when regional variations in electoral support are caused primarily by variations in the strength of autonomist parties.

The first condition may arise when the party systems in several regions of the state are more skewed towards the left or the right than the overall multilevel party system. Parties of the right may feel tempted to advocate more left-wing positions when they are competing in a predominantly left-wing electoral environment and vice versa. In order to enable such strategic electoral choices, one can expect regional party branches to seek maximal autonomy from the statewide party branches in terms of candidate selection, campaigning or regional policy-making.

The same observations apply a fortiori when variations in regional support are due to competition from autonomist parties. Here, statewide parties must not only provide choices with regard to the left–right dimension, but also with respect to how to position themselves on matters dealing with regional autonomy

Variations in the size of regional electorates

Regions can be distinguished from each other on the basis of more than their socio-economic or cultural distinctiveness alone. All multilayered states are to some extent asymmetric insofar as their regions are not equally significant in electoral terms. For instance, taken together Scotland, Wales and Northern Ireland make up less than 15 percent of the UK population, whereas in Germany North Rhine-Westphalia alone is more populous than all of the East German *Länder* combined. It is not difficult to see how differences in demography may be reflected within federal party organizations. For instance, from the viewpoint of the German SPD, North Rhine-Westphalia (NRW) is not only a traditional electoral stronghold but also houses the SPD regional branch with the largest membership base. Therefore, one may assume that the NRW SPD wields more influence (participation) in the statewide party than the other regional branches. On the other hand, the German SPD may be compelled to keep a closer eye on the NRW party branch than on any of the other branches since the outcome of regional elections in NRW will send larger shockwaves through the German multi-level party system than elections in, say, Bremen (this was exemplified in 2005, when then SPD Chancellor Schröder triggered the dissolution of the federal parliament after his party lost badly in NRW regional elections). Because of this interdependence, the autonomy of the NRW branch (organizationally and in policy terms) could be lower than that of the Bremen branch and its electoral campaign may be steered more by the statewide party. For the same reason, it is sometimes said that Scottish regional party branches can get away with more because Scottish voters represent a relatively small share of the electorate and Scottish politics is not frequently reported in the London-based UK political press (van Biezen and Hopkin, 2006). Smallness, however, should also weaken their capacity to participate in statewide party affairs.

Statewide party organizations, simultaneity and cycles

The way in which statewide party organizations operate internally may be affected by the timing of regional relative to statewide elections. Three scenarios are possible: statewide and all regional elections coincide (a situation which Kris Deschouwer has referred to as 'vertical simultaneity'), all regional elections coincide ('horizontal simultaneity') but are held independently from statewide elections, or each or at least a clear majority of regional elections are held separately (and separately from statewide elections).

Where statewide and regional elections coincide, the process of candidate selection for both sets of elections may coincide or is at the very least coordinated between the two levels. The same applies to drafting party programmes for statewide and regional elections (Deschouwer, 2003 and 2006a: 296–7). Consequently, the autonomy of the regional party branches is likely to be lower and the coordinating role of the statewide party is likely to be stronger. When statewide and regional elections do not coincide but all regional elections are held simultaneously, the statewide party is likely to take an exceptionally high interest in the election, given that the regional elections will be perceived as a crucial popularity test for the incumbent central government. Consequently, the statewide party may wish to coordinate regional campaign themes and intervene in processes of regional candidate selection. Finally, the autonomy of the regional branches should be highest where regional elections take place independently from statewide elections and are held independently from each other.

In the event of non-simultaneity, the timing of a regional election relative to that of a statewide election is likely to be of significance. Where statewide and regional elections do not coincide, the propensity of the statewide party to intervene is likely to be larger the closer the election is held after, but especially before, the statewide election. In the latter case, the election will be seen as an important indicator of future statewide electoral performance; in the former case it will be seen as a confirmation of past statewide electoral success or failure (Deschouwer, 2006a: 297). One may add that regional elections can also gain in relevance the more they generate direct and immediate policy repercussions at the statewide level. The best example occurs when a German regional election tilts the balance in favour of the incumbent central government or opposition parties in the German second chamber. Whenever a regional election takes on such a character, the German media will give it more attention and the party leaders of the statewide incumbent or opposition parties will more likely appear during the campaign, seeking to influence the regional party programme and to intervene in the process of government formation.

Finally, it is sometimes suggested that the choice of electoral system – proportional representation (PR) or majoritarian – affects the vertical integration of statewide parties and the autonomy of their regional branches. PR systems tend to centralize powers within the party organization whereas majoritarian systems typically provide a stronger role for local or constituency associations, especially in the process of candidate selection. Yet the effect of the electoral system on the autonomy of the regional branches of multilevel parties must be carefully studied from party to party. For instance, an important aspect of candidate selection in majoritarian systems takes place at the constituency level, whereas party executives play a comparatively larger role in drafting lists for PR elections. If the drafting of lists for statewide or regional elections is coordinated at the *regional* and not the statewide party level, the autonomy of the regional branches remains intact. In fact, such a party would be more decentralized than a statewide party with the ability to amend candidates for central or regional office who were proposed by subregional constituency associations.

The choice of electoral system has a more profound effect on whether it is necessary to put together coalition governments after elections. Since plurality elections are more likely to produce a clear winner, the 'need' for statewide parties to interfere in the formation of a regional government is expected to be much lower than if regional elections are held under PR.

Statewide party organizations: Party ideology, development and incumbency

Incumbency

The autonomy of regional party branches is not fixed. Whether or not the statewide and/or regional branches of a party hold office is likely to have a profound effect on the level of regional-party branch autonomy. The Table 0.3 summarizes the four possible configurations. We discuss the hypothesized repercussions of each configuration for the level of autonomy of regional branches and their participation in the statewide party in turn.

A party is most vulnerable to central–regional disagreements when its central and regional party branches participate in government (scenario 1). Internal party disagreements could generate genuine policy disagreements and produce deadlock or contradictory public and party policy. Therefore, the statewide party may want to constrain the autonomy of the regional branches while avoiding open conflict by strengthening their participation in statewide party affairs. The statewide party branch is expected to keep a close eye on the campaign themes which the regional party develops. Conversely, the autonomy of regional party branches in campaigning, preselecting candidates and, where appropriate, regional coalition-building or developing deviant party policy should be highest when the statewide party and its regional branches occupy the opposition benches at both levels

Table 0.3 Combination matrix government and opposition

	Statewide party branch in government	Statewide party branch in opposition
Regional party branch in government	Scenario 1	Scenario 2
Regional party branch in opposition	Scenario 3	Scenario 4

(scenario 4). However, regional party branches are likely to participate less in statewide party matters since the possible consequences of a lack of intra-party coordination between levels are less damaging.

We hypothesize that a regional branch which participates in a regional government but cohabits with a statewide party in opposition should have considerable autonomy (scenario 2). Due to its role in government, the regional party branch has access to informational and material resources which the statewide party branch is lacking. The policy-making expertise of regional office-holders could be of enormous benefit to the statewide party. Therefore, their participation in the statewide party is likely to increase as a result. In contrast, a regional party branch in opposition which cohabits with a statewide party in office (scenario 3) is more constrained in taking issue with statewide party policy. Such a stance would clearly undermine the authority of the statewide party where it matters the most: in government. Therefore, the statewide party may seek to limit the level of regional-party branch autonomy, without involving the branches to the same extent in statewide party affairs as in scenario 1.

Party ideology

Not all party ideologies are equally supportive of regionalism. One can at least hypothesize that statewide parties that are more supportive of region-alism or territorial politics are also more likely to organize internally along regional lines. Therefore, the more a party favours territorial autonomy, the stronger are its regional party branches and the stronger is their involve-ment in statewide party matters. On the whole, Labour and Conservative parties are expected to be less receptive to regional autonomy than Liberal or Christian Democratic parties. Mass parties in origin (though in the mean-time catchall or even cartel parties), labour parties are externally created and have continued to use their broad links to trade unions as a means to mobi-lize electoral support (Krouwel, 2006: 254). Furthermore, Social Democratic parties are inclined to prioritize 'interpersonal' solidarity rather than territo-rial autonomy. For instance, several representatives of the German SPD who participated in the Parliamentary Council (1948) to debate a draft West German constitution vehemently opposed federalism (Niclauß, 1998). To give another example, in the UK several Labour Party politicians (including prominent Scottish or Welsh Labour figures, such as the later party leader Neil Kinnock) rejected devolution when it was first proposed in the 1970s.

By contrast, the resistance to territorial autonomy among Conservative par-ties reflects their concern to uphold traditional notions of sovereignty. Among pluri-national states, sovereignty is more closely associated with statewide symbols such as the monarchy, the central parliament, the military, a major-ity language and, where appropriate, the reverence for empire (in which the majority nation took a lead role). Each of these values is linked more closely with a centralized than a decentralized political regime. On such grounds, and because of that party's historical connection to Francoism, we would expect the Partido Popular to be the more centralized of the two major Spanish statewide parties. However, in the UK the structure of the Conservative Party is not necessarily the least decentralized of the statewide parties. Although the Conservatives were united in their opposition to devolution (at least until 1999), until 1965 the Scottish Conservatives – then known as the Scottish Unionist Party – were a quasi-independent party that was only loosely associated with the Conservative Party in England and Wales (Seawright, 2004; Hopkin and Bradbury, 2006). Its Scottish identity was played out handily during the 1950s, when a British Labour government embarked upon nationalization policies which affected Scottish-run businesses and council-run services (Seawright, 2004). In the 1955 statewide elections, the party polled 50.1 percent of the Scottish vote. Yet, with Conservatives in power in London and the British Empire in decline, the capacity to pull the Scottish vote waned, and by the mid-1960s the party had lost much of its electoral appeal in Scotland.

Christian Democratic parties should be distinguished from Conservative parties. Although frequently characterized as mass or catch-all parties, Christian Democrats generally support '*subsidiarity*'. This doctrine, which originates in Catholic thought, supports policy-making at the lowest possible level. Therefore, Christian Democratic parties could be expected to be more supportive of regional branch autonomy and policy-making than Social Democratic parties (Schmid, 1990; Dachs, 2003).

Finally, so-called Liberal parties should be more open to internal dissent, discussion and deliberative decision-making. For instance, the British Liberal Democrats have been a federal party for a long time, both in their internal organization and in their preferred political structure for the UK (a legacy which dates back to Prime Minister Gladstone's proposal in the 1880s to give Ireland Home Rule within a UK federal system). The same observation applied to the Austrian Liberals before the party drifted into more populist and even extreme right-wing waters (Höbelt, 2002). However, in Germany, the electoral success of the Liberals (FDP) was primarily built on their status as a kingmaker in federal, though less so in regional, coalition-building. Furthermore, the party never developed a significant membership base. When it did so in East Germany shortly after unification (partially due to the enormous popularity of foreign minister Genscher there), the internal party organizational and decision-making structures remained quite centralized and elitist. In the view of Hopper, the party's refusal to adjust its organizational structure has contributed to the rapid decline of support for it in the East and the declining influence of the East German party branches within the Liberal statewide party organization (Hopper, 2001).

Party development and institutionalization

The above examples suggest that by itself ideology is not a reliable predictor of party organizational decentralization or campaigning. There is always a contextual element that needs to be taken into account. For instance, since the PSOE was outlawed during the Franco regime and deprived of executive power at the statewide level until December 1982, regional party branches could be involved more easily in the building of the post-Franco party structures (Gunther, Montero and Botella, 2004; but Fabre and Mendez-Lago in this volume). For some regional party chiefs this influence outlived the entry of the PSOE into central government (after which the PSOE became a more centralized party). Regional barons used their party influence to extract policy concessions from the statewide government. One could argue that, due to its origins in the Spanish political system, the PSOE was bound to develop a more decentralized organizational structure than its Conservative arch-rival. Statewide electoral successes of the PSOE accelerated a process of organizational centralization, just as the centralized nature of the German FDP has been attributed in part to its long-standing role as a kingmaker in statewide elections (Hopper, 2001). Similarly, since the German SPD did not take part in a federal coalition until 1966, the regional party branches (which often participated in regional coalitions) built up an important reservoir of policy expertise that came in handy when Willy Brandt steered the party towards federal electoral victory. Brandt, who once headed the Berlin regional government, recognized the relevance of regional party branches and leaders in presenting the SPD as a credible alternative to the Christian Democrats at the statewide level (Lösche and Walter, 1992: 234–5). The autonomy of the regional branches even increased after Brandt became party president and successfully pushed through internal party and ideological reforms. Simultaneously, the party (and the people at large) looked upon federalism as a more favourable institutional device (Conradt, 2005: 274).

Finally, although path-dependent logic makes parties inimical to structural change, parties also operate in an increasingly volatile environment, and unlike other 'public institutions' (for instance, ministerial departments or agencies) are subject to direct and recurrent electoral accountability. It has been suggested that, in order to cope with these new external challenges, most West European parties developed from *mass* into electoralist *catch-all* parties and by now have acquired the features of *cartel* parties (see Krouwel, 2006 for a comprehensive overview; Katz and Mair, 1995 for an exploration of the cartel party; and Detterbeck, 2005 for a powerful critique). In cartel parties power typically moves away from the party organization (especially the party activists) to the party office-holders. However, a second feature relates to the vertical *stratarchy* of different party levels. According to this thesis each level (statewide or regional) should be free to devise its own political strategies and strategic questions, including candidate selection and policy-making (Katz and Mair, 1995: 21; Detterbeck, 2005: 174–5). However, one could hypothesize that the degree of decentralization and concomitant strategic divergence will depend on how the party was organized in the past. Arguably, for parties that developed into strong and centralized mass parties it will be less easy to adapt their organization and strategy to a decentralized state structure.

Overview of the contributions

In the previous sections, we set out an ambitious research agenda with respect to studying multilevel party systems and the organization, strategy or policies of statewide parties which compete in statewide and regional elections. The chapters in this volume do not apply this framework to each of the West European federal party systems or the statewide parties which are vying for votes and office within them. Instead, we present evidence from five important federal or quasi-federal states of Western Europe: Belgium, Germany, Italy, Spain and the United Kingdom. Our chapters are comparative in the sense that each of them focuses on the electoral performance, strategy or organization of more than one statewide party. Some chapters deliberately adopt a cross-national approach by combining evidence from Belgium and Spain (Deschouwer), Spain and the UK (Fabre and Mendéz-Lago), Spain and Germany (van Houten, Ştefuriuc). Other chapters present evidence from individual country studies, but always with a broader theoretical or comparative framework in mind. The order in which the chapters are presented roughly respects the threefold structure of the analytical framework outlined above.

Party system analyses

A first group, consisting of two chapters, is concerned with an analysis of multilevel party systems. In the first contribution, Kris Deschouwer addresses Caramani's nationalization thesis by testing whether nationalization can be observed where it is expected the least: Belgium and Spain. Both states have undergone a rather radical regionalization or even federalization process in recent decades and therefore the question arises whether we can observe any effect of the regionalization of their political systems on the outcomes of statewide elections. Deschouwer develops a set of measurements to establish (1) whether the outcome of statewide elections reflects regional differences and (2), if so, whether the territorial heterogeneity of statewide electoral results has been *increasing* over time. Although the Belgian parties are no longer statewide, their inclusion is warranted, since parties still behave as 'party families': ideologically related parties from both sides of the language border end up together in federal government or opposition, at least until 2007. Furthermore, since the Belgian statewide parties split during the period between 1968 and 1978, but the electoral time series goes back to 1949, we can indeed consider to what extent the split of the parties coincides with or is rather preceded by a regionalization of national electoral results.

Deschouwer's chapter is concerned with developments in the statewide party system in two states which have decentralized in recent decades. In their contribution, Hough and Koß consider whether similar developments can be observed in Germany, a more 'stable' federation in terms of the scope of regional autonomy in recent decades. In contrast with Deschouwer, the authors analyse electoral trends in the statewide *and* regional party systems. In doing so, they pay attention to the concern that, even if no significant trends in the 'regionalization' of the statewide party system may be observed, voters could nonetheless increasingly display features of 'multilevel' voting behaviour, that is, approach regional elections without clear reference to statewide party politics. By adopting a multilevel approach, Hough and Koß analyse the effect of German unification on the integration of the German party system. Their analysis compares electoral trends before and after unification and, in the case of the latter, also compares developments between the 'old' and the 'new' German *Länder*.

The organization of statewide parties in the context of a multilevel system

A second group, consisting of five chapters, is concerned with how statewide parties organize in light of having to compete for votes and office in a multilayered structure. The first three of these chapters provide a general overview on how statewide parties have adapted their organization to the regionalized or federal nature of the state in which they operate.

In the first contribution Detterbeck and Jeffery build upon the preceding analysis by Hough and Koß. They focus on the shockwaves that German unification sent through the German political system and especially how it prompted a recalibration of German federalism. However, contrary to Hough and Koß, their unit of analysis is the adaptation of the statewide parties, not the German party system. Since unification, Germany has become a much more territorially heterogeneous society. The authors analyse the extent to which the German statewide parties have organized differently as a result.

In the next contribution, Jonathan Hopkin provides one of the first accounts – if not the first – of the territorial organization of Italian statewide parties. His analysis provides meaningful insights into the assumed relationship between the gradual decentralization of the state and adjustments in the internal organization of statewide parties. Like the chapter on the German parties (in which unification features as a 'critical juncture'), Hopkin distinguishes between two radically different periods. However, the critical juncture is related less to specific changes in the territorial organization of the state than to the implosion of the old party system and the change of electoral system in 1993. Therefore, the effect of regionalization on the party system is considered separately for the First Republic and the Second Republic.

In a third contribution, Fabre and Méndez-Lago focus on the territorial organization of the leading UK and Spanish statewide parties. The degree of autonomy of the regional party branches ('self-rule') is compared with their levels of participation ('shared rule' or 'vertical integration') in the statewide party branch. The authors present the evidence in light of some hypotheses that were outlined above: what are the effects of constitutional asymmetry, of incumbency at the statewide and regional levels and of party ideological traditions on how these statewide parties organize internally?

The fourth chapter in this group revisits the UK case, but focuses on one important aspect: candidate selection. Candidate selection, Gallagher and Marsh once famously said, is the 'secret garden' of politics (Gallagher and Marsh, 1988). That garden has become less secret in recent years, as more publications have become available which analyse how parties select candidates for statewide elections (Rahat and Hazan, 2001; Bille, 2001). In his contribution, Jonathan Bradbury sheds light on how the British statewide parties adapted their candidate selection procedures since they have had to organize for UK devolved elections. In doing so, his analysis 'corrects' the statewide bias which has thus far prevailed in most research on candidate selection. He also considers the link between constitutional asymmetry (Scotland versus Wales) and party ideology in selecting candidates for regional elections. Bradbury challenges the hypotheses that the cartelization of parties coincides with a more stratarchical relationship. Relying on more recent writings of Katz (2001), he argues that, in parties which adopt a more cartelized profile, central party elites do not refrain from pushing through candidate selection reforms for electoral reasons.

In the final contribution to this section, Frederik Verleden analyses the conditions under which the Belgian statewide parties split along linguistic lines between 1968 and 1978. The break-up of statewide parties in a unitary political system poses an important puzzle for analysts who posit a causal link between authority migration and party system (de)nationalization. The contribution by Verleden suggests that to solve this puzzle we must consider 'authority migration' *within* party organizational structures and not just within the state as a whole. More specifically, to what extent were the Belgian statewide parties already organized as 'federal' or 'confederal' parties before they broke up, and what triggered their break up?

Campaign strategy and policy

The final section brings together four chapters which focus more broadly on the relationship between the statewide party and its regional branches in a context of having to fight elections (campaign strategy) and to make policy at different levels and distinctive territorial political contexts.

The first contribution, by Pieter van Houten, applies a 'principal–agent' framework to demonstrate the intricate relationship between the statewide and the regional party branches on policy issues that touch the core of regional autonomy. van Houten first considers to what extent the German statewide parties sought to influence the views of the party-controlled *Länder* governments when these were asked to formulate their position on some proposals affecting their own financing. He then turns to the highly sensitive negotiations between the Spanish Social Democrats and their semi-autonomous regional party branch on revising the Catalan Statute of

Autonomy in 2005–6. By focusing on three policy issues of intra-party con-
tention, Van Houten investigates the conditions under which the statewide
party principal can or cannot assert 'his' autonomy vis-à-vis the regional
agents.

The next chapter in this cluster by Irina Şterfuriuc stays with the German
and Spanish case studies, but focuses on a different dimension of regional
party branch autonomy, namely, regional coalition-building. Spanish and
German regional elections are held under proportional representation (albeit
skewed in a majoritarian direction in the former case), and as a result frequently necessitate the building of regional coalition governments. But can
regional party branches build the coalitions of their choice, or are they constrained in this respect by the desires of the statewide party? The relatively
high level of interlocking between the statewide and regional policy levels
in both polities provides statewide party branches with an incentive to
prefer the 'politically most reliable' (read most party-politically congruent)
coalitions at the regional level also. Yet regional party branches may opt for
incongruent coalitions because the outcome of regional elections leaves them
with no choice or because they prefer such coalitions for electoral or policy
reasons. Relying on interviews with key policy-makers in two Spanish and
two German regions, Ştefuriuc considers why and under what conditions
regional party branches are likely to opt to form regional coalitions that are
incongruent with statewide coalitions.

The final two chapters in the section focus specifically on the electoral
strategy of statewide parties in regional elections in multinational states.
Campaign strategies are analysed by studying the content of party manifestos for statewide and regional elections. To this end, both chapters
analyse regional party manifestos, using the well-known methodology of the
Comparative Manifesto Project (CMP). Rather than copying the CMP issue
categorization, Bart Maddens and his team redefine issue categories in a way
which makes them more amenable to the comparative analysis of *regional*
party manifestos. For each statewide party, issue profiles are drawn up which
map the *salience* (that is, the frequency) with which certain issue categories
(for instance, social security or foreign policy) are listed in their manifestos
for statewide and regional elections. In addition, each issue is screened for its
position (direction) on the regionalist issue, that is, for the views that parties
adopt with regard to the current levels of regional autonomy (institutional
dimension) and to the strengthening of a regional (cultural or linguistic)
identity. Combining salience and position generates a measure of *directional
intensity*. In the first of two contributions, Maddens and Libbrecht analyse the
strategy of the Spanish statewide parties with regard to the regionalist issue,
that is, the extent to which statewide parties support either regional autonomy or regional culture and identity in regional and statewide elections.
In a second contribution, Fabre and Martínez consider the strategy of UK
statewide parties with respect to their salience profiles overall (that is, on all

the issues in a party manifesto) and with respect to the directional intensity on the regionalist issue.

The editors' conclusion to this volume seeks to tie the various approaches together and, where possible, to address (some of) the hypotheses that were outlined above. It also identifies unresolved puzzles or additional questions on party (system) research that were raised by the findings presented in the various contributions to the volume.

1
Towards a Regionalization of Statewide Electoral Trends in Decentralized States? The Cases of Belgium and Spain

Kris Deschouwer

Regions and electoral politics: Three approaches

The general and long-term picture of electoral politics in Europe is one of gradual nationalization. We now have considerable empirical evidence to support this view (Caramani, 2004). The evidence shows an increasing statewide territorial homogeneity of electoral support for the parties on offer, at least in general elections. There are several explanations for this long-term trend, but they basically boil down to the idea that national party competition has been spread and institutionalized over the entire territory of the state. Voters are therefore responding to national or statewide factors: nationally defined mechanics of the party system, national government policies, and national events (see also Caramani, 1996).

This all illustrates the crucial importance of the state and of its territorially defined political community as the central structure of modern politics, as the forum for political participation and policy-making. Parties and pressure groups as well as notions like citizenship and legitimacy are deeply rooted in the state as an institutional environment. The process of state formation and boundary closure is of crucial importance for understanding modern (party) politics (Flora et al., 1999).

If this institutional environment is indeed so important for understanding the way in which politics functions the gradually changing institutional architecture of politics must have highly visible effects on political actors and strategies. If we are today witnessing a move towards a more 'regional Europe' and towards a (re)invention of the regions as meaningful levels of decision-making then the effects on (among others) party politics must be evident.

The general mood in the literature since the late 1980s is undoubtedly one in which the regional factor is being explicitly acknowledged, especially in countries where regions are fairly new or where they have recently received more substantial competencies (for instance, Harvie, 1994; Keating, 1998; Loughlin, 2001).

For party politics or, more broadly, electoral politics this leads logically to three possible types of analysis. The first is the analysis of the regional level itself: regional elections, regional parties, and regional party units. The new level is analysed according to its own logic, with its own electoral system, its own parties and party system, and its own pattern of competition (for instance, De Winter and Türsan, 1998; Hough and Jeffery, 2006c). This regional level can of course never be understood outside its national context. Regionalist parties have a programme that questions the status of their region in the national state, and regional sections of statewide parties need to deal with these demands. Yet the analysis of the regional level of party politics is to a large extent a single-level analysis, dealing with party interactions and voter behaviour at the regional tier of the national state.

A second type of analysis looks more explicitly at the *interaction* between the regional and national levels. A typical example of this approach is the notion of second-order election, originally coined to explain how elections to the European Parliament are actually fought according to the national logic and given meaning according to the national logic (Reif and Schmitt, 1980; Reif, 1984). The notion of a second order refers explicitly to a hierarchy, to a core level influencing the other level. The idea that elections at different levels tend to give meaning to each other, depending on their place in each other's electoral cycle, is, however, older than the first elections to the European Parliament (see Dinkel, 1977), and has now expanded beyond the analysis of European elections (for instance, Heath et al., 1999; Jeffery and Hough, 2003; Pallarés and Keating, 2003).

The idea of interacting levels has also found its way into the analysis of political parties. New research is conducted on the way in which political parties coordinate their activities and strategies between levels (campaigns, coalition formation, vertical integration of the party organization, and relations with typically regional or regionalist parties) (for instance, Hopkin, 2003). The regional level is thus brought in as a meaningful level for party politics. The national level is not the only level at which electoral politics is relevant, and voters are therefore mobilized and respond to party politics at both the national and the regional levels (Lancaster, 1999). Parties need to adapt to this new and more complex multilayered institutional environment, just as parties need to adapt to (older) federal systems (for instance, Hadley et al., 1989).

In this chapter we wish to explore a third approach. It links directly to the notion of the nationalization of electoral politics, and tries to look at the consequences of the (re)invention of the regional level for the processes of nationalization. Indeed, if the regional level is important there is always more than one level in the institutional environment of electoral politics. And rather than looking at the way in which regional electoral politics are different from or influenced by national politics one can try to see to what extent national electoral politics is affected by the presence of the regional level. Our research question is therefore: *can we see an effect of the regionalization of political systems on the outcomes of national or statewide (general) elections?* If that is the case national election results are likely to display a larger and, especially, increasing variation or heterogeneity across the regional units of the state. In other words: is there evidence of a slowing down of the nationalization processes or even of a 'denationalization' of national electoral politics in states with a strong regional tier?

We will explore this regionalization of national electoral politics, that is, the effects of the regional factor on the national electoral game in two countries, namely, Belgium and Spain. The two cases were selected because they have both recently gone through processes of constitutional change that have clearly redefined their territory. In Spain the granting of substantial political powers to the Autonomous Communities as part of the democratization following the end of the Franco regime from the outset created a political system in which the political parties have to be aware of regional differences. The regional party systems in Spain display a high degree of variation, mainly due to the presence of a fairly large number of regional parties. The importance of the regional level for electoral politics has also been clearly illustrated by the high degree of dissimilarity between regional and national elections (Jeffery and Hough, 2003; Pallarés and Keating, 2003). We expect to see the development of national electoral politics that reflects the institutionalization of the regional fact in Spain.

Belgium has in the course of the last few decades also been transformed from a unitary state into a complex federal-type system, taking into account the ethno-linguistic differences between the Dutch speakers of north and the French speakers of the south of the country (and of the awkward location of the 'frenchified' capital city of Brussels in the northern region). Moreover, there are no more statewide political parties but only parties competing in their own language group (see Verleden in this volume for a detailed analysis). Even for national elections the electoral arena is split into a northern one and a southern one. That should lead to a strong regionalization of national electoral politics.

For the two countries we will ask two related questions. First we try to see whether and to what extent *national electoral outcomes reflect regional differences*. Since we look at decentralized countries we do assume that we will find such regional differences. The second question is then: do these differences increase over time? If the regional factor and the regional level have become more important in the course of the last few decades we should see an *increasing regionalization* or territorial heterogeneity of national electoral politics in Belgium and Spain.

The two countries are, however, also quite different, and in answering the questions we will sometimes need to rely on different indicators. One of the crucial differences is the number of regions. In Belgium, although there are three language communities (Dutch, French, and German) and three regions

(Flanders, Wallonia, and Brussels), the division of the country is basically one between north and south. This bipolar logic means that the national level is the aggregation of the two parts of the country, and that any comparison of a region with the national level is simply a comparison of one part with the other. In Spain, by contrast, each region can indeed be compared with the rest of the country.

Belgium

Belgium seems to be an obvious case of strong regionalization of electoral politics. Indeed, between 1968 and 1978 the three major Belgian parties – Christian Democrats, Liberals and Socialists – each divided into two separate unilingual parties, competing only with the other parties of their own language group (except for the central Brussels constituency). Subsequently, all new parties were created in one or the other language group, even if some of these new parties – the Greens in particular – are present on both sides (but as two different party organizations). Therefore, Belgian parties cover only a limited territory since not a single (significant) party is present in all of the constituencies.

As a consequence there are two party systems. Voters of each language group are confronted (via unilingual mass media) with patterns of competition that are specific to that one language group. In the north the party system is highly fragmented. For decades after the Second Word War the Christian Democrats were by far the dominant party of Flanders. Today four parties are relatively close to each other: Christian Democrats (CD&V), Liberals (Open VLD), Socialists (SP.a), and the right-wing populists (Vlaams Belang). There is a smaller Green party (Groen) and – flashing up at the 2007 elections – a breakaway Liberal Party (List Dedecker).

In the south the party system comes closer to a two-party mechanism; until 2007 the Socialists Party (PS) was the largest party, a position it has (temporarily?) ceded to the Liberal Party (MR) in the 2007 general elections. Christian Democrats (CDh) and Greens (Ecolo) are much smaller and the right-wing populist FN is close to insignificant.

This split party system should be a strong factor working against nationalization. Voters receive information and major cues about what happens in politics only within their own language group. The political personnel are different in north and south, and important politicians – including those with the ambition of becoming a member of the federal government – compete only in their own language group.

At first sight it might even seem quite pointless to take Belgium as a case where regionalization of electoral politics can be tested. That it is regionalized indeed goes without saying. If there are no national parties national results can only reflect the regional factor. It is indeed striking that election results are read and interpreted at the level of the language group and not at the national level. Official results will obviously report the scores obtained by the parties in Belgium at large, but media on both sides and the parties themselves give meaning only to the results obtained within the language group in which they are competing.

Belgium's self-image is also one in which the discourse of 'increasing difference' prevails. The general belief is that the north and the south of the country are constantly growing further apart, favouring different policies, and displaying different attitudes and political cultures. It leads to a constant questioning of the sustainability of the system. It is of course not easy to be responsive to the electorate if it is completely split and sends different regional messages to the federal level of decision-making.

Yet the Belgian political system (still) exists, and its existence does mean that national factors remain present in the way in which it functions. Federal elections are held (in principle) every four years and produce a federal bicameral parliament and a federal government. One of the most important characteristics (before 2008 at least) of the federal government is its symmetrical composition. Parties belonging to the same ideological family either govern together or end up together in federal opposition. That means that the federal cabinet (which according to the constitution must be composed of an equal number of ministers from each language community) produces a clear division not only between governing and opposition parties but also between party *families* in government and opposition. The competition for government thus retains a similar character in both communities. Even if there is a specific dynamic in each party system, the parties of the same family go to the polls on both sides of the language border either as parties of the incumbent government or as parties of the opposition. If this is a meaningful element it could have a homogenizing effect on the electoral fate of party families all over the Belgian territory. While there is an extremely differentiated campaign in north and south there is also a symmetry that introduces a homogeneous element to the campaign.

In the analysis of the Belgian case, we will therefore take the party *families* as the unit of analysis. Looking at the individual parties can lead – as said above – only to the conclusion that there is full and complete regionalization. And this needs to be kept in mind for the further discussion of the Belgian case. Using the party families is also a choice than enables us to present a truly longitudinal analysis, since the party families can be seen and measured irrespective of the presence of a unitary party. We can look at the dynamics before the splitting of the national parties in the 1970s, at what happens during this falling apart, and at what happens from then until the present.

We will compare the electoral results since 1946 in the two major regions of the country: Flanders and Wallonia. That is not the only way to divide the country. Indeed, the regional division does not fully coincide with the division into language communities. For Flanders the electoral results of the

Flemish region are almost the same as those in the Dutch-speaking (Flemish) community. The only difference is the votes for Dutch-speaking parties in Brussels. Since more than 97 per cent of the votes for Dutch-speaking parties originate from the Flemish region and not from Brussels this difference between region and community is very marginal. On the francophone side matters are slightly more complicated. Indeed, the congruence between Wallonia and the French-speaking community is smaller. Between 15 and 20 per cent of the votes for francophone parties originate from Brussels. However, we will look at the Walloon region alone. Opting for the linguistic community would mean that we have to be able to count the francophone votes in Brussels, and this is possible only after the split of the Belgian parties. Before the split the unitary Belgian parties received votes in Brussels, but it is impossible to know from which language group they came. We also leave out the Brussels region. The problem here is that it was not possible – until 1995 – to aggregate election results to the level of what is known today as the Brussels region. The electoral cantons in Brussels – the lowest level at which votes are counted – included local communities of the present region of Flanders. That also means that the results for Flanders are not absolutely perfect: until 1995 some of the votes in Flanders (a very small proportion, however) were cast in cantons that include parts of Brussels.

Three of the traditional parties have recently decided to form electoral alliances with smaller parties. The francophone Liberal Party (MR) since 1995 has been an electoral alliance of the Liberal Party and of the Brussels Party of Francophone Defence (Front des Francophones, FDF). It is impossible to single out the votes for each party since they are cast for a common list. Thus, we opted to count all the votes as votes for the Liberal family. In Flanders the regionalist party Volksunie fell apart in 2001 (Wauters, 2005). Two new parties were created: a left-liberal party called Spirit and a conservative and more clearly regionalist (actually separatist) party New Flemish Alliance (NVA). For the federal elections of 2003 and of 2007 Spirit formed an electoral alliance with the Flemish Socialist Party. In 2007 the NVA presented common lists with the Christian Democrats. In both cases the votes were also considered to be cast for respectively the Socialist and the Christian Democratic family in the north.

Party families in Flanders and Wallonia

If the level of support for each party family is different in north and south that must add up to a different overall result in Flanders and Wallonia. The question here is then: is this difference increasing? Do the two regions grow further apart when their citizens vote in national elections? This can be tested in a very straightforward way. For each election since 1946 we calculated an index of dissimilarity, computed like the volatility index (Pedersen, 1979) for comparing two subsequent elections in the same area. We sum up the differences per party family and divide the total by 2. The result of this

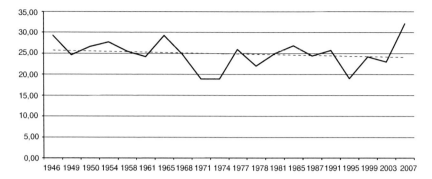

Figure 1.1 The dissimilarity between general/statewide election results per party family in Flanders and Wallonia (1956–2007)

can be seen in Figure 1.1. It shows in the first place that the difference between the two regions is quite impressive. Electoral results in north and south really are different from each other. The graph shows the post-war evolution, but pre-war election results show the same gap between the regions (Ştefuriuc and Deschouwer, 2007).

The evolution over time is one of fluctuation. There are three high points: 2007 with a dissimilarity index of 32.1 per cent, 1946 with 29.3 per cent, and 1965 with 29.2 per cent. Both the oldest and the youngest results belong to this highest trio, and the linear trend is close to a flat line. Therefore, we must conclude that electoral results in Flanders and Wallonia are very different, and that they have always been different. It is not the reform of the institutions granting autonomy to the regions and language communities that has created the differences. The institutional reform, rather, acknowledged these differences. The second conclusion is – rather surprisingly – that the differences are not increasing, at least not if we look at the full period. The four most recent elections show an increase. In 1995 the regional parliaments were directly elected for the first time, and since then one can indeed say that the national election results have moved further apart. But 1995 is not the date from which the Belgian party system and the Belgian public opinion split. And it is of course a little early to assess the dynamics created by the adding of the regional elections, especially since in 1995 and in 1999 the regional and federal elections were organized on the same day, producing close to identical results. The peak in 2007 can also partly be explained by the presence and sudden success (6.4 per cent of the Flemish votes) of the breakaway Liberal Party LDD. We have counted it as a separate party, not as one belonging to the Liberal family.

Table 1.1 breaks down the index of dissimilarity per election year. The figures are thus the difference between the results of each family in Flanders and Wallonia (for the dissimilarity index the sum of these differences is

Table 1.1 The difference between electoral results in Flanders and Wallonia per major party family (absolute values of the difference between the percentage of votes obtained in Flanders and in Wallonia)

	CD	SOC	LIB	COM	REG	ECO	XR
1946	29.1	8.9	1.6	16.0			
1949	20.0	14.1	1.6	9.0	3.2		
1950	26.6	18.6	2.0	5.3	0.0		
1954	21.5	19.0	0.9	5.2	3.9		
1958	21.5	18.4	0.6	4.4	3.4		
1961	19.4	16.8	0.4	5.3	6.0		
1965	19.3	10.6	8.8	8.6	10.0		
1968	18.1	8.5	10.5	1.5	6.7		
1971	17.0	15.7	1.9	0.4	1.9		
1974	17.0	15.7	1.9	0.4	1.9		
1977	18.2	16.7	4.6	4.2	7.6	0.6	
1978	16.7	15.7	0.5	3.9	2.7	1.06	2.0
1981	12.5	15.5	0.5	2.9	10.7	1.98	1.77
1985	12.1	15.6	6.5	2.0	12.7	0.0	2.2
1987	8.3	19.6	3.5	1.2	12.2	0.9	3.0
1991	4.4	19.6	0.6		8.3	5.6	8.1
1995	4.9	13.5	2.3		7.3	3.2	6.01
1999	5.6	14.0	1.4		8.2	6.8	10.5
2003	5.8	12.5	3.2		4.8	3.4	12.4
2003	5.8	12.5	3.2		4.8	3.4	12.4
2007	13.9	13.2	12.4			6.5	13.4

divided by 2). A closer look at these figures immediately reveals that the *meaning or content* of the more or less stable difference has been changing quite dramatically. In 1946 there is a difference of almost 30 per cent between the Christian Democrats of the north (polling 56 per cent of the votes) and the south. Another major difference is the left vote, with a 15 per cent difference for the Communists and another 9 per cent for the Socialists. This huge gap between the Christian Democratic results has gradually narrowed, mainly due to the spectacular decline of Christian Democracy in Flanders, which in 2007 again polled – this time in alliance with NVA – almost 30 per cent of the vote.

The Liberal parties have always been rather close to each other, with again the 2007 result showing quite a difference. In 2007 the francophone Liberals realized their best score ever, while the Liberals in Flanders lost heavily (see also below). Between the two Socialist parties there has always been a difference of 10 to 20 per cent. The story of the regionalist parties in north and south is also somewhat different. Regionalism developed a little earlier in Flanders and survived for a longer time, only to disappear – at least in its electorally visible aspect – in 2007. Another enduring difference between Flanders and Wallonia is right-wing populism. It is very strong in Flanders, with close to 20 per cent of the votes in 2007, while the FN polls only 5.5 per cent in Wallonia.

Flanders and Wallonia are thus two regions which vote differently in national elections. That difference is large. It has, however, always been large, and it is difficult (and probably too early) to assert that it is increasing. However, the difference has had a different meaning over time, with only a clear gap between the scores of the Socialists and more recently of the right-wing populists as a permanent feature.

Electoral swings

Another important indicator of the nationalization of electoral politics is the territorial homogeneity of electoral swings. If movements up or down are the same all over the territory this means that the voters are responding homogeneously to clues and incentives coming from the national party. If electoral swings vary across the territory it means that voters are rather responding to local phenomena, like a locally differentiated image of the party or local party leaders. We are thus looking for similar electoral changes in all parts of the territory. If a party loses it should lose everywhere. If it loses heavily it should lose heavily everywhere.

For Belgium the analysis of the electoral changes between elections and per party family are very relevant. Indeed, the role of the national government as the crucial link between the two party systems makes the electoral swings an important aspect of the legitimacy of government formation. Although cabinets need only to secure a majority of seats in the national parliament there is a psychological element that cannot be discarded. When a party (or party family) has 'lost' the election, that is, secured fewer votes than the previous time it is much more difficult to claim the right to (continue to) govern. And since party families have until 2008 always governed together in symmetrical national governments a common trend makes it at least easier to legitimize the choices made for cabinet formation.

In the Belgian public debate it is – as we said above – generally accepted that the electoral results in the two regions are increasingly different, sending different messages to political decision-makers. We have already seen that there is indeed a large difference in the results but that this difference is not increasing (at least not until 1995). What about the electoral swings then?

We have computed an index of change per party family and per election, by dividing the results in one region by the results of that same party in the same region at the previous election (election result of party A at time t/election result of party A at time t-1). The index is larger than 1 if a party increased its score and smaller than 1 if it lost votes.

Table 1.2 shows 72 comparable swings (for parties polling at least 5 per cent in their region), with 20 of them conflicting (that is, going in different directions in north and south). Of these 20 no fewer than 9 are for the liberal family. And 11 occur during the period of high ethno-linguistic tensions

Table 1.2 Electoral trends per party family in Flanders and Wallonia (conflicting trends are shaded)

	CD		SOC		LIB		REG		ECO		RIGHT	
	Vl	Wal	Vl	Wal	Vl	Wal	Vl	Wal	Vl	Wal	Vl	Wal
1949	0,92	1,18	0,87	1,04	1,71	1,59						
1950	1,16	1,06	1.10	1.18	0.72	0.78						
1954	0.86	0.90	1.11	1.07	1.14	1.02						
1958	1.09	1.15	0.97	0.97	0.91	0.89						
1961	0.89	0.88	1.07	1.01	1.24	1.13						
1965	0.87	0.79	0.83	0.76	1.37	2.16	1.93					
1968	0.89	0.85	1.06	0.98	0.97	1.05	1.44					
1971	0.97	1.00	0.95	1.00	1.02	0.66	1.12	1.99				
1974	1.07	1.12	0.92	1.11	1.06	0.89	0.90	0.92				
1977	1.09	1.10	0.99	1.02	0.83	1.22	0.96	0.47				
1978	0.99	1.05	0.94	0.94	1.19	0.88	0.71	1.01				
1981	0.73	0.73	0.98	0.99	1.23	1.30	1.36	0.60				
1985	1.08	1.16	1.15	1.09	0.83	1.11	0.79					
1987	0.91	1.02	1.02	1.11	1.06	0.92	1.02		1.19	1.04		
1991	0.86	0.97	0.80	0.89	1.03	0.89	0.73		1.07	2.09		
1995	1.02	1.00	1.03	0.86	1.12	1.21	0.78		0.90	0.76	1.19	2.78
1999	0.82	0.75	0.75	0.87	1.08	1.03	1.19		1.60	1.77	1.25	0.78
2003	0.95	0.91	1.58	1.25	1.08	1.15	0.55		0.35	0.41	1.17	1.13
2007	1.06	1.03	0.69	0.81	0.78	1.10			1.63	1.71	1.06	1.00

(Trend for parties reaching at least 5 per cent in their region)

of the 1960s and 1970s. For the Greens – which were never a single party in Belgium – the trends have always been the same.

If we leave out the 1949 elections – comparing with the first post-war elections of 1946 – it is clear that something changes in 1968. That is interesting because that is the year in which the first party – the Christian Democrats – fell apart (see the chapter by Verleden). From the early 1960s ethno-linguistic tensions were very high on the agenda, meaning that parties of the same family in the north and in the south defended very different views on the future structure of the Belgian state. The varying responses of the electorates are a logical consequence of that. The 1990s were a decade with fewer clashes between the two language groups and with a stronger emphasis on economic, social, and financial issues. These brought parties of the same family in the two regions much closer to each other. And except for the liberal parties the trends are then again quite similar.[1]

Is the regionalization of the Belgian state then a source of increasing heterogeneity of the electoral swings? The answer is basically negative. The causality goes rather in the other direction: the differences between north and south that are translated into different results and – over two decades – in conflicting trends have led to the decentralization and the creation of autonomous regions and language communities. Once these were put in place, the differences between the members of the same family in the north and south became less marked. The 'nationalizing' factor, that is, the symmetry of the federal government, then seems to be a stronger force than the regional differences.

Spain

In Spain the most obvious indicator of the presence of an important regional level with its own electoral dynamics is the variety of party systems among the regions and the differences between regional and national elections. The crucial ingredient of these differences is the regional parties. Of all the Spanish parties only a few cover the whole territory (mainly PSOE, PP and IU). Most of the parties (but these are small parties seen from the national level) limit their activities to one or two regions. The institutional set-up of Spain also allows for more regional variation. The 'vertical' logic, in which the Autonomous Communities each receive their own autonomous statute from the centre, and the differences from the early days between regions on the fast track and regions on the slower track towards autonomy all allow for some considerable variation between the regions (Moreno, 2001). In some regions like Catalonia or the Basque Country the regional(ist) parties are major players in the game. For Spain our second question will therefore be more important. If there is indeed a high level of regionalization of national electoral politics can we see and say that this is increasing? Is there an ever stronger impact of the regional factor on national elections?

Territorial homogeneity of the results

The first question is the more general: are the electoral outcomes of the parties homogeneously spread over the territory, and more in particular over the Autonomous Communities? To check this we need to break down national election results per Autonomous Community. The data we used are those published by Caramani (2000) and – for 2000 and 2004 – by the Spanish Ministerio del Interior.[2]

In order to see whether the results of a party are homogeneously spread over the Autonomous Communities we compute a *Cumulative Regional Inequality Index* (CRII) (Rose and Urwin, 1975). It actually measures whether the territorial distribution of voters within a party matches the territorial distribution of the electorate as a whole. If for instance a country is divided in five constituencies with each 20 per cent of the voters the electorate of a party also has to be equally divided between these constituencies for the index to equal zero. If a party gathers most of its voters in only one constituency and hardly any voters in the other constituencies its CRII index will be high, meaning that the party support is heterogeneous.

The formula for the CRII is the following:

$$\Sigma \ (E_i \ / \ E_t - P_i \ / \ P_t) \ / \ 2$$

with E_i = proportion of the electorate registered in constituency i
E_t = the total number of registered voters in the country
P_i = the proportion of the voters of party P in constituency i
P_t = the total number of voters of party P in the country

There are two important advantages of this index. In the first place it allows us to make comparisons between parties. It is not affected by the size of a party. The second advantage is that it takes into account the size of the constituencies over which the index is computed. Large areas – in our case Autonomous Communities with a large number of voters – have more weight than Communities with a smaller number. In Spain, where there is quite some variety in the size of the Communities, this is an important guarantee for the validity of the measurements.

Figure 1.2 shows the evolution since 1977 of the CRII values for UCD (until 1982), of the Partido Popular (PP) and of the Socialist Party (PSOE). The figure also gives a weighted total for all the parties participating in national elections. This weighted total shows immediately that there is no increasing heterogeneity of the party results in Spain. The linear trend of the total line is fully flat. The trend line for the UCD is not very surprising and also – for Spanish politics today – not very important. It shows how the decline of the UCD did not occur evenly in all Communities. Before fully disappearing in 1986 it still scored quite well in 1982 in Galicia and in the Canary Islands, but had almost or fully disappeared in Madrid, the Basque Country and Catalonia.

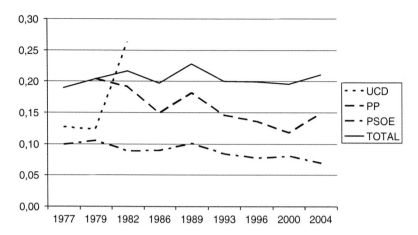

Figure 1.2 Territorial heterogeneity of the major statewide parties in Spain (CRII values)

The new Conservative Party PP starts with rather heterogeneous results, and then rapidly covers the Spanish territory in a fairly homogeneous way. The PSOE was from the very beginning a party with a more homogeneous result, and it still is today. However, it did move further – albeit more slowly than the PP – towards even more homogeneity. The conclusion can thus be that Spain displays some considerable regional variation in its electoral results, but that *this variation is not increasing over time*.

To evaluate the degree in which regions produce electoral results that are different and specific for the regions we need to use a bottom-up measure. That should tell us to what extent the result in one Autonomous Community differs from the nationwide results. Since these nationwide results also comprise the results in the region to be analysed we propose to compare the regional results in each Autonomous Community with the results in the country *minus* those in the Autonomous Community for which we measure the specificity. For comparing the regional results with the results in the rest of the country we also use a dissimilarity index based on the volatility index. While in the case of Belgium we compared the two regions for Spain we measure the dissimilarity between the results in one region and the national results without that region. The results are listed in Table 1.3.

We see indeed that some of the Autonomous Communities have electoral results that are very different while others have results that are more or less the same as in the rest of the country. The most specific regions though are the Basque Country, Catalonia, The Canary Islands, Galicia, and Navarre (and also the two small entities Ceuta and Melilla). The question here is however whether these specificities increase. Indeed, if there is an increasing

Table 1.3 The regional specificity of national elections in Spain (volatility index comparing Autonomous Community with rest of the country) – highest scores per region are shaded

	1977	1979	1982	1986	1989	1993	1996	2000	2004	Avg
Andalusia	10.79	17.76	17.35	20.09	25.23	18.73	17.66	18.33	20.26	18.47
Aragon	16.00	15.63	13.38	13.35	13.82	19.29	16.13	15.02	13.83	15.16
Asturias	11.86	12.82	14.45	11.59	13.23	10.77	11.18	10.54	12.17	12.07
Baleares	19.47	17.55	20.72	15.59	20.45	18.55	15.16	16.37	17.10	17.88
Basque Country	40.03	50.53	54.09	54.54	59.72	49.07	46.51	38.37	45.18	48.67
Canary Islands	27.10	35.25	23.91	20.61	22.65	25.74	25.24	30.02	24.33	26.09
Cantabria	15.57	19.43	17.95	12.28	15.47	14.21	13.21	13.25	14.18	15.06
Castilla-La Mancha	13.91	15.11	13.56	13.93	17.20	15.59	14.08	15.92	14.26	14.84
Castilla y Leon	22.29	21.39	20.91	19.80	21.14	15.31	15.80	13.79	13.28	18.19
Catalonia	38.11	30.27	27.30	33.33	36.22	37.14	35.93	35.60	39.79	34.86
Extramadura	17.57	18.52	11.14	12.99	16.39	14.00	12.90	14.47	13.71	14.63
Galicia	28.59	31.04	27.54	23.44	23.46	19.48	23.26	29.59	21.28	25.30
La Rioja	18.58	21.31	19.81	14.37	16.04	14.17	13.57	11.36	13.72	15.88
Madrid	12.29	12.58	17.19	14.31	20.93	16.59	19.65	14.34	13.61	15.72
Murcia	12.75	13.29	15.05	13.34	13.48	12.99	11.73	15.55	20.89	14.34
Navarre	37.87	35.56	24.18	19.56	24.52	14.63	18.47	16.50	17.97	23.25
Valencia	11.89	11.53	34.83	10.50	11.57	12.04	11.66	12.11	15.69	14.65
Ceuta	16.08	25.34	13.63	13.77	21.88	20.11	22.08	30.76	21.35	20.56
Melilla	24.80	25.34	16.84	22.54	30.23	20.76	18.28	27.57	16.70	22.56

regionalization of electoral politics in Spain these regions should generate more regionally specific results. And that is not the case.

Only in the case of Catalonia and Murcia is the last election the most specific one. For Murcia this is an exceptional score that needs to be confirmed. The most recent score for Catalonia it is a little higher than the score for 1977, but Catalonia has always had relatively high scores. For the other important regions the highest dissimilarity scores are found in 1989 (Basque Country and Andalusia), 1979 (Galicia and Canary Islands) and 1977 (Navarre).

Electoral swings

Finally, we have also looked at the electoral swings in Spain. This allows us to check whether the parties move in the same direction between elections in all the Autonomous Communities. We computed again an index of change: votes for party at t1/votes for party at t-1. And for each election year we compute whether this index is varying between the Autonomous Communities. To this end we use a standardized coefficient of variation; this is the standard deviation of the index of change divided by the average of

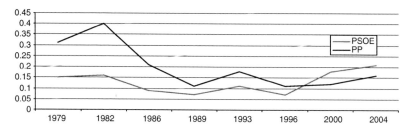

Figure 1.3 Heterogeneity of electoral swings in Spain

the index of change. The division by the average standardizes and thus neutralizes the magnitude of the swing. If a party loses or wins a lot the standard deviation is also higher; dividing by the average controls for this.

Figure 1.3 presents the evolution of the electoral swings for the PP and the PSOE. These swings were quite high in the late 1970s, but then rapidly declined. The two last elections showed again a little more heterogeneity, but still much lower than in the 1970s and the 1980s. The PSOE was more homogeneous from the beginning, while the PP – which stabilized and institutionalized later than the PSOE – remained at a higher level of heterogeneity.

If we look at the *direction* of the swings the picture is one of fairly large homogeneity. The last three elections can illustrate nicely what is going on. In 1996 the PSOE lost slightly (index 0.97) while the PP won (index 1.13). The PP won everywhere, except in Isles Baleares (0.97), while the PSOE lost in most regions but not in Aragon, Asturias (both 1.01), Catalonia (1.13), and Valencia (1.00). Only Catalonia is thus really deviant.

In 2000 there is a little more homogeneity. In 2000 the PP won again (index 1.13) while the PSOE lost more heavily (0.85). The PP lost votes only in Aragon (0.97) and in the two small units Ceuta (0.88) and Melilla (0.97). The PSOE lost everywhere, except in Madrid (1.04).

And 2004 is – as far as the direction of the swings is concerned – very homogeneous. The PSOE won clearly (1.33) and lost only in Extramadura (0.95). The PP lost everywhere, except in Extramadura (1.08), Ceuta (1.24), and Melilla (1.10). The general picture is one of parties moving in the same direction in a great majority of the regions. The deviant results of Ceuta and Melilla are, given the small size of both communities, of course not very important.

Conclusion

This paper has presented data on two countries. It is a first attempt to tease out the notion of regionalization and to see how it can adequately be measured. We chose Spain and Belgium because we thought that these are countries where regionalization would be evident.

The results are not very encouraging for those who believe that the presence of (strong and important) regions has clear and increasing effects on national electoral politics. For Belgium we must of course acknowledge the absence of national parties, which is a very strong indicator of a purely regional logic. Yet looking at the party families has revealed a number of slightly surprising results. In the first place we have seen that the party landscapes in north and south are very different, but that this difference is not becoming more important but rather of a different kind, more complex. We have also seen that the electoral swings in north and south have been diverging during a specific period: between the late 1960s and the early 1980s. Before and after this period the general logic is one of parties of the same family moving up and down together in north and south. Since 1995 there seems to be an increase in the differences again, but with only two federal elections not coinciding with regional elections so far it is a little early to call this a new and enduring trend.

For Spain we have found the expected presence of a fairly strong regional variety in the national results. But this variety is not increasing. It has – as in Belgium – always been there and remains rather stable. We have also seen that for the two major statewide parties – PSOE and PP – the electoral results tend to become more homogeneously spread over the Autonomous Communities. The homogeneity is greater for the PSOE than for the PP, but both parties seem to move towards increasing national homogeneity. Electoral swings were high for both parties at the first elections, but have been gradually going down since. The 2000 and the 2004 elections show more heterogeneous electoral swings, but the direction of the swing is basically the same in all the Autonomous Communities. And that means that we have a regionalized country with regional specificities present in national elections, but with a trend moving rather in the direction of increasing nationalization.

2
Territory and Electoral Politics in Germany

Dan Hough and Michael Koß

Introduction

Modern party political competition, as this volume illustrates, occurs in ever more complex settings. Long gone are the days (if, indeed, they ever existed at all) when parties could craft one political package that was suitable for more or less all electoral contests. Parties now have to mould, shape and articulate their demands in a multitude of ways to make them relevant to different sets of voters possessing differentiated sets of interests for elections to different sets of institutions. At the vertical level, federal institutional arrangements have traditionally been used to permit voters to voice their territorially specific interests in substate elections. Long-established federal states (such as the US, Australia, Canada, Germany and Switzerland) have recently been joined by states such as Belgium, the UK, Spain and Italy – to name but four – in creating, or rejuvenating, genuinely significant multilayered institutional frameworks. Increasing divergences in wealth, interests and even identity awareness *within* nation-states have also prompted parties to mould their political profiles and messages in more subtle and focused ways in order to appeal to electors who rely less and less frequently on the pillars of class and partisan alignments in shaping their votes.

Political scientists have not always been the most adept at making sense of the changes (or nuances, in the case of older multilevel states) in organization, policy and strategy that parties have adopted in coming to terms with these challenges. Parties are all too frequently viewed as unitary actors with specific sets of aims and methods. Such criticisms can also be made of attempts to make sense of what voters make of these different electoral environments. While attempts to understand voter attitudes to mid-term polls in the US (Tufte, 1975; Erikson, 1988) and elections to the EP in Europe (Reif and Schmitt, 1980; van der Eijk et al., 1996) have undoubtedly gone some way to highlighting how electors deal with multilevel challenges, a concerted theory of voting behaviour in different institutional contexts is still noticeably lacking. The decision of Tony Blair, the former UK Prime Minister, to devolve power to a newly (re-)created parliament in Scotland and an assembly in Wales has prompted a generation of UK scholars to at least attempt to take up this (not inconsiderable) challenge. Although most scholars would be quick to say that data sets in the UK are small and attempts at theorising from them are very much works in progress, one particularly interesting attempt to understand the new dynamics of party political competition stems from a research team in mid-Wales centred on Richard Wyn Jones, Roger Scully and Dafydd Trystan. They have developed a framework for understand voter behaviour that is based on what they term 'multilevel voting' (Wyn Jones and Scully, 2006; see also Trystan et al., 2003). This approach suggests that sub-state elections in states with meaningful regional authorities are not necessarily subject to what Reif and Schmitt would call 'second-order' influences alone. These polls lie somewhere between first order and second order and therefore illustrate sets of characteristics that can be particular to either of the arenas. Strong regional identities, cultural traditions and socio-economic peculiarities may prompt voters to think rather more about whom they cast their votes for in *all* elections in that territory than has previously been perceived as being the case. While some second-order traits may be evident, such as lower turnouts and an increased tendency to vote for smaller parties, there may also be significant interest in the election itself, and votes could quite plausibly be being cast in such a way as to grant politicians at the substate level legitimacy to shape substate-level solutions to the problems of the day. But the primacy of 'first-order' considerations among those voting cannot be assumed as a given; it is most likely to hold when voters are *not* able to identify relevant considerations within the particular electoral context to guide their voting decisions. In other words – as Heath et al. argued in 1999 – second-order considerations may be less dominant, for example, in local council elections in the UK, if people can be mobilized around local issues (Heath et al., 1999). And in the elections to *Land* parliaments in states such as Germany, with its (in comparative terms) relatively powerful regional tier, there may be substantially greater scope yet for many of those voting to identify matters in the substate arena on which to shape their voting decisions.

Research conducted elsewhere (Hough and Jeffery, 2006b; Jeffery and Hough, 2009) illustrates that some of the characteristics of the multilevel voting that the Welsh team discusses may well be prevalent – particularly since 1990 – in the Federal Republic of Germany. Although the same parties contest all types of election, and voters do not generally cast their ballots in radically different ways across the levels, disparities between statewide and substate election results in individual *Länder* appear to have increased since unification (Hough and Jeffery, 2006b). Pre-1990 German voters largely cast their ballots the same ways no matter what the electoral contest (European, federal, *Land*, local). Yet this nicely symmetrical pattern appears to have been disrupted and complicated by forces set in motion when Germany unified in 1990. Given the pointers highlighted in the evidence accrued thus far, it is therefore certainly worth investigating in more detail whether, and to what extent, the notion of multilevel voting has any mileage in the German case.

There are good reasons to expect that it might, and even should, have. Germany possesses a myriad of well-developed territorial identities and, since unification, has become quite diverse in socio-economic terms. It also, as was indicated above, has a significant tier of substate government in the shape of the 16 *Länder*. Yet most analyses of territorial politics in Germany tend to stress that if territory matters, then it matters most within the context of the East–West cleavage that unification has spawned. Eastern 'differentness' (not to mention 'difficultness'), so the theory goes, gives it undue influence in shaping German electoral outcomes. The party system that has developed in the Eastern states since unification is indeed quantifiably different from, and territorially more differentiated than, that which exists in the Western states. The traditionally strong socio-economic and religious cleavages that shape(d) electoral competition in the pre-1989 FRG either facilitate altogether different electoral outcomes in the East and/or simply play a much less significant role than is the case in Western Germany. Furthermore, rather than 'settling down' over time, the East German party system continues to display systematic differences from the statewide party system and from those that exist in the ten substate parliaments across Western Germany. This goes, at least superficially, against the general train of thought in contemporary electoral politics in Europe, which tends to stress how – slowly, and in nationally specific ways – processes of nationalization tend to overcome regional peculiarities in shaping voting behaviour (Caramani, 2004). Processes of homogenization – built on events being shaped within a statewide context and voters getting used to framing their own political existences within the discourse of statewide politics – therefore squeeze out substate specific shapers of the vote. We aim to analyse this apparent paradox in a little more detail.

More specifically, this chapter attempts not only to test whether there is evidence of multilevel voting in Germany, but also to directly build on, and bounce off, the contributions by Klaus Detterbeck and Charlie Jeffery, and Kris Deschouwer to this volume. Detterbeck and Jeffery's contribution sets out an overarching framework to facilitate a systematic exploration of the role of territory in the German statewide parties. It illustrates how these parties have adapted to German unification and the growing territorial heterogeneity of German society. Deschouwer's contribution, meanwhile, is concerned with analysing whether and how the regionalization of national elections is taking place. It relies on putting constituency data from national elections under the analytical microscope in order to test hypotheses related to the processes of territorialization in the national arena. Our chapter takes a different tack, dealing mainly with variations in electoral behaviour on the basis of differences in voting for statewide/substate elections. We do this by briefly analysing the mechanics of the German party system, illustrating how territorially specific issues, interests and influences – particularly since unification – have contributed to producing different party landscapes and different electoral outcomes. We then move on to illustrate that the East–West divide is by no means the complete story in terms of the influence of territory on German party political competition. To measure differentiation across space in statewide elections we employ the Pedersen Index. To analyse differentiation in each of Germany's 16 *Länder* we build on ideas of multilevel voting by introducing analysis based on the weighted mean deviations of party performance and expected vote shares in different electoral contests. Taken together, these measures give a strong indication that the differences in party performance across space in statewide elections are supplemented by differences in electoral outcomes across a vertical dimension; in other words, territorial distinctiveness has contributed to producing not just differing electoral results in statewide elections across all Germany but also in *Land* elections, where voters can and do differentiate between parties based on their position in substate party systems. Territorially specific issues and cleavages therefore not only contribute to an increasing *horizontal differentiation* in voting behaviour across Germany, they also have a strong effect on the *vertical choices* that voters make across the levels. Finally, we speculate on what this may mean for German electoral politics in the future.

The German party system post-1990: Developments at the horizontal level

For most of the post-war period the German party system at the statewide level – and largely also at the substate one – remained perhaps the most solid and unspectacular in Europe. Within 15 years of the introduction of democratic elections, minor parties were largely sidelined and a 'two-and-a-half' party system had, by 1961, become the norm. Two larger parties – the SPD on the centre-left and the CDU/CSU on the centre-right – were each dominating their respective sides of the political spectrum, and only a smaller, liberal, Free Democratic Party (FDP) remained alongside them in the Bonn parliament. Voting behaviour remained stable and levels of party identification high – in statewide and substate polls alike (Roberts, 2006).

The calm world of German electoral politics received the first of two major shocks in the early 1980s when the Greens began forcing their way onto the political scene. They entered parliament on the back of a slow – but significant – loosening of the links between voters and parties. Voters were becoming more volatile, and the SPD was confronted with a new challenger for votes on its left flank. The entry of the Greens into the Bundestag in 1983 also had the effect in the short term of tying the FDP to the CDU/CSU, but in the longer term of raising the prospect of new 'red–green' coalitions (Lees, 2000; see also Hough and Jeffery, 2006b: 123–4).

The second shock came in the form of unification and the expansion of the FRG party system to include the former citizens of the GDR. Although both the Christian Democrats and the Social Democrats expanded quickly into the Eastern states, they were not able to dominate political and electoral competition in the same way that they have historically done in Western Germany. The stabilization of the Party of Democratic Socialism (PDS – recently renamed the Left Party) as an Eastern German regional party, periodic rises (and – as a rule – falls) in support for right-wing parties such as the German Peoples Union (DVU) and the National Democratic Party (NPD), and the much smaller vote shares achieved by the FDP and Greens have ensured that three relevant (in Sartori's sense, cf. Sartori, 1976) parties tend to exist across the region. This is in stark contrast to the ten Western legislatures, where until recently the Left Party was not represented at all and the FDP and Greens (and occasionally the Republicans) normally have fair chances of achieving more than 5 per cent of the popular vote. The existence of two structurally different 'regional party systems' has been for the most part uncontested.

The reasons for such a differentiation lie in the inability of the Western parties to incorporate differing Eastern German attitudinal and value positions into their political platforms. This originally surprised many analysts who, at the time of unification, posited social-psychological models of electoral behaviour suggesting that as the two Germanies came together the Western parties were likely to simply expand into virgin electoral territory and subsequently dominate political activity (Bürklin and Klein, 1998: 168). No matter that Easterners had had no direct experiences of the Western system of political interest articulation and East German society was not likely to be rooted in the mosaic of cleavage divides that characterized West German political and electoral competition; the Western parties were clearly convinced (as were many academics) that they could mould and shape such apparently rootless terrain to their advantage (Weßels, 2000: 132). Through the 1990s the limited ability of the Western parties to set the agenda and articulate the particular concerns of Eastern Germans became ever more apparent. By 2005, the two main *Volksparteien*, the CDU and SPD, were scraping together barely half of the votes in the Eastern states (55.8 per cent) compared with a historically low but nonetheless respectable 73.5 per cent in the Western states (see Table 2.1).

Elections that have taken place in the late 1990s and early 21st century reveal that the initial alignments of the Eastern electorate were, and still are, weaker than had been initially anticipated. Since 1990 there has been a steady drop in the number of voters who claim to identify strongly, or reasonably strongly, with a particular party; at the time of unification, around 70 per cent of Western Germans regarded themselves as having some sort of party identification, while – perhaps surprisingly, given that they had not actually lived in the FRG at that point – as many as 60 per cent of Easterners also saw themselves as strong or reasonably strong party identifiers. A fall to

Table 2.1   The 2005 Bundestag election in Eastern and Western Germany

	Germany		Western states		Eastern states	
	Vote share (%)	Change since 2002	Vote share (%)	Change since 2002	Vote share (%)	Change since 2002
SPD	34.3	−4.3	35.1	−3.2	30.5	−9.4
CDU/CSU	35.2	−3.3	37.5	−3.3	25.3	−2.9
FDP	9.8	+2.4	10.2	+2.6	7.9	+1.5
Left Party	8.7	+4.7	4.9	+3.8	25.4	+8.5
Greens	8.1	−0.4	8.8	−0.6	5.1	+0.4
Others	3.9	−0.9	3.5	−0.7	5.8	−1.9

barely 40 per cent in the East in the mid-1990s – largely as a result of increasing dissatisfaction with the fallout from unification – saw the gap between the two regions open, before, interestingly, it narrowed again through the late 1990s and into the 21st century. In the run-up to the 2005 election 50–55 per cent of Eastern Germans and 60–65 per cent of Western Germans (depending on the exact wording of the question) saw themselves as psychologically attached to one of the parties, illustrating that even in an era of increased dealignment the majority of voters do (still) exhibit some sort of party identification (Arzheimer, 2002 and 2005).

Electoral volatility nonetheless remains higher in the East than it does in the West, as Easterners appear more prepared to vote for the party which they perceive to best represent their interests at any given time. Volatility is most typically measured using Pedersen's index of volatility, which calculates the net change in each party's seat or vote share from election to election (at whatever level of analysis one chooses). The total change in the percentage of seats and/or votes won or lost by all parties is then added together and divided by two (Mainwaring and Scully, 1995: 6). The implications of high levels of electoral volatility are that electoral outcomes are naturally more erratic and that, in states that are newly democratized, establishing legitimacy can be more difficult and governing therefore more complicated.

A look at the Pedersen Index in Eastern and Western Germany since unification reveals a number of interesting trends (see Table 2.2). It is no surprise to see that volatility is consistently more pronounced in the Eastern states. Scores for the four elections in 1994, 1998, 2002 and 2005 range from 10.4 to 13.5 and are clearly in a different league from the scores in Western Germany (5.1 to 7.2). The scores across the five 'authentic'[1] Eastern *Länder* group together reasonably well, generally around the 10.5–15 mark, with only the 1994 score in Mecklenburg–Western Pomerania slipping into single figures. A similar grouping occurs in Western Germany, although at a lower level (around 4–9), with few outliers either above or below this. However, the trends evident when the two regions are directly compared are a little

Table 2.2 The Pedersen Index in post-1990 Germany

	1994	1998	2002	2005		1994	1998	2002	2005
Bad-Wüt	5.5	7.1	6.9	7.2	Brandenburg	15.9	10.7	13.8	12.3
Bavaria	5.4	4.9	11.6	9.3	MV	8.9	12.3	15.5	10.7
Bremen	6.6	7.1	6.1	8.2	Saxony	13.0	17.6	14.3	12.4
Hamburg	6.4	6.9	5.8	7.2	Sax-Anhalt	13.3	13.0	10.1	14.8
Hesse	3.6	6.9	6.0	7.6	Thuringia	13.3	14.7	17.2	13.8
Lower Sax	5.2	9.0	4.3	5.5					
NRW	6.6	4.9	6.4	5.0					
RP	5.1	4.8	6.5	7.5					
Saarland	7.2	5.0	8.4	19.2					
Sch-Hol	5.9	7.1	4.1	5.8					
West Ger	5.1	6.1	6.2	7.2	East Ger	12.6	13.5	10.4	12.3
Germany	6.0	7.5	6.6	8.1					

different; the Western states have seen a steady increase in their Pedersen Index scores since 1990, moving from 5.1 in 1994 to 6.1 in 1998 and 6.2 in 2002. The 2005 election saw a further increase, up to 7.2. This steady pattern towards further volatility in voting behaviour is not evident in Eastern Germany. The scores may indeed be higher (indicating that there is more volatility in real terms), but there is no such pattern of increasing scores: 12.6 in 1994, 13.5 in 1998, 10.4 in 2002 and 12.3 in 2005. This may, on the one hand, be taken as evidence of a stable pattern of instability in Eastern Germany and of increasing changes in voter preference (if from a much lower level) in Western Germany. On the other hand, it is clear that the 2005 election – at least in the Western states – was not a 'normal' one. The Left Party has competed in elections in both regions since 1990 in the guise of its predecessor, the PDS – but up until 2005 it never managed to poll more than 1.2 per cent of the vote in the West. This changed in 2005. Popular opposition to Chancellor Gerhard Schröder's package of labour market and welfare reforms from a vocal minority of left-wing critics from his own party (the SPD) prompted a new 'Electoral Alliance for Social Justice' (WASG) to be constituted in 2004. This movement did not form in time to run for election in 2005, but had a clear effect on the electoral outcome by running some of its members on the open lists of the Left Party (which changed its name precisely to illustrate its openness to WASG members). The decision of former SPD Finance Minister Oskar Lafontaine to run on a Left Party ticket further enhanced the party's profile and contributed to the party obtaining a highly respectable 4.9 per cent of the vote in Western Germany (Hough, Koß and Olsen, 2007). Lafontaine's presence clearly prompted the massive leap in the Pedersen Index in the Saarland (19.2 in 2005), illustrating how outliers in West German data can often be linked to the influence of a local matador; it is no coincidence that Gerhard Schröder's home state of Lower Saxony registered its highest score in 1998 (9.0), the year he ran for the chancellorship for

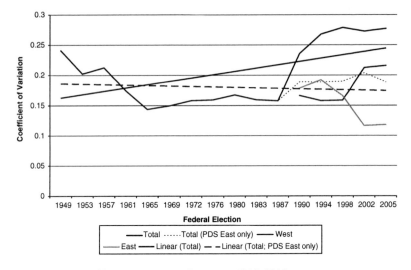

Figure 2.1   Regional heterogeneity in Germany, 1949–2005

the first time, or that the highest Bavarian figure (11.6) came in 2002, when a CSU candidate, Edmund Stoiber, ran for Germany's top office.

The Left Party did not have such a dramatic effect in the Eastern states as it already enjoyed strong vote shares across the region. And, in spite of the advances made in the Western states in 2005, the Left Party still remains the most noticeable expression of East German differentness. It is not only ideologically anchored in East German society, it is also sociologically and organizationally rooted there.

The importance of the regionally strong Left Party in understanding statewide election results in Germany is also evident if we look at another tool for measuring variation in election results across space, namely, the standardized coefficient of variation. This figure is simply the standard deviation of the results per party in the different states in the same statewide election divided by the statewide result, as Deschouwer argues elsewhere in this volume. One noticeable advantage of this measure over others is that it enables us to compare the performances of single parties and not just the differences between regions. Figures 2.1 and 2.2 show these results. The general finding varies depending on whether one includes the Left Party's results in Western Germany. If one chooses to do this,[2] then the pattern is very clear. Levels of regional heterogeneity in party performance across space are greater today than they have ever been in post-war Germany. Even if one takes the Left Party in Western Germany out of the equation – an equally understandable thing to do given that the Left Party remains a small actor that is bound, given its strong performances in the East, to skew our results

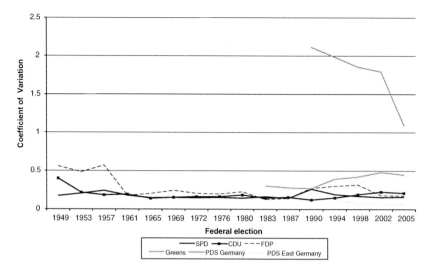

Figure 2.2 Regional heterogeneity in Germany, 1949–2005: all parties

a little – then we see that the figures are 'merely' increasing at almost the same pace as they have been doing since the heyday of electoral homogenization in 1965, the (linear) trend line pointing only slightly downwards. These findings are indicative of the overall importance of the Left Party when it comes to interpreting regional heterogeneity in the German party system.

Figure 2.2, furthermore, shows the important role of two other parties in pushing regional heterogeneity in Germany, namely, the FDP (both in the formative years of the Federal Republic and again since 1987) and the Greens (mainly since 1990). We have left out the Left Party for Western Germany here because it would have made the party a crass outlier, showing coefficients of heterogeneity between 1.1 and 2.1. A case of increased heterogeneity all round then, it would appear? Not quite. Figure 2.1 also illustrates, even more interestingly, that whereas heterogeneity of results was greater in the Eastern states after 1990, it is now – and has been since approximately 1998 – far more obvious in the Western states. This remains the same even if we exclude the Left Party from the results for Western Germany, although regional heterogeneity decreases after 2002.

These trends can also be explained by looking at the different relationships that Eastern voters have with political parties in general. Voters in the Eastern states are more willing to vote based on short-term factors such as their attitude towards a particular chancellor candidate or sets of salient policy issues, and this prompts more uniform swings for or against particular parties. This is in marked contrast to the period 1990–8, when faith in Helmut Kohl as the 'Chancellor of Unity' prompted a proportion of a much more

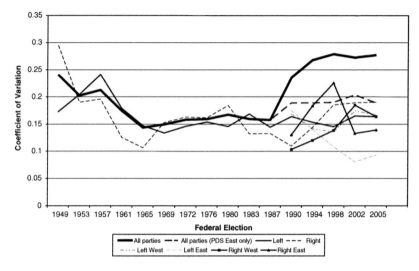

Figure 2.3 Regional heterogeneity in Germany, 1949–2005: Left-Right

non-aligned electorate to remain loyal to the CDU. Such loyalty has, for many citizens, long since evaporated. In comparison, Western Germany appears far more heterogeneous, remaining divided into a largely social democratic north and a more conservative south.

One intriguing aspect of Germany's relatively stable pattern of instability is the destination of voters who choose to switch their votes between elections. Germany's party system has developed into a bloc system, with a centre-right pole (CDU/CSU and FDP) battling against a centre-left (SPD and Green) or even out-and-out left (centre-left plus the Left Party) one. Germany's proportional electoral system, as well as its consensual political culture, have strongly facilitated this development, and it is something that voters are highly aware of. It is nonetheless worth asking whether voters tend to stay within their bloc or whether there is evidence of cross-bloc switching. This will give us a further indication of the nature of Germany's stable pattern of instability in that it illustrates whether voters still think in terms of supporting one party within a bloc or whether electoral volatility extends to jumping the ideological divide. In other words, are recalcitrant SPD voters likely to vote for a party such as the Greens or the Left Party that is ostensibly within the same bloc, or is there evidence that they could cross the left-right divide and support out-and-out political opponents? Figure 2.3 elaborates on this and shows trends for the party blocks. The CDU/CSU and the FDP are regarded as being on the 'right' throughout all of these calculations while all other parties are placed on the 'left' (except for the period 1969–82 when the FDP clearly joined the 'left' camp when it governed with the SPD at the statewide level). Post-1990, and particularly since 1994, variation has been greater in the right camp than in the left. This comes as no surprise given that the CDU has polled erratically in the East and much more consistently in the West. Compared with the overall heterogeneity of all parties, we find a far more stable picture between blocs. Given that Peter Mair argued that we can speak of party system change only when the balance between party blocs changes (Mair, 1997: 68 f.), we find little evidence of significant party system change in Germany – another feature of the stability behind the change in German party politics. We also tend to find a far more stable picture between left and right than between East and West, and it appears that, although German regions are becoming ever more vocal in articulating their 'differentness', the parties still appear to serve as genuine mediators in all of these debates.

The German party system: Developments at the vertical level

Most of the systemic differences discussed above have received at least some coverage in analyses of East German differentness. Three parties of roughly similar electoral strength compete for votes in statewide and substate elections in the Eastern states, compared with two large parties and two, latterly three smaller ones in the Western states. This East–West territorial cleavage – and the much weaker alignments that are linked with it – are also visible if one takes a look at voting behaviour at the substate level. Territory has a role to play in *Land* elections in two main ways: (1) politicians can successfully buck (or at least partly counteract) national trends to their own advantage if they campaign on platforms that voters in their *Land* can relate to and (2) there is qualitative evidence – for each of the main parties – that territorially specific factors can prompt voting behaviour across the levels that is simply more volatile than is the case in Western Germany (see election reports in *German Politics* and *Zeitschrift für Parlamentsfragen* for more evidence of this). In the East German case this can frequently lead, for example, to startling successes for far-right parties in the subnational arena while they remain marginal, at best, in statewide polls.

A way to unpack some of the deeper trends that may exist is to measure the differences in performance of the five main statewide parties across *Land* and federal elections over time. More specifically, do some parties perform better at one level than they do at others? And are such inter-level differences more prevalent in particular areas of Germany? Is there evidence of a decoupling between the two levels or between the vote shares of particular parties across the two levels? Recent research has illustrated that some parties across Europe – notably regionalist or nationalist parties such as the CiU in Catalonia, the SNP in Scotland and PC in Wales – do indeed seem to do better in substate elections than they do in national elections (Wyn Jones and Scully, 2006; Pallarés and Keating, 2006; Bromley, 2006). Voters appear

Table 2.3   Mean of expected vote share (as a percentage, weighted)

	1949–2005	1949–1990	1990–2005	1990–2005 (West)	1990–2005 (East)
SPD	–0.9	1.6	–2.7	–1.0	–4.1
CDU/CSU	2.1	–1.6	4.6	3.6	6.7
FDP	–1.3	–1.0	–1.5	–1.6	–1.3
Greens	–0.2*	–0.2**	–0.1	0.2	–0.7
Left Party			2.2	–0.2	3.7
All parties	–0.3	–0.3	0.5	–0.02	0.8

* 1982–2005.
** 1982–90.

willing to support nationalist/regionalist parties in their more 'natural home' in substate parliaments or assemblies. How does Germany fare?

Table 2.3 reveals information about the direction of these hypothesized decoupling processes. We have calculated the mean of the expected vote share[3] for each of the parties in Eastern and Western Germany since 1949. We also differentiate between East and West. In other words, one can see the extent to which actual election results differ from our expected results in numerical terms. A mean figure below 0 indicates that a party performed less well at the substate level than it did at the statewide one. A mean figure above 0 indicates the opposite: a party is polling better at the substate level than it is in the statewide arena. Subsequently, the further the value away from 0, the weaker is the coupling of substate and state election results for that particular party. The mean percentage of expected vote also shows the *direction* of change between results in statewide and substate elections. We simply calculated the average of the percentages of the expected results. The SPD's figure of 1.6 percentage points between 1949 and 1990 probably has much to do with the fact that it was in opposition at the statewide level for most of this period, while the CDU/CSU's score of (−1.6 percentage points) has at least something to do with its long tenure in the national government. The FDP's underperformance in almost all *Land* elections indicates that it was basically regarded as an actor on the statewide level, helping the CDU/CSU (and earlier the SPD) to govern.

While interesting, the performances of the individual parties are, again, not the whole story. It is the lack of a post-unification pattern – particularly in the Eastern states, although this is also true to some extent in Western Germany – that makes multilevel voting such a prevalent phenomenon across the East.

As Table 2.4 illustrates, pre-1990 there are strong links between the election results at both levels for the three parties that dominated German political life for the vast majority of this period, namely, both of the main catch-all parties (CDU/CSU and SPD) and the Free Democrats. The only exception to

Table 2.4 Mean of expected vote share (as a percentage, weighted) at the Land level

	SPD		CDU/CSU		FDP		Greens		Left Party
	1949–1990	1990–2005	1949–1990	1990–2005	1949–1990	1990–2005	1949–1990	1990–2005	1990–2005
Bad-Wüt	1.4	−2.9	−1.9	0.2	−0.1	−1.3	−0.2	1.0	—
Bavaria	0.3	−1.9	−3.0	3.4	−1.3	−2.9	1.7	0.1	—
Bremen	1.7	−6.7	−3.1	6.8	−1.0	−2.0	−3.0	−0.3	−0.6
Hamburg	2.0	−2.6	2.0	2.1	−2.8	−2.9	1.1	−0.2	—
Hesse	3.5	−0.9	−2.8	5.1	0.4	−1.9	2.3	0.1	—
Lower Sax	0.8	−0.8	−0.5	3.2	−1.6	−1.2	1.3	0.9	−0.1
NRW	2.9	−0.5	−1.9	2.2	−0.3	−0.5	−1.2	1.3	—
RP	1.3	4.1	−0.8	−4.1	−1.0	0.1	0.1	0.3	−0.1
Saarland	1.3	−8.0	−3.3	18.1	−0.3	−2.0	−2.0	−0.2	−0.1
Sch-Hol	1.3	0.7	−0.8	−1.4	−2.1	−1.7	−2.1	−1.0	—
Brandenburg		1.5		−2.4		−2.2		−1.4	5.3
MV		0.6		0.2		−1.0		−0.7	1.0
Saxony		−10.2		17.7		−2.9		−0.7	4.4
Sax-Anhalt		−3.3		−0.8		2.3		−0.2	3.6
Thuringia		−9.0		18.6		−2.9		−0.7	3.9

this is the Greens, where a degree of diversity exists – in half of the Western states they perform better at the substate level, while in the other half this is reversed. The better performance in the substate arenas in Lower Saxony, Hamburg and particularly Hesse probably reflects their willingness to cooperate with the Social Democrats in government in those three states, indicating that, when a party is not in government in the statewide arena but does take part in substate coalitions, it is likely – in the long term – to benefit electorally from the territorial profiling it can inevitably undertake in the *Land* arena. There is nonetheless a remarkably high degree of uniformity across states and across levels during this period.

Post-1990 this stable pattern starts to unravel – although only slightly. Of the 40 cases (4 parties that compete in both periods in 10 Western *Länder*), the level of decoupling is greater than it was pre-1990 in 25 of them. There are, however, a fair number of genuine outliers; the CDU/CSU's strikingly better performances in the Saarland stand out (as do the SPD's poor performances there), much like the Christian Democrats' much better results in Bremen's substate elections (likewise the SPD's poorer showings there too). The CDU/CSU has improved its performance in substate elections in NRW but the SPD has clearly improved its standing in *Land* elections in Rhineland-Palatinate. There are explanations for these phenomena. First, local politicians have made an impact – more specifically, Oskar Lafontaine's departure not just from the Saar's *Land* arena but also from the SPD itself has contributed to drops in support in what used to be his 'home' state, while former SPD leader Kurt Beck has proven to be a very successful minister president in Rhineland-Palatinate. Secondly, the SPD's dismally low approval ratings during its seven-year tenure in national government caused it to lose a succession of *Land* elections as voters punished the federal government in substate polls. This is probably the main reason why we see so many minus figures appearing before the SPD's post-1990 values.

The smaller parties have seen less change in their scores, reflecting perhaps voter willingness to 'punish' or 'reward' politicians in the major parties for the performances in either statewide or, occasionally, the substate arena. Even though it has not been in national government since 1998, the FDP continues to struggle to get its message across in substate elections. It is perceived as a party with a national role and continues to poll much better in these elections, with only one exception, namely, Rhineland-Palatinate (again), where it performs marginally better in substate elections, most likely on account of its long-standing coalition – the only one of its sort left in the whole country – with the Social Democrats in that state. The Greens, meanwhile, continue to present something of a mixed picture characterized by remarkably little decoupling. Figures for the Left Party are included, but given the low proportion of the vote that it polled in the Western states until recently, it should not be too surprising to see that decoupling is not an issue for the Socialists. Most interestingly when one looks at the smaller parties, the vote shares of both the Greens and the FDP appear no more decoupled than before 1990.

If we turn our attention to the East, then the picture is altogether different. There is no uniformity of catch-all party scores across the states, and we frequently see large differences in the percentage points that they register. The small parties do, however, perform worse in substate elections and, in contrast to the performance of the major parties, much more consistently (particularly the Greens). Neither the FDP nor the Greens mobilize protest support in substate elections; in the East that goes either to the far right or, under certain circumstances, to the Left Party. The Left Party's scores are also striking; it clearly does much better in the substate arena across all of Eastern Germany, particularly in Brandenburg (where the party has never governed), although not so well in Mecklenburg-Western Pomerania (where the party was in power for seven years and where substate and statewide elections have a tendency to fall on the same day). The picture therefore is something of a confusing one of instability (and decoupling) for the major parties, stability (and much less decoupling) for the minor parties as well as systematic patterns of better support at the substate level for the Left Party.

Conclusion

This chapter has thrown light on the role that territory plays in shaping both the party system and electoral outcomes in Germany. It has illustrated that, although party competition and voting behaviour in statewide and substate elections are more differentiated in Eastern Germany than they are in the Western states, the picture is rather more complex than it may at first appear. It is no surprise that party system volatility across space, as measured by the Pedersen Index, is consistently more pronounced in the East than it is in the West. However, the trends evident when the two regions are directly compared are a little different; the Western states have seen a steady increase in their Pedersen Index scores since 1990, while such a steady development towards increasing volatility in voting behaviour is not evident in Eastern Germany.

Post-1990, and particularly since 1994, variation in the support for blocs of parties has been greater on the right than on the left. This comes as no surprise given that the CDU has polled erratically in the East and much more consistently in the West. Compared with the overall heterogeneity of performance by individual parties, we nonetheless find a far more stable picture between blocs. Given that party system changes are frequently seen as being of genuine significance only when voters are prepared to cross the bloc divide, we find little evidence to suggest that such significant party system change is taking place in Germany now. If we do not take into account the Left Party in the West, then regional heterogeneity – even when we look at individual parties – has remained stable since 1949. We also tend to find a far more stable picture between left and right than between East and West, and it appears that, although German regions are becoming ever more vocal in articulating their 'differentness', the parties still play an effective role in mediating territorial differences within the political process.

We did not find a great deal of evidence to support theories of multilevel voting in the pre-1990 period. The election results of both the SPD and the CDU/CSU (as well as the FDP) showed strong similarities across the levels, and there is little evidence to suggest that voters thought (and acted) differently in the various electoral arenas. There was a strong link between *Land* and federal election results, and only the Greens – arising as they did to deliberately challenge the prevailing consensus that the three other parties epitomized – bucked this trend. Post-1990 we do, however, see rather more evidence of voters taking different cues in different arenas. This is clearly not a case of *Land* contests becoming first order; but some of their characteristics do appear to have rather more 'first-order-ness' about them. But, while this shift is noticeable and quantifiable (in terms of election results), this clearly should not be taken to mean that the mirror is completely broken. The increased role of personalities is likely to have prompted some of the decoupling at the vertical level, while the variations in socio-economic status and cultural identity across the country are likely to have contributed to greater variety in electoral outcomes in horizontal terms. The East, of course, remains much less subject to uniform trends than the West per se.

What we might in fact be seeing is a slow process of the West becoming rather more like the East than many Westerners would perhaps like to admit. Voters across the whole of the republic are gradually becoming more volatile. This development is gathering speed (if from a low level) in Western Germany, whereas in the East this stable instability has long since embedded itself into the electoral process. This, in other words, may in fact be more evidence of some form of 'nationalization' taking place; this process is not linear and it is not uniform, but the dynamic nonetheless appears to have been set in motion.

3
Rediscovering the Region: Territorial Politics and Party Organizations in Germany

Klaus Detterbeck and Charlie Jeffery

Introduction

This chapter explores the interconnections of two of the defining features of post-war German politics as they flex and adapt to the long-term implications of German unification: a distinctive federal system widely characterized as 'cooperative' federalism, and a party system in which a small number of parties for a long period monopolized representative politics.

For decades, the interlocking of federal-level and *Länder* politics has been the hallmark of German federalism. While the federal level over time accumulated responsibilities for uniform, statewide legislation, it remained dependent on the political and administrative cooperation of the *Länder* in the implementation of its laws. In that process the *Länder* lost most of their primary legislative competences (now restricted largely to education, culture and the media), yet gained political strength from participation in federal-level politics. In particular the legislative power of the Bundesrat – the federal-level second chamber composed of representatives of *Länder* governments – grew as the scope of federal-level legislation grew, tightly interlocking the two levels of government (Scharpf et al., 1976; Schmidt, 2002). In other words, the federal level and the *Länder* both agreed to prioritize cooperative shared rule over autonomous self-rule (Elazar, 1987; Watts, 1999).

These institutional structures of cooperative federalism were able to work relatively effectively, despite the many potential veto points they produce,[1] for two reasons. First, they reflected a particular social and political context which emphasized statewide equity (what the German constitution calls a 'uniformity of living conditions') at the levels of both elite and public opinion. This normative commitment to statewide equity was in part a legacy of a post-war reconstruction process which prioritized goals of national mobilization and integration focused on economic renewal, political stabilization and the integration of some 12 million or so refugees and expellees from East Germany and formerly German-speaking parts of eastern Europe. It also reflected the relative absence in West Germany of politically significant ethnic, linguistic or religious cleavages on a territorial basis and – at least from the 1960s onwards – of politically significant regional economic disparities (Jeffery, 1999a: 131–4; Schultze, 1999: 174–6).

Cooperative federalism worked, second, because of two features of party politics which underpinned the commitment to statewide equity (see, *inter alia*, Lehmbruch, 1976; Grande, 2002; Detterbeck and Renzsch, 2003):

- From the early 1960s through to German unification, party competition at federal and *Länder* levels was both concentrated on a small number of parties and strongly congruent across the levels. Only three parties (supplemented by the Greens from the early 1980s) were represented in the Bundestag and the *Land* parliaments; moreover, with few exceptions, patterns of government and opposition at one level were replicated at the other level.[2]
- These parties organized in a highly integrated way across the levels.[3] They developed programmes, policies and strategies which were consistent across both federal and *Länder* politics. And they established networking channels and decision-making fora which provided much of the infrastructure for the complex bargaining processes of the interlocked federal system.

(Leonardy, 2004)

Since 1990, however (and arguably beforehand, at least in incipient manner; Jeffery, 1999b), cooperative federalism has become contested as new patterns of territorial politics have emerged. This 'new territorialism' (Jeffery, 2005) has begun to recalibrate German federalism, introducing and legitimizing new *Länder*-specific frames of reference for interest formation, representation and policy-making alongside the statewide frame that has been the standard template for the analysis of German politics.

We set out the features of this new territorialism in the next section. We do so in order to set in context the central purpose of this chapter, which is to explore the implications for party politics of a less interlocked federalism. While there has been a lively debate on the growing amount of asymmetry and incongruence in multilevel party competition in Germany (see, *inter alia*, Sturm, 1999; Jeffery, 1999a; Detterbeck and Renzsch, 2003; Hough and Jeffery, 2006b; see also Hough and Koß in this volume), little work has been done so far on the organizational responses of German parties to processes of territorialization.

We argue that there is a double tendency at play. On the one hand *Land* parties – that is, the substate branches of statewide parties – are increasingly willing to diverge from statewide party positions in order to tailor their appeal to specific *Land* conditions. On the other hand, *Land* parties still value a strong presence within their federal party's organizational structure. This indicates that they continue to value integration across levels of government for reasons of intra-party coherence. However, the disintegrative

challenges posed by the new territorialism make this task both more difficult and less rewarding.

The recalibration of German federalism

German federalism has encountered an unaccustomed and fundamental challenge since 1990: to reconcile a new and stark territorial social diversity with
a federal system geared to the aspiration of 'uniform living conditions'. This
new diversity has in particular, but not only, to do with Eastern Germany. Any
perfunctory trawl through the relevant socio-economic indicators, like those
on GDP per capita and unemployment, confirms the obvious: the objective
needs of East Germans are different from those of West Germans. The six
Eastern *Länder* are stuck at the foot of the economic league table. On all the
indicators, the worst-performing Western *Länder* do better then the best
performing Eastern *Länder*.

Those economic indicators map on to, and reinforce, a collective sense of
difference, an East German identity whose roots lie in the GDR past, and
which has been recast and reaffirmed by the material dislocation of the post-
unity era (Hough, 2002: 77–80). The net outcome is the emergence of Eastern
Germany as a 'space' for a distinctive territorial politics – more egalitarian,
more statist – than in the West (Hough, 2002: 106–7). There is ample confirmation in public attitudes data. Though East Germans acknowledge that in
many respects the situation in the East has improved massively since 1990
(Bürklin and Jung, 2001: 683), there remains a sense among Easterners that
the inherited power relations of the society they joined in 1990 are loaded
against them. East Germans are more likely to see their relationship with
West Germans as one of conflict than vice versa. East Germans have different, and more pessimistic, evaluations of the 'provenness' of the German
model of the social market economy and the 'social justice' it delivers, and
are less likely to favour market solutions to policy problems or to think the
level of social policy expenditure is high enough (Bürklin and Jung, 2001:
687–95). And these socio-economic concerns underline a perception that
neither *Länder* governments nor, in particular, the federal government are
responsive to East German concerns (Grube, 2004: 166).

One outcome of these perceptions of difference and disadvantage has
been a series of ameliorative measures through which the federal government allocates special and asymmetric benefits to the East, in particular in
the Solidarity Pact II negotiations in 2001 (Jeffery, 2003: 37–9). But, importantly, the special features of the East also create claims on the Western
Länder to fund the special needs of the east. That claim is institutionalized
in the federal system by the fiscal equalization process. Fiscal equalization in
Germany is intended to put all the *Länder* in a position, despite differences
in economic structure and performance, to deliver uniform living conditions on their territory. It is a powerful expression of commitment to

statewide solidarity. But the territorial distribution of resources is an inherently contentious issue, and has become so all the more since unification. In 2004 €6.7 billion was transferred from economically stronger to economically weaker *Länder*. A small group of southern *Länder* – Bavaria, Baden-Württemberg and Hesse) accounted for 88 per cent (€5.9 billion) of that total transfer. 80 per cent (€5.4 billion) of the total transfer ended up in East Germany.[4]

Unsurprisingly, the period since unification has seen heightened territorial sensitivities about the allocation of resources. Debate about the costs and benefits of statewide equity, or uniform living conditions, has become more vivid and polarized between donors and recipients. In these circumstances, rhetoric about 'our money' has in some places come to resonate strongly with territorial identity. Bavaria is the most obvious example, where discourses of regional distinctiveness – based in traditions of statehood, political Catholicism and agrarian nostalgia – have become more prominent and have been instrumentalized as an argument for greater autonomy and self-reliance (or, in other words, less solidarity with the rest). Other *Länder* have also, though less vigorously, hopped on the bandwagon of territorial politics, particularly those with better economic situations. The southern *Länder* of Bavaria, Hesse and Baden-Württemberg have been persistent advocates of a reformed, more 'competitive' federalism which would better match their specific territorial interests.

Though there is no definitive single statement of this more competitive federalism advocated by the 'rich south', a number of features stand out (Jeffery, 2005: 97):

1. A restatement of the normative purpose of the federal system from one geared to equity and solidarity in a statewide frame to one focused more on self-reliance, innovation and autonomy in a narrower *Länder* frame.
2. A commitment to 'disentangling' the relationships of the federal level and the *Länder* by rolling back the scope of statewide legislation, restoring primary legislative competences to the *Länder*, and limiting the role of the Bundesrat as a linchpin of interdependence between the two levels.
3. A commitment to 'incentivize' innovation and self-reliance by reducing the level of transfers – that is, solidarity – from wealthier to weaker *Länder* in the fiscal equalization system.
4. A concern, in sum, to allow greater diversity of 'living conditions' between the *Länder*.

The 'rich south', both singly and at times in concert, has sought repeatedly since 1990 to advance this agenda, pressing its claims in the post-unification constitutional reform debate in the early 1990s (Jeffery, 1995), in the Solidarity Pact negotiations on fiscal equalization in 1993 (Mackenstein and Jeffery, 1999 and 2001; Jeffery, 2003), and in the various stages of the federalism reform negotiations of the mid-2000s (Holtschneider and Schön, 2007). They have achieved some movement both on the allocation of legislative competences and on the obligations of fiscal equalization, though constitutional change in Germany is a notoriously sticky process. They have also tried to exploit more fully the leeway the current distribution of powers and fiscal capacity gives to do it 'their way', Sinatra-style, especially in regional economic policy, but also in related fields like higher education and 'cultural' policy more generally.

German federalism has become more complex as new territorial calculations become more important. An asymmetrically dependent 'poor East' and an autonomy-focused 'rich South' have introduced new lines of cleavage around which distinctive territorial interests are expressed, challenging older commitments to uniformity and solidarity.

The scope for expressing these territorial interests has been amplified by changing patterns of party competition in *Länder* elections since 1990. The PDS/Left Party has consolidated its position as a regional interest party for the East, bringing an additional player to the game. In addition, new volatilities of voting behaviour – interpreted by some as a new territorialism on the part of voters (Hough and Jeffery, 2006b) – have complicated coalition formation. Since 1990, as a result of electoral arithmetic, expediency or both, the SPD has worked in coalition in the *Länder* with the CDU, the FDP, the PDS, the FDP and the Greens together in a 'traffic light' coalition, the anti-establishment Stattpartei (in Hamburg), as well as running single-party and SPD-Green minority governments 'tolerated' by the PDS in Mecklenburg-West Pomerania.

This diversity of coalition alignments has made it difficult to replicate the Bundestag government–opposition divide in the operation of the Bundesrat. At any one time since 1990 there have been coalitions (and therefore Bundesrat delegations) which cross-cut party alignments in the Bundestag. The weakening of federal–*Länder* congruence in government formation has made it more difficult to mobilize the Bundesrat on party lines and opened up greater scope for decision-making by coalitions of territorial interests than on the basis of statewide party discipline interconnected with that in the Bundestag (Renzsch, 1999; Hough and Jeffery, 2006b: 130–2).

In sum, though the federal system has seen only limited formal change resulting from the various post-1990 reform initiatives, in practice it has changed significantly. Table 3.1 sets out these changes. Regional economic disparity and a sharpening sense of territorial social cleavage have challenged the inherited normative commitments of post-war federalism, leading to growing pressures to disentangle a federal structure geared to delivering statewide equity. These changes have been paralleled and reinforced by new incongruences in party competition between the federal and *Länder* arenas.

Those divergent dynamics of competition at different levels of government raise a question that has been curiously under-researched in the German

Table 3.1   The recalibration of German federalism since 1990

	Pre–1990	Post–1990
Institutional	Interlocked federalism	Tendency to disentanglement
Normative	Statewide equity	Challenge of competitive federalism
Social	Homogeneous	New territorial cleavages
Economic	Limited disparities	Wide disparities
Party competition	Congruent across levels	Dissimilar across levels
Party structure	Integrated across levels	Integration across levels under challenge?

case: how political parties which operate on a statewide basis reconcile the tensions of a conventional logic of party competition in a single statewide political arena with that of the increasingly diverse set of territorial political logics in the political arenas of the German *Länder*. What follows is a first attempt to explore that tension systematically and capture any dynamics of disintegration of party structure across levels of government in Germany. We start by setting out the broad pattern of territorial structures of the main German parties and the factors that impact on intra-party coordination across levels. Then we explore evidence for recent change in a) the autonomy of *Länder*-level branch organizations of the major parties and b) the integration of *Länder* party branches in federal-level party structures.

Territorial structures of German parties

German parties are internally federalized, that is, they have *Land*, district and local organizational levels, each with its own statutes, structures, personnel and resources. As branches of statewide parties, the lower party units possess some autonomy to govern their own affairs.[5] At the same time, they are also involved in the decision-making processes of their federal party. This multilevel party organizational structure has evolved to correspond with the arenas of electoral competition and parliamentary decision-making in Germany. Moreover, the legal framework of the 1967 Party Law, which cleared the way for massive state regulation and state funding of political parties, requires some kind of a vertical division of powers within parties to satisfy the constitutional obligation of intra-party democracy (Gabriel, 1989: 66–7; Poguntke, 1994: 186–90).

Parties as federal systems in miniature

The logic of adapting party organization to the structure of the federal system, along with the legislative requirement for internal decentralization, has led over time to processes of organizational convergence, particularly between the two major parties, the SPD and the CDU (Gabriel, 1989: 67). For the Social Democrats, the challenge was twofold: to accommodate a traditionally centralist party ethos with internal decentralization and to transfer organizational power from the traditional intermediate party level, that is, the smaller party districts (*Bezirke*), to the *Land* parties. Until the 1960s the SPD either had no party branches at *Land* level or at most loose confederations of the smaller party districts within the *Land*. Since then, *Land* party organizations have increasingly sought, in some cases with rather limited success, to supplant the district level (Gabriel, 1989: 67; Lösche and Walter, 1992: 203–5).

In the SPD heartland of North Rhine Westphalia (NRW), after a prolonged struggle, the four powerful party districts, now transformed into 'regional associations' (*Regionalverbände*), lost many of their powers on staffing and finance to the *Land* organizations in 2001; however, the new party 'regions' kept control of candidate recruitment for party lists and the right to send delegates to *Land* and federal party conferences.[6] The party reformers argued that strengthening the *Land* party (now branded as 'NRWSPD') would be a more effective way of organizing for *Land* elections, of cooperating with the party in the *Land* parliament, and of pursuing *Land* interests in the federal party and vis-à-vis the federal government (on the assumption of SPD participation) (Detterbeck and Renzsch, 2003: 265–6).

For the Christian Democrats, the process of adaptation was different. The (newly formed) post-war party developed in the *Länder* first, with considerable organizational, social and programmatic heterogeneity. While this was consistent with the programmatic principle of subsidiarity and the catch-all approach of the CDU, party cohesion was inevitably low and mainly organized around the personal leadership of Konrad Adenauer (Schmid, 1990: 54–8; Bösch, 2007). The federal party, founded only in 1950, remained weak and poorly integrated with the relatively autonomous substate branches until the late 1960s. Only then did party reforms strengthen the extra-parliamentary federal party organization and gave it a coordinating role vis-à-vis the federal parliamentary party and the *Land* parties (Schönbohm 1985; Schmid, 1990: 150–8).

In some of the *Länder*, similar to the SPD, CDU *Land* party branches were established late and/or had to deal with strong smaller party districts within their territory. Competition between district units is particularly pronounced in the CDU in Baden-Württemberg (where the *Land* party was formed in 1971), North Rhine Westphalia (formed in 1986; the two former *Land* parties were split into eight districts) and Rhineland-Palatinate (formed back in 1947). In Lower Saxony there are still, formally speaking, three autonomous *Land* branches of Brunswick, Hanover and Oldenburg.[7] In practice, however, they compete for influence within a confederal 'CDU in Lower Saxony', which they combined to form in 1968 (see Schmid, 1990: 75–117).

In both the SPD and CDU, the five East German Land branches are organizationally weak. The East German branches enrolled just 8.8 per cent of the total party membership of the CDU in 2006 and a mere 4.1 per cent of the SPD's membership.[8] No East German branch approaches the organizational density (the ratio of members to voters) of even the weakest West German branch in either parties (Niedermayer, 2007). The SPD and CDU resemble much more the model of cadre party in the East, revolving around their parliamentary parties (Grabow, 2001), rather than the *Volkspartei* model of the West, with a large, albeit declining membership (of around 550,000 members each) and an extensive and differentiated extra-parliamentary structure.

Both the FDP and the Greens have comparatively small membership bases, of 65,000 and 44,000 members respectively. Unlike the *Volksparteien* they have only a small number of ancillary organizations representing different socio-economic interests (youth, student and women's sections in particular) (Poguntke, 1994: 200–2). In both parties, there is a certain ambiguity between a decentralist party ethos and a rather weak infrastructure at the *Land* level (Vorländer, 2007: 285–7; Probst, 2007: 184–6).

The bulk of the PDS's 60,000 members and organizational infrastructure are concentrated in the East (Niedermayer, 2007), where strong *Land*-level parties sit somewhat uneasily with party traditions and socialist thinking (Koß and Hough, 2006). After the recent merger with the WASG (Labour and Social Justice – the Electoral Alternative) in 2007, the new Left Party has around 70,000 members, three-quarters in the East. Though the Left Party is predominantly Eastern in terms of membership, programmatic outlook and parliamentary representation – with currently 127 seats in the Eastern *Land* parliaments, 23 in Berlin and 7 in the West – the party is strategically committed to 'Western expansion'.

Despite the differences between German parties, the general picture shows organizations which are multilayered and vertically integrated. All the major parties, except the Bavarian CSU (but including the PDS in its new guise), seek parliamentary representation and government responsibility across the state; all have functioning federal structures, shaped by their specific party trajectories. As we will see in more detail below, the *Land* party levels possess important autonomous powers and are strongly involved in federal-level party structures. German parties mirror the structure of the federal system. As cooperative federal systems in miniature, they are able to aggregate territorial interest and develop common positions across levels of government (Renzsch, 1998 and 2004). In doing so, parties have become deeply interconnected with the federal system.

This was particularly true with respect to the Bundesrat. Party discipline on the one hand helped to solve conflict between levels and between *Länder* and simplified majority-building in the Bundesrat. On the other, party discipline in the Bundesrat made it possible to present united fronts of support for and opposition to the federal government. In times of divided majorities this seriously hampered the capacity of the federal government to push through its policy agenda (Lehmbruch, 1976 and 2000; Jeffery, 1999a; Renzsch, 2004).

Incentives and disincentives for intra-party coordination

Whatever the consequences for federal outcomes, vertical party discipline (that is, between federal and *Länder* levels) rests on certain preconditions. Party actors need both an organizational infrastructure and political incentives to hold the various components of the party organization together. Our argument is that changes in the environment in which the German parties operate – the recalibration of the federal system – have made intra-party coordination much more difficult. If those changes weaken incentives for coordination, we would expect to see changes to the structures and processes of vertical integration within these parties.

The main incentives for intra-party coordination are shared rational interests and shared ideologies and identities (Filippov et al., 2004: 184–213). From a rationalist perspective, parties organize to maximize their success in terms of votes, office-holding and policies (Strøm, 1990). Working within a system of cooperative federalism, maintaining party unity across levels is likely to be promote all of these party goals. Avoiding intra-party conflict and presenting an unambiguous message to voters may maximize electoral success, enhance the success and credibility of office-holders, and facilitate the pursuit of policy commitments.

To the extent that parties are understood as more than rational-efficient organizations, party ideologies, party traditions and partisan identities come into play (Lipset and Rokkan, 1967; Ware, 1996). From a comparative perspective, German parties have traditionally placed a strong emphasis on programmatic debate and broad programmatic formulas. Shared party values and political 'projects' drawn from party ideology – whether 'social justice', 'liberal freedom' or 'the social market economy' – have served to unite party leaders and activists across the territorial levels, all the more so since party identities and belief systems were deeply embedded, dating back to the subcultural origins of the German parties in their respective socialist, liberal and Catholic milieux in the 19th century. The idea of party as political community was very strong in the German context and remained a powerful framework for accommodating internal conflict into the post-war era (Lösche, 1994; Wiesendahl, 2001: 614–17).

However, there are a number of ways in which these sources of vertical party discipline have come under increasing pressure in recent decades. First, as noted above, the symmetry of federal and *Land* party systems has given way to a more regionalized frame of party competition. Similarly, both social and economic heterogeneity and the diversity of *Land* policies have grown. With these changes it has become more difficult for the German parties to identify shared rational interests across the levels and across the *Länder*. Policy issues may now have different saliencies in different places, policy solutions may look different according to specific *Land* circumstances. What may be a strategic option or even necessity in East Germany may have no relevance to party competition in the West. Rationally speaking, the federal party and the different *Land* parties may be better off in pursuing their own distinct strategies and policies.

Second, party ideology has lost force in facilitating internal cohesion. This is the result of a number of complex developments in the post-war era (Mair, 1997: 19–44). In the German case, both the CDU/CSU and, by the late 1950s, the SPD adopted a 'catch-all' approach to electoral politics. This was a response to a changed social environment compared with the fundamental cleavages and struggles of the Weimar Republic. But it also helped erode long-term party loyalties as traditional programmatic goals were relaxed, with the general programmatic outlook of the *Volksparteien* and their profile in government gradually becoming increasingly similar (see Schmidt, 1985 and 2001). Since the late 1980s this tendency has intensified. As the scope for policy discretion available to national governments has become more limited, due to factors like globalization, European integration and government inertia, ideologically informed political agendas have become ever more difficult to discern (Mair, 1997: 131–6). In these senses party ideology is now much less of a glue holding the various levels of the party together.

Third, partisan identification has become weaker, with weakening partisanship acting as a primary source of electoral instability. There are now more German voters, particularly in the East, who cast their ballot according to short-term calculations, or abstain or switch party votes between elections (von Beyme, 2000: 43–63; Scarrow, 2002: 79–86). Partisan de-alignment has also contributed to the regionalization of party competition at the *Land* level. Volatile voters are more likely to vote differently at different levels and to punish the party in federal government for unpopular policies in midterm elections (Burkhart, 2004).[9] More importantly for this discussion, the decline of partisan identities has two sets of repercussions for party activists and leaders. First, there is some evidence that there has been a shift in the motives for joining a party. New party members are said to follow a more instrumental logic, often related to personal career motives or specific policy goals, rather than being driven by an affective sense of partisan belonging and more easily amenable to party discipline (Niedermayer, 2001; c.f. Biehl, 2005: 218–26). Second, party elites may become more responsive to short-term changes in public opinion. Being able to respond in a flexible way to the short-term demands of voters has become an important asset in electoral terms. Again, this short-termist outlook may undermine the capacity of parties to generate vertical party discipline. Managing party consensus and compromise across levels becomes more difficult if the party at each level is focused on the demands of different electoral arenas.

So far, we have identified sources of increased tensions within the vertically integrated German parties. We have also argued that incentives for intra-party coordination have become weaker over time. We now move on to look at recent organizational developments to see how far these shifting parameters have been reflected in changes – both formal and informal – to the structures of German parties. We focus in turn on the two dimensions of the relationship between federal and *Länder* parties that are commonly distinguished in the literature (Dyck, 1996: 160–3; Thorlakson, 2001: 4–8; Deschouwer, 2006a: 291–300; Swenden, 2006: 155–71; van Biezen and Hopkin, 2006: 14–36): the degree of autonomy enjoyed at the *Länder* level, and the level of integration of *Länder* branches in the federal-level party. On the former, we look at: (a) the selection of candidates and party leaders; (b) party finances; (c) party programmes and policies; (d) election campaigns; and (e) government formation. On the latter, we discuss: (f) the interlocking of party structures; (g) the inclusion of *Länder* party leaders in federal party structures; and (h) the integration of party careers across levels.

The autonomy of land parties

Selection of candidates and party leaders

In Germany, the lower party levels have always jealously guarded their role in candidate recruitment (Gabriel, 1989: 68–9), and have continued to do so since 1990. As electoral law regulates the nomination process in detail, selection procedures within different parties have been both similar and stable over time (Poguntke and Boll, 1992: 368–71). The 'mixed member proportional' electoral system used for federal elections and in most of the *Länder* has led to a dual process of candidate selection: constituency candidates are nominated by local party conventions, while list candidates are chosen by *Land* (or party district) party conferences.

Despite attempts to make nomination procedures more open and democratic, local and regional party elites still play a decisive role.[10] Constituency candidates need a well-entrenched local power base; holding local party office is thus an important asset for *Land* and federal politicians. Party lists are typically the result of complex bargaining processes between the various social, political and regional groupings within a *Land* party; incumbents and constituency candidates are often awarded safe positions on the list (Poguntke, 1994: 189; Borchert and Golsch, 2003: 154–5). Occasionally, candidate selection has been contested between party wings, particularly within the SPD and the Greens (Padgett, 1994: 15–16). However, in general, *Land* party executives have managed to accommodate intra-party conflict through effective balancing of factions and organizations.

The upper party levels – the federal party in the case of *Land* party lists, the *Land* level in the case of constituency candidates – do not have much influence on selection procedures. The electoral law provides regional and federal party executives with a veto power on constituency candidates; in practice, this has no relevance. Federal and *Land* parliamentary parties have to live with their 'rebels' as long as these have support from their local selectorates (Poguntke, 1994: 189; Schüttemeyer, 1999: 48–9).

Parachuting has become more important since the late 1990s. SPD *Land* parties and some in the CDU introduced reforms in the 1990s to allow *Land* executives to place non-party experts on prominent list positions; however, even in these (rare) cases, *Land* party delegates have the final say (Beil and Lepzy, 1995: 39).

The one serious restriction on the autonomy of the local and regional selectorates has been the introduction of gender quotas by federal party conferences. The Greens follow a policy of gender parity, as does the Left Party in principle, while the SPD introduced a 40 per cent quota for women on party lists in 1988, and the CDU a non-binding quota of 33 per cent female candidates in 1996; only the FDP and the CSU have not made similar moves (Poguntke and Boll, 1992: 373–4; Scarrow, 1999: 349–50).

The *Land* parties are also autonomous with respect to the election of their party leaders. Open attempts by the federal party to influence the election of *Land* party leaders would be seen as most unusual. *Land* prime ministers (Ministerpräsidenten) and opposition leaders in the *Länder* parliaments regularly serve as *Land* party leaders.[11] The party law stipulates that the party conferences at each territorial level are responsible for choosing the party chair, his or her deputies and the other members of party executives (Poguntke, 1994: 190). By and large, this practice has prevailed. In recent years, parties have occasionally used (non-binding) member ballots for choosing their party leader or their top candidate in election campaigns (Beil and Lepzy, 1995: 21–4; Scarrow, 1999: 348–9).[12]

Party finance

Germany has been among the pioneers of state funding of political parties. Since the late 1950s state subsidies for parliamentary parties, election campaign costs and party foundations have grown substantially (Poguntke, 1994: 191–7; Ebbighausen et al., 1996: 141–270). One of the most remarkable effects of public funding has been the financial decoupling of party levels. Whereas the federal party levels are financed primarily by the state, local branches depend strongly on membership fees and donations, with the intermediate *Land* level falling somewhere in between. Both federal and *Land* parties have used public money primarily for investing in more professionalized election campaigns and for employing more staff in their party headquarters (Nassmacher, 1989: 250–1).

State subsidies account for around 30 per cent of total party income, but contribute between 60 and 80 per cent of the budget of the federal party level (Nassmacher, 1989: 254; Pierre et al., 2000: 14; Poguntke, 2001: 268). There has been a gradual shift in public funding towards the federal level. At present, some 80 percent of direct state subsidies are channelled to the federal parties, with the remaining 20 per cent going to *Land* party headquarters (Ebbighausen et al., 1996: 440–1).[13]

This is not to say that *Land* parties are financially dependent on their federal counterparts. Indeed, particularly in the CDU and SPD, it is the federal level that is underfinanced. Studies of both *Volksparteien* have shown that the *Land* party level has a substantially higher share of the total party income (Schmid, 1990: 142–4; Lösche and Walter, 1992: 234–5). This is mainly because, alongside public funding, *Land* parties have better access to 'private' membership fees and donations.

Membership fees are divided between party levels according to ratios decided by federal party conferences (Poguntke and Boll, 1992: 336–7). In the SPD, where fees still account for one half of the total income, only some 15 per cent stays with the federal party; *Land* and local parties each receive over 40 per cent (Lösche and Walter, 1992: 235). In the CDU, the situation is similar. The bulk of member fees – around 40 per cent of total party income – remain with the *Land* and local parties, though the federal share was increased during the party's financial crisis in 2000 (Bösch, 2005: 180–3). Donations, which are particularly important for FDP, CSU and CDU budgets, are retained at the party level which received the money. Again, this tends to benefit the local and the *Land* party budgets (Lösche and Walter: 1992, 235).[14] Finally, *Land* legislative salaries and public subsidies to the parliamentary parties in the *Länder* have been extended significantly over the last few decades (Greß and Huth, 1998: 96–107; Borchert and Stolz, 2004: 4–5). This has given substantial additional resources to the *Land* parties in terms of staff, expertise and organizational infrastructure.

In sum, the financial autonomy of German *Land* parties is pronounced (although there are 'horizontal' variations between different *Länder* branches). Official party reports show that *Land*-level branches have a higher share of the total party income and a smaller share of total expenditures than the federal level.[15] While the former is mainly due to the broader access to a variety of income sources, the latter reflects the costs of more capital-intensive and professionalized election campaigns at the federal level and the costs of prestige federal party headquarters (Nassmacher, 1989: 247–56; Detterbeck, 2002: 133–8 and 215–9). Their relative financial autonomy allows *Land* party branches to attune organizational infrastructure, electoral campaigning and programmatic development to the specific context of the *Land* concerned.

Party programmes and policies

In formal terms, *Land* party programmes and the public policies pursued in office are exclusively the domain of *Land* party organizations. *Land* party executives and party conferences and *Land* parliamentary parties, in particular their government ministers (if in office), are the key decision-makers. To varying degrees, *Land* parties have developed an organizational infrastructure (party committees, expert groups, hearings and so on.) to develop the party programme and specific *Land* policies (Schneider, 2001: 399–400).

Formal programmatic autonomy allows for political heterogeneity within German parties. All the major parties have a spectrum of more left-leaning or more conservative, more pragmatic or more ideological *Land* party organizations (on the CDU, see Schmid, 1990: 132–7; more generally, Oberndörfer and Schmitt, 1991). Quite often, these positions are stable over time, reflecting *Land* party traditions, regional political cultures, socio-economic context and strategic patterns of *Land* party competition (Schmid, 1990: 137–41; Schneider, 2001: 402–4; Debus, 2006: 5–6).

However, programmatic heterogeneity has been contained within limits. Common ideological positions, shared political goals and the electoral need to present a united party line have favoured a general convergence of federal and *Land* party programmes. Moreover, cooperative federalism provided strong incentives for parties to agree internally on policy issues. Coordinated action, that is, pursuing a single party line in parliamentary and intergovernmental arenas, strongly enhanced the potential for policy success. As a result, resolving disputes and facilitating intra-party bargaining on common policy stances became one of the central objectives of vertical integration in Germany parties (Renzsch, 2000; Detterbeck and Renzsch, 2003).

Rather than insisting on programmatic autonomy, *Land* parties competed for influence on federal party positions. As Schmid (1990: 194–251) has shown in the case of the CDU, federal-level programmatic innovation in areas like social policy, education, the media or technology policy originated in *Land* parties. Holding government office at *Land* level significantly enhanced the capacity of *Land* branches to shape federal party programmes.

However, maintaining consensus on programmes and policy positions has become more difficult with the recalibration of German federalism after 1990. The institutional scope for autonomous *Land* policies has grown with reforms in the structure and practice of the federal system. And regionally distinctive patterns of party competition suggest a growing demand for distinctive policies. At the same time, the ideological and social cohesion of German parties has eroded (see above). In such a context, we might expect *Land* parties to adopt programmatic positions which are increasingly different from both the federal party and the party in other *Länder*.

Analysing election manifestos on both levels in the time period from 1994 to 2006, Debus (2006 and 2007) reveals empirical evidence for this hypothesis. While *Land* parties remain in ideological proximity to their federal counterparts, *Länder*-level programmes vary significantly. For example, while a majority of CDU *Land* parties (in particular, Baden-Württemberg and Hamburg) favoured more interventionist economic policies than the federal party, some *Land* parties (Hesse, Berlin, Schleswig-Holstein) called for fuller economic liberalization. With differing intensities, most SPD *Land* branches (in particular Hesse, Lower Saxony and Saarland) advocated more left-leaning economic policies than the federal party; however, East German SPD *Land* branches tended to be more moderate than their Western comrades.

Equivalent programmatic differences between federal and *Land* parties in other policy areas are also discernible.

Moreover, *Land* parties change their policy positions more quickly than federal parties. While some movement seem to be induced by the unpopularity of federal policies, other changes in election manifestos could be read as testing new electoral markets and coalition alternatives at the *Land* level.[16]

Differentiated, competitive strategies appear increasingly important in the programmatic development of *Land* parties. *Land*-level parties are increasingly using their formal autonomy to respond to *Land* electorates in more distinct ways and/or to position themselves vis-à-vis other parties according to *Land*-specific competitive (or cooperative) logics. In both the CDU and SPD, as well as in the smaller German parties, *Land* branches have taken advantage of their formal rights to determine programmatic positions as they see fit. While this has happened in both major parties to a similar degree, this may be more problematic for the Social Democrats given their stronger tradition of programmatic cohesion.

Election campaigns

There is a similar pattern of differentiation in *Land*-level campaign strategies. Land-level parties control *Land* election campaigns, with activities being coordinated by a campaign team around the Land party leadership supported by professional agencies and consultants to optimize media and marketing performance. While there is a strong focus on the lead candidate, that is the potential Land prime minister, in both SPD and CDU/CSU, local activities are arguably more important in Land elections than in federal campaigns (Sarcinelli and Schatz, 2000; Soyke, 2006).

The federal party leadership is typically involved in strategic planning and providing organizational and financial assistance, particularly vis-à-vis weaker *Land* organizations. Federal leaders regularly appear in *Land* election campaigns, give speeches and support the lead candidates in the *Länder*. While it is the *Land* party that ultimately decides whether to accept federal advice and help, political context is of crucial importance for determining the impact of the federal party level. One the one hand, the availability of resources will be a decisive factor. Strong *Land* parties, with access to government resources and a sound membership organization, will be more autonomous in their campaign strategies than weak branches fighting the election from the opposition benches. On the other hand, the federal party will be more interested and thus more active in some *Land* elections than in others. The size of the *Land*, the timing of elections, majority constellations in the Bundesrat or the closeness of an electoral race are among the most important factors here (Sturm, 1999: 203–11).

In a similar vein, the saliency of federal issues in *Land* election campaigns will result from a complex interplay of external factors, like public debates, media agenda-setting and electoral timing, and internal factors, including the strategic choices of both federal and *Land*-level parties. In some cases, *Land* parties will have a strong interest in promoting federal issues. Parties in federal opposition have often tried to take advantage of unpopular federal policies in *Land* elections. In other cases, *Land* parties will try to focus on *Land*-level issues. Successful or poor *Land* government records, the qualities of regional candidates and contentious regional policy issues have been centre stage in many *Land* elections (for examples of both, see Decker and von Blumenthal, 2002).

We lack systematic data to evaluate changes in strategic campaign choices. However, case studies have shown that *Land* parties are quite sensitive to unfavourable federal trends (often referred to as '*bundespolitischer Gegenwind*', an 'ill wind from federal politics'). This sometimes led to *Land* campaigns which were either fought in ostensible distance from or even outright resistance to the federal party, as, for example, in the cases of the CDU in Baden-Württemberg in 2001 and the SPD in Lower Saxony in 2003. In both instances, governing *Land* parties tried to counteract federal 'ill winds' by focusing on the records of their *Land* prime ministers, Erwin Teufel and Sigmar Gabriel respectively, who openly criticized their federal-level parties (Grotz, 2004: 65–6; Lösche, 1998: 76–8). There have also been incidents where *Land* parties have asked unpopular federal politicians to keep their distance from *Land* election campaigning.

For both the FDP and the Green Party, which often lack well-known *Land* politicians, prominent federal party leaders are important assets in *Land* election campaigns; this is also true for the PDS/Left Party, which, however, can build on a stronger local presence in East Germany.

Though so far there have been relatively few detailed case studies, we can assume that the autonomy of *Land* parties in election campaigns has gained in strength, for two reasons. First, regionalized patterns of party competition will demand specific programmatic and strategic answers. For example, the potential strength of the Left Party has varied considerably between West and East, and is likely to do so also between West German *Länder* after the merger with the WASG. As a consequence, the extent to which SPD *Land* parties face competition from the left varies significantly. In such a context, differentiated, decentralized decision-making on campaign strategies is the most likely outcome.

Second, reforms to the operation of the federal system have increased *Land* autonomy in some policy areas. With growing potential to do things differently, *Land* parties may increasingly need to give tailored, *Land*-specific answers to policy questions. We can expect voters to be more focused on *Land* politics and *Land* party elites to be more willing to act as regional advocates.

Government formation

As noted earlier, the heterogeneity of government formation in the *Länder* is one of the most distinct features of party competition in the *Länder* since

1990. Due to the greater diversity of *Land* party systems, *Land*-level coalition-building has become both more autonomous and more 'promiscuous' (see Sturm, 1999, 201–2; Detterbeck and Renzsch, 2003: 262–3). This is in marked contrast to pre-unification patterns, particularly in the period between 1969 and 1989. With the SPD/FDP federal government taking office in 1969, the final breakthrough of patterns of congruent coalition formation occurred. The main institutional incentive to build congruent coalitions at both levels is the weight of the Bundesrat in the federal legislative process, which makes the majority in the second chamber a valuable 'prize' of party competition (Jeffery, 1999a: 135–7).

While earlier attempts by CDU-led federal governments to structure *Land* coalitions along identical party lines met with only limited success, from the early 1970s on *Land* government constellations which were inconsistent with the pattern of government and opposition in the Bundestag became very rare exceptions (Lehmbruch, 1976; Jun, 1994). Congruence resulted from three developments. First, during the 1960s a process of concentration had taken place in both the federal and *Land* party systems; with just three (or later, with the Greens, four) parties left, there was limited room for manoeuvre in coalition formation. Second, single-party governments became much more common after 1970 with several *Länder* seeing the same party win several successive terms of office. Third, the German parties deliberately renounced strategic options in the *Länder* that would have been inconsistent with their federal political alignment (unless using new coalition opportunities in the *Länder* to prefigure a change of government coalition at the federal level).[17]

Since 1990, a rather colourful patchwork of single-party governments, grand coalitions, red–green, red–red (SPD/PDS), red–yellow (SPD/FDP) and bourgeois (CDU/FDP) coalitions and some (rarer) three-party coalitions has emerged. As incongruent coalitions regularly use Bundesrat 'abstention clauses'[18] to prevent disagreement over federal issues, majority building in the Bundesrat has become more fluid and less subject to federal-level party discipline (see Jeffery, 1999a: 156–60). Currently, however, the strong position of the Christian Democrats in the *Länder* does not leave much doubt about Bundesrat majorities.[19]

With the growing regionalization of party competition, *Land* politicians have claimed more rigorously the formal right to decide on their own which solution best matches regional circumstances. There have been several instances where *Land* parties have opted for a coalition partner against the (informal) advice of the federal party leadership (Kropp and Sturm, 1999: 41–2).[20] However, with an eye to ideological proximity, Bundesrat decision-making and voters' perceptions, *Land* parties remain strongly influenced by the federal patterns of government and opposition. Congruence remains a powerful determinant of government formation in the *Länder* (see Pappi et al., 2005; Debus, 2006).

Yet there now is an increased likelihood that either arithmetic necessities or strategic innovations will lead to **Land** coalitions that do not mirror federal patterns. Such coalitions have most frequently been formed in East Germany. Given the weakness of the FDP and the Green Party there, several CDU–SPD grand coalitions were formed in order to prevent the PDS from entering *Land* governments (Kropp and Sturm, 1999). The SPD has been more willing to innovate – or show 'promiscuity' (Mair, 1997: 134) – in coalition formation. While this may have provided it with a strategic advantage in party competition, it has also led at times to serious conflicts between party levels and within individual *Land* party branches.[21]

The autonomy of substate branches with regard to government formation has increased since 1990. While internally the federal party leadership will still make its preferences clear, *Land* party elites now have more arguments at their disposal in claiming a free hand in coalition bargaining.

Integration of the Länder in federal-level parties

Interlocking of party structures

In German parties, vertical linkages are evident in all three 'faces' of parties (Katz and Mair, 1993): membership organization, the parliamentary party and the party headquarters. All German parties have unitary membership structures. Members usually join the local party branch and are then automatically members of the federal party. Membership fees are shared between party levels. In line with a constitutional obligation (Article 21 of the Basic Law) to practise intra-party democracy, lower party levels are represented at higher party levels, allowing for a decision-making process which operates in principle from the bottom up. So local branches send delegates to district and *Land* party conferences, and lower party branches nominate delegates for federal party conferences. Party conferences at the different levels are formally responsible for the election of party executives and the adoption of party programmes. With some nuances, there is broad structural similarity among the German parties here (Poguntke and Boll, 1992: 341–68). Unsurprisingly though, the internal political weight and the democratic openness of party conferences vary substantially between the parties. In particular, the participatory tradition of the Greens produces party conferences which are less controlled by the party leadership and more prone to surprising results (Poguntke, 2001: 264–5; Probst, 2007: 183–6).

Vertical integration is also an important feature of the parliamentary groupings of German parties. The Bundestag caucuses are organized along functional and territorial lines. Thus, alongside working groups of the experts in a specific policy field, all members of a particular caucus elected from a certain *Land* meet regularly in their '*Land* group' (*Landesgruppe*). Their aim is to coordinate political parties' regional interests within the Bundestag and vis-à-vis the Bundesrat (Renzsch, 2000: 58–60; Leonardy, 2004: 188–9).

The parliamentary leaderships of a party at the European, the federal and the *Land* levels meet several times a year. Specialist working groups reflecting ministerial responsibilities also link the different levels of the 'party in public office' (Leonardy, 2004: 190–1). Bundesrat sessions are preceded by party round tables, in which representatives of *Land* governments controlled by that party meet, supplemented in some cases by representatives of the party in federal government (where relevant), the federal party, the party in the Bundestag and *Land* parliamentary parties (Leonardy, 2004: 186–7).

Finally, there are substantial linkages between federal and *Land* party headquarters. Certain tasks important to both levels necessitate permanent channels of communication, for example the organization of federal election campaigns and the preparation of party meetings. With their stronger apparatus, federal party headquarters can provide services and expertise for *Land* offices.[22] This may range from legal advice, campaign assistance and training of staff members to organizational infrastructure and temporary secondments of personnel (for the SPD, see Lösche and Walter, 1992: 200–11). We may expect a continuum on which, depending on circumstances, federal help will either be highly welcome or seen as intrusion upon *Land* party autonomy.

On all three 'faces' of the German parties vertical linkages are deeply entrenched. Cooperation between party levels, involving processes of bargaining and conflict management, has become strongly institutionalized. This may explain why we have not seen significant changes since 1990. While there may now be more potential for conflict, the membership organizations, the parliamentary parties and the party headquarters at federal and *Land* levels remain strongly interlocked.

Inclusion of land party leaders in the federal party

One of the most remarkable features of German parties is the strong pattern of inclusion of *Land* party leaders in federal party executives. Heading the membership organization and directing the federal party headquarters, German party executives are powerful, in particular in defining party strategies and policy positions. While federal party executives were the domain of federal ministers and legislators in the 1960s, *Land* politicians have taken on important party offices at the federal level since the 1970s. With very few exceptions, these *Land* politicians were regional 'heavyweights': *Land* prime ministers and cabinet members or *Land* opposition leaders, all of whom often also served as *Land* party chairs or deputy chairs. Both the CDU (in the 1970s and after 1998) and the SPD (in the 1980s and 1990s) have tended to include more *Land* party 'barons' in their federal leaderships while in opposition, when the federal party lacked power and resources (Schüttemeyer, 1999: 53–4; Detterbeck, 2002: 66–8).[23]

In the CDU, all *Land* prime ministers are, if not elected directly by the federal party conference, *ex officio* members of the federal party executive and the smaller executive committee. In addition, all *Land* party chairs are *ex officio* members of the federal party executive. Apart from these institutional prerogatives, which reflect the strong federal ethos of the CDU, both the recent period of federal opposition (1998–2005) and the current strength of the party at the *Land* level are reflected in the composition of the CDU executive committee elected in 2006. Twelve of the 24 members are representatives of the *Land* parties. Among them are 10 *Land* prime ministers, 3 holding the position of federal deputy party leaders.

In contrast, the power balance within the SPD has been tilted more towards the federal party since the late 1990s. With the party in government at the federal level since 1998, while losing a series of elections at the *Land* level, the federal parliamentary party came to dominate the SPD. In addition, for a variety of contingent reasons, the supply of ambitious *Land* party elites looking for positions in the federal SPD was limited. In 2007, nearly one half (22 out of 45) of the federal party executive were federal government ministers and parliamentarians. One third of the federal party leadership (15 out of 45) represented the *Land* parties. Within the executive committee – chosen from within the elected party executive – there is a similar picture, with 4 out of 13 members (30.8 per cent) being *Land* politicians. However, the current party leader, Kurt Beck, rose to that position while serving as *Land* prime minister. He is the latest in a series of recent SPD party chairmen with an identical (Engholm, Scharping, Lafontaine, Platzeck) or similar (Schröder) *Land* government background (Detterbeck, 2004).[24]

As regards the smaller parties, *Land* party elites also have a role in federal party bodies. In the FDP party executive of some 40 members, 16 seats are reserved for representatives of the *Land* branches (Poguntke and Boll, 1992: 357). The Green Party established a (reformed) national council in 1991, which brings together the 15 members of the federal executive committee with representatives of the *Land* party executives and the Green parliamentary groupings at the European, federal and *Land* levels (Poguntke and Boll, 1992: 360–1; Koß, 2006). Within the PDS and its successor, the Left Party, leading *Land* politicians from the East German *Land* parliaments and party boards have made their way into the federal party executive, at times exercising considerable leverage over federal party matters (Koß, 2006; Neu, 2007).

The inclusion of leading Land politician in federal party bodies is an essential feature of vertical integration within German parties. Changing balances of power between the party levels obviously have an effect on the strength of inclusion at any given moment. Yet, there are no signs that the multilevel character of parties' federal executives has become weaker in the period after 1990.

Integration of party careers

Movement and linkages are the two major ingredients of integrated party careers (Borchert, 2001). In integrated career patterns, politicians move from one political level or institution to another over time; they may also hold various party and public offices at the same time.

In the German case, most political careers start, often on a part-time basis, at the local level. The vast majority of *Land* legislators has held local public office (75 per cent) and/or local party office (61 per cent) before being elected at the *Land* level (Borchert and Stolz, 2003: 158). Many *Land* and federal politicians keep a seat on local party executive boards as a sound 'home base' for reselection (Borchert and Stolz, 2003: 165–6; Best and Jahr, 2006: 72–3). However, there is surprisingly little career movement between the *Land* and the federal parliamentary arenas. At the end of the 1990s, just 15 per cent of federal MPs had previous experience in *Land* parliaments. This figure has fallen over recent decades from 25 per cent in the mid-1960s (Stolz, 2003: 230–1). With the increased professionalization of *Land* parliaments, in terms of salaries, time budgets and staff allowances, the *Land* level has obviously become a more enduring career choice (Greß and Huth, 1998; Borchert and Stolz, 2003).

As for movements in the other direction, even fewer federal legislators subsequently 'descend' to the *Land* level. A mere 3 per cent of all members who have entered *Land* parliaments since 1990 have had previous experience at the federal or European level (Best and Jahr, 2006: 72–3). Having reached the Bundestag, few parliamentarians choose to return to the *Land* parliaments. Thus, most German politicians remain at the political level at which they were first elected to a full-time professional position in the public sphere (Borchert and Golsch, 2003: 156–7; Stolz, 2003: 228–33; Best and Jahr, 2006: 72).

Only at the very top is there a different pattern. A majority of federal Chancellors (Kiesinger, Brandt, Schmidt, Kohl, Schröder), most chancellor candidates and many federal ministers have been recruited from *Land* government positions. Some *Land* prime ministers and cabinet members have previously served in the Bundestag (see Schüttemeyer, 1999: 51–5). However, such vertical linkages do not necessarily stem from upward and downward mobility. A very strong feature of the German case, as we have already seen, is office accumulation via parties. *Land* party elites combine *Land* public office, *Land* party leadership and federal party leadership simultaneously (Schmid, 1990: 158–66; Herzog, 1997: 311–18). While staying at the parliamentary level where they started their full-time professional careers, they nevertheless provide for close cooperation between party levels.

Most politicians have first been elected to the *Land* party leadership before they take on a position in the federal party executive. There is a clear logic to this sequence as nearly all *Land* members of the federal party leadership are elected or appointed federally *because* of their leading position at the *Land* level. We see more diversity with respect to the sequence of accumulation of party offices and public mandates. While sometimes party positions are springboards to public office, these offices may constitute in their own right a basis for representation in the party leadership (see Detterbeck, 2004).

In sum, there seems to be a tendency towards a stronger separation of parliamentary careers between the political levels. With the federal reform of 2006, it may also become more attractive to serve as *Land* legislator as policy discretion has grown at the *Land* level. However, integrated patterns of political careers have remained strong after 1990. At the top political level, the recruitment of government personnel has continued to create movement between *Land* and federal political arenas. Within the parties, the vertical accumulation of party and public offices provides for close linkages between *Land* and federal party branches.

Conclusion

This chapter has explored how German parties have responded to the recalibration of German federalism. Our general argument is that the autonomy of *Land* party branches has grown while the levels of vertical integration of *Land* parties with the federal party have remained high.

With respect to the autonomy of *Land* parties, formal organizational competencies which had existed before are now being used more systematically with a stronger focus on specific regional contexts. We have mainly argued that within a changed political context, in which patterns of party competition have become more regionalized and in which there is more scope for autonomous policy-making by the *Länder*, decision-making within the parties has become more decentralized and fine-tuned to specific *Land* circumstances. There are no substantial differences between the two major parties, the CDU and the SPD.

However, this is not to say that the federal and *Land* branches of the German parties are now widely divergent from one another with respect to party programmes, campaign strategies or coalition choices. *Land*-specific responses remain within the spectrum of their federal parties.

We have also argued that the second dimension of vertical party linkages, that is, the integration of substate branches into the federal party, has not declined since 1990. Despite growing heterogeneity and the subsequent potential for conflict between party levels and between *Land* organizations, German parties have by and large attempted to maintain their close cooperation.

Why is this so? Our answer would be that there are still many incentives for parties to organize as integrated multilevel organizations. Despite recent changes, German federalism still has interlocked structures and the Bundesrat remains an important organ in federal policy-making. *Land* elections are still largely shaped by federal issues; second-order effects, while arguably weaker since 1990, are still visible. Voting behaviour and party strategies may increasingly but still do not generally follow a clear-cut distinction between federal and *Land* elections. Finally, vertical integration within German parties remains strongly institutionalized.

However, incremental party change is likely to continue. The recent reforms to the federal system have increased the potential for policy divergence between the *Länder*. With this, the autonomy of *Land* politics may become more pronounced and *Land* parties may seek more vigorously to go their own way.

4
Decentralization and Party Organizational Change: The Case of Italy*

Jonathan Hopkin

Introduction

This chapter examines the relationship between the process of political decentralization in post-war Italy and the Italian party system, and, in particular, the impact of decentralization on parties' internal organizations. The Italian Constitution of 1948 established a regional tier of government which was immediately established in selected territories, and extended to the rest of the country a little over two decades later. Further reforms in a decentralizing direction were made in the 1990s and 2000s. This evolution of the territorial shape of the Italian state has changed the institutional context in which Italian party politics is conducted, and territorial politics has become a central part of the political debate. Our aim here is to provide a preliminary analysis of the effects of these developments on the parties themselves and the distribution of power between national and subnational party leaderships. We proceed by generating some basic hypotheses on the impact of decentralization on party organizations, then go on to summarize the process of institutional change itself. The rest of the chapter examines how party organizations have reacted to the changing institutional context.

Decentralization and party organization

After a long period of neglect, the study of territorial politics within political parties has attracted the interest of many political scientists in recent years, as the profession has sought to make sense of the apparently generalized trend towards decentralization in Western democracies. As a result, there is a growing literature seeking to document and explain the ways in which political parties adapt to decentralizing institutional change (see for example Hopkin, 2003; Chhibber and Kollman, 2004; Deschouwer, 2006a). Our theoretical expectations are derived from this literature, which in the most basic sense envisages party organizations responding to decentralization of the state by decentralizing some of their own internal structures. Party organizations have a tendency to reflect the territorial distribution of state power, because there are strong incentives for them to do so: decentralization often creates new electoral arenas for which centralized parties lack adequate territorial units, and it creates new arenas of government formation and policy-making, which require parties to make decisions at a new level of territorial organization. All other things being equal, decentralization reforms should therefore provoke some degree of decentralization of party organizations, although the organizational legacies of a previous, more centralized context can obstruct change and limit the scope of internal restructuring (Hopkin and Bradbury, 2006).

The logic of this argument is that politicians are essentially power-seekers who aim to maximize their access to political resources and influence, within a set of institutional constraints. When new regional institutions are created, subnational political elites will often demand greater powers to be delegated from the centre in order to compete effectively in elections to the new institutions, and to develop strategies of coalition-building and policy-making tailored to the interests of the party's regional organization, rather than simply execute decisions taken at the national level. Although these demands may be focused mainly on enhancing the power and status of the party subnational elites themselves, national leaders may well have an interest in agreeing to this delegation, since regional party leaders are likely to have a greater understanding of the dynamics of the political game at the subnational level. For these reasons, the formal distribution of power within parties tends to reflect the distribution of electoral resources and control over public office. This argument has been taken still further by Chhibber and Kollman (2004), who argue that the party system itself is likely to change as a result of decentralizing reforms, because regionally based parties become more viable.

However, the literature on party organizations also suggests factors which tend to stabilize party organizations and limit the effects of institutional reform. Organizational change is costly in terms of time and effort, and undermines the influence of some organizational actors. Internal decentralization weakens the degree of control of the national party leadership over the territorial organization, and makes it more difficult to present a unified front in the national political arena. Opening up the prospect of a redistribution of power within a party risks destabilizing the organization and provoking a much greater degree of delegation than national party leaders are prepared to accept. Often, lack of agreement on the new organizational model and lack of trust between competing party elites can block change, and obsolete party rule books can persist despite not reflecting the real balance of internal power. In sum, decentralizing reforms can have unexpected consequences depending on a variety of institutional factors.

Rather than testing predictions, this chapter will assess some evidence from the Italian case of organizational changes resulting from decentralization, and draw some tentative conclusions of more general interest. We will attempt to gauge the degree to which decentralization has enhanced the autonomy of the subnational elites of national political parties, by assessing how decisions on the management of subnational party structures are taken. A first step is to analyse the institutional context in order to understand how reform changes the incentives available to party actors.

Decentralization in Italy

Italy is a complex but useful test case for this purpose. The Italian case combines a substantial degree of territorial homogeneity with a tradition of the centralized institutions of a unitary state which have recently been reformed to give greater powers to subnational units known as regions (*regioni*). Italy therefore offers a clear case of institutional change in a decentralizing direction (albeit with a number of complexities and uncertainties) with a set of quite distinctive political, economic and socio-cultural circumstances in different regions. We would therefore expect decentralization to make a difference to national political parties' internal distribution of authority.

Like other large national states in Western Europe, Italy comprises territories with deep historical differences. Such was the cultural heterogeneity of the peninsula that it is estimated that only around 10 per cent of Italians actually spoke the Italian language at the time of unification.[1] Added to this linguistic diversity, different regions had been dominated before unification by a variety of different foreign powers: the Spanish Habsburgs and Bourbons had governed the South in the Early Modern period, while much of the North fell under Austrian domination in the pre-unification period. Finally, for a variety of reasons including geographical proximity to different markets, the North was more economically advanced than the South at the time of unification, a situation which has persisted through the history of the unified state. This set of historical legacies ensures that Italy remains a far from homogeneous or uniform country, leading to the expectation that political decentralization will have substantial effects in the Italian context.

The initial administrative model established by the unified state in the late 19th century was inspired by the centralized French model (Ziblatt, 2006), in which the national territory is divided into small and similar-sized portions (departments in France, provinces in Italy) which are controlled directly by the national government through the presence of centrally appointed 'prefects'. Through this hierarchical system, the centre can, in theory, impose uniformity on political and administrative practices throughout the state. Although in practice this system was not particularly successful in imposing uniformity in the Italian case, it did establish a bureaucratic and legal tradition which tended to centralize decision-making and discourage distinctive patterns of government in different territories. At the same time, the inability of this centralized state to achieve genuine control established a practice of clientelistic relations in which local notables negotiated directly with the central authorities, securing local order in exchange for bureaucratic favours (Tarrow, 1977; Panebianco, 1984). This weak but centralized state model is therefore the starting point for the development of democratic politics in post-war Italy.

The decentralizing reforms experienced by Italy since the Second World War can be crudely divided between two broad phases. A first phase began with the approval of a new democratic constitution in 1948. The Constitution established a regional tier of government, which would have administrative responsibilities and some limited legislative powers (subordinated to the primary legislative role of the Italian Parliament) (Putnam, 1993). However, only 4 of the 20 regions were created immediately: Sicily, Sardinia, Val d'Aosta and Trentino-Alto Adige were established as regions with 'special statutes', giving them greater autonomy than that envisaged for the remaining regions, including exclusive legislative authority in some policy areas. The 15 'ordinary' regions (Friuli-Venezia-Giulia, another 'special' region, was created in 1963) were not established until 1970, partly at least to avoid providing a power base in the institutions for the Italian Communist Party (PCI), the strongest political force in some of the central regions (Bull, 1994). These 'ordinary' regions had complementary legislative powers, subordinated to the framework legislation produced by the Italian Parliament in Rome. Although the actual devolution of powers and resources to these institutions was a slow and tortuous process, ultimately this wave of decentralization led to responsibility for much of education and health policy, as well as regional transport, research and innovation, and local policing being passed down to the regional level. By the early 1990s, regional government spending amounted to around 10 per cent of Italy's GDP (Putnam, 1993: 6).

An analytical (rather than chronological) distinction can be drawn between these reforms, which gradually implemented the provisions of the 1948 constitutional text, and a further set of changes deriving from the 'earthquake' that shook the Italian political system in the early 1990s, ushering in what has become known as the 'Second Republic'. Between 1992 and 1994 an acute political crisis, involving a threatened collapse of the state finances, a judicial offensive against political corruption, a mafia terror campaign, and a reform of the Italian electoral system, effectively dismantled the centre-right coalition which had governed Italy in various guises since the war. Among the multiple causes of this crisis was the electoral growth of the Northern League (*Lega Nord*), a radical right-wing populist party advocating the independence of the prosperous North from the less developed South of the peninsula, which League politicians blamed for Italy's problems (Mannheimer, 1991; Biorcio, 1997; Diamanti, 1993 and 1996). The success of the League fatally undermined the Christian Democrat Party by robbing it of its electoral base in the North-East, and placed the territorial structure of the state at the top of the political agenda. In the bipolar politics of the new Italian party system the League held a pivotal position, ensuring that the other major parties quickly became responsive to demands for decentralization.

This 'second phase' of decentralizing reforms therefore takes place in a different context. Rather than a relatively consistent delegation of policy areas to a set of fairly similar subnational units, the second phase is composed of reforms which fit into a broader debate about improving the performance of Italy's political institutions, such as changes to electoral rules, and reforms which respond to the secessionist threat of the League, and which therefore at least to some extent open up the possibility of a clear differentiation between regions. Centre–periphery dynamics were affected by the 1993 reform of electoral laws governing local elections, which introduced the direct election of mayors of large cities under a two-round majority system (Baldini and Legnante, 2000); further reforms in 1995 and 1999 introduced a similar system at the regional level, which directly elected regional presidents and reinforced the position of the regional executives (Baldi and Baldini, forthcoming). Although not explicitly a decentralizing move, this reform enhanced the status of local and regional political leaders vis-à-vis national party leaders, and therefore created centrifugal pressure within the parties. In terms of the broader debate on the shape of the state, the key change has been the constitutional reform passed by the centre-left Amato government in 2001. This reform removed central government controls over regional legislative powers, gave some powers that were previously concurrent exclusively to regions, and gave regions the power to legislate in all areas not explicitly reserved to the state. In the context of the Italian political scene of the turn of the century, this reform implied the prospect of regions with most resources enhancing their powers beyond the possibilities of the poorer regions (Vandelli, 2002; Esposito, 2003). Further decentralization was envisaged by a set of constitutional amendments proposed by the Berlusconi government, which were rejected in a referendum shortly after the government's electoral defeat in 2006.

These two phases of reforms – which here we describe as the regionalization of the 'First and Second Republics' – have led to significant changes in the way Italy is governed, although it remains a unitary state in which central government retains significant reserved powers. These reforms have come about in different circumstances with varying implications for parties' autonomy, but in all cases pose concrete dilemmas for Italy's main political parties, almost all of which field candidates throughout the national territory (with the exception of the League). These dilemmas stem in part from the transfer of policy competences to the subnational level, and in part from the changes to electoral politics resulting from the emergence of multilevel governance. The rest of this chapter will offer some examples of how these dilemmas have played out in practice.

Regionalization in the 'First Republic'

Although the 1948 Italian Constitution contained strong regionalizing components, the Christian Democrats (DC), the dominant governing party until 1992, managed to impose a minimalist reading of the constitutional provisions for two decades until pressure from the parties of the left (Socialist PSI and Communist PCI) forced the creation of the 15 'ordinary regions' in 1970. This implies that the process of regionalization did not coincide in time with the institutionalization of the major Italian parties, which developed as relatively centralized organizations in the immediate post-war period (Poggi, 1968). Our expectation, therefore, would be that the regionalization process should have some effect on the degree of centralization of political authority within the parties, resulting from the electoral legitimacy and control over real levers of power available to regional-level party elites.

However, this rather straightforward hypothesis immediately runs up against the complexity of centre–periphery relations in the Italian parties. First of all, rather than regionalization being the result of peripheral mobilizations against central state power, the extension of regional government in the 1970s owed much more to the political competition between rival national parties at the national level. In other words, regionalization was the result of bargaining between nation-level elites of articulated and centralized nationwide parties, in particular between the PCI and the DC. The PCI in this period was if anything an extreme case of internal centralization, given its tradition of 'democratic centralism', in which decision-making authority was concentrated in the party executive. Moreover, the regions where the PCI was likely to have access to real political power at the regional level (central regions such as Tuscany and Emilia-Romagna) could not be considered in any sense 'peripheral' to the party structure; on the contrary, these regions were the party heartlands which provided most the party's electoral support and therefore an important portion of its national-level elites.

A second point worth bearing in mind is that the Italian parties' internal articulation, which centralized power around national-level party leaderships, was in many ways more formal than real. The DC in particular was unable completely to centralize internal authority relations because of its initial organizational weakness which led it to co-opt clientelistic structures at the local level, especially in the immediate post-war period. This situation, in which 'the politicians (we)re local bosses using their parties as their own exclusive electoral machines' (Allum, 1973: 66) reversed the centre–periphery relationship, as local elites often had strong control over packages of votes at the grass-roots level, and could use this control to demand autonomy from national party authority (see Tarrow, 1977; Zuckerman, 1979). Fanfani's efforts to institutionalize the party in the 1950s had a centralizing effect by 'modernizing' clientelistic practices (Chubb, 1982; Leonardi and Wertman, 1989). As state spending grew, flows of resources for local patronage depended increasingly on decisions made in central ministries, and the DC's organization began to reflect this, with a much greater articulation between centre and periphery. However, local power bases still retained importance in the DC as the regionalization process got under way in the 1970s, and party leaders used their influence in local fiefdoms to further their political careers in the party structures at the national level. A similar scenario was valid for the PSI, but rather less so in the case of the PCI, where autonomous political resources were less crucial to the party's internal career structure and the national party executive was able to dominate internal decision-making to a significant degree (Guadagnini, 1984: 597; Panebianco, 1984: 113–15). In any case, local political experience was a key element in political recruitment well before the regionalization reforms, and local party federations were a key locus of power within the parties (Kogan, 1975).

There is nonetheless some evidence that the regionalization process led to shifts in the internal equilibria within the most important Italian parties. First of all, the emergence of a new layer of elective politics and a new tier of elected politicians affected parties' patterns of recruitment, although not dramatically. Research carried out in the early 1980s suggested that the regional tier had become part of the 'career ladder' of aspiring politicians, with many regional councillors moving on to stand for the national parliament (Cazzola and Motta, 1984). This pointed to the regional institutions acting as a kind of 'apprenticeship' for aspiring national leaders, much as the local level had often served as a necessary first stage in national political careers. However, the total number of regional councillors moving to the higher level remained relatively small – a little over an eighth of the total of regional representatives (Cazzola and Motta, 1984: 622) – meaning that many ambitious politicians bypassed the regional level. This suggests a lack of relevance of the regional level for broader internal power struggles, perhaps not surprisingly given the slow pace at which powers and resources were transferred to the regional level in the 1970s and early 1980s. Local power resources, relating to the municipal level of government and influence within the provincial federations of the parties, appeared more important than regional-level resources in battles between national leaders of the major parties. However, even in the early 1970s some impact of regionalization on internal party dynamics could be detected. Kogan (1975) reported that in some regions of the Centre and North the DC's regional elites had established substantial political autonomy from the national leadership, and that even the disciplined PCI had co-opted key regional leaders into the national leadership structures in recognition of their growing influence. Although Kogan also presented evidence of national interference in regional affairs, and his data do not lead to any clear trend in the level of autonomy enjoyed by the regional elites, this research covering only the first two years after the first regional elections suggests that the deepening of the reforms would be likely to provoke a reaction.

Later research offered some confirmation of this. Putnam surveys of local elites revealed that regional party leaders were perceived as growing in influence between the regional reforms of 1970 and 1989, mainly at the expense of municipal leaders. In these surveys, the share of respondents reporting the perception that regional leaders controlled regional council nominations grew from 10 per cent to over 30 per cent, while the share reporting the perception that they decided regional coalition formation grew from just over 50 per cent to 80 per cent (Putnam, 1993: 39–41). Significantly, this growth in influence was perceived to be at the expense of local rather than national elites, suggesting a recalibration of peripheral power balances rather than of the centre–periphery relationship. However, these surveys also showed that local elites increasingly questioned national party discipline during this period, with growing support for the possibility of different coalition strategies in different regions (Putnam, 1993: 42). These subjective data are backed by objective evidence that coalition changes at the national level were less frequently followed by similar crises at the regional level as the regionalization process advanced between 1970 and 1990 (Fedele, 1990, cited in Putnam, 1993: 41).

The shifting balance of power within the parties did not generally take the shape of formal organizational reforms, such as statutory changes giving regional leaderships greater powers. However, the regionalization process inevitably changed internal dynamics, particularly because by the 1970s Italian parties had become increasingly absorbed in state institutions through the well-known mechanism of *lottizzazione*, the spoils system whereby public officials tended to be party appointees, and their roles in the state bureaucracy conflated with their positions within party organizations (Panebianco, 1984: 126–7). The regionalization process – not surprisingly given the voracious appetite of the Italian parties for state resources – led to the creation of a new layer of bureaucracy and of public appointees which the parties could guide and control. The creation of a regional tier of government therefore had the effect of creating a new group of party operatives, with their own interests and strategies. Moreover, although the regional tier initially lacked financial autonomy and therefore had limited material resources, its growing role as a 'broker' between central and municipal governments gave it substantive influence and therefore enhanced the position of the regional elites within their parties, particularly at the expense of the local level (Panebianco, 1984: 127; Dente, 1997: 181). National party leaders were therefore faced with the emergence of 20 sets of regional elites, rather than the innumerable distinct municipal and provincial leaderships, which were not necessarily easily controlled but were unlikely to pose a serious challenge to national leaders' authority.

The expansion of the policy and administrative responsibilities of the regions further boosted the position of the party regional elites by giving them power over significant public services, most notably the national health service, one of the biggest ticket items of the Italian welfare state, which was largely devolved down to the regional level by the 1990s, although regional responsibility for health care also involved extensive delegation to the local level, and in particular the Local Health Authorities (*Unità Sanitarie Locali* or USL) which acquired increasing autonomy as a result of the administrative reforms of the 1990s. These changes in the territorial structure of the public services increased the control of local elites over the distribution of public resources (Putnam, 1993), and it has emerged from the judicial investigations of recent years that the decentralization of health services created opportunities for local elites to use public money for the purposes of mobilizing electoral support.

Patterns of corrupt activity by party politicians offer one window for observing the change in the internal power structure of Italian parties during this period of decentralization. Extensive research by scholars such as Donatella della Porta (della Porta, 1992; della Porta and Vannucci, 1994; della Porta and Pizzorno, 1996) analyse in some detail how different levels of party elites interacted in the kinds of corrupt and clientelistic exchange mechanism that became endemic in the Italian 'First Republic'. Although not necessarily a reliable indicator of the internal power arrangements, the examination of these corruption networks suggests that decentralization had not undermined the essentially unitary nature of Italian parties in the 1980s and early 1990s. In numerous cases, the choice of which firms would benefit from public contracts in exchange for bribes (the proceedings of which in part financed party activities) often required the approval of party leaders at the national level (della Porta and Vannucci, 1994), with national party treasurers, and even party secretaries themselves, playing a direct role. In one characteristic example, the corrupt networks around the Socialist Party (PSI) in Milan often bypassed the formal territorial structures of the party, with an informal party 'treasurer' coordinating the payment of bribes and interacting directly with the party leader Craxi (della Porta and Vannucci, 1994: 236–8). Similarly, in the Christian Democrat Party (DC) corrupt financing was channelled through the party's internal factional structure, with the factions each having their own territorial networks which directed corrupt earnings to factional leaderships at the national level (della Porta and Vannucci, 1994: 236). Even though key competences had been delegated to the regions, the weight of the existing territorial structures (especially the provincial federations and the local authorities) and the lack of discretionary budgeting available to the regions prevented the 'meso' level of party structures challenging the national leaderships.

In the particular case of the Socialist Party, the period of state decentralization from the 1970s to the early 1990s coincided with a dramatic *centralization* of internal power in the party. With the help of his period as Prime Minister, Craxi transformed the PSI into a 'presidentialist' party, weakening the old party organization based on the factions, leaving a lightweight structure of local electoral machines under the direction of an authoritarian leader (Pasquino, 1986; Hine, 1989). The PSI is perhaps exceptional among the major parties, having a smaller electoral base and weaker structure in the first place. However, there is relatively scant evidence of any significant decentralization in the other major political forces. The DC had a complex structure in which local power resources served as a basis for political careers within the party's distinct factions; for example, Ciriaco De Mita, national party secretary in the mid-1980s, had a power base in Irpinia, in the Campania region. Indeed, De Mita, in part at least for instrumental reasons of his own, attempted unsuccessfully to develop greater autonomy for the regional structure of the party in the 1980s (Baldini, 1998). However, the implications of corrupt financing for the distinct factions were also managed at the national level, with local party leaders handing over sums of illegally gathered money to the national administrators, who would then redistribute it back to the party federations (della Porta and Vannucci, 1994: 428). Although it is difficult to establish any general patterns on the basis of the fragmentary evidence available on corrupt financing, the heavy involvement of national leaderships in these matters is difficult to square with any claim of decentralization or regionalization of these major governing parties.

The case of the Communist Party (PCI) is rather different, both because of its exclusion from the institutions of national government until the mid-1990s, and because of its formally highly centralized structure inherited from the 'democratic centralism' of the immediate post-war period. The PCI did not recognize any organized factions, and the party programme was tightly controlled by the national party executive, following the Leninist-inspired organizational model of Communist tradition, until the 1980s (Ignazi, 1992: 85–6). A relaxation of the party's strict ideological discipline in the 1980s rapidly modified this situation, partly in response to demands from the party grass roots for greater participation in decision-making. This trend was accentuated with the transition from the PCI to the new 'post-communist' formation the PDS (Party of the Democratic Left), which aspired to align itself with contemporary European social democracy and adopted a less centralized organizational model which recognized, for example, the possibility of different currents of opinion within the party (Ignazi, 1992; Baccetti, 1997). However, there is no clear evidence that this had any relation to the decentralization of the Italian state, and the organizational changes in the party did not clearly redistribute power to the regional level. Instead the PCI's transformation into a democratic left party responded to the international decline of Communist ideology and the demands of the left electorate for a party capable of responding to changing needs and demands.

In sum, the evidence available suggests that the 'first wave' of regionalization in the Italian 'First Republic' had relatively little effect on the formal rules or internal balance of power in the main Italian parties. Such organizational changes as took place in this period did not result in a straightforward shift of power from the national to the regional level, and in any case can for the most part be better explained by reference to other social, economic and ideological developments.

Regionalization in the 'Second Republic'

The 'second phase' of decentralization in Italy has coincided with a period of dramatic change in the country's party system which is only tenuously related to the transfer of powers to the regional level. The collapse in 1992–3 of the major governing parties in the post-war period – the DC, the PSI and small centre parties – resulted from a combination of corruption scandals and judicial activism, a successful campaign for electoral reform, and a financial crisis of the Italian state (see for example Bardi and Morlino, 1994; Morlino, 1996; Gundle and Parker, 1996; Bufacchi and Burgess, 2001). The emergence of a new regionalist political party, the Northern League, certainly contributed to the pressure on the existing government coalition by making inroads into the Christian Democrat's electorate in the North and undermining its ability to respond to the crisis. However, the most immediate cause of party breakdown was the judicial offensive against the First Republic's system of corrupt exchanges, which placed a substantial proportion of the DC and PSI elites under investigation (Newell, 2000). These parties were effectively 'decapitated' by the anti-corruption drive and ceased to function normally, which in itself indicated an inadequate development of the parties' territorial structures, which were unable to operate without direction from the national leadership.

Gauging the effects of institutional change in this second phase therefore faces two major difficulties. First, the lack of continuity in the party organizations makes it impossible to trace changes in party structures over time: the DC and PSI ceased to exist, and new parties took their place (albeit integrating some of the same elites), while the PCI transformed into the PDS (later DS, Left Democrats) which was a very different organization, not least because of a schism which resulted in the formation of a further party, the PRC (Party of Communist Refoundation).[2] Second, there are many competing potential causal variables of the changes in party organizations after 1992, above and beyond decentralization. Public financing of parties was abolished by referendum (although later re-established), the PR electoral law was replaced by a largely majoritarian system, and the judicial activism of the 1990s along with a much tighter fiscal environment completely transformed the redistributive strategies of Italian political elites. Having established these caveats, we can cite several institutional changes in this period which had decentralizing effects on the parties.

First, the electoral reform of 1993, and the concomitant reforms of elections at the regional and local levels, had consequences for parties' territorial organization. On the one hand, the switch from PR to a largely single-member district system for the elections to the national parliament had, if anything, centralizing effects on party organizations. Given the fragmentation of the

Italian party system, which persisted despite the changes in the parties them-selves, single-member districts created powerful incentives for parties to form pre-electoral alliances in which they would agree to support each others' can-didates in single-member contests. This enhanced the role of parties' national leaderships in candidate selection, since reciprocal arrangements of *désistement* require coordination at a higher level than the electoral district (Pappalardo, 2001). On the other hand, the reform of local and regional electoral laws in a majoritarian direction had the opposite effect. The new law for elections to regional assemblies in the 14 'ordinary' regions retained the pre-existing PR list arrangement for 80 per cent of the seats, but offered a 'majority premium' to the winning coalition, as well as directly electing the regional president (see Vassallo, 2005). This 'presidentialization' of the regional executive clearly reinforced the position of regional leaders (especially winning candidates) with regard to the national party elites. A similar reform to the electoral systems for municipal elections in large cities strengthened the position of directly elected mayors – who have proved to enjoy high re-election rates (Legnante, 2005: 71) – in much the same way.

The powers of regional governments also changed in the 'Second Republic'. First, on the basis of existing constitutional provisions, regions gained greater powers in their main areas of responsibility, in particular the health service. A key feature of this extension of regional powers was the so-called Bassanini laws of 1997–8, which among other things decentralized many functions of the public administration from the central government to regions and local authorities in the areas of health, education, planning and environmental policy. As a result of these and other measures, the subnational share of gov-ernment spending doubled from 15 per cent to 30 per cent from the mid-1990s to the mid-2000s. Another important reform in the same period was the establishment of a regional business tax, the IRAP, which provided regions with an unprecedented (although still limited in comparative terms) degree of fiscal autonomy, trebling regions' share of total tax receipts from just under 5 per cent in 1996 to over 15 per cent less than a decade later (Gold, 2003: 117–19). Although the central state retained significant control over fiscal resources, which acted as a significant constraint on the regional level, these reforms undoubtedly enhanced the importance of regional institutions in the Italian political system. As well as extending the expenditure controlled by the regions, the reforms gave much greater discretion over spending deci-sions in areas such as health and transport than had previously been the case (although this was accompanied by the imposition of much greater audit control than had been the case before the reforms) (Badriotti, 2007).

A second important development is the constitutional reform of 2001, which rewrote Title V of the Second Part of the Italian Constitution (the part dealing with the territorial organization of the state) in a clearly decentral-izing direction. The most significant feature of this reform is that it reversed the centralizing bias of the 1948 text by specifying the central state's reserved powers and those areas where competence would be concurrent between state and regions, and leaving exclusive legislative competence for all other areas in the hands of the regions. Although in the absence of major fiscal reform this change has not yet revolutionized the role of regional governments, by constitutionalizing regional autonomy in important policy areas it enhances the status of the regional institutions (Vandelli, 2002; Cammelli, 2003).

Tracing direct causal effects of these various developments on party organizations is beyond the scope of this chapter, but some consequences of the recent movement towards greater decentralization can certainly be detected. The most visible change is the greatly enhanced status of subnational political leaderships. The direct election of presidents of regions has given them a personalized legitimacy, which is reflected in generalized use of the term *governatori* ('governors') in the press and in political debate (derived from the term used for the heads of state executives in the United States). The regional presidents' position is also aided by the majority premia winning lists in the regional elections receive, which give them greater chances of maintaining stable governing coalitions than was the case in the past (Baldini and Vassallo, 2001). Regional leaders have therefore become powerful personalities on the national stage, capable of challenging the national leaderships of their parties.

This is particularly striking in the case of the centre-right parties. *Forza Italia*, the electoral vehicle of Silvio Berlusconi, is a highly personalized party in which the formal organizational rules provide no scope for internal dissidence or territorial differentiation (Hopkin, 2005), yet Roberto Formigoni, the President of the prosperous and populous Lombardy region, is a clear if perhaps unique exception to this monolithic picture. Although elected on the *Forza Italia* ticket, Formigoni has followed an independent political line, forming social and political alliances with a much broader range of interests than those contemplated by the national-level electoral alliance led by *Forza Italia*, the 'House of Liberties' (*Casa delle Libertà*) coalition. Similar dynamics can be seen in the other major centre-right party present throughout the national territory, namely, National Alliance (*Alleanza Nazionale* – AN), which, despite its highly centralized tradition (as the heir to Mussolini's Fascist Party) and strong national leader (Gianfranco Fini), was unable to prevent the regional president of Lazio, Storace, following an independent political strategy which set him in open opposition to the national party leadership. Although these examples are also consistent with the relatively low cohesion of Italian parties generally in the most recent period, it is safe to suggest that the 'Governors' were strengthened vis-à-vis the national parties by the growing status of their office. Indeed, on the territorial issue itself the regional leaders have been more than willing to express opposition to national party policies. Most notably, the regional presidents of the centre-right coalition – Formigoni the most vocal among them – joined the rest of the presidents in openly criticizing the devolution project proposed by the Berlusconi government in 2001, because of its lack of any serious reform of regional finance.

The increasing status and autonomy of regional presidents has opened up space for political figures outside the normal patterns of party recruitment. This is particularly visible in the centre-left, with two regional 'governors' emerging from outside the party structures as representatives of civil society sympathetic to the centre-left parties, after the institution of the direct election of the regional presidency. In the North-Eastern region Friuli-Venezia-Giulia, coffee entrepreneur Riccardo Illy first won the mayoral office of Trieste and then used this as a platform to win the candidature of the centre-left for the Friuli regional presidency in 2003. In Sardinia, internet entrepreneur Renato Soru has a similar trajectory. Although close to the Left Democrats (DS), Soru instead formed his own political movement, *Progetto Sardegna* (Project Sardinia), and on this basis won the support of the centre-left parties for his successful candidature for the regional presidency in 2004. The implications for the centre-left parties' national leaderships of their parties supporting effectively non-partisan figures to govern two major regions should be clear; this suggests a 'hollowing out', rather than a strengthening, of the parties' territorial organizations.

Similar dynamics can be observed at the local level, where large cities have also adopted a more personalized electoral system with victorious mayoral candidates receiving direct support and reinforced majorities. In the midst of the crisis and transformation of the Italian party system in the early 1990s, the emergence of strong and directly elected mayors in major cities such as Rome, Milan and others for a time appeared as a substitute for the fading national-level parties; the term 'party of the mayors' (*partito dei sindaci*) was coined to reflect their new-found political weight. Although the re-emergence of a national party system has recalibrated the balance of power, the mayoral office of major cities is a crucial political resource, to such an extent that ambitious politicians have begun to seek mayoral office as a prelude to national political careers; the examples of Francesco Rutelli, mayor of Rome and subsequently leader of the centre-left Margherita party, and his successor as mayor Walter Veltroni, now leader of the newly formed centre-left *Partito democratico* (Democratic Party) are eloquent in this regard. Although levels of autonomy are not always clearly visible, the independent power resources of local political leaders do become clearer in situations of conflict. A stark recent example of this is the election of Massimo Cacciari as mayor of Venice in 2005: previously mayor with the support of the centre-left in 1993–2000 (and recognized as a key figure among the 'party of the mayors'), he decided to stand again, against another progressive candidate already selected by the centre-left coalition, the well-known prosecuting magistrate Felice Casson. Despite most of the national parties of the centre-left throwing their support behind Casson, Cacciari won in the second round of voting, in a scenario reminiscent of Ken Livingstone's election as mayor of London as an independent in 2000.

This changing balance of power inside the Italian parties and electoral coalitions, with a much greater relevance for subnational elites, should not be exaggerated. Electoral politics in Italy is still strongly influenced, if not exclusively dominated, by national-level elites and the central leaderships of the major parties. Most strikingly, the largest Italian party, *Forza Italia*, remains a highly centralized organization, notwithstanding the presence of an exceptionally powerful regional leader such as Formigoni. The territorial structures of the party are fragile in the extreme, as is demonstrated by the party's weak showing in regional and local elections (Diamanti, 2003), and its political strategies are decided not only at the national level but by a very restricted circle around the all-powerful leader Berlusconi (Hopkin, 2005). Similarly, the merger in autumn 2007 of the two main parties of the centre-left, the former Communists in the DS and the progressive Christian Democrats in the Margherita party, appeared as a manoeuvre agreed among national-level elites without the clear participation of the parties' regional leaderships. The territorial balance of power within the new formation remains unclear, but its creation itself suggests a prevailing control of national political dynamics by the national party leaderships.

Concluding comments

The Italian case offers some evidence in favour of the proposition that decentralization can enhance the power of subnational elites within the organizations of nationwide political parties. The changes to the electoral system at regional and municipal levels after 1993, and the ongoing process of delegation of increasingly important policy competences to the regional level, in particular since the 1980s, appear to have strengthened the position of subnational party elites, particularly those that win election to leadership positions in the subnational institutions. However, the effects of decentralization, it can be argued, have been less acute than might be expected, and changes in the territorial balance of power have not always resulted from the kinds of development identified in the literature. For example, the process of regionalization in Italy between 1970 and the early 1990s does not appear to have had a dramatic impact on the parties' internal structures, and even the growing role of subnational elites after the early 1990s had as much to do with changes in the national party system and in the electoral systems used as with decentralization of policy responsibilities. The safest conclusion is that political decentralization will tend to induce some decentralization within political parties, but this effect is contingent on a number of further variables relating to parties' internal organizational inertias and the broader dynamics of party competition in the political system as a whole.

This conclusion may be disappointingly ambivalent in terms of the paucity of its predictive power, but it does have rather clear theoretical implications. The Italian case does suggest that the incentives for political aggregation deriving from the territorial structure of the state – the key explanatory variable in the rational choice institutionalist approach to our research question in this volume – are seriously incomplete as a basis for predicting the effects of decentralization on political parties. Put simply, these incentives may encounter countervailing incentives from other features of the opportunity structure, institutional or otherwise; and whether or not parties respond strategically to these incentives depends on their own internal dynamics as complex, plural organizations. In short, we cannot understand how parties respond to decentralization unless we have a profound and nuanced understanding of the parties themselves as key political institutions in their own right.

5
Decentralization and Party Organizational Change: The British and Spanish Statewide Parties Compared

Elodie Fabre and Mónica Méndez-Lago

Introduction

As explained in the Introduction, the existence of several levels of party competition represents a particular challenge for statewide parties. On the one hand, they must present policy platforms for statewide elections aimed at attracting support from across the state and defending some version of the 'national or statewide interest'; on the other hand, regional elections create more space for regional issues. These parties are confronted with the strategic dilemma of having to compete to appeal to the whole electorate in statewide elections and to regional sections of this electorate in regional elections. In multinational countries such as Spain and the UK, statewide parties are, moreover, competing against minority nationalist or ethnoregionalist parties which politicize territorial issues and tend to emphasize the conflicting aspect of their region's relations with the centre. Territorial differences increase the odds of policy divergence between the central and regional levels.

This chapter investigates the effects of the development of a regional level of party competition on the organization of statewide political parties in two prominent European states, namely, Spain and the UK, which have recently decentralized competences and functions to regional governments. Spain has become one of the most decentralized countries in Europe, with an open-ended process of decentralization that started after the transition to democracy in the late 1970s and early 1980s, and has awarded its regions considerable levels of self-government (Aja, 2003). The more recent devolution of power in the UK has also provided Scotland and Wales with important, albeit uneven, levels of autonomy in the management of their own affairs. In both countries, this process of decentralization took place under pressure from ethnoregionalist or minority nationalist parties, which often advocate further institutional changes in favour of regional governments. These parties put pressure on the organization and strategy of statewide parties, as they fuel regional grievances against central government and political actors identified with it.

In Spain, the Socialist PSOE (*Partido Socialista Obrero Español*) and the Conservative PP (*Partido Popular*) both have government experience at the central and regional levels, while the smaller *Izquierda Unida* (IU) has been a minor coalition partner in a number of regions. In the UK, the Labour party is in power at the central level and was the leading coalition party in Scotland and in Wales until the regional elections of May 2007. Since the devolution of 1999, the Conservative Party has remained the second largest party in general elections. Between 1999 and 2007, the Liberal Democrats were in coalition with Labour in Scotland, as they had been for a briefer period in Wales (2000–03). Following the regional elections of 2007, Labour formed a minority government in Wales and the Scottish National Party pushed Labour out of power in Scotland, where it leads a minority government supported by the Greens on some issues.

In order to evaluate the degree of centralization of statewide parties, this chapter uses a number of indicators falling into two categories that refer to the distribution of powers in a federal system defined as a combination of 'self-rule and shared rule' (Elazar, 1987). The autonomy of regional party branches in the management of regional party affairs ('self-rule') is evaluated via the selection method for regional party leaders and candidates to regional elections and the determination of party policy for regional elections. A statewide party can have a 'regionalized' organization which gives regional party branches some level of autonomy to manage regional affairs while letting the central party have some authority to intervene at the regional level or veto other decisions. The most decentralized type of party organization would be one in which each level is responsible for its organization and the management of elections at its level, independently from the other strata of party organization.

'Shared rule' refers to the level of involvement of the regional units in central decision-making, which can provide regional party branches with opportunities to see their problems and interests taken into account at the central level. It is measured through the participation of regional branches in statewide party organs and processes: participation in the selection of the party leader; inclusion of regional representatives in statewide party organs, and in particular in the party executive; and candidate selection and formulation of the party's policy for general elections.

The analysis of multilevel party organization springs from a variety of sources. Party statutes are an important source as they tell 'the official story' of a party's organization and the way it wants to be perceived (Katz and Mair, 1992: 7), but they are only a framework within which party actors can manoeuvre and are not always fully complied with (Sartori, 2005: 84). As a result, we went beyond the analysis of party statutes and used resources in the literature on these parties and data from interviews conducted in both countries.

The first part of the chapter will briefly present the context in which statewide parties compete, the challenges they face in a multilevel setting and the types of factors that are expected to affect party organization, such as the territorial structure of the state and the distribution of competences between the levels of government, the distinctiveness of regional party competition, and levels of regionalism and identification with the regional identity. The description of the organization of six statewide parties with reference to these factors is developed in the second part, which focuses mainly on formal processes. Finally, the most striking organizational traits of the parties as well as the most relevant factors will be highlighted in the final part.

Multilevel party organization in the UK

All three main statewide parties have adapted their structures to that of the newly devolved state in the sense that they have territorial subunits in Scotland and Wales. With the exception of the Conservative Party in Wales, each of the British statewide parties actually already had regional structures for Scotland and Wales. The Liberal Democrats inherited the federal structure of the old Liberal Party (Curtice, 1988: 104) and gave its regional branches (called 'State parties') a considerable amount of autonomy that truly became reality with devolution. The Liberal Democrats advocate a federal Britain and have applied these principles to their organization.

Until 1999, the regional levels of the Labour Party were merely appendages of the National Executive Committee (NEC). Devolution has not led to a particular reorganization of the party and has produced only minor constitutional changes relating to the selection of candidates for regional elections (see Bradbury in this volume). The Scottish and Welsh Labour parties have nevertheless become more important in terms of prerogatives and staffing, but their links with the central party remain important, in particular through the role of the regional offices, which remain staffed by central party employees.

Finally, the Conservative Party has also adapted its organization to the newly devolved institutional setting. Some asymmetry remains between the Scottish and Welsh parties, mainly due to the very different histories of the party in the two regions. Until 1965, the Scottish Conservatives were an independent party, and they maintained a separate organization on the ground and the ability to select candidates for Westminster elections. The 1997 reform of the organization of the Conservative Party integrated the Scottish National Union with the rest of the party and created the Welsh Conservative Party. Because of the more recent development of the Welsh party and its more limited resources, the Welsh Conservatives are weaker than their Scottish counterparts.

Involvement of the regional party branches in statewide party organs
Selecting the party leader

The British parties have chosen different forms of one-member-one-vote (OMOV), which means that the regional branches and leaderships do not have any special role. The Liberal Democrats are the only party to elect their leader exclusively by membership ballot. The Conservative Party also ballots its membership, but only after the parliamentary party has drawn up a shortlist of two candidates. In 2003, Members of Parliament (MPs) hijacked the process and chose to back a single candidate. The Labour Party ballots its members, but their vote represents only one third of the electoral college. The other two thirds are respectively for affiliated organizations, such as trade unions and socialist societies, and for the parliamentary party. Overall, the most influential actors are the MPs who back leadership candidates, even though the members can sometimes upset the expectations of the MPs, as in the Conservative Party in 2001.

Participating in the running of the statewide party

The British Labour Party is the only party that does not provide for any representation of its Scottish and Welsh parties on its National Executive Committee (NEC). The Conservative Party Board includes the chairman or his or her deputy of its Scottish and Welsh branches among its 15 to 17 members. Likewise, the Federal Executive Committee of the Liberal Democrats provides for the presence on one representative from each of the Scottish, Welsh and even English parties. In addition, Scottish and Welsh members of the devolved elected assemblies can attend the national conference of their respective parties. However, their role and their voice are relatively limited, as they are clearly outnumbered by MPs and other representatives of other party sectors. Party conferences have moreover seen their importance decrease, in particular in the Conservative and Labour parties, as parties became more leadership-driven and conferences became more media-friendly events (Stanyer, 2001; Kelly, 2001). Overall, these statewide organs are relatively uninterested in Scottish and Welsh affairs and are rather more concerned with English matters (interviews with party officials; Laffin and Shaw, 2007).

It could be argued that Scotland and Wales also have representatives in the persons of the senior party leaders: former Labour leader Tony Blair was born in Scotland, the Labour leader Gordon Brown is also a Scotsman, former Conservative leader Michael Howard is a Welshman, and former Liberal Democrat leaders Charles Kennedy and Menzies Campbell are Scotsmen. However, involved in British politics as they are, they do not necessarily want to advance the interests of a particular region against the rest of the country. In addition, statewide party leaders do not always seem to be aware of the intricacies of devolution.

Participating in statewide electoral processes

In Britain, statewide party programmes are often elaborated in several steps, involving varying degrees of intra-party consultation and party conferences; and the actual drafting of the manifestos is done by a small group at the level of the party executive. The role of the regional party branches and regional leaders is generally limited by the formal processes of the parties' conferences (in which English representatives form a large majority), the influence of the statewide party and parliamentary leaderships, and the composition of executive party organs.

Devolution has nevertheless brought about some changes through the increased importance of regional manifestos for general elections. While most parties had Scottish and Welsh general election manifestos before devolution, the practice is now generalized across the board. In order to take the changes in policy competence and divergence between Scotland, Wales and England into account, the regional parties are involved in the process of drafting these manifestos. The Labour Party consults its Scottish and Welsh branches on the content of the regional manifestos, basing policy on devolved matters on the programmes elaborated in the regions, but the NEC remains in charge of drafting them. The Scottish and Welsh Liberal Democrats develop their own general elections manifestos in consultation with the statewide party. They develop policy on devolved matters, explain the financial consequences for the region of the budget prepared by the federal party and present the use they would make of these resources in the region. Finally, the situation is more complex for the Conservative Party, as it reflects the asymmetrical nature of devolution. The Scottish party is responsible for everything that relates to the devolved areas in the general election manifesto, while the British party is in charge of the general policies over matters in which Wales obtained executive devolution, and the Welsh party can adapt the details of these policies to the regional context.

With respect to candidate selection for general elections, the statewide parties follow different practices. The Labour Party's selection process is a statewide process overseen by the NEC. The NEC establishes a statewide shortlist of candidates from which the constituency Labour parties can choose, but the grip of the NEC on this process is very strong (Seyd and Whiteley, 2001: 82). In Scotland and Wales, the regional executives implement the process on behalf of the NEC following the rules it has established. The NEC also retains a final say over the selection, but there is little evidence of central party intervention (Laffin and Shaw, 2007). With the Liberal Democrats, by contrast, the selection process is the responsibility of the regional parties ('State parties'). The Scottish and Welsh parties establish their own procedures (although they are more or less identical to those implemented in England) and candidates panels, from which the local parties choose their candidate. Finally, the Conservative Party has an asymmetrical process. While candidate selection in Wales is supervised by the statewide selection committee, a Scottish Candidates' Board appointed by the Scottish party assumes the functions of the national committee in the region. Again, constituency associations elect their candidates from a shortlist drawn up by these selection committees.

Self-rule at the regional level
Leadership selection

The Scottish and Welsh Conservative and Liberal Democrat leaders are elected by ballot of their regional party members. Both parties left their regional branches free to select their own leaders. In the Labour Party, the leaders of the regional parliamentary parties have become de facto leaders of the regional parties, especially once they became first ministers in their respective regions. None of the current Labour regional leaders has been elected by the usual Labour electoral college. The leader of the Labour group in the National Assembly for Wales, Rhodri Morgan, was selected by his parliamentary colleagues after they forced his predecessor's resignation. This challenge to the sitting First Minister Alun Michael was a real show of independence and defiance of the Welsh party vis-à-vis the central leadership, which was held responsible for the election of Michael as a leader in 1999 (Rawnsley, 2000: 247–50, 359–60). No such controversy occurred in Scotland. Twice having to choose a new leader while in power and in less than 28 days (the maximum time allowed for the Scottish Parliament to elect the Scottish first minister), the Scottish Labour Party also had to depart from the rule. In 2001, Jack McConnell was elected leader, unopposed, by the party's Members of the Scottish Parliament and the Scottish Executive Committee. Unlike in Wales (and London), Scottish leaders have been selected without much direct intervention from the central party leadership, even though Prime Minister Gordon Brown is said to keep a close eye on what happens in Scotland (Lynch and Birrell, 2004: 186; Laffin and Shaw, 2007).

Participation in regional party competition

Because of the electoral system, two types of candidates have to be selected for Scottish and Welsh elections: constituency and list candidates (see Bradbury in this volume). The Labour Party requires that the NEC approves the lists established by the regional parties, but the central party has no authority over the selection of constituency candidates. In 1999, the selection process in Scotland became the subject of controversies regarding attempts by the central party to control the procedure in order to make sure that the selected candidates would be sufficiently 'New Labour'. This strategy nevertheless succeeded only to a limited extent, as a number of left-wingers eventually made it to the list (Shaw, 2001; Laffin and Shaw, 2007). By contrast, the Scottish and Welsh Liberal Democrats select their own candidates: the regional parties establish a list of approved candidates, from which the constituency associations can choose, and the lists are established by membership ballot in the top-up areas. The Welsh and Scottish Conservative parties select their candidates in the same way, with selection panels established at the regional level and regional lists drawn up by membership ballot.

The British parties leave their regional branches rather free to develop their own programmes. The rules for drafting of the regional manifestos are generally the same as those existing at the statewide level. The Scottish and Welsh Labour parties develop their own programmes and adopt their own policies for devolved issues, and the actual manifesto is drafted by a small group of party officials and elected office-holders (Lynch and Birrell, 2004: 183). When Labour is in power at Westminster, the Secretaries of State for Scotland and Wales are included in regional party executives and the joint policy committee that elaborates the programme, and they act liaison officers, representing the central party in the regions. A larger degree of divergence was noticeable in the 2003 elections (Hopkin and Bradbury, 2006). The Scottish and Welsh Liberal Democrats are highly independent and preciously guard their freedom to make their own political choices. The situation within the Conservative Party is again asymmetrical: the Scottish party is more autonomous than the Welsh party, mainly because it is older and has more resources and fewer links with the central party. The most prominent policies of the UK party have nevertheless been adopted by both Scottish and Welsh parties (Lynch, 2004: 389). In Scotland, however, former leader David McLetchie allowed the party 'to find a moderate, centre-right, almost Christian democrat voice' (Hassan and Warhurst, 2001: 222).

Comparison

Overall, we see that each of the statewide parties has adapted its structure to the decentralization of the state, albeit to varying degrees. We find that the input of the regional party branches into statewide processes is rather limited in all three main British parties. Policy making for statewide parliamentary elections is a prerogative of the central party, and the regional branches have a limited input in the process. What is more, the representation of these regional branches in the main decision-making organs of the party is generally restricted to a handful of members, compared with a larger presence of party members and public office-holders. The Liberal Democrats are clearly the party that provides for the most systematic representation of the regional branches in the central party. This limited integration of regional units at the centre is not entirely unexpected, as Scotland and Wales represent a much smaller number of constituencies than England. All the parties have given their regional branches important powers in their respective arenas. We also see a certain level of variation in the autonomy of the regional branches.

The Liberal Democrats accord a high degree of autonomy to their regional branches, irrespective of the nature and scope of decentralization. The Conservatives and Labour also give a high degree of autonomy to their Scottish and Welsh branches, which can select their candidates and formulate their own programme for regional elections. However, the Welsh branch of the Conservative Party is traditionally closer to and also more dependent on the central party. In spite of this official autonomy, attempts by the central parties to influence their regional branches are not uncommon, in particular in the case of Labour. However, since the central party successfully removed Alun Michael from the leadership of the party and the position of First Minister, the Welsh Labour party has shown greater independence (Hopkin, 2003: 233). Likewise, the Scottish Labour Party diverged more from the central party line in 2003, with McConnell emphasizing 'Scottishness' and adopting controversial positions on tuition fees, foundation hospitals and free care for the elderly, even though some of these policies were concessions made to the Liberal Democrats as part of their coalition agreement (Hopkin and Bradbury, 2006: 144; Laffin and Shaw, 2007).

The Labour Party is the party that has found it the most difficult to adapt to the new devolved reality of Britain. Because the party is in power in central government, it finds it difficult to accept that its positions are opposed by Labour regional governments. Moreover, the party's past experience of internal ideological strife and the reforms it went through in the 1990s strengthened the centralization of power within the party (Shaw, 1996: 191), and the leadership is unlikely to relinquish this power easily. Finally, the party's social-democratic creed means that it has a tradition of centrally imposed policies that could limit its willingness to decentralize power (Deschouwer, 2003: 220).

Ideology could also explain the Liberal Democrats' adoption of a federal type of organization, as liberal parties are traditionally supporters of power dispersal and decentralization. The fact that the Conservative Party has consistently been in opposition since the start of devolution and so far has had little hope of winning in regional elections may explain why it has been more inclined to leave its regional branches with some room for manoeuvre, although they have used it to a rather limited extent. Overall, the regional branches of the three British statewide parties have stuck to the main principles of the parties and accepted most of the key policies of the central parties, confirming the thesis of the 'franchise contract' according to which a common identity, a 'label' based on adherence to a number of principles, beliefs and policies, unites all the levels of party organization (Carty, 2004).

Multilevel party organization in Spain

The three main statewide Spanish parties are organized according to the political-administrative structure of the state,[1] that is, they are present at the local, provincial, regional (in the 17 Autonomous Communities) and statewide levels. Both IU and PSOE see themselves as federal organizations, whereas the PP statutes define its structure as decentralized and regionalized. The statutes of United Left not only define the party as a federal structure but mention federalism as an organizing principle, and the regional branches can decide autonomously on how to organize (respecting the general principles established in the Statutes).[2]

The Catalan Socialist Party (*Partit dels Socialistes Catalans*, PSC) is not formally a regional party branch but an independent party, which since 1978 has been in a stable coalition with the PSOE. In terms of its representation in the central PSOE, the PSC is treated like any other regional party branch, but it has generally enjoyed a greater degree of influence and certainly more autonomy than any other federation.[3] There is a similar case in the PP, which dissolved its party structure in Navarre in the early 1990s after reaching an agreement with the moderate regional party *Unión del Pueblo Navarro* (UPN), making the UPN the representative of the PP in this region.

Party sections at the subnational levels tend to mirror the organizational structure of the national level in the three parties. Whereas the three parties formally have decentralized structures, there are in fact big differences in the way they work and the extent to which they develop the two principles of 'federalism': shared rule (that is, participation of subnational levels in decision making at the federal level) and self-rule on the part of the subnational entities.

Involvement of the regional branches in the statewide parties

Selecting the party leader

Regional sections of the three statewide Spanish parties formally participate in the election of the party leaders through their representation in party congresses, although in some cases these just rubber-stamp decisions taken by a previous leader or by informal consultation. In the PSOE, only the (subregional) provincial party sections are directly represented in party congresses, but the provincial sections coming from the same regional party branch tend to act as one on votes which require collective decisions. The introduction of individual secret ballot for the election of the party's executive and the secretary general (respectively in 1994 and 2000) has contributed to limiting the ability of national and regional elites to influence the outcome of congress elections (see Méndez Lago, 2000: 119). This facilitated the election of Rodríguez Zapatero as Secretary General against José Bono, who had the support of a majority of the regional leaders and was a regional leader himself (see López Alba, 2003).

In the PP, subnational branches formally participate in the election of the party leader through their representation in party congresses. So far their role has been to rubber-stamp the decision taken by the leader. In 2003 José María Aznar kept his promise to stand down after two elections and he chose Mariano Rajoy as his successor (Iglesias, 2003). Rajoy became Secretary General of the party and was elected President of the party in 2004. Finally, the Federal Assembly of the United Left elects the party leader (*Coordinador General*) by an indirect voting system: delegates from the regional party branches choose some members of the Federal Political Council, which in turn elects the party leader.[4]

Participating in the running of the statewide party

In the three statewide Spanish parties there is some formal representation of the regional sections in the theoretically most relevant body in between congresses – the PSOE's Federal Committee (*Comité Federal*), the National Steering Committee (*Junta Directiva Nacional*) in the PP, and United Left's Federal Political Council (*Consejo Político Federal*) – but there is no rule prescribing secure representation in the executive board that really runs the party.

Regional federations try to have representatives in these executive boards, but their limited size makes it virtually impossible to have a delegate from each regional federation (given that there are 17 of them). In all three parties, the leader has considerable room for manoeuvre in deciding who sits in this body, although some relevant differences exist. The Federal Executive Committee (the statewide party executive) of the PSOE is elected by the party congress, but there is usually only one list of candidates resulting from intense negotiations in which territorial, gender and ideological criteria play an important role. In the PP, the president has the prerogative to decide which members of the Executive Committee occupy top offices such as the secretary general and executive secretaries (Astudillo and García-Guereta, 2006: 408). The president also decides which party leaders can attend the weekly informal meetings (*Reuniones de maitines*) where the most important issues regarding party strategy are discussed. In United Left, the General Coordinators of the regional federations are present in the Federal Executive Presidency, but not necessarily in its Permanent Commission (a smaller part of the presidency elected by the federal General Coordinator).

Thus, there are usually some regional party leaders or representatives in the statewide party executives, but not as a result of formal rules. The number of regional representatives depends on several factors. The strength of a regional branch or its leader is a crucial factor, as national leaders are sometimes 'forced' to include leaders from strong regional branches, but there are also examples of leaders of less powerful branches who were included in the national executive in order to balance the territorial interests represented in the executive.[5]

The most relevant organizational development regarding the adaptation to the State of the Autonomies has occurred in the PSOE, with the creation of the Territorial Council (*Consejo Territorial*), a new party body that brings together all the regional leaders (irrespective of whether the party is in regional opposition or government).[6] Its creation was a reflection of the increasing powers of regional leaders, especially those in office in their respective regions, who had gained internal leverage and the capacity to influence statewide policies, strategies and decisions. So far it has had only consultative capacities, and the leaders of strong regional federations therefore still try to influence party policies through the Federal Executive Commission, which is still the most important party body, or through informal channels. Its activities and meetings have also been limited so far, although it has become more influential and more visible to the general public as the forum that sets the 'official' position of the party in relation to the 'State of Autonomies'. This was easier to achieve when the PP was in office, since this organ helped in coordinating the opposition strategies of the PSOE. Since the party has returned to (statewide) government in 2004, the visibility of the Council (along with that of the party in central office, as opposed to the party in public office) has diminished and its meetings have become more irregular. The PP created a similar body in its 2004 Congress, the *Consejo Autonómico* (Autonomous Council) (art. 38). It includes the presidents of the Autonomous Communities where the PP holds office, but as of 2008 it has met only once.

Participation in the statewide electoral process

Party congresses, in which regional party branches are represented, play a very limited role in drafting election manifestos. In all three parties the most important party organ in between congresses (PSOE's Federal Committee, PP's National Steering Committee and IU's Federal Political Council) is in charge of giving the final approval to the election manifesto, so regional sections participate indirectly through their representation in these bodies. Although central authorities are formally in charge of making and approving election manifestos, the statutes of United Left state that they must collaborate with the regional branches. But how this collaboration should develop in practice is not specified (Ramiro and Pérez-Nievas, 2005).

All the parties, especially the PSOE, have experienced increasing difficulties accommodating the demands of their regional branches when drafting policy proposals. Negotiations take place both within party structures and, when a party is in office at any of the two levels involved, in intergovernmental fora. A clear example is water policy, on which there are conflicting views in the different regions (Orte, 2006). These tensions are evident when general elections take place, but they are stronger in regional elections, especially in the regions that hold elections at the same time, since it is easier to notice when regional branches of the same party support divergent policies. In the PSOE, regional branches have used their presence in the Federal Committee and in the Territorial Council, as well as different fora of intergovernmental relations, to try to influence the national policy advocated by the party. In contrast, PP central leaders have retained more power to control the definition of national policy and to ensure that the policies defended in each region do not contradict the general party line.

Candidate selection for general elections is formally a bottom-up process in the three statewide organizations, but the final say over candidatures remains in the hands of central party authorities. Each provincial party branch proposes a list of candidates that is then submitted for approval to a central party body (*Comité Federal* in the case of the PSOE, *Comité Electoral* in the case of the PP, *Consejo Político Federal* in United Left).[7] It is rather uncommon for these committees to change the list proposed by provincial branches, but this should not be interpreted as a sign of autonomy at the subnational level. The influence of the central party authorities is usually channelled through informal pressures exercised before these lists are finalized. As we shall see shortly, the clearest example of this can be found in the Popular Party.

In the PSOE, federal authorities (*Comisión Federal de Listas*) have the power to add names to the lists drawn up by the provincial branches. The *Comisión* must justify any inclusion, and the regional secretary general, a representative from the Provincial Executive Commission and a member of the PSOE's parliamentary group must take part in the debate that leads to it. The Federal Committee has the final say over the composition of lists.

In the PP, the Provincial Election Committee proposes a list of candidates that has to be approved by the National Election Committee. There are not many examples of open conflict over lists because any central intervention usually takes place through informal channels (Astudillo and García-Guereta, 2005: 21). In addition, there is a high degree of ideological congruence between the party elites at different territorial levels, facilitated by the sequencing of party congresses (national–regional–provincial).

Although the formal procedure is similar in IU, in this party there are more examples of open conflict over lists of candidates. This should be interpreted as an indicator of the greater autonomy of regional branches. When this autonomy leads to conflict, it is usually expressed and solved through the procedures established in the party statutes rather than anticipated (and avoided) through informal negotiations, as is often the case with the two major parties.

Self-rule at the regional level

Leadership selection

Formally, both the leader and the different governing bodies at each territorial level of the three Spanish statewide parties are elected in the congresses that take place at each of these levels, although the way they are elected differs among the three parties. In no case is there a membership ballot.[8] As mentioned in other parts of the chapter, the influence of higher party levels is exerted through informal arrangements, and it is common to read about the candidate 'preferred' by Génova or Ferraz (headquarters of, respectively, the PP and the PSOE) in the press. Although control from the 'centre' was substantial in the PSOE during the 1980s and early 1990s, the degree of interference has tended to diminish over time.

The timing of regional congresses, which take place a few months after the national congress, helps to account for the low level of centre–periphery conflict within the parties. This timing facilitates the reproduction of the balance of power achieved at the central level in lower party strata. This is particularly true of the Popular Party, which has placed a great emphasis on internal cohesion and discipline as part of its strategy since the 1990s (Astudillo and García-Guereta, 2006: 408).

IU regional federations display the highest degree of autonomy: each federation has the power to decide how it organizes and how it chooses its leader, provided that it respects the general principles of IU. In fact, many of these branches do not take advantage of this power and thus organizational homogeneity is greater than one could expect given this potential scope for divergence. As for the timing of party congresses, the statutes stipulate only that regional congresses (*Asambleas*) cannot take place at the same time as the federal congress.

Participation in regional party competition

Regional party organizations draw up their own lists of candidates and programmes, and decide upon pre- and post-election coalitions, although central authorities (where regional branches are represented) retain the power to ratify such decisions. For example, the statutes of PP state that it is a serious offence to make pacts or alliances with other political forces without the explicit approval of the hierarchically superior bodies (PP Party statutes 2004, art. 12.h). In IU there is a vague reference to the power of its Federal Political Council to ensure that the federations do not adopt internal rules or support policies that violate the principles set out by its federal organs (art. 38 h, Statutes 2004).

Incentives for coordination are greater in the case of the 13 Autonomous Communities, which hold their elections at the same time, and weaker for the four remaining communities that hold their elections on different dates (Andalusia, Galicia, Basque Country and Catalonia). In addition, the particularities of these regions (especially the Basque Country and Catalonia) in terms of their history, culture and distinctive logic of party competition due to the presence of nationalist parties give the regional branches further incentives to develop their own policies. In the three parties there is a 'framework programme' for the local and regional elections that take place at the same time, but each regional branch nevertheless develops its own programme, which has to receive the final approval of the central party authorities.

The PP is again the party with the highest degree of cohesion and central intervention (mostly through informal arrangements, while regional autonomy is formally maintained). The PP leaves the regions with little room to express their differences. Only in Catalonia, the Basque Country and Galicia have the regional branches been allowed more autonomy (Balfour, 2005: 163), but only when it was in the interest of the central party authorities and their strategy. There are also clear examples of intervention by central party authorities, even in these regional branches.[9]

In the PSOE the degree of actual autonomy varies across the regions. For instance, the Catalan PSC is formally an independent party, and this is clear in the extent to which it can make its own decisions about policies, alliances and so on.[10] In contrast, it is harder for a weak regional branch to enforce its decisions in case of discrepancy. The main resources of intra-party power for regional branches are membership (which is the criterion used to establish the number of representatives in party congresses) and incumbency at the regional level, especially when they are able to obtain more votes in regional elections than in general ones.

In the case of United Left, Ramiro and Pérez-Nievas (2005: 23) point out an interesting development towards greater 'centralization': in 1994 its statutes mentioned for the first time the requirement that candidate lists for regional elections should be ratified by the central party authorities.

Comparison

The three Spanish parties have adapted their structures to the decentralized nature of the state, even though they differ in their degree of decentralization. United Left is the most decentralized party, followed by the PSOE and finally by the PP. Regarding 'shared rule', the three parties have provisions for the participation of regional branches in different statewide organs. The ranking of the parties is the same with regard to the 'self-rule' of regional branches: United Left allows for more autonomy, followed by the PSOE and the PP. In all three parties, particularly in PP and to a lesser extent the PSOE, central party organs retain control or at least have veto power over the most important decisions concerning both statewide and regional political matters. Various factors seem to interact and explain these different degrees of decentralization across parties: incumbency at the central and regional levels, strength of central leadership and presence of intra-party struggles, party ideological tradition and party strategy.

Regional leaders have tended to increase their internal power when they have held office, both in the PP and in the PSOE. Incumbency at the national level is also relevant in order to understand the type of challenges the three parties have had to face: whereas the PSOE and PP have been in government at both levels, United Left has been a relatively marginal party in both scenarios. Thus, potential tension over policies has been more acute for the PSOE, since it has been the party that has been in government at both levels for the longest period of time. In contrast, IU has faced less pressure to homogenize its strategies because it has never held office at the centre.

The strength of central party leadership and the presence of internal divisions also help to explain variations in decentralization across parties and over time: in the 1980s the central party authorities of the PSOE managed to suppress any attempts by regional leaders to question the general party policy. At that time, keeping control from the centre was relatively easy because the process of devolution was just starting, and regional governments were therefore not fully developed. In the 1990s, regional leaders who had held office for some years were able to exert increasing influence within the party.

This development was facilitated by the internal divisions and struggles of the party in the early 1990s and also by the weakness of the central leadership at the end of that decade. Regional leaders' influence has, however, diminished since Rodríguez Zapatero's accession to the leadership, especially as his leadership has become consolidated (Méndez Lago, 2005). Central party authorities still attempt to intervene in regional affairs and manage to exert a great deal of influence in some circumstances, particularly when the decision of a regional party branch goes against the strategy of the central party. These attempts are not always successful, but they tend to work best in the weakest regional branches, that is, those that are not in office, do not get many votes and do not have a large membership base.[11]

Party legacies, traditions and discourses are also important. While United Left has adhered to a federal ethos since its foundation in 1986, and the PSOE reconstructed its organization in 1975 as a formally federal party (even though with little content at that time), the PP has a very different tradition. It has had difficulties both in accepting the creation and development of the *Estado de las Autonomías* and in decentralizing internally. Even though it now describes itself as a regionalized and decentralized party, it stresses very strongly the need for central control and unity of message and strategy. There is an obvious parallel here in the three parties between the principle of party organization and the type of territorial policy defended for Spain.

Finally, party strategy has also played a role. The PP has presented itself as the only true national party in opposition to the Socialist Party's internal diversity and, in their view, lack of ideological coherence across territories. As a result, it tries to stop any demand from regional leaders that might threaten this strategy. The PSOE has responded by making the most of the slogan 'La España plural', which refers to both unity (through the term 'Spain') and diversity ('plural').

Conclusion: Multilevel party organization in Spain and the UK

This chapter has shown that all the parties have adapted their organizations to the decentralized context of government and party competition. None of them has maintained a totally centralized form of organization, and they have all given some powers to their regional branches. Whereas the degree of political decentralization of the state is greater in Spain than in the UK, the Spanish parties are not more decentralized than the British parties. Regarding 'shared rule', the Spanish parties have managed to incorporate regional branches and leaders in central decision-making to a greater extent than their British counterparts.

A noticeable difference between the two countries is the pace of adaptation of the parties to the new scenario of decentralization, which highlights the importance of patterns of party formation and institutional inertia (Panebianco, 1988; Hopkin, 1999). When the process of decentralization started, the Spanish parties had just been founded or refounded after 40 years of dictatorship and were concerned with establishing strong organizations and strengthening their role in the political system. Unity and cohesion became the priorities of all the major political parties, and centralization of power and resources within parties was perceived as the best way to achieve these goals. These organizational traits delayed the pace and extent of decentralization of power within the statewide parties. On the other hand, devolution in the UK occurred in an already long-established democratic system and the parties were already well institutionalized. Moreover, they already had more or less established Scottish and Welsh structures that were 'activated' by the process of devolution and the need to compete in regional elections.

Incumbency at both the national and subnational levels seems to influence the extent to which parties are internally decentralized. Both the PSOE and the Labour Party have been concerned with maintaining party unity and avoiding policy divergence in order to ensure the party's electoral potential at the central level. This has been crucial for New Labour, which has sometimes attempted to fashion a regional political class in its own image in order to minimize policy divergence and cause minimum embarrassment to the central government. The issue of party unity and having a consistent message throughout the country has become crucial for the PSOE, as the PP has started integrating this issue into its strategy, trying to take advantage of the fact that it is a more cohesive party. In contrast, parties without government position and with limited odds of achieving office at the central level have fewer incentives to enforce a strict discipline, as divergence is less likely to be noticed by the electorate. In addition, these parties may benefit from better adapting their strategies to the regional context. This holds in particular for the United Left and the Liberal Democrats. Incumbency at the regional level has contributed to increasing the regional leaders' ability to influence the central party, especially in the two main statewide Spanish parties, where the term 'regional barons' has been coined to refer to regional leaders who usually hold government in their respective arenas. Although the term was first used in the Socialist Party, its use is becoming relatively common in the Popular Party.

Although it has been in power at the central level, the Partido Popular has not been under the same sort of pressure as the PSOE to control its regional branches because its organizational ethos and ideology emphasize cohesion and discipline in a way that has limited the autonomy of the regional branches and the expression of divergence. The same can be said of the Conservative Party. The central party has not exerted the same degree of pressure on its regional branches, yet its regional branches have remained close to the party line. Similarly, liberal ideology facilitated the adaptation of the Liberal Democrats to devolution, as the party values power dispersion and decentralization (Ingle, 1996: 114). Overall, the emphasis on the 'central message' differs between the parties but remains strong, even in the most decentralized parties.

To sum up, both cases show that the decentralization of the state structure has led to the creation and empowerment of regional party structures but that there is no 'perfect correlation' (Riker, 1975: 137) between the type of decentralization and degree of autonomy of regional governments on the one hand, and the type of central–regional relationship within statewide parties and the autonomy of regional party branches on the other. Although it is an important factor, the role of the institutional structure on party organization does not seem to be as strong as the Introduction to the present volume hypothesized. Other aspects that should be considered, but are beyond the scope of this chapter, relate to electoral competition at the regional level: the status of regional elections as second-order or independent elections, the electoral cycle, and the strength of the challenge posed by regionalist and nationalist parties.

6
Devolution and Party Organization in the UK: Statewide Parties and Statewide–Regional Branch Relations over Candidate Selection in Scotland and Wales

Jonathan Bradbury

Introduction

An analysis of the implications of devolution for party organization has to confront the core issue of candidate selection. As Schattschneider famously remarked, 'the nominating process has become the crucial process of the party' (quoted in Gallagher, 1988a: 3). A focus on its complexities will cast considerable light on the nature of statewide–regional branch party relations, as well as the extent of variation in organizational practices between regional branch units. Consequently, in assessing the implications of political devolution in the UK for organization in the major statewide parties, this chapter focuses on their approaches to candidate selection.[1]

The Scottish Parliament and the National Assembly for Wales were both elected for the first time in May 1999. The devolved institutions also departed from the orthodox British principle of simple plurality and used instead mixed member proportional (MMP) electoral systems. This required that two types of candidate be selected: to fight single-member constituencies (73 in Scotland and 40 in Wales) on a simple plurality basis; and to contest multi-member regional constituencies (eight in each of seven regions in Scotland and four in each of five regions in Wales) on a party list top-up basis using the d'Hondt formula. This chapter will focus on approaches to candidate selection in the three key statewide parties – Labour, the Conservatives and the Liberal Democrats.

Section one addresses the theoretical concerns raised by such a study. Section two addresses the pre-devolution historical context. Section three examines statewide–regional branch relations over candidate selection in the Labour Party after devolution; and section four examines relations in the Conservative and Liberal Democrat parties. The focus of analysis is candidate selection in each of the parties ahead of the first two sets of elections to the Scottish Parliament and Welsh Assembly in 1999 and 2003. The paper draws on research published from a study of candidate selection procedures and candidate attitudes in 1999, supplemented by interviews and further research in 2003 (Bradbury et al., 2000a, 2000b and 2000c; Mitchell and Bradbury, 2004; Bradbury, 2006).[2]

Theoretical context

In his comparative study undertaken in the late 1980s Gallagher (1988b: 256–65) cited five major potential stimulants of innovation in candidate selection: changes in the legal framework, government organization, electoral system, political culture and the nature of parties. Our primary concern here is the implications of a major change in government organization, namely, towards decentralization. This raised the fresh requirement of selection of party candidates for constituency and list elections for regional level government. What theoretical assumptions should one make about the balance of power between statewide and regional branches in the statewide parties in developing approaches to candidate selection? There are conflicting possibilities.

Analysts typically start from the assumption that in unitary states statewide branches have the overarching power of setting rules for candidate selection in their parties. Logically, if there is a shift in the locus of constitutional and governmental power to lower levels of government, analysts suggest the likelihood of a general trend towards party decentralization to accompany such changes (Hopkin, 2003; Chhibber and Kollman, 2004). This approach can invoke a number of conceptual images. Eldersveld (1964) suggested that governmental decentralization enhances the stratarchical nature of parties, as the allocation and exercise of powers within parties are redistributed to simultaneously maintain both the unity and the internal balance of parties. Carty (2004) emphasized the degree to which statewide branches will seek to sustain control over the overall party identity and programme, but might franchise out powers on certain issues, such as candidate selection, to their regional branches as part of a new party 'accord'. Laffin and Shaw (2007) invoke the concepts of stratarchy and informal party accord in their account of Labour Party adaptation to devolution after 1999.

Alternatively, one might emphasize the expectation that the statewide branch will maintain significant influence over party organization, despite governmental decentralization. Here one needs to take note of theories of party change since the 1960s. Both the catch-all party thesis (Kircheimer, 1966) and the cartel party thesis have suggested that the pressures of electoral competition on established parties have led them to the novel development of increased statewide branch control. This need not cover candidate selection. Katz and Mair (1995) in their original cartel party thesis emphasized the requirement of statewide party leaderships to develop stratarchic relationships, with local parties being in charge of local affairs, so as to leave the leadership with the autonomy to focus central control on more important issues. However, Katz (2001, 292) raised the specific problem of the apparently contradictory requirements of perceived local control and necessary statewide branch influence in the very important 'local affair' of constituency candidate selection. He suggested that a cartel party's statewide branch would keep the act of candidate selection at the local level but would in practice seek to strongly influence its outcome. He suggested that party reform would involve, first, an 'increased involvement by the central party in candidate recruitment and in setting and limiting the options among which local selectorates will choose, at the same time broadening the range of groups from which candidates may be recruited', and secondly, 'a movement of local candidate selection procedures and selectorates toward greater inclusiveness, in particular away from choice by local party officials and formal party meetings and toward selection by broad based ballots'.

These arguments suggest that reform of candidate selection in major statewide parties has been mainly shaped by central party elites for strategic reasons: central approval systems were introduced to structure and control the nomination process to get candidates amenable to party leaderships; gender balance procedures became a key innovation to enhance the social representativeness of candidates and thus make parties more electable; and one-member–one-vote (OMOV) procedures were introduced to empower a non-active membership, malleable to party leadership cues, and to disempower local activists who may stand in their way. As Mair (1997) argued, behind the façade of recent democratization in many West European parties lies the growth of 'powerful elite influence in practice'. Both Conservative Party and Labour Party statewide branches have been attributed with such strategies both generally in relation to party organization and specifically in relation to candidate selection (Peele, 1998; Seyd, 1999).

Katz (2001, 291) recognized that statewide party interference in selection procedures for a particular institution which is firmly entrenched may be very difficult and counterproductive. However, he suggested that this tendency may be most clearly manifest and observable in the 'attempted manipulation of new electoral systems rather than the reduction of established local prerogatives within a stable system'. Clearly, the need to select candidates for new devolved institutions in Scotland and Wales presented an opportunity for such concerted intervention by statewide parties. In following this line of argument, we may, of course, focus solely on theorizing control incentives for elites in the regional branches of statewide parties. But it might be suggested that regional branches that operated in such a way would give a purchase for the statewide branch to maintain an influence on selection. We may also expect that statewide branches that had developed control over candidate selection at a statewide level would be reluctant to relinquish control in the devolved setting. In such circumstances, the relative degrees of control of local selection by the regional party branch or the statewide branch might be very hard to discern, but nevertheless we might expect a basis for continued statewide branch influence.

Having questioned the automatic assumption that party decentralization will follow government decentralization, it is important to consider a range of further factors that may shape our expectations of party approaches to candidate selection after devolution. These, too, raise different possibilities. First, there are the implications of the particular form of government decentralization introduced. In federal analysis Chandler (1987) and Scharpf (1995) highlight the useful distinction to be made between dual federalism and joint federalism. Dual federalism, by creating a clear division of powers and separate arenas of party competition, suggests that national parties should decentralize and operate in distinct forms at different levels of government. Joint federalism, in contrast, features a much greater degree of overlap in resources, powers and arenas of electoral competition between levels of government, inspiring a logic for statewide parties to still control regional branch party organization. In so far as federal analysis is relevant to the UK, devolution sat somewhat ambiguously between these ideal types. On the one hand, considerable autonomy was bestowed to the Scottish Parliament in primary legislation and executive authority: on the other, the Scottish Parliament remained virtually entirely grant-resource-dependent upon Westminster. Similarly, the Welsh Assembly had significant autonomy over the implementation of legislation, while not having primary legislative powers and being entirely resource-dependent upon Westminster. Neither case suggests a clear case of either quasi-dual or joint federalism with its consequent expectations for party adaptation. That said, the asymmetry of the UK devolution settlements remains important, the more 'dual' nature of devolution for Scotland suggesting greater party decentralization than in response to the more 'joint' nature of devolution for Wales.

A key second issue is the extent of the perceived territorial threat to the state from political decentralization. Where it is not associated with a territorial threat, then statewide party branches are likely to be relaxed about granting autonomy to regional party branches; where it is so associated, there is a strong territorial management imperative to sustaining statewide party branch control over regional party branches. In the case of the UK advocates of devolution as a force for reconsolidation have had some cause to be relaxed about its territorial implications. On the other hand, there are profound sceptics. Notably, Urwin (1982) characterized the UK as an old union state which, despite its success, remained highly vulnerable to the centrifugal effects of its various national identities. Political devolution as a means of accommodating Scottish and Welsh national identities could fragment the state and potentially break it up. This implied the need to impose statewide control over regional units in a variety of contexts, including statewide parties, if devolution was not to undermine the state. Bulpitt (1983) argued that this placed problematic pressures on statewide institutions, which historically had been unwilling because of the paucity of resources relative to other commitments to intervene strongly for very long in the governance of the territorial periphery. UK central governors were used to running the state according to an ideal type 'dual polity' in which the periphery was largely governed directly by local elites whom the centre had to trust, while centre governors enjoyed the relative autonomy to get on with more important things such as running an empire or, latterly, retaining a global role. This suggested the possibility that while statewide institutions, including parties, would be very anxious about the territorial implications of devolution, they would seek to engineer conditions in which they did not normally need to intervene in regional branch organizations, resorting to 'gunboat diplomacy' only in the event of crisis.

A third key factor is the premise that devolution is likely to stimulate a new set of party system dynamics. Evidence of regional elections across a number of countries has shown that autonomist or nationalist parties tend to perform better in regional elections than in statewide elections, with consequent challenges for the statewide parties. In the case of Scotland and Wales devolution provided new opportunities for the Scottish National Party (SNP) and Plaid Cymru. If statewide party branches were going to adapt to the new substate political environments, it was logical to expect that they would need some autonomy, including over candidate selection, in order to compete. New demands upon regional party branches also arose from the fact that devolution incorporated another of the potential stimulants to party innovation listed by Gallagher, namely, electoral reform. The MMP electoral systems created the novel candidate selection task of list selection, with which statewide party leaderships were not familiar. MMP also provided much greater potential for differential party performance at the regional level and for coalition government, adding further to the challenges of adaptation for regional party branches. Electoral system innovation, therefore, compounded expectations of greater autonomy for regional party branches in adapting to the new party system and electoral contexts.

Such expectations are not, however, definite in their implications. It is equally possible in responding to regional political contexts that regional party branches will work against the general political strategies of statewide party branches and cut across habits of central leadership control. Statewide party leaderships might seek to resist such dynamics. It should also be noted that the need to select list candidates raised questions. It was possible that regional party branches could assume control and indeed, as Gallagher (1988b) argued, ensure that joint constituency procedures sustained the decentralized basis of selection. However, list selection has commonly been associated with increased leadership control to get preferred candidates selected (Epstein, 1980). On these grounds, the use of MMP electoral systems in the Scottish Parliament and Welsh Assembly, incorporating regional lists, provided the potential for leadership control in regional party branches over candidate selection. This might remain insulated from statewide influence but equally it gave a potentially useful purchase for statewide branch party influence as well.

A fourth factor in determining candidate selection is the different ideologies of territorial politics across the parties that shape approaches to party organization. In the UK case, the clearest positions are those of the Liberal Democrats and the Conservatives. The former is committed to a federal state and has a federal party constitution that pre-dates devolution. In contrast, the Conservative Party is a clear Unionist party, with little innate sympathy for government decentralization. This was reflected in a unitary party constitution prior to devolution. The Labour Party before devolution presented a more complicated picture. It had been the party that had led the campaigns for devolution. However, some party campaigners used a nationalist rhetoric or promoted a more avowedly socialist politics than was possible in a UK framework, while others saw devolution as simply offering the scope to solve Scotland's and Wales's problems closer to home. In the run-up to devolution there had appeared little ideological dissonance between party representatives at the British and Scottish/Welsh levels in the Liberal Democrats and the Conservatives, but significantly more in the Labour Party. This suggested the greater potential scope for Labour Party regional branches to seek autonomy, simultaneously provoking more statewide party incentives to intervene directly than in the other two parties. When it came to candidate selection this also raised stronger expectations in the Labour Party of national and regional party branch elites cooperating to screen out ideologically undesirable candidates who were on the nationalist or left wings of the party (Scarrow et al., 2000).

Finally, it is important to consider the extent to which parties are parties of government. Parties in office, particularly where they are in office at different levels, have strong incentives to sing from the same hymn sheet so as not to undermine policy programmes. Where they are not in office at different levels, they have stronger incentives to capitalize on all opportunities presented at different levels of government irrespective of apparent contradictions between statewide and regional branch party positions. During the early years of devolution the parties had contrasting experiences. Labour was in government at the UK level from 1997; was the major party of the coalition government in Scotland during 1999–2007; and in Wales led a minority government during 1999–2000, a coalition during 2000–3, a majority government 2003–5 and a minority government 2005–7. Meanwhile, the Conservatives were one of the two major statewide parties, but were not in government at either UK or Scottish/Welsh levels. The Liberal Democrats were part of the coalition government in the Scottish Parliament 1999–2007, and were part of the coalition in the Welsh Assembly between 2000 and 2003. They remained, however, a distant third party force in UK politics. Given these different records the incentives for close control appeared to be much stronger in the Labour Party than in either of the other two parties.

Overall, the primary assumption is still that other things being equal government decentralization will be accompanied by party decentralization. Government decentralization does not customarily inspire pathological fears of territorial separation that undermine party decentralization. Regional party system dynamics generally make it logical to devolve powers to regional party branches to help them be competitive in the new situation. Indeed, the challenge of Scottish-only and Welsh-only nationalist or autonomist parties meant that it was likely that regional party branches of statewide parties would need space to be electorally competitive. The relatively small size of the Scottish and Welsh electorates and the role of the London-based media added to the need for regional party branches to do more to be heard in regional electoral contexts. A trend towards decentralization of party organization might vary between Scotland and Wales, not least because of the asymmetry of the devolution settlements and levels of MMP. More devolution and a more pluralist party system in Scotland implied a clearer set of pressures for party decentralization in Scotland than in Wales. Decentralization might also vary between parties based on party traditions and role in government. But overall the pressures for party organization decentralization were strong.

Yet we have also noted the potentially powerful countervailing pressures towards statewide branch influence over regional branch parties. These arise where we consider the degree of party centralization that had built up at a statewide level to be strong, creating an expectation of statewide party control over branch units even when government decentralization occurs. Countervailing pressures also arise where we consider the level of government decentralization to be relatively less substantial, where there are indeed pathological fears of territorial separation, where regional branch operations in electoral competition cut across statewide party priorities too much, and may be strongly embedded in statewide party traditions and self-perceptions as parties of government irrespective of whether they are currently in power. Nevertheless, Bulpitt's perceptions of the relatively limited resources of statewide branches raises a cautionary note that even where it occurs control of regional branch units may be more on a selective basis than a consistent one.

This chapter will seek to assess these theorized expectations against the evidence of approaches to candidate selection prior to the 1999 and 2003 elections to the Scottish Parliament and National Assembly for Wales. This cannot be done in a vacuum. The next section addresses developments in statewide parties on candidate selection prior to devolution as a basis for understanding the degree of statewide party central control which each party had already established over candidate selection. Of course, such a review is of theoretical significance itself, as analysts have emphasized the importance of previous historical trajectories of parties in their approaches to party organization for shaping how they respond to further major external stimulants to change (Panebianco, 1988; Katz and Mair, 1995; Hopkin and Bradbury, 2006).

Statewide parties and candidate selection before devolution

All three statewide parties in their organizational structures had long taken account of the fact that the UK is territorially a union of England with the other stateless nations of Scotland and Wales as well as Northern Ireland. This meant that, even though there had been no political decentralization prior to 1999 in Scotland and Wales, the British statewide parties were distinctive in already having well developed regional branches. Both the Labour and Conservative parties had Scottish and Welsh party conferences, executives, staff and offices. The secretaries of state or their 'shadow secretaries' for Scotland and Wales, whoever was in power, were the de facto leaders of the regional party branches of the two parties in each country. The Liberal Democrats were even further differentiated, going as far as electing their own regional party branch leaders. The Liberal Democrats were formally a territorially federal party well before devolution, with the Scottish and Welsh party branches empowered to keep their own parliamentary candidates lists and determine their own procedures for selection for the then primary focus on UK elections.

However, while the existence of regional party branches was important in terms of general party organization and election campaigning, this had no significance for candidate selection, even in the Liberal Democrats. Prior to 1999 candidate selection practices in all three parties were uniform across England, Scotland and Wales. This meant that statewide party branches had power over setting candidate selection rules, leaving the other primary focus for candidate selection to be the UK Parliament constituency parties. Surveying research between the 1960s and 1980s Denver (1988) portrayed British parties as distinctive in that, despite having considerable potential for statewide branch central control over selection, the power of the constituency party in selection was particularly strong. Statewide party branches set the rules for selection and in different ways had procedures for vetting potential candidates either before or after selection. However, they all desisted from the imposition of controversial rules, any obvious or consistent screening out of aspirants, or influencing of local selection. This approach was primarily a function of the electoral system, which placed a focus on constituency level organization for the fighting of elections. There was some variation in local procedure. The Labour and Conservative parties used a subset of constituency party members to determine selection. The then Liberal and Social Democrat parties were alone in conducting selection on the basis of constituency one-member-one-vote (OMOV) primaries.

For a long time such approaches raised little dissent, except in the Labour Party where left-wing activism in the early 1980s sought to make constituency selection even more accountable to local activists through mandatory reselection of all sitting MPs. These approaches were also notable for producing substantial similarities in the types of candidate produced by the different parties. Selected candidates were predominantly male, middle class, well educated and experienced, with an average age in their forties. They were also generally more moderate in their political views than local activists. This had the implication for party leaderships of making decentralized selection appear a safe and acceptable means of elite recruitment. The situation, in short, appeared to suit party members and leaders alike.

From the late 1980s to the late 1990s, however, there were debates about three key issues in party candidate selection, which suggested the need for greater statewide party branch intervention. The first and second issues both focused on who was allowed to be nominated as a candidate, and arose from perceived problems of too many poor quality candidates and too many men. Hence, there were debates over, first, the greater use of centrally approved panels of candidates from which constituencies might select as opposed to allowing local party nomination, and second, over what approach might be best taken to overcome the perceived shortage of female candidates, and in particular whether it was appropriate for national party leaderships to introduce procedures of positive discrimination. The third issue focused on the appropriate selectorates within parties and arose from concerns that unrepresentative local activists within parties wielded too much power. Consequently, there were debates about whether statewide parties should insist on local constituency parties selecting their candidates on an all-member OMOV basis (see Norris and Lovenduski, 1995).

The Labour Party wrestled with reform the most, and made a number of changes. First, Labour had been the major party which featured the least statewide party branch control over vetting applicants. From 1988, however, Labour introduced a centrally run preselection approval process, albeit only for by-elections. The general procedure of endorsement after local selection otherwise remained in place ahead of the 1997 general election. Second, Labour was most radical in relation to female representation. In 1993, following various initiatives, the party decided that in half of the winnable seats not held by the party, and in half of the seats where a Labour incumbent retired, the candidate should be a woman. This was to be achieved by the statewide party branch insisting that in specified seats local members should select a candidate from all-women shortlists. As a result the 1997 election returned more than 100 women Labour MPs. A successful legal challenge brought by two defeated male aspirants under the Sex Discrimination Act in 1996 did, however, leave Labour without positive discrimination procedures ahead of future general elections (Perrigo, 1996). Finally, Labour also reformed selection at the constituency level. Although local general management committees (GMCs) retained power over drawing up the shortlists, a simple OMOV party primary procedure was introduced for the 1997 election.

The other parties saw less change. The Conservatives had used a preselection statewide branch approval process for some time and saw little need for further change following the formalization of its procedures in 1980. On female representation the party was also steadfastly against change, believing instead that women should stand on their own merits. The Conservatives did switch to OMOV by the 1992 general election. Even so, despite the statewide party branch encouraging otherwise, constituency associations were in the habit of recommending only one candidate to a final selection meeting. OMOV therefore was often used only to endorse a candidate chosen by the constituency executive council, leaving effective power still with the local activists. Overall, the local constituency party remained substantially and consistently more autonomous in how it chose its candidate than in the Labour Party.

The Liberal Democrats, created after the 1987 general election by a merger of the Liberal Party and the Social Democratic Party (SDP), actually felt the least need for change among the statewide parties. Like the Conservatives they chose their candidates locally from an approved panel drawn up by the statewide party, but again it was uncontroversial. On the issue of female representation, the Liberal Democrats continued an SDP policy of local selection with gender-balanced shortlists. The problem for the party, however, remained the basic one of getting enough decent potential candidates to stand for selection, and enough women to come forward to allow the construction of gender-balanced shortlists. Following the 1997 election only three of the 46 Liberal Democrat MPs were women. They used the OMOV local primary principle for selecting their candidates.

Overall, developments in statewide party branch intervention in party candidate selection on the issues of central approval, gender balance and OMOV procedures were most extensive in the Labour Party. Despite such developments, however, what is significant for our purposes is the fact that statewide branch relations with Scottish and Welsh branches of the Labour, Conservative and Liberal Democrat parties changed little. The rules of candidate selection remained constitutionally a statewide branch preserve, zealously guarded in the Labour Party by the National Executive Committee, and determined by statewide party officials in the Conservative Party. The writ that ran for the relative powers of the party leadership and local constituency party in determining candidate selection did so on a statewide basis. Regional party branches simply helped, where required, in the administration of procedures set by the statewide party branch. In the sense that they had more to do as agents of the statewide branch, notably in the Labour Party, it was solely because statewide branch intervention in selection had itself increased during this period.

Statewide–regional branch relations over candidate selection and the Labour Party

Set against this background, how did the statewide parties address the selection of constituency and list candidates for the 1999 and 2003 Scottish

Parliament and Welsh Assembly elections? Analysis for each of the parties focuses on three questions. First, to what extent were decisions about the selection procedures to use taken by regional as opposed to statewide party branches? Secondly, how much regional branch party control in the procedures was established at the regional level? Thirdly, how much did the statewide party branch control or influence the regional party branch in determining selection at the regional level, or conversely how much autonomy did regional party branches retain? Analysis focuses substantively on the development of party approaches to central approval lists, constituency selection and list selection, and the influence thereon of attitudes to positive action on gender representation or the introduction of OMOV to selection procedures. Experience across the parties varied considerably, and needs to be considered in the context of pre-1999 statewide party experience. A schematic overview of who set the rules and who then influenced candidate selection is provided in Tables 6.1 and 6.2. They are adapted from the presentational approach of Gallagher (1988) in seeking to emphasize the key points of influence over candidate selection in each of the parties. (For a fuller review of the selection procedures for each of the parties, upon which this discussion is empirically based see Bradbury et al., 2000a, 2000b, 2000c.)

Table 6.1 Who sets the rules over candidate selection in statewide parties? Locus of significant influence over rule-setting

	Scottish/Welsh party conference	Scottish/Welsh party executive/leadership	British party executive/leadership
1997 General election	Lib Dem	Lib Dem	Labour Conservative Lib Dem
1999 Scottish/Welsh elections			
Constituency	Labour Lib Dem	Labour Conservative Lib Dem	Labour Conservative
List	Lib Dem	Labour Conservative Lib Dem	Labour Conservative
2003 Scottish and Welsh election			
Constituency	Labour Conservative Lib Dem	Labour Conservative Lib Dem	Labour (partial) Conservative (Wales only)
List	Labour Conservatives Lib Dem	Labour Conservative Lib Dem	Labour (partial) Conservative (Wales only)

Table 6.2 Who picks the candidates in statewide parties? Locus of significant influence over candidate selection

	Party voters	Party primaries (OMOV)	Subset of constituency party	Scottish/ Welsh party conference	Scottish/ Welsh party executive/ leadership	British party executive/ leadership
1987 General election	Lib/SDP		Labour Conservative			
1997 General election		Labour Cons (partial) Lib Dem	Cons (partial)	Lib Dem		Labour
1999 Scottish/Welsh elections						
Constituency		Labour Cons Lib Dem		Labour Cons Lib Dem	Labour	Labour
List		Cons (Wales) Lib Dem	Cons (Scot)	Labour Cons Lib Dem	Labour Cons (Scot)	Labour
2003 Scottish and Welsh election						
Constituency		Labour Cons Lib Dem		Labour Cons Lib Dem	Labour	
List		Labour (Wales) Cons Lib Dem		Labour Cons Lib Dem	Labour	

Both tables suggest that the general trend was towards decentralization in UK statewide parties after devolution, although it was by no means a uniform trend. Table 6.1 indicates that the Labour and Conservative parties saw continuation in a role for the statewide party branches in setting selection rules, although this had diminished by 2003. Table 6.2 suggests that the Labour Party again experienced distinctive patterns of statewide party intervention in intra-party relations over actual candidate selection, although again this diminished between 1999 and 2003. We will look at all of the parties in more detail but start with the most distinctive case of the Labour Party, assessing approaches to selection before each set of elections in turn.

Labour and the 1999 Scottish and Welsh elections

First, who decided the procedures in the first place? There is mixed evidence of decentralization to the regional branch and continued statewide party branch control. On the one hand, the Scottish and Welsh branches of the party each were charged with establishing their candidate selection procedures prior to the 1999 elections. In this sense, there was a formal decentralization to the regional party branches of the responsibility for rule setting. Proposals were drawn up by the Scottish and Welsh party executives and debated at Scottish and Welsh party conferences. However, it should be noted that there was almost complete uniformity in the formal procedures actually chosen between the Scottish and Welsh parties. This reflected the high degree of collaboration of the Scottish and Welsh executives with the statewide Labour Party Parliamentary Selections Review Group in drawing up proposed procedures. It also reflected the formal control that the statewide party's National Executive Committee still held over the ratification of selection procedures. This suggests that the statewide party branch kept a pretty close eye on the decisions that were being taken in the Scottish and Welsh parties.

Second, how much did the regional branch party assert control in the procedures over who was actually selected? While OMOV was used for constituency level selection of the eventual candidates nominated, there was considerable evidence of substantial regional branch party leadership control over all stages of candidate selection. The regional party branch in both countries introduced a preselection approval procedure which established an approved list from which constituency and list candidates had to be chosen. A regional party branch selection board considered nominations to the approved list against agreed criteria and whittled the numbers down to 326 applicants in Scotland and 315 in Wales. After interview 166 applicants made it onto the approved panel in Scotland, a relatively small number given that there were 129 seats to be contested in the Scottish Parliament. In Wales 152 candidates were approved to contest selection for 60 seats. In Scotland there were a number of appeals, only one of which was successful. In Wales there were 13 successful appeals, which took the approved list up to 164.

The regional party branch in both Scotland and Wales also introduced radical new procedures for constituency selection in order to create gender balance. The party twinned constituencies for the purpose of making a joint selection which would then apportion the leading female candidate to fight one seat and the leading male candidate to fight the other. In this way an equal number of female and male candidates was guaranteed across all the constituencies. Where possible, equally winnable adjacent constituencies were to be paired to give women an equal chance of eventual election. The male and female candidates were selected by an OMOV vote across the twinned constituencies, and following the vote a meeting between constituency representatives and successful candidates decided which seat each candidate would actually contest. This represented a significant intervention from the regional party branch into the affairs of constituency selection.

It might be assumed that regional party branches had much less interest in list election, as Labour expected to win very few seats in this way. Nevertheless, in both Scotland and Wales the regional party branch also gave itself considerable discretion over list selection. In each region an electoral conference was held for the selection of each regional list, at which hustings were held for all interested approved candidates. An electoral board made up of party officers and representatives then had the job of drawing up a recommended rank ordered list. It was put to representatives of constituency parties, and the constituency representatives could then approve the list or refer it back to the electoral board for further debate until a regional list was concluded. The final authority, nevertheless, lay with the electoral board.

These approaches suggested initially strong regional branch control in the Scottish and Welsh Labour parties, enabling it to intervene in all stages of selection from approval to constituency and list selection. It was defended on progressive grounds, ostensibly to ensure candidates of a required quality and social representativeness. There were nevertheless criticisms of the ends to which such regional party branch control were put. This takes us on to the third question of who exercised control relatively in the operation of the procedures between regional and statewide party branches. In practice, many observers considered the arrangements provided the capacity for the statewide party branch to impose its influence on these approaches in a number of ways.

The selection boards that drew up the initial approved lists, uniquely among the parties, included both statewide-party nominated members and non-party members, as well as Scottish/Welsh party branch members. Equally, while constituency selection was left ultimately to an OMOV vote, the electoral boards charged with overseeing list selection drew their personnel from both the regional party branch and the statewide party branch. They were composed of members of the Scottish/Welsh executive, the regional party branch general secretary, the secretary of state or representative, and members of the statewide National Executive Committee.

There were then a significant number of allegations of connivance between regional branch and statewide party branch officials in the implementation of the procedures to gain the kind of candidates that the statewide and regional branch party leaderships wanted. This was evident, first, in relation to the approval process. In Scotland, there were many of the view that there was a statewide/Scottish Labour leadership campaign to avoid having dissident Labour Members of the Scottish Parliament (MSPs) who would not be supportive of New Labour policies in Westminster and would seek to lobby for further constitutional change towards more powers for a Scottish Parliament. This raised the spectre of a cull of socialist/nationalist applicants, of whom Dennis Canavan was but the most prominent of a number of aspirants who felt excluded on ideological grounds (Canavan, 1999). They protested at the selection board being chaired by a well-known supporter of Tony Blair, and key interview panels being chaired by another strong party loyalist, Ernie Ross MP. They also claimed that their interviews included individualized questions which imposed a New Labour loyalty test. Even five successful applicants felt sufficiently strongly to publicly criticize the process for its central control and political expediency.

There was also criticism in the Welsh party of the non-approval of the well-known devolution campaigner, Gareth Hughes, and the popular socialist figure, Tyrone O'Sullivan. At the same time the selections board was considered to have 'fixed' approval for preferred candidates. Indeed a very large number of aspirants were admitted onto the approved list, letting through the very candidates who were widely seen as lacklustre but were well connected within the Welsh party. Equally important was the appeals committee that upheld appeals from a number of candidates of similar ilk who had failed even the initial trawl. This approach was extended to doing favours for the statewide branch. In particular, applications to go on the approved list were reopened after the resignation of Ron Davies as leader-designate of the Welsh Assembly Labour Group, and Alun Michael, Tony Blair's preferred replacement, was included. The reopening of applications for Alun Michael at the behest of the statewide party was seen as blatant manipulation. Hence, while there were undoubtedly priorities in the regional party branches that affected approval of nominees, the politics of New Labour and influence of the statewide party branch also appeared to distort the approval procedure in both Scotland and Wales.

The selection of constituency and list candidates was also perceived as being to a significant extent influenced by the statewide party branch. The very fact that twinned constituency selection was introduced in Wales as well after long debate in the Scottish party suggested strong pressures towards conformity that involved the statewide branch. Moreover, in Scotland the apparent ideological bias in favour of New Labour at the approval stage was perceived to be at work again to ensure that the statewide and Scottish regional branch leadership's preferred candidates won nominations. For example, there were accusations that some candidates were 'twinned out' by careful party manipulation of which constituencies were twinned with each other. Margaret Lynch, a failed candidate who defected to the SNP, claimed that all but three selected constituency candidates were 'firmly in the New Labour camp' (*Herald*, 1998). Similar manipulation was not evident in Wales, for in the Welsh party there was more widespread opposition to the erosion of constituency party independence and to the perceived imposition of female candidates. As a result, regional party branch officials were simply often grateful for whatever could be agreed even if it did not meet rational criteria, and there was consequently much less opportunity for statewide branch manipulation.

The significant control of the regional party branch over list selection provided an even clearer point of potential leverage for statewide party influence. Indeed, coming in early 1999 after so much controversy over approval and constituency selection, list selection actually inspired greater criticism of both statewide and regional branch leadership control, as the leadership's use of its powers appeared to be so blatant. The political context was important. In Scotland the regional party branch imposed a rank ordering on Glasgow against the wishes of constituency representatives (*Herald*, 1999). Equally, in the Highlands and Islands, which ultimately produced Labour's only three list MSPs, the party inserted Peter Peacock, a candidate who had only recently become a party member and who had not been chosen by any constituency, at the top of the list.

In Wales, list selection got caught up in the leadership battle between Rhodri Morgan and Alun Michael for the very simple reason that selected list candidates became voters in the leadership electoral college. While party officials made a spirited defence to the effect that list selection ignored the leadership affiliations of aspirants, achieved gender balance and also enhanced ethnic minority representation, there was much that smacked of regional party branch manipulation to assist Alun Michael, the preferred candidate of the statewide party leadership. First, two Wales Executive members of the Electoral Board were open supporters of Alun Michael. Secondly, there was a last-minute decision to cut the number of places on Labour's regional lists from 12 to 4, a decision which it was suggested was due to Michael's realization that longer lists would have created more opponents to him in the electoral college. Third, the Electoral Board imposed lists in three of the regions against constituency representative wishes, and allegedly to create new Michael voters. A majority of the selected list candidates who became new voters in the electoral college to elect the leader were clearly pro-Michael (Flynn, 1999).

Overall, it may still be said that selection procedures in the Scottish and Welsh party branches, and the innovations to provide both for a comprehensive approval process and gender-balance procedures, suggested significant decentralization of party organization and an opportunity to inject some 'new politics' into approaches to candidate selection in both Scotland and Wales (Brown et al, 1998; Davies, 1998). Indeed, the achievements on gender balance in both candidacy and eventual election were substantial, women forming exactly half the Labour group in the Scottish Parliament and numbering 15 out of 28 in the Welsh Assembly. The party kept to the usage of OMOV in constituency selection. Yet to achieve these outcomes the Scottish and Welsh regional party branches introduced highly centralist approaches to selection. All stages of the selection process were then controversial as a result of the perceived openness to statewide as well as Scottish/Welsh leadership influence. It was often impossible to differentiate the relative influence of the two levels but the influence of the statewide leadership was strongly perceived in the determination evident in the original approved lists to promote candidates loyal to the New Labour project and to screen out dissidents. In both Wales and Scotland there was no pretence of a proper democratic procedure for list selection, and in the special circumstances in Wales political expediency to serve the statewide leadership's preferred Welsh leadership candidate appeared to reign supreme. The selection procedures appeared to fall prey to a party machine ultimately interested in getting its preferred candidates selected.

Labour and the 2003 Scottish and Welsh elections

The approach to candidate selection in the Labour Party was a much less high-profile issue ahead of the 2003 Scottish and Welsh elections (for a fuller review of the selection procedures for each of the parties, see Mitchell and Bradbury, 2004). Many constituency MSPs and Welsh Assembly Members (AMs) intended to stand again, and the advantage of incumbency guaranteed reselection almost universally across the parties. In the Labour Party this involved an affirmative nomination procedure which could avoid the holding of a selection contest unless local members wanted it. Nevertheless, there had to be competitive procedures for selection in constituency seats which they did not hold as well as in list selection. An important change in the legislative context for candidate selection had occurred since 1999. The 2002 Sex Discrimination (Election Candidates) Act made it legal to use strong positive action measures, such as all-women shortlists, to ensure the selection of women candidates. Consequently, the degree of party decentralization in how selection procedures were decided upon, the level of regional party branch control over selection wielded at the Scottish/Welsh level and the extent of statewide party influence remained open to development. Again, we need to consider approaches to approved lists, constituency selection and list selection in turn

In the Labour Party, a major change was the effective devolution of the power to set the candidate selection rules ahead of the 2003 elections from statewide party control to regional branch party control. While, constitutionally speaking, powers remained at the statewide level and the statewide

National Executive Committee remained the guardian of such issues, in practical terms in 2001 the Scottish and Welsh parties were given freedom to choose their procedures without coordination from statewide party officials (Labour Party, 2001). In Scotland, with virtually all constituency incumbents standing again and little expectation of increasing their number of seats, the incentive for statewide party control was virtually eliminated. In Wales, despite the fact that several target seats were potentially winnable by new candidates after the poor election result of 1999, there was also little sense of tight party control over candidacy. For example, Labour now accepted Tyrone O'Sullivan as an approved candidate, and he was lined up for the Rhondda constituency until he made the personal choice to stand down and pursue other priorities. This reflected a renewed emphasis on actually winning seats after the losses of 1999, and a relaxation in the Labour Party of concern over the possible influence of maverick figures, like O'Sullivan, if they were actually elected.

This left the Scottish and Welsh regional party branches with considerable autonomy. There was continuity in the use of approved lists, although in both Scotland and Wales the party experienced a good deal less interest than in 1999, and there was little pressure for screening aspirant candidates. There was also continued interest in taking strong positive action to achieve gender balance in candidacy and representation, although the lack of close statewide party branch coordination was reflected in a divergence of approach between the Scottish and Welsh party branches. In Scotland, where all but one of Labour's incumbent constituency MSPs stood for re-election, no special procedure was used to select constituency candidates in other seats; the focus was rather on a special procedure whereby women were placed top of the list in the two regions where Labour stood most chance of winning (Mackay, 2003: 79–80). In Wales, interest in gender parity was more far-reaching and focused on the usage of the new legislation legalizing all-women shortlists in constituency selection. At the Welsh party's conference in March 2002 the party decided by 61 per cent to 39 per cent to divide the 16 seats in which it had to choose a new candidate into two groups of eight determined by order of winnability. In each group it was suggested that three constituency parties have all-women shortlists (Wales Labour Party, 2002). After the elections of Labour's 30 AMs, all of whom were elected from constituencies, 19 were women and just 11 were men (Mitchell and Bradbury, 2004: 295–8).

The Welsh Labour Party also uniquely took steps towards positive discrimination for black and minority ethnic (BAME) candidates. To avoid the perception of regional branch party officials using their own discretion in choosing list candidates, the decision was taken to fill up most list positions with those already selected as constituency candidates, ranked in order of the percentage majority of the vote gained in their seat in the 1999 election. In addition, though the party held a separate all-Wales membership postal ballot to rank approved BAME candidates wishing to stand on regional lists. The five top candidates were then 'zipped' into a reserved place on the regional list equal to their place in the BAME ballot. The procedure was possibly not legal but in practice probably the lack of both the expectation and actuality of winning a list seat dampened down any possible controversy.

Overall, the Scottish and Welsh Labour parties gained a more clearly decentralized control over selection procedures in 2003 than in 1999. The Welsh party, and to a lesser extent the Scottish party, gained no less a reputation for intervention in procedures to achieve desired aims, to the annoyance of some party members who opposed either positive discrimination or the eating away of constituency party power. But, critically, any resentments that were felt in 2003 were not aimed at any perceived statewide Labour Party intervention. The statewide party was notable by its absence from being seen to control or influence the procedures adopted, the approval stage or constituency and list selection. However, whether this represented a permanent retreat of the statewide party on an important issue of party organization remained unclear; importantly, the Labour Party generally avoided any strategic review of statewide–regional party organizational relations. There was instead a form of discretionary devolution of powers on this issue for the time being, leading both to autonomy for the Scottish and Welsh parties and divergence in the procedures adopted by them. Fundamental debates on this were delayed for another time.

Statewide–regional branch relations over candidate selection in the Conservative and Liberal Democrat parties

In the other statewide parties there was also a general trend towards decentralization in party organization. Nevertheless, as Tables 6.1 and 6.2 show there were some notable differences between the Conservatives and the Liberal Democrats and between Scotland and Wales, as well as changes over time. This section looks at the Conservatives and Liberal Democrats in turn.

The Conservative Party

The Conservative Party's approach to selection procedures in both Scotland and Wales provided comparatively limited evidence of substantial decentralisation to the regional party branch in 1999, although more out of indifference than calculated central control. Such an approach was conditioned by the fact that the Scottish and Welsh party conferences had no policy-making role, and organizational reform following the 1997 general election defeat came too late to have a bearing. Hence, in both countries the selection procedure was devised by the party chair and vice chair of the regional branch party units, following the advice of their senior officials, but only after consultation with Conservative Central Office in London. Consequently, while technically made in Scotland and Wales, decisions over the selection procedures adopted ultimately took place within an organizational structure still strongly dominated by the statewide party branch.

In drawing up these proposals the regional party branch officials on the whole did not try to assert new measures of control over the party. There were no substantial innovations in the approved candidate procedures. Indeed, the problem was not so much the screening of candidates as attracting them in the first place. Equally, constituency selection occurred in the conventional manner, and the power of the constituency party was also evident in the fact that in both Scotland and Wales the potential candidates for list selection were limited to those who had been selected to stand in constituencies. The job of regional list selection was thus limited to that of rank ordering from among these doubly favoured candidates, a task undertaken in both Scotland and Wales within the regional party branches. A statewide-level approach, which sustained the power of constituency selection, with little statewide party intervention to set new or discriminatory rules, was thus largely perpetuated in the approaches of the Scottish and Welsh branch parties to selection for the Parliament and the Assembly.

Nevertheless, it is important to note that there were some differences between the Scottish and Welsh parties in how they determined selection procedures. For constituency selection, the Scottish party insisted on a minimum number of candidates to be considered by constituency parties at each stage of the selection process, and a minimum of two for consideration by the full local association. This was to prevent a local executive putting just one candidate forward for approval by the membership. Indeed the Scottish party's candidates' board retained the right to add to the candidates put before both a constituency executive council and a local OMOV vote if necessary. Equally, for list selection, while the Welsh party held regional hustings and voting was on the basis of OMOV, in Scotland it was decided that rank ordering of list candidates would be undertaken by a joint council formed for each of the electoral regions. This was made up of Scottish party branch appointees and the constituency chairs for each specific region.

This intervention by the Scottish party varied in its significance. The greater strictures over the openness of constituency selection were of relatively limited significance. Constituency parties still provided the main source for finding potential candidates for the approved list in the first place, and then ultimately selecting those who would stand for election. Intervention in list selection was more controversial, as the joint council procedure in effect determined who would have a better chance of being elected to the Scottish Parliament. All 18 of the Conservatives MSPs after the 1999 elections were elected from regional lists. Given that it was dominated by the Scottish party hierarchy, the system smacked of Scottish party control. However, as far as the Scottish party was concerned, this procedure still only selected from among candidates that had already been selected at constituency level on an OMOV basis. It was simply efficient to be able to use the joint council approach for rank ordering rather than going through OMOV again. There was no evidence of the statewide party using even this limited lever of Scottish party branch control to influence selection. In practice, most internal party criticism, such as it was, focused not on the issue of how much power the statewide and Scottish/Welsh levels of the party had to decide the procedures, or whether there had been any statewide party influence over selection, but on the general lack of a new approach to candidate selection at any level of the party. This focused particularly on the party's disinclination to address the issue of gender balance.

Overall, ahead of the 1999 elections the Conservatives for the most part appeared to simply adapt Westminster selection practices. Except for the need to devise approaches to list selection, it was business as usual. The reliance on decentralized constituency-based selection appears to have remained intact, and intervention by neither the regional party branch in Scotland and Wales nor the statewide party branch appeared to be a priority. The party was still essentially still reeling from its defeat in the 1997 general election, and there were much bigger issues occupying leaders and officials than how candidates were selected to go down to expected defeats in 1999. Formally, the statewide branch therefore retained a substantial say and influence over selection procedures. There was, nevertheless, some asymmetry as the Scottish approach to constituency and list selection did indicate some greater assertion of Scottish branch party control over selection procedures where it mattered and where the opportunity most readily presented itself, that is, over list selection, even when expectations of electoral success remained limited.

Ahead of the 2003 elections the Conservative Party moved more towards decentralization in approaches to candidate selection, though clearly so only in the Scottish party branch. As part of the response to the 1997 election defeat, and to increase its electoral appeal in Scotland, the party in Scotland held a major review of its organization, resulting in the Strathclyde Report in 1998 (Scottish Conservatives, 1998). Following this, the party in its Scottish–British relations adopted a confederal constitution, which inter alia gave the Scottish party control over candidate selection procedures and power to maintain its own list of approved candidates for both Scottish Parliament and Westminster elections. There was, however, no parallel development for Wales. Debate in the Welsh party after 1997 simply resulted in the creation of a Welsh board of management, which was, nevertheless, subordinate to the party's British board of management.

Paradoxically, following these developments, the party's selection procedures in Scotland and Wales converged rather than diverged. The Conservatives in Scotland introduced OMOV postal ballots for regional selection, thus echoing the Welsh party's use of an OMOV procedure, and responding to criticism of Scottish branch party control of list selection in 1999. As a result of this move, the scope for statewide party control of candidate selection in either Scotland or Wales was very limited since, irrespective of the degree of decentralization to the Scottish or Welsh party, the challenge of actually getting enough good candidates remained formidable, and ordinary members ultimately determined both constituency and list selection.

The Liberal Democrats

In contrast to both the Labour and Conservative parties, the Liberal Democrats decided to settle the power to decide candidate selection procedures for the Parliament and the Assembly on the Scottish and Welsh parties from the start. This reflected the fact that the Liberal Democrats were a federal party, and represented a clear case of party decentralization in party organization to echo government decentralization. Equally, Scottish/Welsh party branch approaches gave little indication of either regional or statewide branch control. The party in both Scotland and Wales set up an approved list. In Scotland about 200 applied and in Wales about 100, of which about a third were women. The vast majority of applicants were approved in both countries. Constituency selection gave power of selection to constituency parties, tempered only by the adoption of an equal opportunities approach to gender balance in selection, which laid down that half the shortlist should be women. Selection was on the basis of OMOV (see Scottish Liberal Democrats, 1995). When it came to list selection, both the Scottish and Welsh party branches used regional committees, made up of constituency representatives, to draw up the gender balanced shortlists, and selection was then by OMOV either by post or in person at the local hustings meetings. As a result of these approaches, which gave no levers for party influence at the regional level, there was little scope for statewide party influence either.

That said, as is evident from this summary, the clear decentralization of party organization and lack of statewide party intervention did not lead to much divergence in practice between the Scottish and Welsh parties. Indeed, in their approaches to candidate approval, constituency selection and gender balance both regional party branches followed established UK party practice in Westminster candidate selection. There were only three differences. First, in approving candidates the Scottish Party introduced the option of 'commending' candidates. In this way the Scottish party branch could recommend particularly talented candidates who may not be 'insiders' to local parties in winnable seats. Secondly, OMOV worked slightly differently in constituency selection. In Scotland, all members were sent a postal vote after hustings meetings were held, while in Wales postal votes had to be applied for. The former approach was considered to slightly enhance the openness of competition for candidacy. Finally, in list selection the Scottish party decided that voting should determine the ranking of only the top three places. The other nine places were filled with other approved candidates. In Wales, however, regional voting produced a rank-ordered regional list of five candidates. This left the regional lists to be topped up with a further seven candidates.

The significance of these minor differences points in the direction of the Scottish party being interested in ensuring a greater degree of Scottish party branch influence over how members selected their candidates. In this sense, there was some asymmetry between the Scottish and Welsh parties, as there was with the Conservatives, pointing in the direction of the Scottish central party being more interested in influencing events. Nevertheless, these were still relatively minor differences, and there was no evidence of statewide branch influence in either Scotland or Wales. Overall, Liberal Democrat approaches were marked by continuity and consensus with past practice. This meant that constituency selection was decentralized to constituencies, and in list selection an emphasis was placed on the perceived democracy of the process. That procedures did not follow a branch or statewide party agenda in either Scotland or Wales is borne out by the frustration of some party officials over female representation. While 3 of the 6 Liberal Democrat members of the Welsh Assembly proved to be women, this was more by luck than judgement. In Scotland, the party achieved only 3 women out of 17 MSPs.

Ahead of the 2003 elections the Liberal Democrats provided evidence simply of continuity in statewide–regional party branch relations. The decentralization of power over candidate selection was sustained. The party kept the same selection procedures, including the provision for gender-balanced shortlists, used in 1999. In Wales, there was simply a move to copy the Scottish party and to use a full postal ballot to ensure the openness of local selection, despite the added cost that this entailed. There was no evidence of the statewide party seeking to intervene in candidate selection.

Conclusion

The opening suggestion of this chapter was that an analysis of candidate selection would cast considerable light on the nature of statewide–regional branch relations in the major statewide political parties following devolution. The chapter presented a number of theoretical perspectives suggesting expectations of both decentralization and centralization in party organization. What actually occurred in practice, and in what ways were the contrasting expectations borne out? Overall, there would appear to be four principal conclusions.

First, the tendency in all three major statewide parties over the period of two sets of devolved elections was towards decentralization to the regional party unit. This covered both the drawing up of candidate selection procedures, and the degree of control and influence over the key issues of candidate approval and constituency and list selection. By the time of the 2003 elections, the statewide branch in all three parties had a residual or no role in such matters, with the exception of the Conservatives in Wales where the statewide–regional party relationship could still properly be called that of a unitary party culture. This appeared to generally back up assumptions of decentralization in party organization following significant governmental decentralization. It also appeared to sustain the significance of how devolution creates new party systems that press regional party branches to assert autonomy and to select candidates required to compete effectively at that level. These pressures demonstrably produced stratarchic (or franchising) effects in all of the parties.

Secondly, that said, the Labour Party did not take a direct route to this position. Ahead of the 1999 elections there was evidence of statewide party influence at all stages of candidate selection. This appears to bear out assumptions that statewide party branches can be concerned about the impact of their regional branches' activities on their own fortunes. This can be accentuated where the party concerned has worries about the assertion of ideological positions contrary to those expressed by the statewide party – in this case more Scottish and Welsh nationalist and left-wing political positions than those expressed by New Labour at the statewide level. It is further accentuated when the party is a party of government, emphasizing the need for unity of message in office. Labour's approach also appears, though, to bear out the assumptions that, while the broader politics of territorial management can be deeply influential on the internal affairs of a political party, the statewide party does not have unlimited resources to impose control, and is equally aware of the damaging consequences for electoral fortunes at the devolved level if control is sustained over the long term. This calls to mind the relevance of Bulpitt's sceptical reflections on the resources and activities of statewide political units in the UK: that they are weak relative to their expectations and aspirations and, in the usage of their relatively limited resources, they have to be careful about making interventions in peripheral politics. In this context, party elite territorial management in the Labour Party may be better characterized as a focused one-off intervention in 1999 to structure the nature of the party's representation in Scotland and Wales for a generation, which used up considerable political resources. Once the job was done the statewide party leadership retreated. But for such occasional 'gunboat diplomacy' this was likely to be the prevailing approach for the foreseeable future.

Thirdly, there is some asymmetry in the extent of decentralization to regional party branches, with clearer decentralization to Scottish party branches than Welsh party branches paralleling the greater governmental decentralization to the Scottish Parliament than the Welsh Assembly. This is evident in the case of the Conservative Party, where constitutionally the powers of the Scottish party are different from those of the Welsh one following the Strathclyde report in 1998. Again, the Conservative Party did not take a direct route to this outcome; the differentiation reflecting the realization that a failure to perceptibly adjust to the transformation of Scottish politics that devolution involved would leave the party in a parlous state. The constitutional significance of devolution in Wales did not have quite the same impact on Conservative Party thinking. One might also make the case that the Scottish Labour Party has had a greater interest in asserting quasi-constitutional autonomy than the Welsh party (see Bradbury, 2006), although by 2003 there was little practical difference between the powers of the Scottish and Welsh party branches on this issue. In the Liberal Democrats, a party looking forward to federalism all round, there was no difference at all between the Scottish and Welsh party branches.

Finally, these conclusions taken together appear to bear out the enduring influence of historical trajectories. While all of the parties ended up with decentralization of powers to the regional party branch over determining candidate selection rules, each of them was constrained by distinct party constitutional traditions. The actual approaches of regional party branches to candidate selection were also generally grounded in the previous statewide party branch approach. In the Labour Party, for example, there had been distinctive Scottish and Welsh party units before devolution but it had been in the main a territorially centralized party, and after devolution in developing the powers of regional branches there was no wish to confront fundamental generative issues of party constitutional change. Consequently, party decentralization took place on the basis of discretionary devolution. Equally, it is interesting to note that regional party branches used their new powers in as interventionist a manner as the statewide party branch had done before, notably in promoting gender balance. Likewise, the Conservative Party had previously been constitutionally quite territorially centralized, and party decentralization still strongly reflected the influence from this in Wales. Clear constitutional decentralization of powers for the Scottish party probably reflected the party's capacity to make pragmatic adjustments to electoral needs north of the English–Scottish border. Even then, both the Scottish and Welsh party branches in practice sustained the highly constituency-based approach to selection developed by the statewide branch. In the Liberal Democrats party decentralization was entirely in keeping with the party's pre-existing federal constitution and federal party political culture. Equally though, there appeared barely any differences in the approaches followed to candidate selection between those of the regional party branches and those of the statewide party.

Overall, it is apparent that the assumption that statewide parties set candidate selection rules on a statewide basis and Denver's (1988) observation that in the 1980s Britain was distinctive in having 'centralized parties with decentralized selection' both have to be substantially revised. Even before devolution, Denver's analysis needed to be revised to note the greater activation of central power in the Labour Party, and the development of decentralized selection across the parties more at the behest of the mass membership than local party activists. Post-devolution, we need to recognize that statewide party candidate selection has become both *more* multilevel and multiform, with decentralization to regional branches in each party, though noting differences between Scotland and Wales and between different parties. In that there are Scottish and Welsh level 'centres', the activation of the central capacity for control is now also being undertaken at the Scottish/Welsh party branch level as well, again particularly in the Labour Party.

7
Splitting the Difference: The Radical Approach of the Belgian Parties

Frederik Verleden

Introduction

One of the peculiar aspects of the Belgian federal system is its lack of statewide political parties. All parties are regional, whether or not they qualify as autonomist parties (Caramani, 2004; De Winter, Gómez-Reino and Lynch, 2006). Mainstream political parties (Catholics, Socialists and Liberals), traditionally major statewide forces, all fell apart during the 1960s and 1970s, each giving birth to two distinct and completely autonomous 'sister parties', one for each linguistic community. Furthermore, this regionalization of the 'Belgian' party system preceded the institutional process that transformed the unitary framework into a federal one, culminating in the 1993 new constitutional article: 'Belgium is a federal state, made up of Communities and Regions.' Therefore, *'The Belgian experience does not support the thesis that changes in the territorial structure of the state cause shifts in the territorial structure of the party system'* (Swenden and Jans, 2006: 880; emphasis added). Indeed, most theories concerning political parties in federal systems assume parties to be reactive: they 'seem to be expected to adapt quasi-automatically to the structure of the state, mimicking its overall structure' (Deschouwer, 2006a). More explicitly, Chhibber and Kollman (2004: 21) argue that the level of party aggregation depends on territorial structures and the importance of subnational governments (see also Thorlakson, 2007). In other words, the federalization of the country ought to precede the transformation of the party system. The Belgian case seems to defy this.

In this chapter I seek to demonstrate why and how the 'unravelling' of the Belgian statewide party system occurred and how it influenced the transformation of the Belgian state into a federation. I will show how the growing salience of the Dutch–French language divide sparked the rise of autonomist parties which in turn put the organization of the statewide parties under strain. The split of the Christian Democrats placed this party family into a competitive advantage vis-à-vis the other leading statewide parties, that is, the Socialists and Liberals, whose split was just a matter of time. The chapter

145

illustrates the 'suddenness' of these splits and the (in hindsight) mistaken assumption that parties of the same family would 'reunite' once the electoral success of the autonomist parties which they were meant to combat had disappeared. I also demonstrate that some mechanisms to pacify relations between the two language communities *within* the formerly statewide parties were *exported* to pacify relations between these communities in some key institutions of the Belgian centre (parliament and executive).

The chapter takes a chronological approach and mainly covers the period between 1930 and 1980. For each time period we systematically discuss developments within the Christian-Democratic/Catholic, Socialist and Liberal party families. However, in the final section I briefly consider the long-term repercussions of the split party organizations (and systems) for the dynamics of Belgian federalism

The recognition of Dutch and the adaptation of the statewide parties (1893–1945)

The Dutch–French language divide already featured prominently in Belgian politics decades before Belgium started its transformation from a unitary into a federal state. The basic feature of this linguistic issue – the territorial partition of Belgium into a Dutch-speaking north, Flanders, and a French-speaking south, Wallonia – has existed ever since Belgian independence in 1830. However, the ruling classes at the time, whether in Flanders or in Wallonia, spoke French. The governance of Belgium as a unitary centralized and exclusively francophone state was not a political issue as long as politics was limited to the wealthiest (Witte et al., 2000: 43). Furthermore the dominant cleavages of the 19th and early 20th century centred on the appropriate demarcation between state and religion (Catholicism) or between employers and workers. The democratization of politics (universal adult male suffrage in 1893 and 'one man one vote' in 1919) brought about a fundamental change. The French-speaking political and social elite was now confronted with the demographic preponderance of the Dutch-speaking Belgians of Flanders. In the future, the unitary state – and its political system – would have to cope with a linguistic duality, French versus Dutch.

The very first laws aimed at satisfying the growing 'Flemish Movement' were adopted at the end of the 19th century. They recognized the use of Dutch in public affairs in Flanders, next to French. However, the refusal of the Belgian centre to enforce these laws persuaded some key members of the Flemish Movement to collaborate with the Germans during the First Word War. In the aftermath of the Great War nearly all political forces accepted that a 'national' solution to the linguistic issue was imperative. An entirely bilingual state was strongly opposed by the French-speakers. Wallonia had always been a French-speaking region; therefore, to impose a bilingual regime would be seen as a step back. Initially, the king and the French-speaking elite hoped to keep Flanders bilingual. Yet the Flemish Movement had become sufficiently strong to impose its will: Flanders should become an exclusively Dutch-speaking region. A series of 'language laws' followed: administration (1921), education (1932), judicial (1935) and military (1938) affairs would be conducted exclusively in Dutch in Flanders, in French in Wallonia, both languages coexisting in Brussels. The Belgian territory was divided in two distinct, legally recognized, monolingual regions: Flanders and Wallonia (Witte and Van Velthoven, 1998: 92–109).

The first attempts at linguistic pacification were limited to mere law-making, in particular to regulate the use of languages in the public sphere. Nothing was altered in the constitution. Dutch-speaking Flanders and French-speaking Wallonia had their own territory, but no proper institutions. Belgium kept its unitary framework: one national parliament and government. Federalism was deemed perilous, a threat to national unity. Yet the creation of language zones also institutionalized the cultural divergence between the two regions. In the long run French lost its culturally dominant position in Flanders, ultimately fostering the emergence of different societies underpinned by completely separate media (Billiet et al., 2006: 914). This gradual cultural divergence was further enhanced by the policy of 'cultural autonomy'. Cultural autonomy, a claim of the Flemish Movement, implied that, as Flanders was recognized as a Dutch-speaking region, the Dutch or Flemish community should be able to decide for itself on matters such as language, culture, arts and so on, without going as far as federalism. And as well as having different languages, Flanders and Wallonia differed in another aspect: Wallonia was a predominantly leftist, socialist region, whereas the Catholic Party stood strongest in Flanders. As a result, the Flemish Movement had strong ties to Catholicism whereas regionalism in Wallonia (or the Walloon Movement) was closely linked to Walloon socialism.

Political parties would have to deal with this evolution. The decision to set up monolingual regions implied that the French-speaking political elite lost its legitimacy as a representative of Flemish constituencies. Instead, Flanders would be represented in Parliament by (albeit usually bilingual) Dutch-speaking politicians, a process that was completed well after the Second World War (Gerard, 1999: 169). Politicians elected in the Flemish constituencies came to see themselves as representing 'Flanders' as well as Belgium. Because of this the linguistic duality intensified inside the political parties. Statewide political parties – especially the Catholics and the Socialists – were increasingly confronted with the linguistic subdivision of the Belgian territory. Consequently, they needed to adjust the party organization in order (1) to allow the coexistence of two political elites, and (2) to deal with the linguistic territorial division. On top of this, the combination of the linguistic territorial subdivision and the Belgian electoral system encouraged regional rather than national electoral strategies. The territorial level for the distribution of seats – with a formula of proportional representation – was the electoral district (there were

30 of them for the Chamber of Representatives) and the provincial (that is, subregional) level. All electoral districts (apart from Brussels) and all provinces (apart from Brabant: partly Dutch-speaking, partly French-speaking and bilingual Brussels) were situated within one of the linguistic regions. Autonomist parties, Flemish or Walloon, could limit their participation in elections to electoral districts in only one of the linguistic regions. One such party to emerge in Flanders during the inter-war period was the Flemish National Party, the *Vlaamsch-Nationaal Verbond* (VNV). The party reacted strongly against the reluctance with which some of the language laws were observed, but combined this with an extreme right-wing agenda. It fielded candidates in the Flemish electoral districts and in Brussels. The presence of linguistically homogeneous electoral districts and of a relatively significant (extreme right-wing) Flemish nationalist party meant that the statewide parties increasingly competed in two-party systems rather than in a single Belgian one.

The electoral breakthrough of the VNV complicated the coexistence of two linguistic communities within each party. By 1936, the Flemish nationalist party was polling 13 per cent of the votes in the Flemish electoral districts. Its success came at the expense of the Flemish sections of the national political parties. As a result, the latter advocated a distinct Flemish course for their party in order to counter the Flemish nationalistic rhetoric of the VNV. Flanders, as a predominantly Catholic region, was the electoral backbone of the Belgian Catholic Party. The electoral swing in favour of the Flemish nationalists posed a special threat to the Catholics. Therefore, the Catholic Party was the first national political party to experiment with a 'dual' party structure, as early as 1936, after parliamentary elections that registered a significant swing from the Catholics to VNV in Flemish constituencies. The shock of 1936 convinced the Catholics of the need to equip themselves with a proper party structure which would enable them to regain lost electoral ground. In fact, before 1936 there was no such thing as a Catholic party, yet there were several Catholic organizations, for instance the conservative Federation of Catholic Associations and the Christian Labour Movement. Apart from a Catholic parliamentary party group, there was no organization worth mentioning that guided Catholic party politics on a day-to-day basis. It was decided at the end of 1936 to set up two party structures: the *Katholieke Vlaamse Volkpartij* (KVV) in the Flemish constituencies and the *Parti Catholique Social* (PCS) in Wallonia, each with its own name, organization and party president. In the elections of 1939, they presented separate electoral lists in the bilingual constituency of Brussels. Together, the KVV and the PCS made up the 'Catholic Bloc of Belgium', with a statewide leadership consisting of two party presidents and a statewide party executive. Only the party congress of the entire 'Bloc' could alter party statutes, including those of the PCS and the KVV. This way the KVV could present itself as a Flemish party against the VNV, while preserving unity with the francophone Catholics (Gerard, 1985: 485–90). The most important feature of the 1936 party reform was its confederate framework. The party statutes guaranteed both linguistic communities equal representation in the party executive, in fact leading to a reciprocal veto.

The creation of different language wings within a party before 1945 was not confined to the Catholics. The Socialists underwent a similar process, although this process was not linked to the rise of the VNV. The Socialists – the *Belgische Socialistische Partij* (BSP, Dutch name), *Parti Socialiste Belge* (PSB, French name) – was the oldest Belgian organized political party. The party structure dated from the party's creation in 1885. The party was organized as a cluster of local socialist federations, corresponding to the electoral districts, grouping in turn the socialist pillar organizations, such as trade unions. The party always emphasized its social agenda and treated the language issue as a problem of secondary importance usually not subject to binding party guidelines. In this way, the Socialists created some latitude to cope with internal disagreements on the matter. However, during the inter-war period the party structure was forced to address the coexistence of the two language groups within the party. Before 1919 (reform of male suffrage: one man one vote) the Socialists were relatively insignificant in Flanders. Thereafter, the party developed a substantial Flemish following, including figures such as Camille Huysmans, who championed Flemish demands for language laws (Hunin, 1999: 219–22).

Merely letting the Socialist representatives decide freely on language matters would not suffice, as tension within the party was building up on the language laws of the inter-war period. The party sought a preliminary internal compromise between its Flemish and francophone wings. Inevitably, this led to increasing Flemish and Walloon sensitivities within the party. Party statutes were altered to guarantee a regional balance inside the Bureau, the central party executive: Flemish and Walloon party federations were to be represented equally (Parti Ouvrier Belge, 1926: 98). Further adaptations were made in 1933 with the installation of a party presidency and a dual party secretariat. The party president and vice president were chosen from different linguistic communities. The secretariat – controlling all technical matters regarding the party – was now directed by two figures, one for each language group. As well as these checks and balances, the Flemish and Walloon sections were given some freedom of action. The Flemish or Walloon federations could meet separately and even hold separate party congresses. The Flemish federations did so in 1937, the Walloon sections (jointly with the francophone Socialists from Brussels) in 1938 (Claeys-Van Haegendoren, 1967: 319–20).

The above paragraphs have demonstrated that, at least in the Catholic and Socialist parties, the driving forces which led to the dissolution of a statewide party system and to Belgian political parties in the 1960s and 1970s were already at work before the Second World War.

Twenty years of respite (1945–65)

The political context

The first two decades after the Second World War brought a period of respite for the 'traditional' political parties. During the war, the radical wing of the Flemish Movement, including the VNV, turned once again to collaborating with the Germans. This discredited the entire Flemish Movement after the war. The radical wing was eliminated as the state repressed extreme right-wing collaboration forces after the war. Flemish nationalism was (for the time being) politically dead in 1945 (Witte and Van Velthoven, 1998: 131–5). However, a new Flemish autonomist party, the *Volksunie* (People's Union), was created in the mid-1950s but gained no more than a single seat in the parliamentary elections of 1954 and 1958. Linguistic tensions were manifold, yet until the 1960s remained subordinate to the ideological and confessional cleavage between Catholics and non-Catholics: the constitutional crisis concerning the position of King Leopold III (the 'Royal Question', 1945–50) or the 'School war' concerning subsidies to Catholic schools (1950–8).

Yet the confessional cleavage also had a linguistic undercurrent, for instance, in the case of the Royal Question. Being a predominantly Catholic and royalist region, Flanders favoured the return of King Leopold to power after the Second World War. The political left demanded abdication after the end of the war because the king refused to side with the allies in 1940, acting against the advice of his government. A referendum was called in 1950 to end the stalemate. A majority (57 per cent of all Belgians, 72 per cent in Flanders yet only a minority in Wallonia and Brussels) backed the king. A wave of protests in Wallonia ultimately forced Leopold to step down in 1950, which was seen in Flanders as a huge humiliation.

Renewed tensions between the language communities escalated at the beginning of the 1960s. The socialist 'strike of the century' of 1960 failed to bring down the government, largely because Flanders did not share the fervour of Wallonia's socialist trade unions. Furthermore, since the late 1950s Flemish politicians had been demanding a redistribution of parliamentary seats according to the latest census. As a result, Flemish constituencies would have more seats than Wallonia and Brussels combined. The fear of an *Etat belgo–flamand* became tangible: a widespread feeling among the French-speaking Belgians of being reduced to an irrelevant minority in the unitary state.

Political mobilization along linguistic lines was triggered by a new series of language laws, ironically proposed as the 'final solution' to the language quarrels. The language laws of 1962 and 1963 fixed the boundaries of the language zones, until then determined by decennial language censuses. The establishment of a fixed boundary prevented a further expansion of the legally bilingual Brussels area into the suburbs situated in Flanders. These laws were the most significant legacy of a coalition government of Catholics and Socialists (1961–5), headed by Prime Minister Lefèvre. However, this government also sought to prepare constitutional reforms, in particular the granting of cultural autonomy to the two language communities and the need for majorities within *each* language group in parliament for adopting certain types of legislation. Ultimately, these constitutional changes would not be approved until 1970, but they dominated much of the institutional debate in the 1960s.

The language laws in particular proved highly controversial. They provoked stiff opposition from French-speaking politicians in the capital, who supported extending the territory of the bilingual capital into Flanders (the decennial language censuses would have benefited the French-speakers: as a result of a process of suburbanization, many French-speakers moved from the predominantly French-speaking capital to the Flemish suburbs). The renewed attention to the language issue led to an upsurge of electoral support for ethno-regionalist parties, yet this time on *both* sides of the 'linguistic frontier'. The Flemish nationalist *Volksunie* repeated and even went beyond the electoral performance of the pre-war VNV: 3 per cent of the Flemish vote in 1958, 5 per cent in 1961, 12 per cent in 1965 and 17 per cent in 1968. A novelty in the elections of 1965 was the rise of an autonomist party also in Wallonia: the *Rassemblement Wallon* (RW) polled 3 per cent of the Walloon vote, gaining two parliamentary seats. Three years later, the RW managed to obtain 10 per cent of the vote in the Walloon electoral districts. Finally, the *Front Démocratique des Francophones* (FDF), a new francophone party, operated in the capital and strongly opposed the 1962–3 language laws. It polled 10 per cent in the Brussels electoral district in 1965 and 18 per cent in 1968 (Buelens and Van Dyck, 1998: 52 and 56–7). The successes of such francophone autonomist parties were unprecedented.

The response of the statewide parties: Adapting the national party structures

The themes of the ethno-regionalist parties differed according to the linguistic region. Whereas the *Volksunie* still campaigned for the cultural and political emancipation of Dutch-speaking Flanders in a state dominated by a francophone elite, Walloon regionalists were demanding some sort of constitutional check on the Flemish majority in Belgium. The FDF – which agitated against the Flemish claims for linguistic parity in Brussels – sided with the Walloons. From 1961 to 1968, the Belgian statewide parties lost tens of thousands of votes to autonomist parties; who presented themselves only to a fraction of the Belgian electorate, to one of the linguistic communities, or in a single electoral district (the FDF in Brussels). Apart from the presence of autonomist parties at the francophone side, this situation was in many ways a repetition of the 1930s, when the electoral swing to the Flemish nationalists dislocated the national party system. The responses of the statewide parties before and after the Second World War, in terms of both electoral strategy and internal party organization, showed substantial similarities. As far as the party structure is concerned, they can be summarized as (1) setting up checks and balances between French- and Dutch-speaking politicians within the central party structures, so that no language community would be capable of unilaterally dominating policy-framing, (2) creating two 'party wings' within the statewide party, each with some degree of autonomy and the ability to present the party to the Flemish or francophone electorate with a more out-spoken Flemish or francophone profile. However, in the aftermath of the Second World War (in which Flemish nationalism was heavily discredited) the parties centralized, if only briefly.

The Catholic Party

Driven by post-war Belgian patriotism, the Catholics opted in 1945 for a unitary political party in a unitary state. The KVV and PCS were replaced by the *Christelijke Volkspartij* (CVP, Dutch name) or *Parti Social Chrétien* (PSC, French name). The CVP-PSC defined itself as a 'Belgian' party: Politically, Flemish nationalism had disappeared and the party distanced itself from the Walloon Movement, which had a leftist image and thrived in the aftermath of the war. Regarding the party organization, the CVP-PSC abandoned much of the dual structure of 1936, though not all of it. The party was directed by a single party congress, National Committee (party executive) and party president. Yet the party executive was still divided evenly between Dutch- and French-speaking members, although the CVP-PSC gained many more votes in Flanders. Each language group of the National Committee – 'wings', as they were called – had its own president and could even meet separately. Yet, apart from the possibility of adjusting party programmes to the peculi-arities of each linguistic region, these wings lacked proper competences. However, the competences of the party wings would be extended whenever party unity was endangered by matters dividing Dutch- and French-speaking Belgians (Beke, 2005: 75–7).

   In 1951, just after the denouement of the Royal Question, the compe-tences of the language wings were extended as a gesture towards the Flemish part of the CVP-PSC. The next step was sparked by a growing assertiveness on the part of the Flemish CVP-PSC members of parliament. The Flemish CVP parliamentarians acted as a Flemish pressure group during the forma-tion of a new government, after elections in 1961. Before long plans were afoot for a new reorganization with further autonomy for the two party wings. The reasons for the heightened tensions in the National Committee were twofold. First, considering that Flanders was the electoral stronghold for the Catholics the emergence of a Flemish nationalist party was seen as a direct threat. The CVP-PSC had prevented the re-emergence of such a party by placing former nationalists on their lists for the elections of 1949. Yet, by the 1950s, the Flemish wing was becoming nervous about the renewed appeal of Flemish nationalism. In 1958 the Flemish CVP-PSC even consid-ered forging an electoral alliance with the *Volksunie*. Second, as a result of the language laws which were announced by the new coalition government elected in 1961, French–Dutch divisions would dominate the political agenda for some time to come. Consequently the two wings of the CVP-PSC had to reach a compromise in the National Committee on the language issue. This proved to be easier said than done. In the end, the result – the language laws of 1962–3 – sparked serious divisions between the two language groups inside the party. In its search for a final solution, the government then set its mind upon a constitutional reform to complement the language laws.

Amidst an escalation of linguistic tensions, the CVP-PSC suffered severe losses in the 1965 elections. The immediate response was a further loosening of the national party structure by the end of 1965. Each wing could advance its own opinion on a wide range of political issues, especially those relating to linguistic quarrels. The reform of the party structure was inspired by *constitutional* proposals of the CVP-PSC according to which the Flemish and francophone communities in the state should be able to decide separately on matters regarding culture and language (Beke, 2005: 363, 396, 444 and 464–71). In parallel, and as in 1936, the party could once again speak with two voices. This arrangement made it all the more difficult to reach an understanding in the National Committee whenever the viewpoints of the Dutch and French speakers were opposed. The issue of dividing the bilingual Catholic University of Leuven/Louvain led to a breakdown in the National Committee in February 1968. The Flemish wing opposed the presence of a francophone section (Université Catholique de Louvain) within the city of Leuven (situated in the Flemish linguistic region), whereas the French party wing strongly defended it. Ultimately the bilingual university split into two sections and the francophone section was moved 30 km to the south across the linguistic border (to the city of Louvain-la-Neuve or 'The New Louvain'). Parliament was dissolved over the matter and the two party wings decided to present themselves as separate political parties at the polls. A bilingual CVP-PSC list in Brussels was countered by a single PSC list. Indeed, the drive for the 1968 split was a chiefly francophone one (CRISP, 1970: 4–10). The French speaking wing felt uncomfortable being part of a national party now that the Flemish wing had overruled the francophone veto in the National Committee.

With hindsight, February 1968 was a watershed in the process of breaking up the statewide parties along linguistic lines. The end of the unitary CVP-PSC set a powerful precedent for other statewide parties. Yet matters were not that clear in 1968. Unable to satisfy both opinions on the Leuven question, the National Committee of the CVP-PSC ceased to exist. CVP and PSC were to be fully autonomous political parties, but, as in 1936, a statewide association was retained. A statewide president, with a statewide party study centre and party secretariat, encompassed both parties. Immediately after the elections, CVP and PSC were anxious to cooperate, as the largest parliamentary group traditionally nominated the Prime Minister. In 1969 both parties called party congresses to confirm the autonomous course of February 1968. The new CVP-PSC structure – with a common link, albeit minimal – was an adaptation of the party structure to the Belgian bifurcated party system following the success of ethno-regionalist parties in Flanders, Brussels and Wallonia. The framework of the state, on the other hand, remained unitary.

The Socialist Party

Like the Catholics, the Socialists were not very keen on keeping up a high regional profile after the Second World War, especially on the Flemish socialist side. The Socialist Party maintained the pre-war organizational reforms, such as the possibility of separate congresses, but the desire of Flemish socialists to present themselves as 'Flemish' rather than Belgian was lukewarm. For them, Flemish nationalism was tarnished by wartime Nazi collaboration. Walloon Socialists had fewer problems presenting themselves as Walloon, as the 'leftist' Walloon Movement was free from this prejudice. The francophone Socialists held a party congress of their own in 1947 and animated the post-war congresses of the Walloon Movement. The 1945 Walloon Congress, with an important Socialist delegation, even openly favoured federalism. Yet the Socialist national party structure was not really questioned. The language quarrels of the 1960s would change this. Because of the previously mentioned anxiety about the Flemish demographic and increasingly also economic strength in the state, a Walloon regionalist party emerged, demanding federalism. This was particularly threatening to the Walloon Socialists, as many Walloon regionalists originated in the *Mouvement Populaire Wallon*, a pressure group espousing both federalism and socialist economic reforms, founded by the socialist trade unionist André Renard. Overt militants of Walloon regionalism were excluded from the Socialist Party in 1964 (Falony, 2006: 81–7). The Socialists suffered severe losses in the 1965 elections. On top of this, the internal difficulties mounted as the Socialist Party had to present its opinion on the constitutional reform initiated by the Lefèvre government (see above).

A congress seeking to unite the language wings on the issue of constitutional reform failed. A further plan advocating regional devolution was accepted in 1967 at separate congresses of the Flemish and Walloon federations. The quest to devolve socio-economic autonomy to the Regions (Flanders, Wallonia and later also Brussels) as opposed to two language communities was indeed driven by the Walloon Socialists, as they wanted to obtain socio-economic instruments to revamp their decaying industries. However, the party statutes had been modified a few years earlier: as from 1963 half the party executive was nominated by the Flemish and Walloon federations, the other half by the (unitary) party congress. Party reform and party drafts for a new constitutional framework often came at the same time, as they were frequently prepared by the same committees. The Walloon congress of 1967 decided to create a 'Comité Permanent des Fédérations

Wallonnes du PSB': a permanent committee for concerted Walloon action, distinct from the statewide party bureau or executive (Geldolf, 2006: 209 and 211–16). The impetus for internal regionalization was thus predominantly francophone.

However, in Brussels, where numerical strength favoured the francophones, the Flemish Socialists quit the bilingual constituency party. A row over drafting the Socialist list in the 1968 elections – Flemish candidates were placed in inferior positions – led to a split in the Brussels federation. The Flemish Socialists presented themselves as 'Rode Leeuwen' ('Red Lions': red for socialist, the lion refers to the Flemish anthem and crest) with a list of their own in the Brussels electoral district. The party was able to confine the schism to the capital, recognizing henceforth two Socialist federations in Brussels (Mares, 2006: 63–71). The final element in restructuring the party consisted of a dual party presidency. When Léo Collard planned to step down as party president, Flemish federations claimed his succession. All presidents since 1945 had been francophones, with Flemish vice presidents at their side. Unable to reach an understanding, the Flemish and the Walloon federations decided in 1971 that each should separately choose a president. The two presidents would jointly run the party. The BSP-PSB thus entered the 1970s as a national party, but its organization gravitated towards bifurcation.

The Liberal Party

The Liberal Party (traditionally secular and business-oriented), the smallest of the three statewide parties, was also the last party to organize itself as a structured party. Membership cards were only introduced after the Second World War (D'Hoore, 1989: 88). It was not until 1961 that the loose federation of liberal electoral associations and members of parliament was transformed into the *Partij voor Vrijheid en Vooruitgang* (PVV, Dutch name) or *Parti de la Liberté et du Progrès* (PLP, French name). As long as the liberals lacked a solid party leadership, there was little problem of balancing the two languages communities at the top of the party. Besides, the Flemish influence in the party was considerably smaller than in the Socialist Party or the Catholic Party. The liberals had their grass roots among the francophone elite of the capital and other major towns. In Flanders, the Liberal Party was until the 1960s the last refuge for those politicians and voters who rejected the enforcement of Dutch as the official language in public affairs. In the 1971 elections liberals were still openly seeking votes among the French speakers living in Flanders (Boeynaems, 1972: 252, 257 and 268). As Brussels francophones dominated the party, the Liberals were not very fond of territorially fixed language laws, advocating national unity and 'linguistic freedom' instead. However, it would be a mistake to describe the party as unanimously opposed to the cause of Flemish emancipation. The Flemish Movement comprises some liberal pressure groups. Although the party leadership usually belonged to francophone Brussels circles, in 1951 – after the

Royal Question – it was agreed to rotate the presidency of the party on a linguistic basis (D'Hoore, 1989: 87).

In October 1961 the Liberal Party transformed itself into the PVV-PLP amidst rising tensions among Flanders, Brussels and Wallonia. Apart from creating a centralized party organization, the Liberals renewed their party programme in order to attract conservative Catholics. With regard to the language laws of the Lefèvre government and its planned constitutional reforms, the PVV-PLP staked everything on Belgian unity, opposing all proposals for devolution or federalism. The refusal to help the government in its plan to change the constitution was a matter of electoral strategy – the PVV-PLP withdrew from the negotiations just before the 1965 elections – but it also enabled the Liberals not to take a stand themselves. All internal dissension over the matter was to be avoided, because of the campaign in favour of national unity. Yet the Flemish Liberals supported the policy of the Lefèvre cabinet. They were certainly not pleased with the 'linguistic compromise' which the PVV-PLP leadership imposed at the party congresses of Liège (1966) and Knokke (1967). This compromise scaled back the 1962–3 language laws. However, the entire operation – the creation of the PVV-PLP and the adoption of a unitary stand – was conducted by a Flemish party president, Omer Vanaudenhove. Electoral success also helped contain the language issue. The 1965 election brought an overwhelming victory for the party, doubling its score of popular vote. The planned constitutional reform was stalled, a new coalition of CVP-PSC and PVV-PLP (1966–8) focused on economic affairs. When this government fell in February 1968 over the split of the Catholic university in Leuven, the PVV-PLP hoped for a repetition of 1965 and campaigned for national unity in an election dominated by the French–Dutch language issue (and the split of the CVP-PSC). The gains that were hoped for did not materialize and the status quo was seen as a defeat. As Belgian unity clearly was no longer a vote winner, internal criticism of the 'linguistic compromise' soon emerged and regionalist sympathies increased within the party.

After the 1968 elections, a centre-left cabinet composed of CVP-PSC and Socialists and headed by Flemish Catholic Prime Minister Gaston Eyskens (1968–71) sought to implement the constitutional reform previously outlined by the Lefèvre government. Since the government lacked the required parliamentary majorities to amend the constitution, it required the support of the Liberal opposition. The Flemish Liberals, unlike in 1965, were determined to cooperate on such a reform. National party congresses in 1969 and 1970 were unable to find common ground. The proposed boundaries of a future bilingual 'Brussels region' divided Flemish and francophone Liberals. When the matter was voted in parliament, the former sided with the government, the latter against it. The divisive issue had far-reaching effects for the PVV-PLP, because traditionally Brussels was a Liberal stronghold. The francophone Liberals in Brussels were staunch supporters of an enlarged bilingual region and strongly opposed the fixed language frontiers of 1962–3. Uneasy about their inferior position, the Flemish Liberals left their bilingual Brussels federation. They created a federation of their own at the end of 1969, nicknamed the *'Blauwe Leeuwen'* (Blue Lions), following the Socialist example. The PVV-PLP was now confronted with the same problems as the other two statewide parties: stalemate at the top of the party regarding language matters (as with the CVP-PSC in February 1968) and a split in Brussels (as with the BSP-PSB in the 1968 elections). The answer was a speedy transformation of the centralized party structure.

Omer Van Audenhove, figurehead of Belgian unity, stepped down as president in 1969. That year, Flemish, Walloon and Brussels Liberals were equally represented in the party leadership, and were also allowed to meet separately. After the Flemish Liberals backed the government in 1970 in its decision to confine the territorial borders of the Brussels capital region to 19 municipalities the (now merely francophone) Brussels federation, in retaliation, cut its ties with the statewide party. The francophone Brussels federation steered its own course, whereas the Flemish and Walloon federations created new structures of their own. Because the Brussels federation was so important, the PVV-PLP developed into a federation of three wings instead of two, unlike the other statewide parties. A permanent committee of the Walloon federations was created in 1970, followed in mid-1971 by the appointment of distinct presidents and executives for the Flemish and Walloon sections. A 'final' reform of the statewide party statutes was announced but shelved for the time being. In spite of the disintegration of the statewide party level, the PVV-PLP went to the polls in November 1971 as a statewide party. Both wings (PVV in Flanders, PLP in Wallonia) had their own language programmes, but the overall party manifesto was still statewide, with the exception of Brussels, where the francophone federation competed against a bilingual PVV-PLP list (Prevenier and Pareyn, 1989: 333–40; Prevenier, 1989: 341–9).

The 1970 constitutional reform and the dissolution of the statewide party structures (1972–8)

Political context

The elections of November 1971 ended the parliamentary legislature of 1968–71, which centred on the issue of constitutional reform. The reform was considered by its key framer, Prime Minister Eyskens, as the final move to heal the division between francophone and Flemish Belgians. The 1970 reform granted cultural autonomy to the language communities – a Flemish demand – and protected the francophone minority against a Flemish majority. The latter was accomplished by a range of institutional innovations: (1) governments were to be composed equally of Dutch- and French-speaking politicians; (2) members of both houses of parliament were assigned to a

Dutch or a French 'language group', according to the region in which they were elected; (3) three quarters of each language group could halt the law-making process whenever a proposal was deemed to harm its interests; (4) basic laws regarding relations between Flemish and francophones were to be approved by a majority in each language group, in addition to an overall two thirds parliamentary majority.

The language groups in parliament served as cultural (legislative bodies) with the aim of enacting 'cultural policies' for the French and Dutch language communities. As such, their creation complied with earlier legal measures which established a complete separation of the Dutch- and French-speaking broadcasting systems (1960) and split the national education and cultural ministry into two ministries for culture and education (1961). Hence, the reforms of 1970 transferred legislative competences in culture and languages from the parliament as a whole to the assembled Dutch and French language groups of both houses of parliament, known as 'Cultural Councils'.

Apart from a proper territory and a legislature made up of members of the national parliament, the linguistic communities lacked proper institutions or financial resources. Yet as well as the Cultural Councils of the two communities, the 1970 constitution envisaged the creation of three 'Regions' (Flanders, Wallonia and Brussels). As indicated above, regions with a form of socio-economic autonomy primarily responded to the demands of the Walloon Movement, which hoped that proper institutions for economic policy would counter the decline of Wallonia's outdated industry. Eyskens envisaged that Regions would remain clearly subordinate to the centre; hence they would provide for a form only of economic devolution. The creation of Regions was a concession to Walloon pressures and secured Walloon support for the parallel creation of Communities, a Flemish demand (Martens, 2006: 771). The 1970 reform did not envisage federalism, as Eyskens admitted (De Ridder, 1989: 248). Only afterwards did it become obvious that this was just the first of a series of constitutional reforms leading to a federalized Belgium. According to most political actors of that time, the 1970 reform was no beginning: it was the final stage of a reform process. In the words of Eyskens, it was a solution 'meant to last for 30 years'.

The constitutional strategies to resolve the language quarrels (language parity in the government, separate French- and Dutch-speaking ministers for education and culture, language groups inside parliament) resembled the checks and balances at the top party echelons. The Cultural Councils, composed of central parliamentarians from the two language groups, could be compared with the autonomous party wings. Party change and institutional adaptation were clearly linked. Growing intra-party dissension in the 1960s was accelerated by the need for the statewide parties to present their plans for the pending constitutional reform. As the latter was deemed as good as finished in 1970, it was not unrealistic to consider that the internal adaptation of the statewide parties had been completed also. The constitution created linguistic checks and autonomy within the framework of still central institutions. Similarly, the three statewide parties preserved a national dimension in the November 1971 elections. The BSP-PSB was a fully national party, albeit with a dual leadership and two Brussels federations. Nominally, the PVV-PLP was still a unitary party, albeit with a rebellious francophone federation in Brussels. Since 1968, the CVP and PSC presented themselves as separate forces, but retained a common structure with a national CVP-PSC coordinating chairman. Even a bilingual CVP-PSC list was presented in Brussels. Yet the dissolution of the party system went on. By the time of the next parliamentary elections in March 1974, the national structures of the CVP-PSC and PVV-PLP had been dissolved. At the end of 1978, the BSP-PSB was torn in half. What had happened?

The parliamentary elections of November 1971 were another disappointment for the statewide parties. Neither the majority parties (Catholics and Socialists), which brokered a constitutional solution, nor the PVV-PLP opposition gained ground. The francophone PLP wing even lost heavily. By contrast, all autonomist parties grew stronger. The *Volksunie* polled 20 per cent of the Flemish vote, *Rassemblement Wallon* a similar share of the Walloon vote. The FDF even obtained 30 per cent of the vote in the Brussels electoral district. The 'national' compromise did not pay off at the polls at all. Future constitutional settlements would require negotiations between two language communities as much as or even more than between political parties. The 1970 framework institutionalized this requirement by prescribing majorities in each language group for significant constitutional reforms. It goes without saying that such a position is anything but comfortable for a political party with two distinct wings, who present themselves at election times to only one of both language communities. The entire decade after the 1970 reform was dominated by ongoing institutional negotiations, which explains why the drive for dissolving the national parties did not cease.

Furthermore, if each new problem dividing the Dutch and French communities could trigger a party split, an equivalent incentive to take a 'Belgian' stand was lacking. Each 'national' solution was open to criticism from the ethno-regionalist parties, stressing how 'the other side' had benefited from it. Only in the bilingual Brussels electoral district could politicians hope to profit from a 'unitary' position, gaining both Flemish and francophone votes. Prime Minister Vanden Boeynants did so in 1968, with a CVP/PSC list in favour of Belgian unity. But everywhere else close ties with the other language community were no help against the ethno-regionalist campaigns of the *Volksunie* or *Rassemblement Wallon*. Formally severing ties with the national party structure was a strategy to regain some of the electorate lost to the autonomist parties. Besides, although a government needed only a simple parliamentary majority to survive, the mandatory linguistic parity requirement secured the presence of francophones inside government, whether or not they hung on to the national party structures. One of the – unintended – consequences of the 1970 reform was thus the accelerated end of 'Belgian' party politics.

The split of the statewide parties

Within a year of the 1971 elections, the national structures of both the CVP-PSC and the PVV-PLP came to an end as domestic politics was dominated by the failure to conclude the constitutional reform: the special majorities that were needed to establish the Regions were lacking. After yet another electoral success for the *Volksunie*, the CVP chose to change course: Wilfried Martens was elected party president in March 1972. An overt federalist, his elevation to the presidency aimed at regaining votes lost to the Flemish nationalists. It marked a profound change in strategy for a party which still avoided the word 'federalism' in its party platform. By the end of the year, the new leadership of the CVP made it clear that the 1970 reform signified merely a first step in transforming the state. As a result of this change of course and of other problems pitting francophone against Flemish viewpoints, Prime Minister Eyskens resigned in November 1972.

The PSC had also changed its strategy in 1972. Traditionally, the PSC stood for Belgian unity. A new party president, Charles-Ferdinand Nothomb, now announced a 'Walloon' stand. Otherwise the PSC would get stuck between the RW and the federalist CVP of Martens. Nothomb called for deliberations of all francophone parties or party wings to counter the Flemish demands. With regard to the CVP, the PSC wanted parity instead of being the junior partner. Nothomb opposed the dominance of Flemish politicians in the remaining national CVP-PSC structures and provoked the resignation of the national CVP-PSC coordinating chairman Robert Houben. The political crisis of November 1972 served as pretext for removing Houben, since the CVP had caused it (Martens, 2006: 107–12). Houben was not replaced. The end of the national CVP-PSC presidency came to symbolize the end of formal links between both parties. Yet Martens and Nothomb still presented a common electoral manifesto in 1974, a common secretariat existed until 1979, and – according to Nothomb – there had been plans to appoint a new national chairman (Nothomb, 1987: 93–104, 127, 163). However, those plans never materialized, as the constitutional disagreements between Flemish and francophones escalated towards the end of the 1970s.

The national PVV-PLP suffered a similar fate. The francophone PLP wing lost heavily in the 1971 elections and responded by embracing federalism and, like the PSC, defended a Walloon position. Both the PVV and the PLP constituted themselves as fully autonomous party wings in 1972. PVV chairman Willy De Clercq called it 'adapting to the reality of regionalization'. This decision is usually marked as the end of the PVV-PLP; however, the break-up happened a few years later. As with the end of the statewide CVP-PSC, the demise of the statewide PVV-PLP was meant to be only a temporary solution. After the 1972 reform, the PVV and PLP were technically still part of a statewide structure. The PVV-PLP held a national congress that year. It turned out to be the last, as a planned congress to devise new national statutes was cancelled at the end of 1975. Up to 1976 the francophone Pierre Descamps acted as the national PVV-PLP president, yet both wings were fully independent parties by that time (Govaert, 1995: 5–14). The fall of the Eyskens government in 1972 led to another schism. When the Liberals participated in the new Leburton government, the Brussels French speaking Liberals severed their remaining ties with the PLP in January of 1973 to form a party of their own, the Parti Libéral Démocratique et Pluraliste (Liberal Democratic and Pluralist Party). Whereas the CVP-PSC had split into two, the Liberals now had three 'regional' branches (Prevenier, 1989: 349–50).

Seeking to regain the ethno-regionalist vote was a common motive during these operations. The CVP hoped to placate the voters of the *Volksunie*, seen as CVP dissidents (Platel, 1979: 71). The PSC and PLP did their best to make overtures to the *Rassemblement Wallon*. The PSC lost many Catholics to the RW with the split of the University of Leuven/Louvain in 1968 and hoped for their return after loosening its ties with the CVP. An attempt at uniting PSC and RW in a single party failed in 1976. Instead the right wing of the RW merged with the Walloon PLP that year, creating the PRLW. With the founding of the PRLW, any reference to a statewide Liberal party disappeared (D'Hoore, 1997: 17 and 23). Governing with the autonomist parties was another strategy to reduce their appeal. The RW was in government from 1974 until 1977, the *Volksunie* from 1977 until 1979 and the FDF from 1977 till 1980. They all lost votes because of this, especially the RW in 1977 and the *Volksunie* in 1978.

The dissolution of the Catholic and Liberal statewide parties in the 1970s was a gradual process, without a clear moment marking the 'conclusive' split. The end of the Belgian Socialist Party is a somewhat different story. Despite electoral losses to the regionalists and an overt division in Brussels, the BSP-PSB managed to maintain its statewide unity until after the constitutional reform of 1970. Its sudden split in October of 1978 was radical, as Flemish and francophone Socialists severed all formal links at once. The rupture between the two language groups in the BSP-PSB coincided with a renewed attempt to 'conclude' the 1970 constitutional reform since the three Regions – Brussels, Flanders and Wallonia – still existed only on paper (despite efforts to implement Regional in addition to Community devolution in 1970). By 1976, all political parties had presented fresh plans for devolving powers to the Regions, paving the way for federalism (Leton and Miroir, 1999: 126). After early elections in April of 1977, a new coalition of CVP-PSC, the Belgian Socialists and the Flemish and Brussels regionalists (*Volksunie* and FDF) vowed to resolve the pending constitutional problems. Matters had moved on since 1970: the so-called 'Egmontpact' of 1977 envisaged the extension of Community competences, the creation of separate executives and administrations for the Communities and Regions, and in the case of the Regions also the establishment of directly elected assemblies. This was to be complemented with a reform of the Senate and the institution of a 'court of arbitration', an embryonic constitutional court (CEPESS, 1977: 293–303). The plan was controversial in Flanders, despite the support of the *Volksunie*. Pressure mounted on the Flemish parties to alter parts of the 'Egmontpact', eliciting counter-moves from the francophone side. This put the coalition and the sole national party in it, the Belgian Socialists, in jeopardy.

An important reason for the prolonged unity of the Belgian Socialist Party was the antagonism, ever since 1945, between the Flemish Socialists and the Flemish nationalists. Yet in 1977 the new Flemish co-president of the BSP-PSB, Karel Van Miert, chose to stress Flemish interests when negotiating the Egmontpact. The pact faced growing criticism from the Flemish Movement, which claimed that it contained too many concessions to the French-speaking fringe of Brussels. The Flemish hesitations greatly annoyed Van Miert's francophone colleague André Cools (Falony, 2006: 136–8). Party co-president Cools craved for the realization of the pact. The Walloon Socialists cherished hopes of being the dominant political force in the Walloon Region. Ultimately, for Cools a Walloon Region was more important than preserving the national unity of the party since the Flemish wing sided with the *Volksunie* and the CVP when it came to renegotiating the Egmontpact. Furthermore, since the Socialists were the largest party in Wallonia, Cools was quite certain that they would be needed to negotiate further constitutional reforms. So, when the government fell in October of 1978, the pact still in limbo, his decision was swift. The francophone Socialists cut their ties with the Flemish wing and created the *Parti Socialiste* (PS), covering Wallonia and the francophone Brussels federation. The Flemish wing, faced with a fait accompli by Cools, eventually changed its name to *Socialistische Partij* (SP) in 1980.

The sudden decision of Cools to stand alone ended an intra-party momentum towards extending the competences of the party wings. In 1974, the Flemish wing created its own permanent committee (the Walloon Socialists had had one since 1967), anticipating the emergence of a Flemish Region. Both committees were recognized by the party statutes in 1977 (Geldolf, 2006: 507–16). External talks concerning devolution to the Regions were connected with intra-party ones: both wings managed to present a common institutional programme in 1976 (Ceuleers, 1977: 169–70; Brepoels, 1981: 294). The institutional dynamic affected the BSP-PSB in a further way, as was apparent in the lead-up to Egmontpact. Ever since the 1970 reform established special majority requirements, finding majorities within each language group was at least as important as finding a common party platform. Therefore, when negotiating the Egmontpact, the Flemish party president conferred with his colleagues of the CVP and *Volksunie*, whereas in French-speaking Belgium Cools was doing the same with the PSC and the FDF, a situation which was difficult to maintain. At a separate Flemish congress in 1978 – the last one in the unitary party – the Flemish co-president hinted at a 'confederal' party reform. A few months later his suggestion was already outdated (Ceuleers, 1980: 376–82).

With the Socialist split of 1978 came an end to the existence of Belgian statewide party organizations. All former unitary parties have been replaced with 'party families' (see Deschouwer in this volume), each consisting of two 'sister parties'. Many elements still united the former Flemish and francophone 'party wings'. They shared a common ideology, were linked to the same 'pillar' (the trade unions or health care providers retained their statewide character), and since the 1970s collaborated in European party structures. Sister parties even shared the party headquarters inherited from the statewide parties, at least until the 1990s. Some party families even upheld single parliamentary party groups in the central parliament until the 1980s (Leton and Miroir, 1999: 101). The CVP and PSC had a common study centre until 2001. Furthermore, the first generation of politicians from the regionalized parties started their careers in unitary structures and still had many contacts with politicians from the 'other side'. So, since the 1970s Belgian governments have brought together the two parties from a 'party family' (De Winter and Dumont, 2006: 326–7). In other words, the federal government traditionally kept a symmetrical composition (except when an ethno-regionalist party were involved), notwithstanding the split of the statewide parties.

A federation without statewide parties

It was not until October 1980 that some of the proposed reforms of the Egmontpact were realized. Ten years after the 1970 reform, the Flemish and Walloon Regions finally came into being, and the Brussels Capital Region took off in 1988. And starting in 1985, the assemblies of the communities and the regions freely nominated their own executives, distinct from the national government, bringing the completion of the transition from economic devolution and 'cultural autonomy' to federalism even closer (Deschouwer, 2006b: 51). The timing of events can be of huge importance, especially when dealing with the evolution of political institutions (Pierson, 2004). The fact that a federal design was created only *after* the split of the statewide political parties had far-reaching consequences. The split of parties into linguistic segments signified a first step towards more self-rule for each of these segments, not just within the parties (which ceased to exist), but also within the state (which developed from a unitary into a multilayered state of which the linguistic segments were the building blocks). This is not to deny the relevance that state decisions may have had on developments within the party system or the parties (such as the extension of the suffrage, the choice of monolingual constituencies, or the consociational decision-making rules in the federal executive and parliament). However these decisions did not involve a direct 'migration' or 'decentralization' of competencies or authority from the centre to the regions.

Deprived of statewide parties with regional branches, Belgian politics lacked forces which aimed to uphold a 'statewide' stand. The odds were against a return of statewide parties and, with it, a state-centred or 'federal'

view on what the state should look like. To the Flemish Movement, to recre-
ate statewide parties would mean to 'restore a unitary Belgium' whereas the
constitutional checks and balances of 1970 guaranteed the francophone
minority a presence in the national government with or *without* national
parties. The duality of the party system deepened the bipolarity of the
Belgian state structure (Swenden and Jans, 2006: 889). Without electoral districts covering more than one language community, parties have few incentives left to present themselves to the entire country. The break-up of the
statewide parties has for that matter resulted in the disappearance of most
of the autonomist parties, apart from the *Vlaams Belang* in Flanders. Their
role has been assumed since the 1980s by whichever 'traditional' party was
in opposition at the statewide level. The PS in opposition took an aggressive
pro-Walloon stand during the 1980s, incorporating what was left of the RW.
When in opposition, the radicalized Flemish Liberals tried to do the same
with the *Volksunie* in 1992. At the same time the FDF forged an alliance with
the francophone Liberals. The CVP in turn radicalized its Flemish claims
after they ended up in opposition in 1999 by concluding an electoral cartel
with the N-VA in 2004, the successor of the *Volksunie* (De Winter, 2006:
33–9). The political parties which take part in a federal government majority thus nearly always face an opposition which *because* of its opposition role
is free to radicalize its Dutch/French grievances.

However, although the absence of statewide parties accelerated the federalization of Belgium it did not necessarily make policy-making at the
Regional or Community level more important than at the federal level. In
fact, the split in the party system prevented the emergence of two distinct
political elites accountable to different party organizations, each of which
with a task of overseeing politics at different levels of government. Instead,
single party presidents and executives oversee policy-making at both levels of
government. This helps to explain why, even after all regional parliaments
have been directly elected since 1995, regional coalition governments were
still part of *one* major multilevel package deal, determining the composition
of the statewide and regional governments (Swenden, 2002). Hence, parliamentarians are no longer the same at both levels, yet the party organization
is. The urge to guard the same majorities nationally and regionally has not
diminished, otherwise *'The same party (not its regional wing!) would be a partner in government at the federal level, and an opposition party at the regional level.
This leads to a strange but very logical paradox: the absence of federal parties
reduces the political autonomy of the regions'* (Deschouwer, 1999: 106; emphasis
added). Identical coalitions at both levels could be forged with relative ease
in 1995 and 1999, when the federal and regional parliaments were elected at
the same time (vertical and horizontal simultaneity). So, when the Flemish
ecologists were needed in 1999 to build a Liberal–Socialist majority in the
Flemish assembly, they were also invited to join the federal government.
Consequently, the francophone ecologists were brought in as well, in turn,

triggering their presence in the Walloon government. Since 2003 federal and regional elections are no longer held at the same time (although regional elections still coincide). The 2003 federal elections kept the Liberal–Socialist government in place, but the regional elections which followed in 2004 led to new majorities, with the Flemish Christian Democrats controlling the Flemish government, together with the Flemish Socialists and Liberals, while opposing the same parties at the federal level. Similarly, in Wallonia, the Liberals were kicked out of the Socialist–Liberal Walloon government and replaced with the Christian Democrats. Contrary to widespread fears, the federal coalition managed to survive this vertical party incongruence (different coalitions at the federal and regional levels), yet most politicians considered the situation as problematic (Delwit and Pilet, 2004: 64–76).

The problem of managing incongruent coalitions is not only made more complicated by the lack of distinct party organizations within each party for controlling policy-making at the federal and regional levels. In the Belgian bipolar party system, voters and parties hardly distinguish between federal and regional elections since each party covers only one of the linguistic regions. Therefore, political parties presented the same figureheads at the federal elections of 2003 and the regional elections of 2004. In 2003, 40 out of 118 members of the Flemish parliament took part in federal elections. But a year later, 67 out of 113 Flemish members of the federal parliament participated in regional elections (Fiers, Gerard and van Uytven, 2006: 103–6). And in the 2007 federal elections, 75 members of the Flemish parliament appeared on the ballot papers (Weekers et al., 2007: 9). As a corollary, party leaders designated ministers in the federal government that were elected in a regional assembly and vice versa, as was the case with one in three ministers after the 1999 elections (Fiers, Gerard and van Uyten, 2006: 103–6). This blending of the two institutional levels has led to the somewhat derisive remark that Belgium, despite 30 years of constitutional reforms, ended up with a highly complicated institutional framework, yet *in practice* still not a federal one.

Conclusion

The Belgian case defies the assumption of Chhibber and Kollman that shifts in authority from the centre to the regions or vice versa pre-date shifts in the party system. In Belgium, significant developments in the party system triggered the split of the statewide parties, which in turn brokered the federalization of the state. Hence the causality largely runs in the opposite direction. The end of the Belgian statewide political parties was clearly no answer to the transformation of Belgium from a unitary into a federal state. It was not until the start of the 1980s that Belgian politics truly started federalizing the country. By then, statewide parties had disappeared.

Belgian parties were confronted with a twofold challenge. First, ever since the creation of two homogeneous language zones, 'Flanders' and 'Wallonia' had gradually grown apart into two distinct cultural entities. Statewide parties, covering both linguistic regions, suggested consociational mechanisms in order to reconcile this duality. Long before the 1970s, Belgian statewide parties operated in a confederate way, since each language community had some degree of organizational autonomy (as distinct 'party wings') and matters of the statewide party as a whole were subject to a mutual veto power. Second, the electoral system made it possible for autonomist parties to mature, adding further pressure on statewide parties, which already faced increasing difficulties in aligning both party wings on linguistic issues.

The constitutional reforms which started in 1970 did not cause the dissolution of these autonomist or ethno-regionalist parties but merely accelerated the process of statewide party disintegration. Although historians tend to single out symbolic dates, such as 1968 in the case of the CVP-PSC, 1968 was merely the end point of an ongoing development. Parties were responding to centrifugal trends in society and the party system long before then. On the other hand, notwithstanding their split, parties continued to think in terms of 'political families' and in preferring symmetrical coalitions at the federal and regional levels. Furthermore, the Belgian case indicates how changes in the state structure can mimic mechanisms intended to enable the two language groups to live together under one and the same party roof. The consociational decision-making rules in the federal executive and parliament mimicked similar power-sharing mechanisms that were in place within the statewide parties.

The break-up of the statewide parties has perhaps led to two other, arguably less favourable, consequences. Statewide parties can provide a powerful element of 'linkage' or integration into the statewide party system (see Introduction). In Belgium, that element is missing. Furthermore, since the non-statewide parties in Belgium largely operate within monolingual electoral districts, they cannot be criticized for defending 'community selfish' viewpoints. Combined with the presence of linguistically split media, a *genuine* dialogue between the communities does not emerge until after federal elections, when parties from both language groups *must* work together to build a federal parliamentary majority and executive. This helps to explain why the formation of the Belgian federal government elected in 2007 took well over 150 days. If the purpose of a federal system is to provide *stability* or *sustainability*, surely the Belgian party systems and parties are fundamentally flawed (Filippov et al., 2004). Second, and unintentionally, the split of the statewide parties increased the ability of party executives to enforce party discipline. So long as the parties were not split, they had to live with the occasional 'rowdy' or disobedient behaviour of the members of one linguistic group. After they split, disobedient behaviour became much less common because it was more controllable. However, it does not take long before what is deemed a practice becomes a norm.

8
Authority in Multilevel Parties: A Principal–Agent Framework and Cases from Germany and Spain

Pieter van Houten

Introduction

Questions about authority relations in political parties operating at several levels of government are among the central concerns of this volume and of the larger research agenda on territorial party politics. These questions are manifold. For example, where does authority reside in such parties? Does authority vary by issue and context? How is authority exercised? To what extent do national party leaders control and influence the actions of party actors at the subnational level?

Answers to these questions are not straightforward, and require both theoretical and empirical analysis. This chapter aims to contribute to this research agenda in two ways. First, based on insights from a delegation or principal–agent approach, it provides a distinct interpretation of authority relations within multilevel political parties. An implication of this interpretation is that situations in which the interests of national and regional party levels diverge widely – and, thus, in which authority and influence are most contested – are the most appropriate and crucial cases for the analysis of such authority relations. Second, the chapter briefly presents two such case studies: the relation between national and state parties in Germany during negotiations in the early 1990s about fiscal and financial aspects of the German federal system, and the interaction between the Spanish and Catalan socialist parties during the negotiations about a new autonomy statute for Catalonia in 2005 and 2006. These cases indicate the strengths and limitations of control mechanisms available to national parties, and suggest factors that can help to further specify and develop the analytical framework.

Germany and Spain are both states with high levels of decentralization, but with very significant powers and control by the national level. This situation is, to some extent, mirrored by statewide parties in these countries. However, exactly how and to what extent the national leadership in these parties exercises control (or, conversely, regional party branches influence the national party) vary considerably by country and party. The case studies indicate that rules and practices within parties are important, but are not the only relevant factors shaping this variation. First, the territorial organization of the state is crucial, as it determines the channels available to a regional government and to regional party branches to influence decision-making at the national level. German regional party branches have more channels of influence available to them than Spanish regional party branches, which makes national party control more difficult in Germany. Second, the availability of other strategies to influence the incentives of party actors at the different levels needs to be taken into account. Such strategies may include negotiations with other parties to put pressure on a regional branch to adhere to the national party line (as happened in the Spanish case) or using parliamentary and decision-making procedures to influence the possibility of coordination across party levels (the German case).

The next section presents insights from a principal–agent perspective on the relations between different territorial levels within a party organization. The subsequent two sections discuss the German and Spanish cases. The final section summarizes the conclusions from these case studies and their implications for the further development of the analytical framework.

A principal–agent perspective on multilevel authority in parties

Authority in political parties, as in any other type of organization, is exercised in complicated, multifaceted and often informal and barely perceptible ways. One possible approach, which is followed by several contributions in this volume (and by other work on territorial party politics, e.g., van Biezen and Hopkin, 2006; Thorlakson, 2009) is to carefully list and analyse the wide variety of powers of and interactions between different levels in a party organization. This has obvious uses and advantages. It will give a good indication of actions undertaken by parties in a wide variety of situations (daily and routine activities, but also decisions in more particular situations), and it can partly rely on relatively readily available party statutes and practices. It is less clear, however, that such analyses will give a good sense of authority relations between the different levels in a party organization, if we mean by 'authority' the ability to influence and control another person or organization so that this person or organization acts in the interests of the controlling actor. The reason is that, if actions by the controlled or influenced actor are actually sufficiently close to the interests of the controlling actor, then no direct intervention or control mechanism needs to be enacted. In other words, a regional party branch undertaking many activities and making many decisions may appear to be very autonomous, but this may only be because – and so long as – its activities are in the interests of the national party.

This complication in identifying authority (or, more formally, the observational equivalence between the absence of authority and the successful delegation of authority) is a common insight from principal–agent (or 'delegation') approaches to the study of organizations. Delegating tasks and functions can be beneficial – and is indeed necessary – in an organization, but can involve costs for the person or unit delegating the tasks. Principal–agent frameworks analyse such delegation relations from a rational choice perspective (Kiewiet and McCubbins, 1991: Chapter 2; Bendor et al., 2001). Such a perspective can be applied to the analysis of multilevel party organizations, and I have elsewhere developed such a framework (van Houten, 2009). This section indicates the main characteristics of this framework, and discusses its implications for empirical analyses of party organizations.

A principal–agent framework assumes that one actor ('the principal') delegates functions to another actor ('the agent'). Applying this to multilevel party organizations, we assume that the national leadership of a statewide political party (the 'national party') is the principal, and the leadership of a subnational branch of this party (the 'regional branch') is the agent. This is a heuristic device, but seems a reasonable assumption. Political systems in Western Europe are largely 'nationalized' (Caramani, 2004), making a 'top down' approach a priori more sensible than a 'bottom up' one (which might be more useful to understand the historical formation of political parties; see Chhibber and Kollman, 2004). The framework, however, allows for the evaluation of this assumption. If its hypotheses about forms of control and conditions under which these are effective are not supported by empirical evidence in a particular case, then we can conclude that the national party is not the principal in this particular party organization.

We further assume that national party leaders are primarily interested in the party's performance in national elections, and the leaders of regional party branches in regional elections. Moreover, the regional leadership wants to avoid being removed, or overruled in other ways, by the national party leadership. Some autonomy for regional branches can have several benefits for the national party, as regional branches may be better informed and capable of mobilizing voters in the region, and may be seen as a more credible representative of regional interests and the regional electorate. This is particularly important in culturally, ethnically or otherwise distinctive regions. As a consequence, statewide parties can be expected to delegate more powers and competencies in such regions, as well as in more decentralized states.

However, delegation also runs the risk of regional branches acting against the interests of the party as a whole (thus generating 'agency costs' or 'agency slack'). Conflicts of interests between national party and regional party may involve different views on the utility of statewide versus regionally or locally specific political programmes (Müller, 2000), or competition about leadership positions (although this will depend on political career patterns; see Deschouwer, 2006a). Conditions under which conflicts are likely to be most pronounced are similar to those in which delegation is potentially most beneficial, namely, when regions are distinctive and/or have considerable political competencies. The crux of the issue is that, especially in politically distinctive regions, the national leadership may have a desire to control the branch as much as possible to avoid such costs, but has to give it considerable authority and autonomy to obtain benefits. This is the dilemma at the heart of all delegation relations (Kiewiet and McCubbins, 1991; Lupia and McCubbins, 2000).

In such situations, the nature of delegation depends on the ability of the national party to control or induce the behaviour of regional party branches, without sacrificing all possible benefits of delegation. Most importantly, delegation does not need to imply the abdication or transfer of authority. A principal can use various procedures and mechanisms to control agents, although such control will inevitably be imperfect, as control procedures are costly and it is necessary to provide agents with some autonomy in order to reap the benefits of delegation. The analysis of these procedures and mechanisms is at the core of principal–agent frameworks (Kiewiet and McCubbins, 1991). In the case of multilevel party organizations, control mechanisms can include the selection of regional party leaders or election candidates; the establishment of party rules and conventions, such as procedures for the approval of regional party programmes or government coalition decisions, or the creation of central party bodies to coordinate across levels; the use of financial arrangements to control party branches; and various sanctions against regional party actors seen to have acted against the interests of the parties. In short, a wide array of formal and informal institutional arrangements within party organizations can potentially serve as control mechanisms in the delegation relation between national party and regional branches. In addition, institutional arrangements outside party organizations, some of which can be (directly or indirectly) shaped by parties, can also be significant in shaping authority relations between party levels. Relevant arrangements may include state laws and regulations on parties and party finance (Van Houten, 2009), and the territorial organization of the state, that is, the various ways in which different levels of government interact in decision-making procedures.

Although this is a useful general framework, it needs to be further specified to generate more specific arguments and insights, particularly on the specific nature of control mechanisms. Empirical research is crucial for this. But what should empirical work primarily focus on?

As stated at the outset of this section, if the interests of national party and regional branches largely coincide on particular issues, then it will be difficult to determine authority relations in the party by focusing on activities by a regional branch on these issues. The branch may appear to be autonomous and in control, but this may simply be condoned by the national party because it is in its interests to do so. To put it in general terms, agency autonomy can be consistent with control by the principal in the framework presented here. Since this situation may describe many routine and day-to-day activities of party branches, the best strategy for empirical research related to this framework is not to document general competencies and activities of party branches. Instead, it is more useful to focus on specific episodes in which ultimate authority in the party organization is at stake, that is, when the interests of regional and national levels are in stark opposition. This is the motivation behind the selection of the case studies from Germany and Spain in the next sections.

Germany: Party coordination, the Bundesrat and financial issues

Germany is a federal state, but with considerable degrees of centralization. The German federal system is organized mostly along functional lines, which gives the national level decision-making competencies in many areas, although regional governments participate in most national-level decisions. On the other hand, based on the immediate post-war developments in Germany and the constitutional and regulatory framework under which political parties operate, German statewide parties appear to be relatively decentralized with most authority in the hands of subnational (regional and district level) branches.

German parties operate in a highly legalistic environment (Poguntke, 1994). The German constitution and state laws require, among other things, parties to be 'democratic', have implications for the composition of party assemblies and executive, and influence the financial management of parties (mostly through the regulation of public subsidies to parties). Highly relevant for multilevel party dynamics is the stipulation that candidate selection for elections should take place at the subnational level (Lundell, 2004). Germany's statewide parties have organizational structures that mirror the state structure, and regional party branches are formidable organizations (Detterbeck and Jeffery, this volume). These parties, however, are more centralized than this suggests (cf. Jeffery, 1999a: 136). The German Christian Democratic Party (CDU), which was formed in the immediate post-war period, was initially a relatively decentralized party, but over time the influence and organizational presence of the national party has increased considerably (Schmid, 1990). The Social Democratic Party (SPD) was more centralized from the outset in the post-war period, but also strengthened its central party headquarters over time.[1] Factors such as the increasingly centralized and coordinated nature of the German federal system, party finance, the personal influence and role of party leaders, the establishment of various formal and informal coordination mechanisms and forums, and other informal arrangements all played a role in this. One consequence of this, for example, is that national party leaders sometimes play a more important role in subnational coalition formations than formal party statutes indicate (Downs, 1998).

An important impetus behind the drive for more national influence and control within German parties is the participation of regions in the decision-making process at the national level, which is a peculiar feature of the German federal state. The Bundesrat consists of representatives of regional (*Länder*) governments, and is a co-legislator for a large proportion of national legislation. This not only allows regional governments – and, thus, regional party branches – a role at the national level, but also gives national party leaders a direct stake in regional (party) politics. This creates coordination challenges for parties, and raises questions about the authority and control within parties. Parties are obviously crucial actors in the national parliament (the Bundestag), where party discipline tends to be strong and governments generally command a majority for most pieces of legislation. Regional governments are typically composed of representatives of the regional branches of statewide parties, which are, therefore, also members of the Bundesrat. Consequently, parties have an incentive to try to induce and maintain party discipline between their national and regional organizations. Such party discipline is not guaranteed, however, as the interests of regional governments need not coincide with those of the national parties (Detterbeck and Jeffery, this volume).

The German statewide parties have established a whole array of arrangements to facilitate intra-party coordination and compromises in their Bundesrat activities (Renzsch, 1998; Leonardy, 2002; Swenden, 2004: 193–200). These include bodies consisting of all regional government representatives of the SPD or the CDU and some representatives of their respective Bundestag factions, which meet regularly to prepare and discuss issues related to plenary Bundesrat sessions; preparatory meetings by Bundesrat committees members from the same parties; and discussions by party members from both Bundesrat and Bundestag to prepare for sessions of the Concertation Committee (which meets if both chambers are not directly able to agree on a piece of legislation). There are also numerous other forums within each party in which national and regional politicians jointly participate. Leonardy (2002: 193) concludes that these mechanisms help to increase the influence of the national party, but that this influence is not absolute and is moderated by various other factors. In particular, in some instances regional interests diverge so strongly from national party interests that all these existing coordination mechanisms are not sufficient to induce regional party representatives to follow the party line.

Research on decision-making and voting behaviour in the Bundesrat concurs with this. The issue of 'party politics' in the Bundesrat has generated much debate in political and academic circles. Different strands in this debate have focused on the possibility that this will lead to blockades in times of 'contrasting majorities' (when the opposition party in the national parliament represents – through the regional governments in which it participates – a majority of votes in the Bundesrat) and the consequences of this for the German political system (Lehmbruch, 2000), on the ability of party discipline and coordination to facilitate the adoption of difficult and controversial pieces of legislation (Renzsch, 1999; Leunig, 2003), and on the influence of the Bundesrat on the content of legislation as a function of its partisan composition (Manow and Burkhart, 2006). All these arguments and analyses are predicated on the actual existence of party coordination across the two chambers of parliament, and, thus, between national and subnational levels in the party organizations. This coordination, however, is variable. Voting along party lines certainly happens, even if regional and party interests appear to be in conflict, but the extent varies over time and by issue and party (Jeffery, 1999a; Renzsch, 1999; Strohmeier, 2004; Swenden, 2004). For example, the Kohl government in the 1980s was largely able to keep the regions governed by its party on board in the Bundesrat, although this coordination was not easy and unwavering on some economic and financial issues. As Jeffery (1999a: 150) states, 'party-based coordination . . . helped to ameliorate and aggregate territorial interest divergences and filter them into the federal-level decision-making process'. In the 1990s, it appears that such party coordination became increasingly difficult (Jeffery, 1999a: 159).

Intra-party coordination is particularly difficult in the area of fiscal federalism, that is, issues related to how different levels of government are financed and the vertical (between national and regional levels) and horizontal (between regions) distribution of public revenues. On these issues, the territorial interests of regional governments often cut across party blocs, and are directly opposed to the interests of the federal government. As Swenden (2004: 333) indicates, in many situations 'Bundesrat members have pursued interests specific to a region when the fiscal position of their *Land* is at stake'. Party coordination in this area has indeed been limited throughout the postwar period (Renzsch, 1991). However, such coordination has occurred on occasions. For example, coordination between national and regional leaders within the CDU played a crucial role in the adoption of a substantial federal financial reform in 1955 (Renzsch, 1991: 164–8). Similarly, the Kohl government in the 1980s managed on some fiscal federalism issues to get regional governments to prioritize party interests, leading Wachendorfer-Schmidt (2003: 203) to observe that in this period 'party competition entered the fiscal equalization arena'. Nevertheless, it is clear that coordination along party lines on these issues is difficult and an enormous challenge for a party organization. Fiscal federalism issues therefore provide crucial case studies for analysing the nature of the principal–agent relations in a party and the limitations of national-level authority and influence. The remainder of this section discusses one such case: the post-unification reforms of fiscal and financial arrangements in the early 1990s.[2]

The integration of the new regions in Eastern Germany into the federal financial system was one of the most complicated tasks resulting from Germany's reunification. Economic and financial disparities between regions were now much larger than before, and some reform of the system was inevitable. Because of their difficulty and complexity, financial issues were not discussed in the forums established to deal with the implications of unification, but were negotiated directly between the federal and regional governments. The interests of regions (especially the 'old' regions in Western Germany) and the federal state diverged sharply in these negotiations. There was agreement that the new regions required financial support, but the question was how to distribute the financial burden of this. An important aspect of the financial arrangements in Germany is the so-called 'fiscal equalization scheme' (*Finanzausgleich*), which redistributes public revenues from richer to poorer regions. The richer regions in the West wanted to avoid having to transfer more revenues to other regions, or wanted this at least to be compensated by larger money flows from the central state to the regions. The poorer Western regions did not want to lose their transfers, and certainly did not want to contribute much to the financial transfers for the new Eastern regions. The federal government, on the other hand, had an incentive to get the regions to contribute as much as possible to these financial transfers, instead of having to raise taxes or borrow. It is also worth noting that, after 1991, the federal government coalition faced a Bundesrat in which the opposition parties could potentially block decisions if they coordinated their votes across the regional governments in which they participated.

The initial expectation was that the federal government (led by the CDU) would be able to dominate the negotiations, as it might be able to ally with the new regions and some of the poorer old regions (as it had often done in the past in negotiations about financial issues). The opposite happened, however. A final agreement was reached as part of the Solidarity Pact in March 1993. This agreement stipulated the incorporation of the new regions in the existing schemes with only limited changes. The main modifications were a change in the distribution of the sales tax revenues (in favour of the regions) and some minor adjustments in the fiscal equalization scheme. The federal government contributed by far the most to the financial transfers to the Eastern regions.

The regions achieved this by maintaining a common front against the federal government from the start of the negotiations in September 1992. Cooperation between Bavaria (governed by the CSU, a regional Christian Democratic party allied to the CDU and part of the 'government party' bloc) and North Rhine-Westphalia (NRW) (governed by the SPD, and representing the 'opposition bloc') played a key role in this. The initial common stance among the regions was forged by a reform proposal from Bavaria, which NRW supported. After long negotiations, involving a very different proposal from the federal government and various proposals by other regions, it was a variant of the original Bavarian proposal (again supported by NRW) which was accepted by the regions as their position, and subsequently by the federal government.

The common stance of the regions, facilitated by two large regions governed by different parties (Bavaria and NRW), made it impossible for the main statewide parties to coordinate along party lines and use the Bundesrat to impose their party positions on the various proposals. The parties tried to some extent to do this, but to no avail (Altemeier, 1998: Chapter 5; Wachendorfer-Schmidt, 2003: 217–26).[3] This seems a clear case of regional interests trumping party interests, indicating the limitations of the national parties' control over their regional branches in cases where regional and national interests differ significantly (and indicating the extent to which the national parties' role as principals is constrained).

It is necessary to take look more closely at this, however. This becomes especially clear when we compare these negotiations about a long-term arrangement (concluded in 1993) with the negotiations about the refinancing of the German Unity Fund in 1991 (Altemeier, 1998). This fund was established after unification to provide financial support to the Eastern territories until a permanent arrangement for the incorporation of these territories into the federal financial system was reached. A decision had to be made in 1991 on how to refinance this fund. The constellation of national and regional interests was essentially identical to the situation a year later (see above), as was the basic political situation in the Bundesrat (no majority for the federal government coalition). But the process and outcome were very different. Party considerations played a significant role in the negotiations, and an impasse along party lines seemed possible. An agreement was eventually reached when the federal government persuaded the SPD-led Brandenburg government to support its proposal.

A closer look at some differences between these two negotiations provides more nuanced insights into the prospects and limitations of party coordination in situations of conflicting interests. One relevant difference is the strategies of the federal government. In the 1992–3 negotiations, it stuck from the beginning to a proposal that was clearly aimed at trying to split up the regions. This was the outcome in the 1991 negotiations, but the government had been more strategic in the process leading up to this. The hard line from the government in 1992 helped to unite the regions early on in the process (Altemeier, 1998: 187–8). At the end of the negotiations, the government also appeared poorly prepared, leaving the regions' proposal as the only credible one, which it then accepted. A second difference is that there was a subtle difference in the political situation between the two negotiations, which led to different strategies, especially by the federal government. Although in both cases the federal government coalition lacked a majority in the Bundesrat (if voting were to occur along party lines), there was a small difference in its political constellation, which meant that the government parties had a majority in the Concertation Committee (which could be convened in case of disagreements on proposals between Bundestag and Bundesrat) in 1991, but not in 1992. This was one of the reasons that the government's strategy aimed and prepared for the eventual meetings of this Committee in 1991, while in 1992 it tried to avoid the issue going to the Committee by engaging from the beginning in direct negotiations with the regions rather than introducing its proposal through the Bundesrat (Altemeier, 1998: 207–8).

Although it is clear that the diverging financial interests of regions and the federal government were the primary reason for the lack of party coordination in the negotiations about the reforms to the fiscal federal arrangements in 1992–3, these other, more detailed factors are relevant for an understanding of the extent to which party coordination was tried and sustained in the negotiation process. The Spanish case study further reinforces the idea that conflicting interests as such are not a sufficient explanation for the lack of party coordination in this German case study.

Spain: PSOE, PSC and the Catalan autonomy statute

Since the reintroduction of democracy in the 1970s, Spain has become an increasingly decentralized and 'quasi-federal' state. Spanish statewide political parties have both shaped and had to adapt to these developments. Although to various degrees and in different ways, the two main parties – the conservative PP and the socialist PSOE – created territorial party organizations dominated by the national level (Fabre and Méndez Lago, this volume). The national level in these parties can therefore plausibly be considered the principal in the relation between national party and regional branches. But exactly how and to what extent do the central party and its leaders control the regional branches? What are the limits of this control? And if formal mechanisms are not available (or available to only a limited extent) – which, as we shall see, is the case for the Catalan socialists – how can national party leaders influence affiliated regional politicians?

This case study focuses on PSOE, the more decentralized of the two main statewide parties in Spain, and its relation to the Catalan Socialist Party (PSC). First, it briefly highlights the main elements of PSOE's territorial organization, which indicate that a combination of formal and informal mechanisms has facilitated central control over the party in spite of its federal structure. PSOE's relation with the PSC, however, differs from its relation with other regional branches, and has received less attention in the literature on PSOE's territorial party structure. PSC is a formally autonomous party, but has a stable affiliation arrangement with PSOE. As a result, PSOE has been able to influence, and to some extent control, the Catalan Socialist Party. This influence has formal elements (based on the agreement between the parties established in the 1970s), but is exerted largely through informal means. The negotiations about a new Catalan autonomy statute in 2005 and 2006, in which national and regional interests clashed, show that PSOE influence over PSC can be substantial.

The territorial organization of PSOE has been described and analysed in considerable detail elsewhere (see Méndez Lago, 2000, 2005, 2006; van Biezen, 2003: Chapter 4; Fabre, 2008; Fabre and Méndez Lago, this volume). The party has a federal structure, but the national leadership exercises considerable control over the various territorial layers of the party. This is reflected in the party statutes, and is reinforced by Spanish laws and regulations on political parties. For example, the national congress and executive committee need to approve candidates for national elections, while the congress controls party statute changes. The executive committee also needs to approve regional branch statutes, the outcome of regional leadership elections and (less directly) candidate lists and programmes for regional and provincial elections. It also controls the budgetary and financial management of the party. In addition, central party leaders have much influence over the choice of delegates to the party congress, and the congress has lost influence in the party as a whole. Furthermore, the party leader can influence the composition of the national executive committee. Thus, informal procedures reinforce the national-level dominance in the party, especially of the national party leader. The party's *consejo territorial* (territorial council), which was created in 1997, has not significantly changed this situation (Méndez Lago, 2006).

Regional party leaders can nevertheless be influential in the party. Some regional leaders – the so-called 'regional barons' – increased their influence in PSOE after it went into opposition at the national level in 1996 and Prime Minister Gonzalez stepped down as its leader (Méndez Lago, 2005, 2006). The absence of strong national leadership and authority derived from leading the national government, and their own external prestige due to their regional positions, gave these barons the resources to weaken the control and authority of the national level in the party. However, the influence of these barons decreased again after Zapatero became party leader, and especially after PSOE came back into national government in 2004. The formal structure and procedures in the party, backed by informal channels of control when the party is in government, make it difficult for regional branches to solidify their power.

The situation of the Socialist Party in Catalonia – a large and assertive region in the Spanish state – is an exception to this general picture of PSOE's territorial organization (Fabre, 2008). The PSC is not directly part of PSOE's organization, but affiliated to it only as an autonomous party. As a result, it should be in a stronger position to assert its autonomy vis-à-vis the PSOE.

The current PSC was founded in 1978, through a merger of the two branches of the older PSC (until then independent Catalan socialist parties) and the Catalan Federation of PSOE. It has a 'federal' agreement with the PSOE. The PSC operates in Spanish national elections as part of the PSOE, and has generally been the most successful party in Catalonia. It has been less successful in regional elections, however, where it usually came second behind the nationalist CiU party coalition. In general, PSC faced a problem familiar to many branches or affiliates of statewide parties in distinctive and assertive territories. As Keating (2001b: 152–3) puts it, the Catalan socialists 'have been torn between their attachment to their colleagues in Madrid and the need to compete within Catalonia', which has resulted in 'support for a moderate measure of Catalan nationalism within PSC, while criticizing Pujol [the CiU's leader] for attempting to monopolize nationalist virtue and suffering taunts from the nationalist parties that it is a mere branch office of Madrid'.

In the 1980s and early 1990s, when the PSOE formed the Spanish government, it had significant influence and dominance over the PSC (Roller and van Houten, 2003). The 'Catalan lobby' within the socialist faction in the Spanish parliament became gradually weaker. Being the main opposition party to the nationalist Catalan government, and the party's relative better results in national elections, strengthened the 'national' orientation and image of the PSC. Combined with internal dissent and weak leadership, this made it increasingly dependent on the PSOE. On several occasions the PSOE leadership pressured the PSC to compromise its position on the desired territorial structure of the Spanish state, for example, when PSC politicians refused to support a declaration of the Catalan parliament seeking recognition of Catalonia's right to self-determination in 1989. The strong position of the PSOE's leader Gonzalez, both within the party and in the wider public's image of the party, further reinforced the dominance of the national level.

It should be emphasized, however, that this influence was partly achieved through informal mechanisms rather than formalized institutional arrangements. It depended significantly on strong leadership at the national level, relatively weak party leadership at the regional level, the ability as governing party to provide the region and regional party with resources, and the ability to help the regional party achieve good election results (at least in national elections).

The efficacy of these mechanisms decreased in the course of the 1990s. First, after the 1993 national elections, the PSOE was forced to form a minority government with the support of, among others, the CiU (in return for which the Catalan government managed to obtain various concessions from the central government, for which the CiU could take credit). This put the PSC in an awkward situation as opposition party in Catalonia. While this threatened to weaken the PSC's position, it also provided it with an incentive to try to assert itself more as a Catalan party. Second, the PSOE lost the 1996 national election, left the national government, and faced the challenge of renewing and revitalizing the party (Méndez Lago, 2006). This further allowed the PSC to steer a more autonomous course. Third, in the person of Pasqual Maragall, the former mayor of Barcelona, the PSC now had a more popular leader than before. More than his predecessors, Maragall stressed 'regionalist' issues, such as the federalization of Spain and the need to revise Catalonia's autonomy statute. Thus, the influence of the PSOE over the PSC decreased significantly in this period.

Partly as a result of these changes, the PSC's fortunes in regional elections improved. It obtained the most votes, albeit not the most seats, in the 1999 elections, and then won the elections in 2003. After this election it formed a coalition government, in which also a radical nationalist party (the ERC) participated. The position of this government on various territorial issues diverged from the traditional PSOE positions, although these positions themselves – not least under the influence of Maragall and the PSC – were changing. In this same period the PSOE, now under the leadership of Zapatero, improved both its organizational vitality and its electoral prospects. In 2004, helped by the PP government's handling of the aftermath of the terrorist bombings in Madrid, it won the national elections and formed a minority government. The PSOE's support was now potentially useful again for the PSC, which gave the national party more influence.

This set the stage for discussions about the revision of the Catalan autonomy statute, that is, the arrangement, agreed in 1978, which forms the basis of Catalonia's autonomy and relations with the Spanish state. This discussion took up much of the Maragall government's time from 2004 on, and eventually led to its fall in June 2006 (Orte and Wilson, 2008). The revision of the Catalan autonomy statute was a highly controversial political issue in Spain. In combination with developments in the Basque Country (where the regional government tried to assert a right of self-determination for the region), it raised concerns about the future unity of the Spanish state or at least the commitment of Catalonia and the Basque Country – both relatively rich regions – to solidarity with other regions. These concerns were most vocally expressed and mobilized by the conservative PP, the main opposition party in Madrid. This all placed the PSOE leadership in a difficult position. The PSOE has an interest in good relations with, and good election results for, the PSC. On the other hand, public opinion outside Catalonia, pressure from the PP, and pressure from regional PSOE branches in other regions (especially in relatively poor regions, which had clear interests in the continued participation of Catalonia in financial equalization schemes) made a radical revision of the Catalan autonomy stature an unattractive prospect. But a quite radical revision of the statute was exactly what the Catalan government (which included the radical Catalan nationalist ERC and had to anticipate possible criticisms from the main opposition party in the region, the mainstream nationalist CiU) proposed.

After lengthy discussions between the various parties in Catalonia, the Catalan parliament approved – with an overwhelming majority (the only votes against were from the PP) – a draft for the revised statute in September 2005.[4] This version would have implied a considerable increase in Catalan autonomy. Its most salient aspects were the provision that Catalonia would be able to keep a much higher share of taxes raised on its territory than before, and the recognition that Catalonia is a 'nation'. Perhaps surprisingly, in early November 2005, the Spanish parliament (led by PSOE votes) also approved this draft. However, this approval was conditional on the draft being endorsed as 'constitutional' by the relevant committee. Since especially the clause that Catalonia is a 'nation' seemed inconsistent with the Spanish constitution, this endorsement was at best uncertain.

Several months of further debate and negotiations at the national level then ensued (Orte and Wilson, 2008). Although this was done in the shadow of the 'constitutional checks' of the proposed statute, this process was driven mostly by political rather than constitutional concerns and calculations. This is exemplified by the fact that the Spanish parliament subsequently approved the revised draft, allowed a referendum on this draft to go ahead in Catalonia, and implemented the new statute before this new draft was checked for its constitutional credentials. The debates and negotiations led to a revised draft, which watered down the statute on several fronts. Most significantly, it reduced the tax shares that Catalonia can keep and it omits the clause declaring Catalonia a 'nation'. This version was approved by the Spanish parliament in March 2006, with PSOE and PSC representatives voting in support. Subsequently, this revised draft was put to a referendum in Catalonia in June 2006.[5] The PSC campaigned in favour of the draft approved in the Spanish parliament, as did the CiU. On the other hand, the ERC, one of the PSC's coalition partners, did not support the new draft. An overwhelming majority voted in favour of the new statute in the referendum, although with a relatively low turnout.

Most interesting from this chapter's perspective is the question why the PSC supported the revised draft of the statute. The Catalan government (led by the PSC) had invested much in the original draft, and the endorsement by the PSC of the revised draft led to the break-up of the government and early elections.[6] The strategies and pressure from the PSOE leadership certainly contributed to the change in the PSC position, and involved both 'formal' and 'informal' means and channels.

Formally, the PSOE utilized a basic aspect of the agreement between the PSOE and the PSC established in the 1970s, which stipulates that the PSC is autonomous in the Catalan arena while the PSOE sets the agenda for the socialist camp in the Spanish parliament. Thus, although the PSOE leadership appeared to endorse the PSC's position when the new autonomy statute was discussed in Catalonia, it was under no obligation to continue doing this once the issue had moved to the national arena. As the PSC could not, of course, prevent the transfer of the debate to the national arena (indeed, it had to be approved at the national level to be implemented), this established division of labour in the Socialist camp puts the national party in a strong position.

Furthermore, Zapatero negotiated directly with the CiU, the main opposition party in Catalonia, whose support for the revised statute in the Spanish parliament was important and would make PSC support less essential. Eventually a deal was struck, which included a promise that the PSOE would promote a future PSC-CiU coalition in Catalonia (Orte and Wilson, 2008: 21; *El País*, 2006). This deal marginalized the PSC, and put much pressure on its leaders. It became clear to the PSC leadership that the revised statute would be approved by the Spanish parliament. As it now had no possibility to secure a better deal (Orte and Wilson, 2008: 22), and the majority of the Catalan population was likely to prefer the revised draft over no new statute at all, supporting the revised draft became the best option, even if this led to major tension in the Catalan coalition government. Opposing the revised draft would make it unpopular with large parts of the Catalan population and allow the CiU to take credit for the new autonomy statute.[7] Thus, in the end the PSC fell in line with the PSOE position.

Conclusion

The conclusion from the negotiations about the fiscal federalism reforms in Germany after reunification appears to be straightforward: intra-party coordination and control by the national party is unlikely when the interests of regions and the national level clash (as is often the case with issues related to the distribution of fiscal resources). While this is an important – if perhaps somewhat obvious – point, a closer look at the two cases presented in this chapter suggests important nuances and qualifications. Party coordination and national control almost succeeded in the negotiations about the refinancing of the German Unity Fund in 1991. And in Spain, the PSOE managed to significantly influence and change the position of the Catalan Socialist Party in the discussions about a new autonomy statute for Catalonia, which involved both conflicting financial interests between national state and region, and a conflict about the symbolic and emotional issue of Catalonia's status as a 'nation'.

These case studies suggest two points. First, a crucial factor is the overall territorial organization of the state, as this influences the channels available to a regional government (and, thus, to a regional party branch) to pursue its interests. Regions in Germany are directly involved in decision-making at the national level through the Bundesrat. This means that a governing regional party branch has, in principle, two possible strategies when trying to influence national-level decisions: by trying to influence the position of the national party, and by forming an alliance with other regions to form a majority in the Bundesrat (which actually may involve 'horizontal party coordination' between regional branches of the same party). In cases of conflicting interests between national and regional levels of government, this second channel is particularly attractive. By implication, the control and influence of the national party leadership has limitations, regardless of the exact nature of coordination mechanisms and regulations within a party. Regions in Spain lack the second channel, and regional party branches therefore have to rely on 'vertical' party lobbying and coordination. This significantly strengthens the position of the national party.

Second, parties can use strategies that circumvent any internal party rules and coordination mechanisms, but influence the incentives of the national or regional party. The clearest example of this in the case studies is Zapatero's strategy to negotiate and make a deal with the CiU to secure its support for the revised Catalan autonomy statute, which influenced the PSC's considerations. In Germany, strategies to aim for or avoid the activation of the Concertation Committee between the Bundesrat and the Bundestag are another example. Thus, focusing only on internal party rules and practices, and the routine activities and competencies of party branches, will miss aspects which can be crucial to understand the authority of party levels in contested situations.

The principal–agent framework outlined in this chapter can accommodate these issues. The essence of this framework is its focus on national parties' scope for, and limitations on, shaping the incentives of regional party branches. These incentives are shaped by party rules and arrangements, opportunities provided by the territorial organization of the state, and the availability to the national party or regional branches of other strategies to exert power. Further analytical work should focus on establishing conditions under which these various strategies are available and effective. Detailed and crucial case studies can test these claims, and provide further insights. This combination of deductive and inductive analysis is the most promising avenue to further our understanding of these aspects of territorial party politics.

9
Governing Strategies in Multilevel Settings: Coordination, Innovation or Territorialization?

Irina Ştefuriuc

Introduction

Congruence is a characteristic of a government coalition in relation to another coalition. It is the situation in which the party composition of a regional government overlaps with that of the central government. Coalition congruence is an important aspect of coalition politics in multilevel systems. Intergovernmental relations between the centre and the territorial units are at the same time relations *between political parties* (when the government composition is different across levels) or *within political parties* (when it matches). As the regions and the central government share competences in many policy areas, intergovernmental relations and decision-making are thus likely to be affected by congruence or the lack of it. The larger and the more substantive this shared-competence zone is, the more congruence matters.

The general assumption proposed in the literature is that party leaders will, insofar as electoral arithmetic makes it possible, attempt to enter into congruent coalition formulae across levels (Roberts, 1989). This assumption is plausible if we believe that congruent coalitions are more likely than incongruent ones to help parties maintain policy coherence across levels of government. The primary justification for this assumption is that incongruence has generally been associated with stalemate in those policy areas which necessitate joint decision-making between the centre and the regions (Hough and Jeffery, 2006b; König et al., 2003). As Thorlakson (2006: 45) argues, 'pressure for congruent coalitions can occur in response to the institutional incentives of "joint federalism" systems, where a high degree of intergovernmental coordination is required in policy making, and substate governments may potentially block federal legislation'. It has also been argued that, where incongruent majorities occur, intergovernmental relations are more vulnerable to the logic of inter-party conflict (Bolleyer, 2006).

This chapter accepts the argument that institutional interdependence fosters the formation of congruent coalitions, but argues that congruence is only rarely a decisive factor for the formation of regional governments. This is because, first, the possibility of forming congruent coalitions mainly depends on the symmetry of party systems and the similarity of electoral results at the two levels. The greater the party system asymmetry and the less the similarity of electoral results, the less likely it is that congruent coalitions constitute feasible alternatives. Second, for regional party leaders who need to make coalition decisions, congruence is only one factor among others to consider. The greater their decision-making autonomy and the more specific the political dynamic in their region, the less likely it is that they will opt for congruence against all other odds. As Hopkin put it, 'establishing consistent rules for coalition formation within the national-level party may be difficult if some regional elites are expected to forego opportunities to govern at the regional level for the sake of a party line they may not fully support' (Hopkin, 2003: 234–5).

The first section of this chapter expands on these theoretical considerations. It is followed by a section sketching out the structural conditions for regional coalition formation in Germany and Spain. The third section looks in depth at two cases of government formation from each country, unravelling how the political actors involved in the formation process value congruence relative to other office-, policy- and vote-seeking goals. The final section concludes.

Coalition congruence in multilevel settings – a framework for analysis

The existing literature argues that the institutional interdependence between levels of government leads parties to prefer forming congruent coalitions across levels. Nevertheless, I suggest that congruence is not a sufficient explanatory factor for the formation of certain coalition formulae, since (1) the possibility of forming congruent coalitions mainly depends on how symmetric party systems are at national and regional levels and on the similarity of electoral results at the two levels, and (2) regional party leaders who have a certain degree of autonomy might value congruence less than other coalition attributes and thus opt to deviate from the coalition choices of their central party leaders and form alternative coalitions.

Level interdependence and intergovernmental cooperation

The interdependence between levels of government in decision-making comes in different degrees in federal settings. There are few cases of federations in which the levels are completely interdependent, and even fewer in which they are completely independent (Watts, 1999). Most frequently interdependence is tilted towards one point of the relationship – and it is indeed relevant whether the centre is generally more dependent on the regions for decision-making (i.e., when regions have a veto on a substantial part of federal legislation, as in Germany) or whether the regions are more dependent on the centre for decision-making (i.e., when the grey zone of shared competencies is large, as is the case in Spain). In systems where regional governments are involved in decision-making at the federal level, it is mostly the federal government that is interested in the formation of regional coalitions that are congruent with its own composition.

In systems where regions do not act as collective veto players to decision-making at the centre, the formation of incongruent coalitions has no effect on the decision-making capacity of the federal government, and one can therefore expect less pressure from the centre. However, the institutional effects on congruence are seconded by yet another factor, namely, the distribution of power across levels, more specifically the degree of entanglement or interdependence between the central and regional levels. In federal and quasi-federal systems, depending on the policy area, decision-making can take place exclusively at the federal level or exclusively at the regional level, or both levels may share policy-making competencies. Incongruence arises as a potential problem mostly for shared policy-making, where bilateral vertical intergovernmental cooperation between the two levels is required.

In those cases where close bilateral cooperation between the central and the regional governments is necessary, congruence might seem preferable even if the subnational units are not collective veto players for the action of the central government. Congruence will provide the parties involved the intra-party arena with a complementary channel of negotiation to the institutional one. Personal intra-party relationships can mediate intergovernmental conflict and solve disputes in what can be perceived by political actors as a more amiable setting.

Party system asymmetry, electoral dissimilarity and intra-party autonomy

To summarize the argument so far, congruence is preferred by party actors performing in those settings in which the interdependence between governing levels is high, as government congruence allows intergovernmental relations to be conducted partly in the sphere of internal party politics. Furthermore, in those settings where decision-making at the federal level depends on the collective assent of the regional governments, the federal party leadership is most likely to attempt to exert pressure for the formation of congruent coalitions.

But pressure from above is not sufficient. This is because, on the one hand, congruence might simply not be an option due to substantial cross-level differences in party system characteristics and/or electoral outcomes. On the other hand, regional party leaders might have other coalition preferences ranking higher than the congruent formula and, depending on how great regional party autonomy is in coalition politics, they might find it worthwhile resisting the pressure.

Although strongly interlinked, the national and the subnational levels of government are each characterized by certain dynamics of their own. Whether parties enter congruent or incongruent coalitions at the regional level largely depends on how similar the partisan composition of the regional parliament is with that of the national parliament. When parties compete in symmetrical party systems in both regional and national elections, the odds of coalition congruence are higher because parties are faced with the same set of choices regarding governing partnerships. However, the same coalition formula might not be a viable option at both levels if the electoral results of parties across levels are very dissimilar. Thus, one can expect congruent coalitions to occur more frequently where the multilevel party system is highly integrated (i.e., where roughly similar electoral outcomes for statewide and regional elections are found across the state). Likewise, weakly integrated multilevel party systems that feature dissimilar electoral results are more likely to produce incongruent coalitions.

If party system attributes structure the sets of coalition alternatives that are available to regional party leaders, it is their relative decision-making autonomy that finally enables them to opt for congruent or incongruent coalitions from among the available formulae. If regional party organizations have the autonomy to decide about coalition formation, then congruence will be one factor to consider among others, such as policy proximity, previous governing-together experience or office spoils.

Congruent formulae are not automatically chosen by parties even when they are politically viable – or they are not chosen *just because* they are congruent. One must disentangle the strategic value political actors attach to congruence from other considerations pertaining to office-, policy- and vote-seeking. First, parties can be motivated simply by the desire to get (and stay) in office, and a congruent coalition might offer the best mathematical possibility to do so. Congruent coalitions can also be partnerships with parties whose policy profile is closest – in this case congruence might be an advantage, but the primary reason for forming the coalition is likely to be policy proximity. Finally, coalitions are partnerships that are often expected to bring electoral benefits to the participants – and the fact that they are also congruent is of secondary importance.

To recall, congruence acquires an independent value of its own when a large amount of the regional government's activity relies on cooperation with the federal government, but it is difficult to argue that incongruent formulae are systematically disadvantaged in intergovernmental relations to the extent that would motivate actors to choose congruence against all other odds. The best empirical facts supporting this argument are that incongruent coalitions do occur in real life and that congruent regional coalitions rarely break at mid-term for no other reason than a shift in the coalition formula at the federal level. Although congruence is likely to be an important consideration at the time of forming a coalition, autonomous regional parties are unlikely to systematically base their choice exclusively on this consideration.

Structural conditions for coalition congruence in Germany and Spain

The previous section argued that the greater the degree of institutional inter-dependence between levels the more likely it is that coalition congruence will become an important determinant of coalition formation. It also argued that, in producing congruent/ incongruent coalitions, this institutional factor interacts with the extent to which the party systems and electoral results are symmetrical across levels and with the degree of autonomy regional party organizations have in coalition politics.

(a) Institutional interdependence

The interdependence between levels of government takes different forms in Germany and Spain. The 16 German regional (*Land*) governments have the capacity to act as collective veto players at the federal level. The second legislative chamber – the Bundesrat – is responsible for co-legislating in all matters that affect the regions. It has been estimated that about 60 per cent of the federal legislative production is submitted to a vote in the Bundesrat (Reutter, 2006; Watts, 1999). Thus, the federal government is effectively dependent on being able to foster a majority in the Bundesrat.[1]

It must be noted that this majority need not always be partisan. The considerations on which regions cast their votes in the Bundesrat are often cross-cutting partisan lines and, depending on the issue, often reflect the regions' particular territorial interests. As long as a federal proposal is not at odds with these interests, the regions might vote for it even if the federal government is of a different colour (Scharpf, 2005; Braun et al., 2002; Renzsch, 1999). Nevertheless, in recent times Germany has known periods of effective gridlock due to the existence of asymmetric party majorities in the two chambers (Schmitt and Wüst, 2006). As Scharpf (2005: 7) puts it,

> Generally, hard-core (e.g. financial) *Land* interests are unlikely to be overridden by considerations of party loyalty, whereas the strategic motive is most likely to dominate during election campaigns. When that is the case, the German joint decision system turns into a trap in which national policy initiatives are at the mercy of an opposition whose primary interest is in unseating the government of the day.

In contrast, the Spanish institutional setting does not provide the Spanish regions (i.e., Autonomous Communities) with collective veto power in the decision-making process at the national level. The second chamber in Spain acts as a second-reading chamber, rather than being the locus where territorial interests can catalyse. Intergovernmental relations in Spain are almost exclusively bilateral and vertical, between the central government and each of the 17 regional governments (Aja, 2003; Bolleyer, 2006). In such conditions, the balance of interdependence is tilted more in favour of the central government. The Spanish regional governments do enjoy substantive devolved competencies, but the grey zone in which the federal and the regional governments still share prerogatives is rather large (Aja, 2003), making day-to-day tight bilateral intergovernmental cooperation necessary.

The German regional governments also need to engage in close bilateral cooperation with the federal government, given that the bulk of their activity is to implement federal laws (Gunlicks, 2003; Braun et al., 2002). The primary difference between the two systems is that, while the German regional governments collectively have a say on the federal laws they are implementing, in the case of shared competencies in Spain the regional governments have no institutional channels for collectively shaping decisions that are taken at the centre and that affect them directly.

An additional difference is that, while German federalism is highly symmetric (the voting power of the *Länder* in the Bundesrat being weighted according to the size of their population), Spanish federalism presents some clear asymmetrical traits. These are most notable in the fiscal field, with the Basque Country and Navarre benefiting from a special system that endows them with complete autonomy to regulate a series of important taxes, which makes them practically independent from the redistributive financial scheme the other regions are submitted to (Aja, 2003). More recently Catalonia itself also upgraded its fiscal advantages by retaining a higher percentage of several shared taxes as well as increasing the autonomy of the Catalan government in framing tax legislation (Vintró and Padrós, 2007). The Canary Islands also have a special economic and fiscal arrangement according to which special tax reliefs apply to the Canary territory, but overall the fiscal autonomy of the islands is much less than that of the Basque Country and Navarre and, more recently, Catalonia.

So far as general policy-making powers are concerned, although in practice the distinction the Spanish Constitution makes between historical nationalities (Catalonia, the Basque Country and Galicia) and the other autonomous communities is no longer an indicator of different levels of regional autonomy except in linguistic, civil law and sometimes police matters, historical nationalities have tended to develop privileged relations with the central government (Swenden, 2006: 263). This has constituted a source of de facto political asymmetry (Burgess, 2006) and at times the central government policy has found itself depending on the support of regionalist parties from strong regions – Catalonia and the Basque Country. By granting external parliamentary support to minority governments at the national level (during 1993–6 and 2004–8 to the PSOE government, 1996–2000 to the PP government), parties like the CiU and the ERC in Catalonia and the PNV in the Basque Country managed to extract substantial benefits for their home territories.[2]

(b) Party system asymmetry, electoral dissimilarity and regional party autonomy

The degree to which party systems are symmetric and electoral results similar across levels directly affects the possibility of forming congruent coalitions by altering the similarity of the available sets of potential coalitions at the two levels. The two countries under survey here are rather different in this respect. Throughout the post-war period and until the reunification in the 1990s, the Germany party systems were virtually overlapping across levels. Hough and Koß (this volume) and others (e.g., Saalfeld, 2003; Niedermayer, 1998) show that reunification brought important asymmetrical elements that created a cleavage between the party systems in the old Western regions, which remained largely symmetrical with the federal level, and the five new Eastern regions, which developed a different dynamic. The reformed communist successor party, the PDS – now called '*die Linke*' ('the Left') after a fusion with a splinter faction from the SPD – which is rather small at the federal level and has so far been practically non-existent in any of the Western regional parliaments[3], is a strong electoral contender in the Eastern regions. In Mecklenburg-Western Pomerania and Berlin the PDS/Linke has even governed alongside the SPD for two consecutive mandates, and in Saxony-Anhalt it engaged in a parliamentary coalition with the Social Democrats. On the other hand, the Liberals (FDP) and the Greens, which are important and coalitionable in the Western *Länder* and at the federal level are very poorly and unevenly represented in the East.

Party system asymmetry in Spain is caused by a proliferation of non-statewide parties (NSWP). With the exception of the Basque nationalist parties that field candidates in both the Basque and the Navarre constituencies, the other NSWPs are confined to single specific Autonomous Community. NSWPs with proven governing potential exist thus in Catalonia, the Basque Country, Galicia and Navarre, but also in the Canary and Balearic Islands, Aragon, Cantabria, Andalusia and La Rioja – that is, in 10 out of the 17 Spanish regions. Due to a majoritarian twist in the Spanish proportional representation system, only a few of these NSWPs have any coalition potential at the federal level. These have been the CiU and the ERC in Catalonia, the PNV in the Basque Country and the CC in the Canary Islands. None of these parties has ever formally participated in a national cabinet in Spain, but they were part of parliamentary coalition supporting minority single party governments. In all cases (except the Basque cabinet of 1995) this support pattern was congruent across levels.

It is obvious that these party system differences reflect dissimilarities in the electoral results parties obtain in different electoral arenas. Tables 9.1 and 9.2 present the indexes of dissimilarity in Germany and Spain respectively. This

Table 9.1 Dissimilarity index: German federal and regional elections compared (1990–2005)

	F90-R*	F94-R*	F98-R*	F02-R*	F05-R*	Average
Sachsen	13.8	20.86	49.1	50.1		33.47
Thuringia	8.2	4.1	42.5	50.6		26.35
Hamburg	16.5	14.5	16.3	38.2	35.3	24.16
Brandenburg	20.3	19.4	15.5	37.6		23.20
Sachsen-Anhalt	10.5	8.9	18.4	44.6	27.2	21.92
Berlin	5.9	22.3	40.9	29	8.4	21.30
Saarland	9	4.5	26.1	30.9		17.63
Schleswig-Holstein	32.4	13.2	7.2	16.6		17.35
Bremen	10.3	20.3	25.1	16.2	13.4	17.06
Rheinland-Pfalz	21.6	8.2	15.6	21.9		16.83
NRW	18.9	10.4	11.2	23.6		16.03
Niedersachsen	13.4	13.2	7.4	29.5		15.88
BW	22.8	10.4	11.5	NA	15.9	15.15
Hessen	10.6	4.9	14.7	23.2		13.35
Bayern	12.5	8.6	14.5	16.6		13.05
MVP	9	2.9	3.5	3.9	16.9	7.24
Mean values	14.73	11.67	19.97	28.83	19.52	

Note: F stands for national election in the indicated year (e.g., F90 for national elections in 1990) and R* for corresponding regional elections that followed. Exceptionally, due to differences in the electoral calendar, the corresponding regional elections can occur shortly before the reference national elections.
Source: Author's compilation from official electoral results data.

index represents the percentage of votes that were cast in a different direction in a pair of regional and federal elections.[4] As this index cannot disentangle the pure cross-level differences from changes that are due to volatility between elections (Pallarés and Keating; 2003), its values must be treated with caution. It is, however, on average a good indicator of relative regional departures from the voting pattern in federal elections.

This index has higher average values in Spain than in Germany. The differences would probably be sharper if the index were able to account for pure cross-level divergence, as the electoral calendar varies greatly across German regions and inter-election volatility might artificially inflate the results. In any case, the German index shows sufficiently high values to explain why over the 1990–2006 period there were actually no more than 16 coalitions (out of a total of 90 regional governments) that were congruent with the federal coalition at the moment of their formation. Many of the remaining coalitions are still partially congruent with the federal government of the day, at least in the sense of not cross-cutting the government–opposition divisions at the federal level.

Finally, while these characteristics related to the party systems and electoral results structure the sets of *possible* coalition choices, the degree of

Table 9.2 Dissimilarity index: Spanish national and regional elections compared (1982–2004)

	F82-R*	F86-R*	F89-R*	F93-R*	F96-R*	F00-R*	F04-R*	Mean values per region
Cantabria	27.1	41.9	78.3	35.4	35.5	40.9	57.22	45.19
Navarre	54	77.3	12.8	44.5	55	35.3	25.59	43.50
Catalonia	53.67	38.1	36.7	30.4	28.9	28.36	33.93	35.72
Aragon	34	39.2	31.6	20.4	37.2	32.9	18.28	30.51
Canary Islands	35.8	37.2	36.3	20.9	32.1	23.5	22.07	29.70
Balearic Islands	35.2	26.2	31.2	25.7	32	25.4	19.24	27.85
Basque Country	21.2	35.4	16.3	21.1	20.7	40.5	33.66	26.98
Galicia	45.5	24.9	20.3	31	32.4	9.7	15.27	25.58
Andalusia	27.5	26.3	13.7	28.2	8.4	5.5	8.16	16.82
Valencian Community	16.5	25.9	12.7	12.4	18.2	10.4	16.19	16.04
Extremadura	27	19.5	7.9	20.8	6.4	18.1	6.87	15.22
Madrid	11.7	7.6	22	16.6	15.5	10.6	21.39	15.06
Castilla y León	19.8	13.8	9.4	19.5	12.9	19	7.88	14.61
Asturias	5.6	19.1	13.7	14.3	29.5	14.4	5.43	14.58
La Rioja	21.8	16.3	12.7	14.5	10.3	13.8	12.41	14.54
Castilla-la-Mancha	23.1	5.4	11	3.1	23.8	13.8	10.42	12.95
Murcia	11.9	15.1	10.7	15.6	8.8	3.8	6.23	10.30
Mean values	27.73	27.60	22.19	22.02	23.98	20.35	18.84	

Note: Index calculated as in Table 9.1.
Source: Author's compilation from official electoral results data.

regional party autonomy is important for understanding their final *actual* choices.

In Germany decisions over regional coalition formation are formally left to the regional party organizations. Although highly integrated, all parties in Germany have a formally decentralized structure and, while the federal leadership of each party can issue advice and exert pressure regarding regional coalition formation, the regional party decision-making bodies have the formal autonomy to take final decisions on this issue (see Detterbeck and Jeffery in this volume). This formal autonomy enabled, for example, the formation of the first Social Democratic–Socialist (SPD-PDS) coalition in 1998 in Mecklenburg-Pomerania and then in 2001 in Berlin, despite open hostility to the idea within the Social Democratic federal leadership.

The regional provisions in the statutes of Spanish statewide parties (SWPs) give the central party leadership more formal room for intervention in the process of regional coalition building than is the case in Germany. Thus, although the Spanish Social Democratic Party (PSOE) comes closest to a federal structure with significant levels of autonomy for its regional organizations, in practice many of the important decisions need to be approved by the national leadership (Méndez-Lago, 2000; Fabre and Méndez-Lago, this volume).[5] The Conservative Party (PP) formally sanctions all subnational coalitions that have not acquired the prior consent of the national executive of the party (Astudillo and García-Guereta, 2005). Finally, as regards United Left (IU), is concerned, coalition decisions are still controlled by the national leadership as long as the regional federations envisage entering any agreements with the regional organizations of other statewide parties; and attempts to bypass this rule have in the past seen severe sanctions imposed on the regional organizations, which ranged from severe disciplinary measures to outright dissolution (Ramiro and Pérez-Nievas, 2005)[6].

Summing up, the following expectations stand out with regard to coalition congruence in Germany and Spain. Given the larger cross-level asymmetry of the Spanish party systems and the majoritarian character of the national electoral system, which often allows single-party majority governments to form, it is obvious why the bulk of the regional coalitions that emerge are not fully congruent with the government at the national level (see Ştefuriuc, 2009). Nevertheless, it is important to note that, in those cases where a pattern of stable parliamentary exchange was established between the governing SWP and one or more NSWPs at the central level, a parallel arrangement followed suit in the respective home territories of the NSWPs in question. Sometimes such deals were struck against the wish of the regional SWP organization, as in the case of Catalonia where in 1995 the Catalan Socialists were practically forced by the national PSOE leadership to support the minority government of the *Convergència i Unió* (CiU) (Reniu, 2002).

In Germany, due to party system and electoral dynamics, incongruence features more prominently in the Eastern regions than in the Western ones. Overall, however, it is clear that Germany has better structural conditions for congruence than does Spain, not least because congruence can become such an important factor for the capacity of the federal government to pass its legislative proposals through the two chambers. The parties that form the federal government thus have strong incentives to attempt to influence their regional branches' coalition choices towards congruence. Nevertheless, these regional branches have functional autonomy to decide, and the federal leadership has often found itself frustrated in its attempt to impose certain coalition formulae.

At the same time, regional governments in both countries need to engage in extensive cooperation with the central government. Congruence might thus become an important characteristic in the eyes of regional party leaders forming a government, as congruence has a good potential to smooth these intergovernmental relations by insulating them from inter-party conflict.

Whether congruence is decisive in bringing about specific regional coalition formulae is in the end a matter that can only be explored empirically. The best indication of the relative values of congruence and other office-, policy- or vote-seeking considerations is given by the real choices made when several alternatives are available. If we can show that *formateur* parties (i.e. those parties that formally take the lead in forming the coalition government) at the regional level are systematically opting for coalitions that are congruent with the national government despite having a set of viable choices that would better fit policy-proximity or vote-seeking expectations, then we can conclude that congruence trumps any other considerations.

The remainder of this chapter explores in depth four cases of regional coalition formation from Germany and Spain, unravelling the role congruence plays in actors' coalition strategies. The selection includes both congruent and incongruent coalitions and was made in order to ensure sufficient variation in the set of the hypothesized intervening variables presented in this section. The data used come mainly from personal interviews with regional party politicians involved in the coalition negotiation process. Since most of the interviewees hold public functions of high visibility, their anonymity will be preserved.

Spain: Canary Islands (2005) and the Basque Country (2005)

Before proceeding to an analysis of the two cases of coalition formation in Spain, some qualifications are in order regarding coalition congruence. As the previous section noted, it is impossible to form fully congruent coalitions in Spain across the whole range of the Spanish regions. The national government in Spain has always been single-partied, and in situations of minority it has so far relied on the parliamentary support of NSWPs that are uniquely present in their home territories. These parliamentary agreements in times of minority have been replicated in the specific autonomous communities, which indicates that congruent coalitions of parties, be they just parliamentary and not necessarily governing coalitions, may be the solution sought by default.

Nevertheless, in the Spanish case, it is reasonable to extend the definition of congruence to include those situations in which some, but not all, of the governing parties at one level are also governing at the other level (see Ştefuriuc, forthcoming). These situations of partial congruence enlarge the pool of cases in which we can survey the motivations of political actors in choosing particular coalition formulae. With this qualification, for the purpose of this study two recent cases of coalition formation were selected: a fully incongruent coalition in the Basque Country, which does not contain the party that at the time of its formation was governing at the national level, and a partially congruent coalition in the Canary Islands, in which the party taking the lead in government formation explicitly chose the party in central government as a partner.

Canary Islands – congruence first

In 2003 there were few doubts as to which of the two SWPs present in the parliament of the Canary Islands would be approached by the *Coalición*

Table 9.3   Party composition of the regional parliament in the Canary Islands following the 2003 elections

Party	Seats
PP – *Partido Popular de Canarias*	17
PSOE – *Partido Socialista de Canarias*	17
CC – *Coalición Canaria*	23*
FNC – *Federación Nacionalista Canarias*	3
Total	60

* *Coalición Canaria* loses three MPs to a new group formed in 2005, *Nueva Canarias* (NC).
Source: Author's compilation.

Canaria (CC) to form a coalition (see Table 9.3). Congruence has always been a crucial determinant of coalition formation for the regionalists, who make it clear in their electoral campaigns that they always 'go with the party in Madrid', as one of the CC interviewees put it, thus placing much less emphasis on ideological proximity or other classical determinants of coalition formation. Therefore, in 2003, as everyone expected, the CC signed a government agreement with the *Partido Popular de Canarias* (PP-CAN).

The reasons why congruence is important for the regionalists in the Canary Islands are quite transparent. Many of the important policies initiated by the Canary government need to be carried out in agreement and collaboration with the central government – such as health, fiscal or water policies. Furthermore, the islands enjoy a special status in both Spain and Europe, being the outermost European region which benefits from important sums from European Union structural funds. That is why, for the negotiations in Brussels, the CC needs to make sure that the Spanish government gets the best deal for the region. Last but not least, due to its geographic position, the Canary Islands are the main target of illegal immigration from African countries to Spain. Immigration falls within the exclusive jurisdiction of the central government in Spain, and the Canary government cannot address the issue without the consent and support of the central government. A good relationship with the central government is thus essential. The regionalists perceive that this is guaranteed by congruent alliances across levels.

The 2003 coalition revised the formula that had existed since 1995 between the CC and the PP-CAN. This coalition survived, either formally or in the guise of external parliamentary support, until 2005, when the head of the regional government dismissed the Popular Party's regional ministers. His justification was that the coalition with the PP-CAN was undermining relations between the Canary Islands and the central government. In the context of increasing polarization between Spain's two main parties at the national level, the partisan conflict was infiltrating into intergovernmental relations. According to the CC leaders, the PP was using all available channels, including the Canary government, to challenge the central Socialist government.

For the PP, they said, Canary politics had been transformed into just another battleground for the central government–opposition polarization, which was far from being beneficial in a context in which close cooperation was ever more necessary[7].

After the exit of the PP-CAN, a legislative agreement was quickly struck with the Socialist Party (PS-CAN). In broad policy terms, the CC is closer to the Socialists than it is to its previous partner, the PP-CAN. However, this was never cited as a factor in the rapprochement, which further supports the hypothesis that congruence-related considerations come first – as the bulk of the government's action pertains to multilevel politics. As one interviewee put it: 'In general it is not worth it allying with a party that does not hold the power in Madrid, because especially at the regional level there are many decisions which are made in Madrid, for us more important than for the rest of the autonomous communities – for reasons of distance, separation, transport, the African Coast, etc.'

But why not form a real governing coalition with the Socialists, rather than rely on their support on only a few selected policy issues? It was the Socialists' choice not to enter a formal government coalition, a choice motivated by long-term electoral objectives. According to a Socialist interviewee, the Socialists' strategy in the Canary Islands is to attempt to gain sufficient seats to allow them to be the largest force in any governing partnership with the regionalists. They know that otherwise their fate in the Islands will always be decided by government–opposition dynamics at the central level. Thus, by simply tolerating the government, the PSOE could afford to maintain a critical attitude and, once the electoral campaign for the next election had started, it could avoid all blame for any governmental mismanagement and present itself as an alternative governing option.

In the 2007 elections, PS-CAN obtained the largest vote and seat share, and opened negotiations to form a government with the CC. Soon afterwards, the regionalists decided to stop the process and go for a coalition with the PP-CAN, which had as an advantage the fact that they could retain the prime-ministerial position. It is the first time that the CC had relied on considerations other than congruence to make its choice. One can also explain this choice by the fact that the CC was sure of the support of PS-CAN in one of its primary objectives for the new legislature, which was to reform the Statute of Autonomy of the Canary Islands, a project that had been initiated jointly by the CC and the PS-CAN in the previous legislature. Furthermore, as demonstrated above, the CC did not see a problem in switching coalition partners. The coalition with the PP-CAN could be a tactical act in anticipation of the national elections held in March 2008.

The Basque Country – congruence does not matter

The coalition that was formed after the regional elections of 2005 in Basque country is made up of two NSWPs, namely, the Basque Nationalist Party

Table 9.4   Party composition of the regional parliament in the Basque Country following the 2005 elections

Party	Seats
PNV/EA – *Partido Nacionalista Vasco/ Eusko Alkartasuna* (electoral bloc)	21 + 8
PSOE(PSE-EE) – *Partido Socialista de Euskadi*	18
PP – *Partido Popular de Euskadi*	15
PCTV – *Partido Comunista de las Tierras Vascas*	9
EB/IU – *Ezker Batua/ Izquierda Unida*	3
Aralar	1
Total	75

Source: Author's compilation.

(PNV) and *Eusko Alkartasuna* (EA),[8] and the former regional federation of the third Spanish SWP, *Izquierda Unida* (IU), called *Ezker Batua* (EB)[9]. Its history goes back to the previous legislature, where the same formula was chosen. Although the Basque parliament had seven parliamentary groups, the real coalition alternatives were reduced to a maximum of two. One was the incumbent coalition, the formula that was adopted. The other was a coalition between the *Partido Popular de Euskadi* (PPE) and the *Partido Socialista de Euskadi* (PSE). Both would have held a minority status (see Table 9.4).

This second alternative, however, looked highly improbable if the Basque political stage is placed in context. Although in 2001 the two SWPs attempted to form a coalition in the Basque Country to counter the nationalist front, in 2005 a similar coalition was difficult to imagine. Their strategic alliance was becoming untenable in the context of an ever-stronger polarization between the PP and the PSOE in Spain. The approach of the new Socialist leadership to the territorial reform of Spain – based on the principle of a plural, multinational Spain – was strongly at odds with the centralist turn the PP was taking under the leadership of Mariano Rajoy. Thus, after Rodríguez-Zapatero's arrival in central government the dispute between the two main central parties, the PSOE and the PP, reached maximum levels of conflict, which spilled over to the regional arena as well.

The PNV-EA-EB coalition controlled 31 out of the 75 parliamentary seats. It was invested with the support of the Basque communists (PCTV), a support that was granted for the sake of enabling a government to take office rather than any other clear benefits. As the party that offered to represent the voters of Herri Batasuna (the party that was banned in 2002 on grounds of its links with the ETA – Basque separatist – terrorist organization and since then prohibited from participating in elections) the PCTV was excluded from any coalition negotiations. It is not a classical supporting party and it generally votes against all government initiatives in the Basque parliament. It is rather Aralar, a small NSWP with only one MP, and the Basque Socialists (PSE-EE) that support the government on negotiated pieces of legislation and facilitate the passing of the budget bills.

But why not include the Socialists in the government, or come to a stable agreement on parliamentary support? First of all, the coalition had solid experience of negotiating its bills with the opposition, as in the previous legislature it also had a minority status. One could argue that the congruence would make its life easier. However, as the Basque statute of autonomy grants substantially more powers to the Basque government than that of any other autonomous community, the necessity for everyday policy coordination between Madrid and Vitoria, the capital of the Basque Country is also more limited. The Basque government can enact a wide range of policies without having to cooperate with the central government. Secondly, just like in the Canary Islands, the Basque Socialists declared that their coalition strategy rested on the clear principle (officially adopted by the regional party branch) that they would participate in a coalition government only on the condition that the head of the government belonged to their party.

This coalition was also compact from an ideological point of view. Although it contained parties from both the left and the right of the centre, these parties were sufficiently close to each other on the left–right spectrum. More importantly, as all interviewees noted, the coalition partners were on the same side of the territorial divide, which primarily explained why this coalition was formed. Given the primary policy goal of the PNV and the EA, the two largest coalition partners – revising the statute of autonomy of the Basque Country and, possibly along with that, the Spanish state model as a whole – no other coalition would have been consistent with this goal.

Germany: North-Rhine–Westphalia (2005) and Mecklenburg-Western Pomerania (2006)

North-Rhine – Westphalia: incongruent and happy about it

The 2005 regional elections in North-Rhine Westphalia (NRW) had wide-ranging implications for both state- and federal-level politics in Germany. The results prevented the Social Democratic Party (SPD) from accessing government for the first time after nearly 40 years of being in power. By doing this, the results also greatly shifted the majority in the Bundesrat, prompting the federal Chancellor to call early federal-level elections which eventually led to a new coalition taking over in Berlin.

The Christian Democratic Union (CDU-NRW) and the Free Democratic Party (FDP-NRW) started official negotiations to form a coalition government on 26 May 2005, less than a week after the elections. For neither partner was there any doubt about governing alternatives (see Table 9.5). According to one CDU-NRW interviewee this coalition had already been planned several months prior to the election. The coalition agreement was completed remarkably quickly: just three weeks after the start of the negotiations both party assemblies were ratifying the results.

An incongruent formula (CDU-FDP versus SPD-Greens) was thus intentionally chosen in NRW. In the light of the upcoming federal elections, the

Table 9.5   Party composition of the regional parliament in North Rhine-Westphalia following the 2005 election

Party	Seats
CDU – *Christlich Demokratische Union Deutschlands*	89
SPD – *Sozialdemokratische Partei Deutschlands*	74
FDP – *Freie Demokratische Partei*	12
Grüne – *Die Grünen*	12
Total	187

Source: Author's compilation.

CDU-FDP coalition in one of Germany's most powerful *Länder* was projected as a preview of the coalition to be possibly formed at the federal level. Nevertheless, the 2005 federal elections produced surprising results – in terms of electoral support the two main parties ended up very close and the combined vote share of the CDU/CSU and FDP was below the required majority in the *Bundestag*. After tough negotiations, a grand CDU-SPD coalition was formed, with the CDU as the leading partner.

Thus, although the CDU expected that the coalition it formed with the FDP in NRW would soon become congruent with the composition of the federal government, this did not happen. The CDU thus found itself in a theoretically inconvenient position – it shared government at the federal level with the SPD, which was its strongest opposition party in NRW, while sharing the regional government office with the FDP, which in the meantime remained in opposition to the CDU-SPD federal government in the Bundestag. In practice however, the CDU-NRW party politicians did not appear to view this as a disadvantage – quite the contrary.

Interviewees reported two related advantages of incongruence. One is electoral – federal issues (still) play a crucial role in regional elections in Germany. The 2005 *Land* election in NRW was lost by the SPD-NRW also due to the increasing unpopularity of the federal government led by the SPD (Nagel, 2006). Nevertheless, there is evidence that the two types of elections have been becoming more disentangled in recent years (Hough and Jeffery, 2006b). In the eyes, of CDU-NRW politicians, an incongruent regional government is better able to distance itself from the federal record and capitalize on its own policy performance, attempting thus to increase its immunity to the highs and lows of federal politics.

A second advantage pertains to policy making. For neither the SPD nor the CDU was a grand coalition the favourite choice at the federal level. Electoral arithmetic in the two German parliamentary chambers forced them into this formula, which implied substantial policy compromises on both sides. For the CDU, a coalition with the FDP was the openly preferred option. In such a federal context, the CDU-NRW was happy to depart from the federal CDU line and pursue its own policies, even when these were in opposition to those of the federal government. In the words of one CDU-NRW regional MP,

> We have more choices and more chances compared with our party at the federal level. If we had the same coalition at the federal level, we would have had to work under more stringent conditions . . . [Now] we can always say 'we have another coalition partner that follows different ambitions and we are willing to implement these, no matter what you might think about it in Berlin'.

The same politician also argued that congruence would be an advantage if the party had the same positions at both levels, which is not always the case with the CDU-NRW and the federal CDU.

When we turn to CDU's junior partner in NRW, the FDP, a very different perception emerges. FDP-NRW saw no real advantage to incongruence, arguing that congruence was necessary for harmonious policy-making in the German interlocked multilevel context. At the federal level the CDU needed to compromise with the Social Democrats, which adopted a different policy direction from that in NRW. When the policy decisions taken at the federal level applied to the *Land* level, clashes occurred. One FDP-NRW regional MP and party leader described the situation as follows: 'We try to put here the private sector before the state, to have a bit more liberalism in economic matters and on the federal level they do exactly the opposite.'

Although both partners agreed that in general congruence might help in intergovernmental relations, none of the four interviewees could name any specific advantage. Congruence might make things easier, but incongruence does not necessarily complicate relations across levels.

Recording these opposite views on the advantages and disadvantages of (in)congruence from governing partners suggests that what primarily matters is the position of the actor at the two levels. The CDU was in government at both levels and, although under different coalition formulae, by being the leading partner in both the party had a great capacity to influence decision-making within the coalition. By being a relatively small party in opposition to the federal government based on an unusually large majority, the FDP could clearly not have even the slightest influence on federal-level policy. The post-2005 balance in the Bundesrat also worked to the advantage of the federal coalition, the bloc of liberal-conservative states representing only 17 per cent of the votes. In such a situation the FDP, whose stated long-term goal, according to one of its NRW leaders interviewed for this research, was to get back into power at the federal level, obviously saw some of its policy intentions frustrated by the action of the federal government. Although this was not explicitly stated in the interview material, one can easily imagine that the CDU-NRW could 'invoke' incongruence to justify a departure from federal CDU policies which it did not share, but also from FDP ambitions at the regional level which it did not agree with.

Mecklenburg-Western Pomerania – congruence by necessity

In 1998 the SPD in Mecklenburg-Western Pomerania (MVP) took the unprecedented decision of officially forming a coalition with the Party of Democratic Socialism (PDS). Despite heavy criticism from the federal SPD and having to confront internal dissent as well at the level of the regional party organization, SPD-MVP thought it wise to challenge the PDS, which was building a radical opposition profile almost everywhere in the new Eastern *Länder* by offering them governing responsibility. At that time the SPD-MVP did not have much choice – in 1996 bitter personal in-fighting had prematurely finished off a grand coalition government (CDU-SPD) that existed only to keep the PDS out of government. A coalition with the CDU was thus ruled out, and there was no other viable alternative.

The SPD-PDS government survived in office for two full legislatures and constituted an empirical precedent for a Red-Red coalition in the *Land* of Berlin. In 2006, elections left the SPD-PDS formula with only one seat above the required majority, indicating that a smooth continuation was no longer possible (see Table 9.6). According to one SPD interviewee, in the previous legislature the PDS was unable to maintain strict party discipline, some of its MPs voting against government bills on several occasions. The SPD held exploratory talks with both the PDS and the CDU and, given the slim majority and the prospects of government instability along the PDS, eventually started official negotiations for government formation with the CDU.

At that time, the grand coalition had already been in power in Berlin for almost a year. There are no indications, however, that the choice in MVP was strategically motivated by congruence considerations. It was, like its federal counterpart, a coalition born out of necessity rather than preference. Just as in the case of NRW, interviewees in MVP suggested that what really mattered for each party was to be in government at the two levels, not necessarily in congruent formulae. One SPD-MVP leader argued that

Table 9.6   Party composition of the regional parliament in Mecklenburg-Western Pomerania following the 2006 election

Party	Seats
CDU – *Christlich Demokratische Union Deutschlands*	22
SPD – *Sozialdemokratische Partei Deutschlands*	23
PDS/Linke – *Partei des Demokratischen Sozialismus/Die Linkspartei*	13
FDP – *Freie Demokratische Partei*	7
NPD – *Nationaldemokratischen Partei Deutschlands*	6
Total	71

Source: Author's compilation.

incongruence in practice became problematic only when the policy orientations of the governments at the two levels were substantially divergent (for example a Conservative-Liberal federal coalition and a Social Democratic-Left regional coalition) and when, furthermore, the federal government could count on a comfortable majority in the Bundesrat.

Although all interviewees agreed that intergovernmental relations ran more smoothly when the two governments were congruent, due to the easier personal communication between ministers at the two levels, they also suggested that in those decisions which went beyond shared policy preferences and which split the parties along territorial lines congruence was unable to help. The best example in MVP was, according to one interviewee, that despite congruence and despite the additional fact that the federal Chancellor, Angela Merkel, came from the MVP party organization, MVP could not influence the federal decision about a prolongation of the financial solidarity scheme for the Eastern *Länder* beyond 2019. Where the interests of the *Land* collided with those of the federal government, unless that *Land*'s government were pivotal and could shift a majority in the Bundesrat, congruence amounted to no influence at all.

Conclusion

This chapter revises the existing assumption that in federal and multilevel settings regional party leaders will automatically attempt to replicate the coalition governing at the federal level. It is argued here that, although a high degree of interdependence of governments at the two levels projects congruence as a desirable situation, this is rarely sufficient to explain the formation of particular coalitions at the regional level. In part, this is because differences in electoral results and in party systems across electoral levels can produce incongruent starting conditions for government formation. However, even when congruent coalitions are viable options, they might not be the preferred option of regional leaders. Depending on their level of autonomy, regional leaders might thus choose to form territorialized or innovative coalitions, rather than coordinate their strategy with that of their federal party organization.

The empirical evidence presented here shows that institutional interdependence is indeed the single most important factor prompting regional leaders to *appreciate* congruent coalitions. Intergovernmental cooperation is perceived to be running more smoothly when the governments at the two levels have the same party labels. Nevertheless, it is clear this is not always a sufficient reason to opt for congruent coalitions. Furthermore, contrary to the existing expectation that congruent coalitions are most likely to be formed in systems of joint federalism, the evidence presented here points to the conclusion that congruence of coalition formulae is becoming more and more a matter of coincidence rather than strategic choice in Germany, while retaining a certain strategic value in Spain.

There are three factors that explain the findings for Germany. First, it is obvious that the change brought about by reunification of the party systems and the increasing rates of electoral volatility and cross-level electoral dissimilarity pose real challenges to the capacity of parties to maintain a well-coordinated line regarding coalition formation across levels. The strength of the PDS/Linke in Eastern regions, the tendency to punish the parties in federal government in regional elections occurring at the mid- or end-term of the federal legislative period (Hough and Jeffery, 2006b) or the decreasing electoral support for the two main traditional governing parties (SPD and CDU/CSU) (Schweiger, 2007) are trends that directly affect the possibility of forming congruent coalitions. Second, the federal party leadership has a limited capacity to influence coalition-related decisions of their regional organizations. Regional party leaders need to respond to specific political dynamics in their region, and the interview evidence gathered here confirms existing findings to the effect that these leaders often bypass the federal party line in promoting the interests of their region. They also sometimes have different policy preferences from those of their federal party (Debus, 2006 and 2007), which can explain why they form innovative rather than coordinated coalitions. Third, in general, the *individual* (not collective) capacity of German regions to influence federal decision-making is limited, so that forming alliances with the same partners at both levels does not have sufficient strategic value. Furthermore, incongruence comes with certain advantages of its own by allowing regional party branches to develop a differentiated profile from that of the statewide party at the central level. It can also be used to better justify opposition to the federal line in the defence of specific territorial interests.

In Spain, the bulk of the incongruence encountered can be explained by the asymmetry of the party systems and the proliferation and strength of non-statewide parties at the regional level and by the peculiarity of the Spanish national electoral system, which often leads to the formation of single-party majority governments. However, one can observe a consistent pattern of exchanging legislative support across levels in situations of minority national government, sometimes established against the wishes of the regional SWP organization involved. Generally the national leadership of Spanish SWPs appears to be able to effectively constrain the freedom of regional leaders in coalition politics.

But the findings from Spain reveal within-country differences, too. It appears that an important factor is the degree to which the regions need the central government for decision-making. The more dependent the region on the centre, the more congruence becomes a real determinant of government formation and not just a desirable characteristic of it. This is undoubtedly due to the fact that intergovernmental relations still have a largely bilateral character in Spain, and important asymmetrical policy advances can be obtained via (predominantly bilateral) agreements between the central government and (individual) regional governments. [10]

All in all, this research casts doubt on the argument that congruence is on its own a crucial determinant of coalition formation in multilevel settings. Regional party systems and electoral arenas, to the extent that they are characterized by a dynamic of their own, often produce different coalition options in which the coalition that is congruent to that at the federal level is not always the one that regional party leaders prefer. Obviously, the degree to which regional leaders can take autonomous decisions regarding regional coalition politics, and the degree to which coalition congruence can bring them particular office-, policy- or vote-related advantages are important variables that mediate their choice.

10
How Statewide Parties Cope with the Regionalist Issue: The Case of Spain; A Directional Approach

Bart Maddens and Liselotte Libbrecht

Introduction[1]

In Chapter 8, Pieter van Houten considers a 'principal–agent' framework to assess the relationship between the statewide party and its regional branches, with regard to electoral campaigning, candidate selection and policy-making. Van Houten's framework demonstrates how statewide parties vary their territorial strategies in terms of how they organize themselves, campaign and make policy. In this chapter, we will discuss the strategic positioning of statewide parties by focusing exclusively on their campaign content. To this end we have analysed electoral programmes ('party manifestos') for statewide and regional elections in Spain, held between 2000 and 2003. Spain is an ideal case study since the regional assemblies are elected in separate elections and regional party systems have developed which often contain one or more relevant regionalist parties (Pallarés et al., 1997).

Rather than providing a general overview of the issue profile of statewide parties in regional (and statewide) elections, we analyse party manifestos to investigate how statewide parties deal with 'regionalist issues' in statewide and regional elections. Hence, the 'regionalist issue' profile of statewide parties can be considered as our dependent variable. Regionalist issues are issues in which parties take a stance with regard to the present levels of regional autonomy *or* with respect to matters that touch upon regional identity and culture. When parties emphasize the former, we speak of 'regional institutional issues'; where they debate the latter, we speak of 'regional identity issues'. Again, Spain is an ideal test case, given that some regions qualify as 'minority nations' or 'historic communities', thereby sparking a strong interest in regionalist issues. On the other hand, by limiting the analysis to Spain we will be able to control for the influence of some variables, such as the overall institutional design of the system, the configuration of the statewide party system and the general political context at the statewide level.

We rely on theoretical insights from issue voting to *predict* the expected stance of statewide parties with regard to both types of regionalist issues. In the first part of this chapter we demonstrate how issue voting can be of help to predict the strategizing behaviour of statewide parties. Subsequently, we identify a few independent variables which affect how parties treat the regionalist issue, and we demonstrate that the regions in which manifestos are analysed display sufficient variance on these variables. In the final part we present the empirical evidence and test which of our hypotheses hold.

Theory

The strategic positioning of a party with regard to any issue, regionalist or not, involves two different components: a salience component and a positional component. The salience component refers to the degree to which a party emphasizes the issue: it may keep silent about the issue and thereby dismiss it as unimportant, or it may stress the issue and thereby attempt to increase its salience among the electorate. The positional component refers to the substantive content of the party's issue profile, that is, the stance the party takes with regard to the issue.

Research about voting behaviour and party competition used to be mainly concerned with the positional component, under the assumption that parties compete by taking different positions on the same policy dimensions (see Downs, 1957; Enelow and Hinich, 1984). More recent research has emphasized that parties compete not only by taking and adapting a position in the policy space, but also by attempting to manipulate the salience of the policy dimensions. Directional models of issue voting take into account both the policy direction which a party advocates and the intensity with which it does so (Rabinowitz and Macdonald, 1989; Macdonald et al., 1991). Furthermore, apart from making the salience component critical to assessing the role of issues, directional theory also rejects the spatial assumption that the policy stance of a party can be conceived as a specific position on a continuous policy scale. Instead, each issue is assumed to be essentially bidirectional. Issue ownership theory takes this reasoning a step further and dismisses the positional component altogether. From an issue ownership perspective, parties attempt to make the issues on which they are perceived to be most credible critical to the voter's decision (Petrocik, 1990 and 1996). They differ by emphasizing different issues rather than by taking different positions on the same issues. As a result of this lack of positional competition, all issues become valence issues in the sense that only one policy direction is emphasized (Budge and Farlie, 1983a; Budge et al., 1987; Maddens, 1994). In this chapter we analyse regionalist issues on the basis of their *salience* and *position* (directional certainty) and a combination of both (directional intensity) Thus, we broadly adopt the theoretical lenses of directional theory.

With respect to the strategic dilemma described above, a statewide party essentially has three options with regard to the regionalist issue. In terms of salience, it can choose to de-emphasize the issue and attempt to prime other issues from which it hopes to benefit more. This is what Meguid (2004 and 2005) labels a *dismissive strategy*. We call this an 'evasive' strategy with regard to the regionalist issue. If, on the contrary, the party decides not to dismiss the issue, it has two options which both entail a positional element: the party may take either a regionalist direction (in terms of identity and/or autonomy) or a centralist direction. In Meguid's terminology (2004 and 2005), in the former case it opts for an *accommodative strategy* vis-à-vis the regionalist parties, in the latter case for an *adversarial strategy*. Both the accommodative and the adversarial strategies will normally increase the salience of the regionalist issue in the election and thus its impact on the vote.

One of the important variables which we expect to influence the strategies of statewide parties with regard to the regionalist issue refers to the nature of the regional party systems and particularly the strength of so-called regionalist parties therein. Where statewide parties do not face the competition of one or several sizeable regionalist parties, one possibility is that they will try to keep the regionalist genie in the bottle, as a result of which the regionalist issue simply will not materialize in the campaign. But an alternative strategy is to pre-empt the future rise of regionalist parties by occupying the regionalist niche in the electoral market and by emphasizing a regionalist stand, which could be defined as an *anticipatory accommodative strategy*. It seems unlikely that a statewide party would do the reverse and oppose an anticipated regionalist party by stressing a centralist stand. Such a strategy would probably function as a self-fulfilling prophecy and give rise to a regionalist party. On the other hand, once one statewide party has opted for an anticipatory accommodative strategy, the other statewide party(ies) may respond with an adversarial, that is, centralist strategy.

Thus, in the hypothetical case of two statewide parties competing in regional elections, 10 different scenarios can be distinguished, as shown in Table 10.1. The salience of the regionalist issue ranges from zero (when the statewide parties do not face a regionalist competitor and both opt for an evasive strategy) to high (when a regionalist competitor is present and both statewide parties opt for either an adversarial or an accommodative strategy). In 4 of the 10 scenarios, whenever at least two parties emphasize opposite directions, the issue functions as a position issue. If only the regionalist direction is stressed by at least one party (which is the case in 5 of the 10 scenarios), it becomes a valence issue. As argued above, a scenario involving a monopoly of the centralist direction – and a reversal of the valence – is considered implausible, because a statewide party adopting an intense centralist stance would probably pave the way for a regionalist party.

Directional theory also contends that the regionalist vote will be captured by the party that takes the most intense regionalist stand, provided it remains within a region of acceptability, that is, it is perceived as responsible by the

Table 10.1 Hypothetical scenarios of the strategic positioning of two statewide parties in regional elections with regard to the regionalist issue

	Regionalist party	Statewide Party A	Statewide Party B	Status of regionalist issue	Salience of regionalist issue (0–3)
1	REG	REG	REG	Valence	3
2	REG	CEN	CEN	Position	3
3	REG	CEN	REG	Position	3
4	REG	EVAS	REG	Valence	2
5	REG	EVAS	CEN	Position	2
6	REG	EVAS	EVAS	Valence	1
7	–	REG	REG	Valence	2
8	–	CEN	REG	Position	2
9	–	REG	EVAS	Valence	1
10	–	EVAS	EVAS	Non-issue	0

REG = emphasis on regionalist direction, CEN = emphasis on centralist direction, EVAS = no emphasis on regionalist issue.

voters. This implies that a vote-maximizing statewide party faced with a significant regionalist competitor has little to gain from an accommodative strategy that stops short of putting as much emphasis on the issue as the regionalist party.[2] If the statewide party is not prepared to do so – and we can assume this to be the case, given that such a strategy would upset the statewide party – it is left with the options of either downplaying the issue or playing the centralist card. The latter option, however, is probably unlikely to be chosen in a regional election. Due to the inherently regional focus of such an election, we may expect that there will be a certain regionalist atmosphere in the campaign which may cause public opinion to tilt in the regionalist direction. As a result, it may be all the more hazardous for a statewide party to adopt an adversarial centralist stand, thereby swimming against the tide. According to this reasoning, the only choice left is to opt for an evasive strategy and to divert voters' attention to other issues on which the party is perceived to be more credible. This is what we would expect to happen on the basis of issue ownership theory: the owner – for instance, the regionalist party – attempts to increase the salience of the issue, while the other parties attempt the reverse (Scenario 6).

In the cases where no sizeable regionalist competitor is present, issue ownership theory would expect either of the statewide parties to claim the issue and try to obtain a certain level of credibility with respect to defending the interests of the region and demanding more autonomy from the centre. The allocation of issue ownership is assumed to take place on a 'first come first serve' basis, in the sense that the party which is the first to adopt a credible profile on the issue becomes the owner (Petrocik, 1990: 5–6), leaving the other parties with no option but to dismiss the issue (Scenario 9).

On the basis of the arguments discussed above, it seems rather unlikely that a vote-maximizing statewide party would opt for an adversarial centralist strategy, irrespective of whether there is a regionalist competitor in the field. Yet, to apply Meguid's (2004 and 2005) reasoning, it could be argued that a statewide party may still opt for such a strategy in a setting with a regionalist party, notwithstanding that public opinion is expected to lean to the regionalist side in a regional election. The aim of the strategizing party would then be not to maximize its own vote but to harm the other statewide party by increasing the salience of the regionalist issue and thereby giving an advantage to the regionalist party. Such a scenario (Scenario 5) could materialize if there were reasons to believe that the targeted statewide party is more vulnerable to the regionalist party than the strategizing one. That could, for instance, be the case if the targeted party is closer to the regionalist party with regard to other issues, as indicated by its position on the left–right spectrum. In other words, when one of the statewide parties is close to the regionalist party on the left–right spectrum, a statewide party located either at the other side of the spectrum or in the centre might be expected to emphasize the regionalist issue not in order to win votes but to cause the targeted statewide party to lose votes to the regionalist party. This brings in the location of the various parties on the left–right spectrum as a second explanatory variable, after the presence of a regionalist party in the system.

Clearly, the strategies adopted by the statewide parties in the regional arena will also depend on the broader political setting, more specifically, their compatibility with the strategies of the statewide party branch or with other regionalist branches on the regionalist issue. Thus we can conceive of the profile of the statewide party in statewide elections (but also that of regional party branches in other regional elections, especially when these coincide – see Fabre and Méndez-Lago in this volume) as a third independent variable of relevance. It seems unlikely that a statewide party could afford to swap sides in between statewide and regional elections and shift from an intense centralist stand to an intense regionalist one. A statewide party that takes the former position in statewide elections can attempt to downplay the issue in regional elections, but realistically it cannot be expected to play the regionalist card. More generally, the leeway a party has in regional elections can be hypothesized to depend on the emphasis given to the issue in statewide elections. The more intense the party defends either direction in statewide elections, the smaller the odds that a party can take an opposite stand in regional elections.

Finally, we may assume that the degree of autonomy of the regional party branches can influence party campaigning at the regional level. Manifestos for state elections are normally drafted by central party bodies, but there may be important differences as to which body drafts regional party manifestos. It may be the regional party branches alone, the central bodies of the party or both. Although in theory, for electoral reasons, the central party branch may want its regional campaigns to differ from the statewide election campaign, an organizationally more centralized party is less likely to tolerate such divergence than an internally decentralized one.

The case of Spain

As mentioned in the introduction, an analysis of some Spanish regions allows us to test the impact of the independent variables discussed above, while keeping constant a number of other factors: the overall institutional design of the system, the configuration of the statewide party system and the general political context at the statewide level.

For practical reasons, the analysis had to be limited to the (statewide and regional) elections in the period 2000–3, and to the two largest statewide parties, the PSOE and the PP. The PP, due to its Francoist roots and its conservative ideology, has traditionally been the main defender of Spanish unity, while the PSOE has always been somewhat more accommodating towards the regionalist demands. This difference is also reflected in the party organization. But the distinction between the two parties is more blurred than would seem at first sight. There is also a strong centralist tendency in the PSOE, which prevailed when the party was in government in the 1980s (see Fabre and Méndez-Lago in this volume). The PP in its turn was forced to compromise with Basque and Catalan nationalists when it came to power in 1996 (Pallarés and Keating, 2003).

A selection of eight regions was made with the aim of maximizing the variance on the key explanatory variables that were identified above: the nature of the regional party system (and especially the strength of regionalist parties therein) and the relative position of the statewide parties on the left–right spectrum vis-à-vis the regionalist parties. By focusing on the PP and the PSOE, we can also distinguish between a somewhat more centralist and a more regionalist statewide party, in both ideological and organizational terms.

The regions can be roughly divided into four groups according to the strength of the regionalist party or parties. Table 10.2 (adapted from Pallarés, 1994) includes both the percentage which the regionalist parties obtained in all regional elections preceding the investigated period (2000–3) and the average percentage for these elections. A first group contains three regions with strong regionalist parties, obtaining at least about half of the votes (listed as Type I regions in Table 10.2) Five regions have medium-sized regionalist parties, with an average electoral support from just below 20–33 per cent (Type II regions in Table 10.2). Six regions have significant but small regionalist parties which poll generally less than 10 per cent of the vote (Type III regions in Table 10.2). In the three remaining regions, there is no significant regionalist party (Type IV regions in Table 10.2). In most regions, the regional party system is similar to the statewide (quasi-) two-party system: the PP and the PSOE

Table 10.2 Support for regionalist parties in regional elections in the Spanish autonomous communities (percentages of valid votes)

Type of region	Region	1983	1987	1991	1995	1999	Average support for regionalist parties*
I	Basque Country (1980–1984–1986–1990–1994–1998)†	1980 64.47 1984 64.64	67.90	67.39	59.17	55.87	63.03
	Navarre#	43.38	52.08	58.07	67.39	70.93	58.37
	Catalonia (1980–1984–1988–1992–1995–1999)	1980 39.35 1984 51.47	50.18	54.79	50.93	46.81	48.92
II	Canary Islands	16.84	31.91	37.26	37.87	42.38	33.25
	Aragon	20.64	29.54	27.33	25.69	24.82	25.60
	Cantabria	6.67	13.00	40.57	32.8	17	22.01
	Galicia (1981–1985–1989–1993–1997)	12.98	22.97	16.82	18.55	25.11	19.29
	Balearic Islands	22.18	15.41	11.34	17.6	19.39	17.18
III	Valencia	3.09	9.24	14.18	9.82	9.36	9.14
	Andalusia (1982–1986–1990–1994–1996–2000)	1982 5.41 1986 6.78	10.80	5.85	6.7	7.53	7.18
	La Rioja	7.52	6.50	5.47	6.82	5.90	6.44
	Extremadura	8.52	5.86	4.02	3.86	2.85	5.02
	Asturias	–	1.79	2.77	3.22	9.88	3.53
	Castile and Leon†	2.82	3.03	3.07	3.23	5.23	3.48

IV	Murcia	2.85	3.82	3.06	–	–	1.95
	Castilla-La Mancha	–	–	–	–	–	–
	Madrid	–	–	–	–	–	–

Source: compilation of data from the *Archivo Histórico Electoral, Presidencia de la Generalitat Valenciana:* http://www.pre.gva.es/argos/archivo/index.html

*Compilation of data from the *Archivo Histórico Electoral, Presidencia de la Generalitat Valenciana:* average of all regional elections 1980–99, this means 6 regional elections for the Basque Country, Catalonia and Andalusia and 5 for all the other regions. Only if the sum of support for all regionalist parties is ⩾1 this is taken into account, in the calculation of the region's regionalist party support.

These percentages include the votes for the UPN (*Unión del Pueblo Navarro*), which is closely allied with the PP. Both parties have an agreement according to which only the UPN competes in regional elections and only the PP in the state election. It is a matter of dispute whether the UPN should be considered a separate 'regionalist' party. If the party is not included, the percentages change to 28.6 per cent (1999) and 26.9 (average), as a result of which Navarre shifts to the second category.

† The 'regionalist' parties in Castile and Leon are in fact 'subregionalist' parties in the sense that there is a party defending the interests of Castile (*Tierra Comunera-Partido Nacionalista Castellano* – TC-PNC; 1.42 per cent in 1999) and another one defending the interests of Leon (*Unión del Pueblo Leonés* – PNL; 3.81 per cent in 1999). When these parties are considered subregionalist and not regionalist, Castile and Leon drops to Type IV. The *Unidad Alavesa* in the Basque Country defends the interests of the people from Alavés (this party was dissolved in 2005) and is also a 'subregionalist' party. For the sake of consistency this party will also be included in the calculation of the percentage of regionalist votes.

are dominant and compete for an absolute majority of seats. The stronger the regionalist party, the greater are the odds that neither of the dominant parties gets a majority and the regionalist party obtains a pivotal position. Four regional party systems deviate from this pattern as one of the two leading parties is a regionalist party. This is the case in Catalonia, the Canary Islands, the Basque Country and Navarre. Galicia is a borderline case as, up to the 2003 election, the regionalist BNG and PSOE always competed for the second place, with the PP as clear front-runner (Ocaña and Oñate, 2000).

We also have to take into account the fact that important differences exist between the various regionalist parties. Some of these parties can be considered as 'nationalist' (such as the PNV, the CiU, the BNG) in the sense that they proclaim a national status for their autonomous community and consequently have an electorate tending towards an exclusively regionalist identity and an ethno-nationalist attitude. These parties are located on the 'ethno-nationalist' side of a territorial cleavage, forming a separate ideological dimension in the space of electoral competition. Other regionalist parties are regionalist in character simply because they campaign exclusively within the region, but they are likely to adopt a much more moderate stance on extending levels of regional autonomy or appealing to regional identity issues, in tune with the electorate of their region. In these cases, the rise of regionalist parties has resulted from the political opportunity structures created by the new regional institutions and by the particularities of the regional party system. The latter are often related to the fact that the disappearance of the UCD and the CDS created a vacuum on the right of the left–right spectrum, which could be filled by a regionalist party (Pallarés et al., 1997: 167–8).

The 8 regions that were selected for comparative analysis were drawn from each type or group of regions. Given its atypical status as state capital, we decided to eliminate the autonomous community of Madrid. Further, Castile-La Mancha had to be excluded as a possible case because the regional branch of the PSOE did not have a manifesto for the 2003 election. We also decided to limit the analysis to regions with regional elections that do not take place simultaneously with statewide elections, as a result of which the case of Andalusia had to be dropped. Of the 16 other regions, the 3 so-called historic nationalities have separate regional elections (held in 2001 in Galicia and the Basque Country, and in 2003 in Catalonia), while the other regional elections are held on the same day (also in 2003).

Furthermore, the 8 regions represent a broad variety of regionalist parties and hence display diverse patterns of competition between regionalist and statewide parties (see Table 10.3, which presents the situation before the 2000–3 elections). Three of the selected regions have regionalist parties that are located on the centre-right of the political space and compete mainly against the PP. This is most clearly the case in Asturias (Buznego, 1998; Martín, 2003) and Cantabria (Ramos Rollòn, 1998; Molina, 2003), where conservative regionalist parties were formed as a result of a split within the PP, respectively, the *Unión Renovadora Asturiana* (URAS) and the *Unión para el Progreso*

Table 10.3 Position of regionalist parties in eight regions and percentage of vote for regionalist and statewide parties in the 1998–99 elections

	Left/Centre left	Centrist	Right/centre-right
Basque Country (Type I)	**EA (8.7%)** **HB (17.9%)** PSE-EE/PSOE (17.6%)		**PNV (28%)** PP (20.1%)
Catalonia (Type I)	**ERC (8.8%)** PSC-CIPC (38.2%)	**CiU (38%)**	PP (9.6%)
Canary Islands (Type II)	PSOE (24.4%)	**CC (37.5%)** **FNC (4.9%)**	PP (27.6%)
Cantabria (Type II)	PSOE-Progresistas (33.9%)		**PRC (13.8%)** **UPCA (3.1%)** PP (43.6%)
La Rioja (Type III)	PSOE (36,1%)	**PRi (6.4%)**	PP (52,4%)
Asturias (Type III)	**PAS (2.6%)** PSOE (46.7%)		**URAS (7.3%)** PP (32.8%)
Castile and Leon (Type III)*	PSOE (33.9%)		PP (52%)
Murcia (Type IV)	PSOE (36.%)		PP (53.6%)

Bold: regionalist parties.
* cf. note on Castile and Leon in Table 10.2.

de Cantabria (UPCA). An older regionalist party in Cantabria, the *Partido Regionalista de Cantabria* (PRC), is also generally perceived to be as conservative as the PP, partly because it has preferred to ally itself with the PP rather than with the PSOE (Ramos Rollón, 1998: 167–8).

Other regionalist parties are to be characterized as catch-all parties drawing votes from either side of the political spectrum. The best example is probably the *Coalición Canaria* (CC). Until 1993, the Canary Islands had a variety of constantly changing regionalist, in many cases even 'insular', parties. This fragmentation of the political landscape came to an end in 1993, when 6 of the regionalist parties formed the CC. The coalition contains both left-wing and more conservative parties that had managed to capture the sizeable UCD legacy in the 1980s (Hernández-Bravo, 1998; Soriano, 2003). At the end of the 1990s, an alternative and much smaller regionalist coalition was formed in the Canary Islands: the *Federación Nacionalista Canaria* (FNC). This party can also be considered as centrist, as it contains a broad array of mainly insular parties that had either kept out of or split off from the CC. *Convergència y Unió* (CiU) in Catalonia occupies a comparable position as the CC in the Canary Islands. The CiU also originated as a coalition of parties, ranging from the centre-left

(*Convergència Democràtica de Cataluña* – CDC) to the centre-right (the Christian Democratic *Unió Democràtica de Cataluña* – UDC), and has developed as a broad catch-all party, drawing votes from both the centre-right and the centre-left of the political spectrum (Soler Llebaria, 1998; Díez-Medrano, 1995). The Christian Democratic *Partido Nacionalista Vasco* (PNV) occupies a somewhat similar position in the Basque Country. However, when in 1986 its left wing split off and formed *Eusko Alkartasuna* (EA), the PNV lost some of its centrist catch-all character. But during the 1990s the two parties gradually grew closer and in the 2001 regional election they formed an alliance (PNV-EA). At the same time, the ethno-nationalist conflict is so entrenched in the Basque Country that it is extremely difficult to draw a parallel with other regions.

A much smaller centrist party is the *Partido Riojano* (PRi). The party was founded as the *Partido Riojano Progresista* but quickly adopted a centrist profile as indicated by its attempt, in 1987, to form an alliance with the UCD (Fernández Ferrero, 1997: 104). In spite of its modest electoral score, the party plays an important pivotal role in the political system, first allying itself with the PP (from 1987 to 1990) and then shifting its allegiance to PSOE (from 1990 to 1995) (Llamazares and Reinares, 1998: 319–20; Mora, 2003 : 324–5).

Finally, other regionalist parties have to be located on the left wing of the political spectrum and mainly compete with the PSOE. *Esquerra Republicana de Cataluña* (ERC) (Soler Llebaria, 1998) and *Partido Asturianista* (PAS) (Martín, 2003) belong to this category. The Basque *Eusko Alkartasuna* (EA) – whose ideology is sometimes characterized as social-liberal – and *Herri Batasuna* (HB, now banned) can also be considered as (respectively centre and radical) left-wing parties (Llera Ramo, 1998), but in this case, too, the same cautionary note applies as mentioned above (unlike for the other regions the dominant dimension of Basque party competition centres on the regionalist and not left–right issues).

As discussed above, we also expect the profiles of the regional party branches to be constrained by the strategy of the statewide parties. In order to test this hypothesis, we will also analyse the manifestos of the statewide parties in the 2000 state election. We expect that the stands of the PSOE and the PP in this election will slightly tend in the regionalist and the centralist directions respectively. As a result, the leeway of the regional branches to adopt an intense profile in the other direction should normally be limited.

Given what we know about the nature of the regional party systems and the ideological position of the regionalist parties on the left–right spectrum, what could we expect in terms of the strategic positioning of both statewide parties on the regionalist issue?

In the regions where both the PP and the PSOE are in competition with one or more substantial and centralist regionalist parties (Canary Islands and Catalonia, but not the Basque Country where the votes do not float between the PP and the regionalist centre party), directional theory would not expect these parties to target the regionalist competitor with an accommodative strategy, unless they are prepared to surpass the regionalist party in intensity, which is not very plausible. In other words, according to the logic of directional theory, the odds of taking an accommodative strategy are expected to be small in these cases. Instead, the statewide parties will probably try to evade the issue and to prime non-regionalist issues.

In regions where the regionalist–statewide competition is located on either the left or the right of the political space, directional theory (complemented with Meguid's insights) would predict that the opposite statewide party will be tempted to draw voters away from its statewide opponent to the regionalist party by emphasizing the regionalist issue (in either a regionalist or a centralist direction), thereby making it more central to the voter's choice. Cantabria would be the most obvious battleground for the PSOE to attempt such a strategy. The PSOE would be expected to prime the issue so as to draw votes away from the PP to the right-wing regionalist party. An accommodative strategy would be most in line with the PSOE's generally favourable stance towards decentralization. Asturias is another region where a strategy aimed at prioritizing the regionalist issue could pay off for the PSOE, as the tiny PAS hardly has an impact upon the dynamics of party competition and does not pose a big threat to the Socialists. The most likely region for the PP to attempt such a strategy aimed at harming its statewide opponent by priming the regionalist issue is the Basque Country. Because the ethno-nationalist cleavage is so entrenched in this region, votes do not float between the centrist PNV and PP. On the left side of the spectrum there is more fluidity as the PSE-EE (the Basque PSOE, which in 1993 merged with the left-wing nationalist party *Euskadiko Ezkerra* – EE) has stronger links with Basque nationalism (Llera Ramo, 1998). As a result, it could be in the interest of the PP to emphasize the regionalist issue in order to make PSOE lose votes to the regionalists. In that case, an adversarial strategy (taking a strong centralist position) would be the most likely option given the PP's more centralist ideology.

In the regions without a sizeable regionalist party, such as Murcia and Castile and Leon, the statewide parties may opt for an *anticipatory accommodative strategy* – that is, to take an intense regionalist stand – in order to fill this niche in the market and to pre-empt the future rise of a regionalist party. Due to its expected statewide tendency in the regionalist direction, the PSOE is much more likely to develop such a strategy than the PP.

A final explanatory variable was party organization. As shown by Fabre and Méndez-Lago in this volume, the two main statewide parties in Spain, the PP and the PSOE, are both fairly centralized parties, even though the PP insists more on party cohesion and national uniformity than the PSOE. Thus, we may expect more similarity between the issue profiles of its manifestos across the various regional elections and between the statewide and regional elections in the PP than in the PSOE.

Analysis

In this analysis, the profile of the parties will be mapped on the basis of their manifestos.[3] The text of the manifesto was first split into separate statements or quasi-sentences, applying the Comparative Manifesto Project (CMP) guidelines (Volkens, 1992; Budge et al., 2001). Next, the statements pertaining to the regionalist issue are counted. For the purpose of this research we did not apply the CMP coding scheme, but simply identified the statements related to the regionalist issue.[4] The latter were defined as statements that in one way or another deal with the relationship between the regions and the centre, either because they involve the division of competences and/or the balance of power between them (the institutional component), or because they involve policies relating to strengthening the culture, language and identity of either of them (that is, the cultural component). Following directional theory, we cannot limit the analysis to the salience component (as in the CMP approach), but need to 'unpack' their campaign messages according to salience, position and a combination of both (directional certainty). In this section we first consider the salience that is attributed to the regionalist issue (in both its institutional and its cultural or identity dimensions).

Salience

The *salience* of the regionalist issue can be operationalized in a straightforward way as the share of statements or 'quasi-sentences' on regional autonomy and identity in all statements or 'quasi-sentences' in the manifesto.

As shown in Table 10.4, the statewide parties devote on average roughly 5 per cent of the party manifesto to the institutional aspects of the regionalist issue. The identity aspects receive even less attention and have a salience score of barely 1 per cent. Table 10.4 also makes clear that the statewide parties do not systematically devote more attention to the regionalist issue in regional than in statewide elections. The differences between the PP and the PSOE are small on average. While the PP appears to be a little more reticent than the PSOE on the issue in statewide elections, in regional elections it is the PP which puts more emphasis on the issue, particularly with regard to its cultural dimension.

That the mean value of the PP on the institutional dimension is slightly higher than that of the PSOE is largely due to the Basque Country, where the party devoted no less than 10.72 per cent of its manifesto to institutional issues (compared with only 4.57 per cent for the PSOE) and 2.82 per cent on identity matters (compared with 2.46 per cent for the PSOE). The Basque PSOE also devoted more attention to the regionalist issue than in the other regions, but less spectacularly so than the PP. The regionalist issue also features prominently in the Catalan manifestos of both statewide parties, even though the focus of the PP here is mainly on the institutional dimension.

Table 10.4 Salience of the regionalist issue

Type of region	Salience	PP		PSOE			Other	
		Institutional	Identity	Institutional	Identity		Institutional	Identity
	State election 2000	4.86	0.73	5.32	1.05			
I	Basque Country	10.72	2.82	4.57	2.46	PNV-EA	8.75	2.26
	Catalonia	5.13	1.12	5.71	1.76	CIU	6.98	6.04
II	Canary Islands	3.50	0.63	4.82	0.61	CC	11.49	5.03
	Cantabria	3.15	1.87	5.32	0.60	PRC	1.92	3.55
III	La Rioja	2.97	1.67	3.59	0.61	PR	4.92	3.49
	Asturias	3.16	0.72	5.03	1.64	URAS	1.78	3.11
	Castile and Leon	2.37	1.30	3.11	0.55			
IV	Murcia	4.07	0.57	1.89	0.25			
	Mean regions	*4.38*	*1.34*	*4.25*	*1.06*		*5.97*	*3.92*
	Stdv. regions	*2.52*	*0.72*	*1.21*	*0.73*		*3.52*	*1.26*

The extent to which the profile of statewide parties varies across the regions can be assessed on the basis of the standard deviation (bottom row in Table 10.4). While the PP and the PSOE have comparable standard deviations with regard to the cultural component, the PP profile appears to vary more on the institutional dimension. However, this is largely due to the exceptionally strong emphasis placed on the issue in the Basque elections. If we leave aside this region, the PSOE has a somewhat higher standard deviation (1.28) than the PP (0.83), at least on the institutional dimension.

In both Murcia and Castile and Léon, the PSOE in particular applies an evasive strategy and downplays the issue (in both of its dimensions). The PP shows a similar but less consistent tendency. There is a relatively low emphasis on the issue, except in Murcia where the PP seems quite concerned with institutional matters.

In the four other regions (Asturias, La Rioja, Cantabria, Canaries) the most consistent pattern is one in which the PSOE is putting significantly more emphasis on the institutional aspects of regionalism than the PP. Compared with the other regions, the PSOE's concern with the issue is particularly strong in Asturias and Cantabria, that is, the two regions where the PP is under threat from a regionalist party. In these four regions, the PP adopts a relatively low salience profile with regard to institutional matters. But in La Rioja and Cantabria, it puts a relatively strong emphasis on identity matters.

Although our chapter focuses primarily on the statewide parties, it is worth noting here that most of the regionalist parties are not single-issue parties in a sense that they do not focus on the regionalist issue alone. In fact, they devote on average 5.97 per cent of their manifestos to institutional matters, which is hardly more than the shares reported for the statewide parties. But on closer examination there are considerable differences between the regionalist parties. The strongest regionalist parties (CC, PNV-EA, CiU) devote a much more substantial part of their manifesto to the issue (9.07 per cent on average) than the smaller ones (PRC, PR, URAS; 2.87 per cent on average). This difference is less evident with regard to the cultural dimension. The regionalist parties devote on average 3.92 per cent to identity matters, which is considerably more than the statewide parties. However, the Basque regionalist parties do not put more emphasis on identity matters than the statewide parties.

Directional certainty

As well as salience, directional theory takes into account the position which parties adopt with regard to certain issues. Compared with salience, measuring the substantive position of a party with regard to the regionalist issue requires a more sophisticated procedure involving a qualitative assessment of statements according to the directional cues which they provide. Following directional theory (Rabinowitz and Macdonald, 1989; Macdonald and Rabinowitz, 1993: 65), we assume that a party's position can be defined as the probability that a party will prefer one direction (for instance, more competences for the region) over the other (such as more competences for the centre). This probability or 'directional certainty' ranges from minus 1 (certainty that the party prefers one direction) through 0 (probability of preferring one option equals the probability of preferring the other) to 1 (certainty that the party prefers the other direction). For the purpose of measuring this directional certainty of the regionalist issue, a coding scheme was developed distinguishing 5 main categories: (1) centralist, (2) status quo centralist, (3) status quo, (4) status quo regionalist, (5) regionalist.

With regard to the institutional dimension, statements expressing a preference for more competences for the region (category 5) can be considered as clear cues that the party favours the autonomist direction, while the reverse can be said of statements favouring a re-centralization of certain competences (category 1). With regard to identity matters, categories 5 and 1 imply that the party unequivocally proposes to strengthen and promote respectively the regional and the national identity. Category 3 contains neutral or highly ambiguous statements that provide no cue whatsoever as to the preferred direction and can be considered as an implicit stance in favour of the status quo, with regard to either institutional or identity matters. If we take only these categories into account, the directional certainty variable can be measured as the difference between the number of clear directional statements in one sense minus the number of clear directional statements in the other sense, divided by the total number of relevant statements. In this way the certainty would equal (minus) one if all the relevant statements provided consistent directional cues, or zero if all relevant statements fell within the neutral category or if statements in one sense equalled statements in the opposite sense.

From the perspective of directional theory the interpretation of categories 2 and 4 is less straightforward. These statements do not explicitly express a preference for a change of the status quo in either sense, but they contain a positive assessment of the status quo, from a more regionalist (category 4) or a more centralist (category 2) perspective. The status quo is advocated because it is considered to strengthen the identity or the institutions of the region (category 4) or the centre (category 2). While the voter obtains no clear cue as to the preferred policy direction, it can still be argued that he or she may 'hint' which side the party is more sympathetic to. This could be taken into account by weighing these statements by half. Directional certainty could thus be measured as the number of clear directional statements in one sense plus half the number of hints in the same sense minus the number of clear directional statements in the other sense minus half the number of hints in the other sense (the directional balance), divided by the total number of relevant statements.

$$\text{Directional certainty} = \frac{\sum(C_{d1} + (H_{d1}/2)) - (C_{d2} + (H_{d2}/2))}{\sum S_r}$$

with S_r the number of relevant statements, C_{d1} the number of clear directional statements in one direction, H_{d1} the number of hints in the same direction, C_{d2} the number of clear directional statements in the other direction, and H_{d2} the number of hints in that same direction.

At one extreme are the statewide parties in the state election, which have values close to zero, particularly with regard to the institutional issue (minus 0.07 for the PP and 0.08 for the PSOE). This means that it is hard to deduce on the basis of the regionalist sentences in the party manifesto alone which direction either party prefers, even though, as expected, the balance slightly tilts towards the regionalist side for the PSOE and the centralist side for the PP. The parties are somewhat less ambiguous with regard to identity issues. The PP clearly takes a more Spanish nationalist stand in its manifesto (minus 0.35) while the PSOE slightly tends towards promoting the regional identities (0.13).

The regional manifestos of both PP and PSOE contain more cues in a regionalist sense than the manifestos for statewide elections, with regard to both institutions and identity politics. The overall mean of the statewide parties is 0.33 on the institutional dimension and 0.41 on the identity one. In general, both the PP and the PSOE take a firmer regionalist stance with regard to cultural than to institutional matters, that is, they are more restrained in supporting more regional autonomy than in advocating the identity of the region. Another consistent pattern which emerges from the regional manifesto data is that the PSOE adopts a more distinctive stance in the regionalist sense than the PP, with respect to both identity and institutional matters. The PSOE has an average score of 0.43 on institutional and 0.47 percent on identity matters versus respectively 0.23 and 0.34 for the PP.

However, the Basque Country forms a major exception to the general rule. This is most evident for the Basque PSOE: on both counts the directional balance of this party shifts in the centralist direction, especially so with regard to identity issues. With respect to the latter, the party takes an even more explicit centralist stand than the PP which is even slightly more ambiguous than in its statewide manifesto.

Still, if we leave aside the deviant Basque case, the pattern is remarkably consistent across the various regions. The tendency of the PSOE to take a more regionalist stand than in statewide elections is most outspoken in the Canary Islands, Catalonia and Murcia. In Murcia also the PP takes a particularly explicit regionalist stance on both dimensions. On identity matters, however, the PP is at its most radical in Cantabria and on institutional matters in La Rioja. If we set the Basque case aside, the PP is most ambiguous (and hence also closest to its position in statewide elections) in the Canary Islands.

Overall, the PSOE has a higher standard deviation than the PP on both dimensions, indicating that the regional party branches of the PSOE have more strategic latitude to tailor their substantive position to the competitive context.

Finally, as for salience, we have also looked at the directional certainty of the leading regionalist parties. Unsurprisingly, each of them features very high scores on the directional certainty variables (on average 0.73 on institutional matters and 0.67 on cultural matters), indicating that they unequivocally opt for devolving more competences to the regions and promoting regional identity at the expense of national identity (Table 10.5). The only exceptions are the institutional position of the PRC and the cultural position of the CC, which are more blurred than in the other regionalist parties. The most 'nationalist' parties provide the clearest cues to the voters, particularly on the institutional dimension. Among the non-nationalist parties, it is only the PR in La Rioja which is equally outspoken with regard to regional autonomy.

Directional intensity

Directional theory asserts that in order to fully assess a party's strategy on an issue we need to take into consideration its salience and position with regard to that issue. Bringing salience and position together will allow us to draw a measure of *directional intensity*. For instance, if a party unequivocally indicates that it prefers the direction of more autonomy for the region, but hardly emphasizes this stance (in the extreme case, it may mention it just once), its impact on voting behaviour will be very low. Conversely, the same observation applies to a party which places a lot of emphasis on the issue, but conveys highly ambiguous or contradictory messages. Both scenarios result in a low-intensity issue profile, as a result of which the issue will not have a (positive or negative) impact on the evaluation of the party by the electorate. Conversely, an issue will affect the vote only to the extent that a party places sufficient emphasis on the issue and gives out clear directional cues.

The intensity of a party's profile can be measured as the product of directional certainty and the salience of an issue (Macdonald and Rabinowitz, 1993: 65; Rabinowitz and Macdonald, 1989: 118). As this value equals the directional balance divided by the total number of statements in the manifesto (times 100), it is not affected by the number of neutral or ambiguous statements. In other words, a party may devote its entire manifesto to the regionalist issue (and thus arrive at a salience value of 100 per cent), but if there is not even a hint as to the preferred policy direction or if any hints given are contradictory, the intensity will remain zero. Figures 10.1 and 10.2 provide a graphic display of the directional intensity for both statewide parties and the leading regionalist parties in 1 statewide and 8 regional elections held within the 8 selected regions. Figures 10.1 displays the directional intensity the institutional dimension of the regionalist issue, Figure 10.2 does the same for the identity dimension.

Figures 10.1 and 10.2 locate parties on a scale which in theory can range from minus 100 to 100. A party which devotes its entire manifesto to the regionalist issue and makes it clear in every statement that it favours more

Table 10.5 Directional certainty

Type of region	Directional certainty	PP		PSOE			Other	
		Institutional	Identity	Institutional	Identity		Institutional	Identity
	State election 2000	-0.07	-0.35	0.08	0.13			
I	Basque Country	-0.02	-0.20	-0.07	-0.33	PNV-EA	0.91	0.70
	Catalonia	0.28	0.29	0.73	0.62	CIU	0.87	0.78
II	Canary Islands	0.07	0.17	0.62	0.65	CC	0.68	0.49
	Cantabria	0.25	0.57	0.40	0.57	PRC	0.40	0.69
III	La Rioja	0.38	0.42	0.42	0.38	PR	0.87	0.63
	Asturias	0.30	0.45	0.39	0.54	URAS	0.67	0.76
	Castile and Leon	0.25	0.46	0.44	0.62			
IV	Murcia	0.31	0.55	0.51	0.75			
	Mean regions	*0.23*	*0.34*	*0.43*	*0.47*		*0.73*	*0.67*
	Stdv. Regions	*0.13*	*0.24*	*0.22*	*0.32*		*0.18*	*0.10*

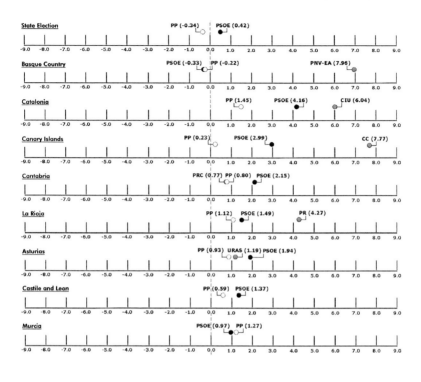

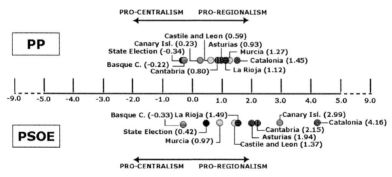

Figure 10.1   Directional intensity on the institutional dimension.

autonomy for the region would obtain a score of 100. Evidently, even region-alist parties – whose scores can be used as a benchmark – remain far below this theoretical upper limit. These parties obtain an average score of 4.67 on the institutional dimension and 2.63 on the identity dimension. However, the differences between the regionalist parties are considerable, particularly on the institutional dimension. While CC (7.77), PNV-EA (7.96) and CiU (6.04)

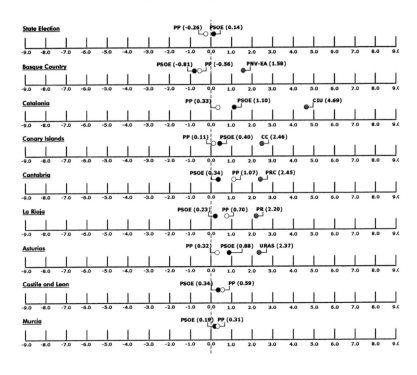

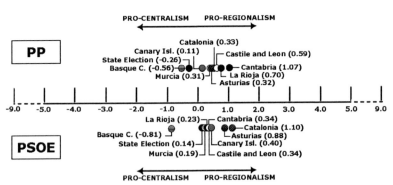

Figure 10.2   Directional intensity on the identity dimension.

have a relatively strong regionalist profile, URAS (1.19), PR (4.27) and PRC (0.77) provide much weaker cues to the voter. The differences are smaller on the identity dimension, as the profiles of the most 'nationalist' among the regionalist parties are less intense than those on the institutional dimension.

The PP and the PSOE adopt an extremely low profile on the regionalist issue in the state election. On both cultural and institutional matters, the PP and the PSOE provide weak cues respectively in a centralist and regionalist sense. Their stance is somewhat stronger with regard to institutions than culture.

In the regional elections both parties tend to shift towards a more regionalist profile, but this tendency is most evident on the institutional dimension. The PP switches from a moderately centralist stance (minus 0.34) to a moderately regionalist stance (0.77 on average). The PSOE intensifies its regionalist stance with regard to the institutional dimension and moves from 0.42 to an average score of 1.84. Thus, in the aggregate, the difference between the two statewide parties remains considerable. As we have seen, this shift is largely due to a change in the substantive positions of the parties, in the sense that they become more explicitly pro-regionalist, rather than to any more emphasis being placed on the regionalist issue.

With regard to identity issues, the differences between the statewide and the (average) regional profiles are smaller. The PP switches from a weak centralist stand (minus 0.26) to a weak regionalist stand (0.36), while the PSOE sharpens its regionalist profile only slightly (from 0.14 to 0.33). The result is that in regional elections both statewide parties have a highly similar profile on identity issues.

At the same time, these averages mask considerable variation between the regions. The differences between the regional party profiles are especially pronounced on the institutional dimension. Also, the latitude for strategic manoeuvring on this dimension is substantially greater for the PSOE than for the PP, as indicated by the higher standard deviation. We already know that this is mainly due to a larger inter-regional variation with regard to the substantive position of the PSOE on the regionalist issue.

The extent to which the PSOE drifts off towards the regionalist end appears to be related to the strength of the regionalist competitor. With the exception of the Basque Country, the PSOE adopts the weakest profile in the regions without a regionalist party. Its profile is most intense in regions with strong regionalist parties (Catalonia: 4.16; the Canaries: 2.99) and somewhat weaker in regions with moderately strong regionalist parties (Cantabria: 2.15; Asturias: 1.94). But the shift towards regionalism does not appear to depend on the strategic position of the PSOE vis-à-vis the regionalist party. In Asturias and Cantabria, the competition for regionalist votes is largely between the PP and the more conservative regionalist parties, while in the Canaries and Catalonia the regionalist parties are more centrist and hence also threaten the PSOE. Yet in each of these cases the PSOE intensifies its stand. At the same time it has to be kept in mind that the stronger stand of the PSOE in these regions is largely due to a qualitative change, as described above. Apparently the presence of a major regionalist party pushes the PSOE to take a more explicit regionalist stance, but not to put more emphasis on the issue.

The strong profile of the PSOE is not always reflected in identity issues. In Asturias and Catalonia, the party takes a relatively clear stance in favour of promoting regional identity, but in the Canaries and Cantabria the party is much less committed in that respect.

Contrary to the PSOE, there is not a single region in which the PP ventures far onto regionalist land. Its institutional stand varies much less between regions than in the case of the PSOE. Variations in directional certainty on regional institutional issues are also less related to the strength of the regionalist parties. The party is most intense in Catalonia, but keeps very aloof in the Canaries, in spite of the dominant regionalist CC. In Asturias and Cantabria, where the party faces a conservative regionalist competitor, its score is only slightly above the mean. Finally, the party adopts its second strongest profile and even surpasses the PSOE in Murcia, of all places: a region in which a regionalist party is completely non-existent.

The PP is even more prudent with regard to the issue of promoting regional identity. Even so, it sometimes leapfrogs a generally low-profile PSOE. This is most clearly the case in La Rioja and Cantabria. Again, there does not appear to be a relationship between the profile of the party and the strength or competitive position of the regionalist party. This is best illustrated by the fact that, in the two regions where this competitive position is similar (Asturias and Cantabria), the PP adopts a fairly different profile.

In the Basque Country, both the PP and the PSOE adopt a very distinct profile. In contrast to their strategy in all the other regions, they take a very cautious centralist stand, with regard to both institutions and identity. As mentioned above, this low profile is largely due to the ambiguity of the positions taken. Apparently, the salience of the ethno-national cleavage in this region compels both parties to give a relatively strong emphasis to the issue, while they do not want to commit themselves clearly to either direction. As a result the deadlock between Basque and Spanish nationalists is not reflected in a clear-cut opposition between centralist and regionalist parties, particularly because the PP, contrary to what could be expected, does not unequivocally play the Spanish card.

On the basis of the data we can now attempt to fit the regions investigated into the typology presented in Table 10.1.

Scenario 10 would seem to apply to Murcia (Type IV) and Castile and Leon (Type III). In these two regions a significant regionalist party is lacking and both statewide parties opt for an evasive strategy. Apparently, in neither region does the PP or the PSOE attempt to draw votes on a regionalist basis and claim the issue. Still, it is noteworthy that, even in these regions, the parties shift substantially towards the regionalist pole. They take a relatively clear-cut stand in favour of promoting regional identity, but hardly emphasize this.

Scenario 4 appears to have materialized in the cases of Asturias (Type III), Cantabria (Type II) and the Canary Islands (Type II). Each of these regions has a significant regionalist party (Type II regions in particular), and, with respect to the institutional dimension of the regionalist issue a more evasive (PP) and a more accommodative (PSOE) statewide party. With regard to identity, both statewide parties generally keep fairly aloof in these regions, expect for the PP in Cantabria (and to a lesser extent in La Rioja) and the PSOE in Asturias, where they put some stress on a fairly explicit regionalist position.

The Basque Country (Type I) would seem to fit Scenario 6, with a regionalist party and two low-profile statewide parties. On a closer look, however, the statewide parties do not particularly de-emphasize the issue. The PP even puts an exceptionally strong stress on the issue. Yet neither party makes an unequivocal choice for either the adversarial or the accommodative strategy. The scheme presented above, based on Meguid's conceptual framework, does not take this possibility into account.

Finally, Catalonia (Type I) appears to illustrate the first scenario. Confronted with a strong regionalist competitor, both statewide parties go to some length to accommodate the claims for more autonomy. Even so, the PSOE goes much further than the PP, which remains relatively ambiguous. And both parties, but particularly the PP, are much less committed with regard to identity politics.

In sum, the data strongly suggest that the regionalist issue generally functions as a valence issue. No party was found to opt for an adversarial strategy and to take an intense centralist stand on the issue. Parties adopt either an intense regionalist or a evasive/ambiguous profile.

Discussion

The analysis confirms that statewide parties generally take a more regionalist stand in regional than in statewide elections. They do not put more emphasis on the regionalist issue, but rather take a less ambiguous stand in favour of devolving more competences to the regions and promoting regional identity. In the case of the PP, this implies a switch from a moderately centralist stance in statewide elections to a moderately regionalist stance in regional elections. Statewide parties take either an ambiguous or a regionalist stand on the issue, but never opt for a head-on confrontation with the regionalist parties by taking an unequivocal centralist stand. Even in the Basque Country, where the conflict between Basque and Spanish nationalists is deeply entrenched and sometimes violent, both statewide parties refrain from adopting an adversarial strategy vis-à-vis the ethnonationalist parties. This somewhat goes against the conventional wisdom that the PP adopts a polarizing strategy in the Basque Country.

The PSOE appears to have more latitude for strategic manoeuvring than the PP. On average, the regional party branches of the PSOE diverge more from the stand taken in statewide elections than those of the PP. The inter-regional variations in strategy with respect to the regionalist issue are also greater in the PSOE than the PP. Moreover, these inter-regional differences are easier to explain on the basis of the variations in the competitive political context. More particularly, the stronger the regionalist party, the more inclined the PSOE is to adopt a more intense stand on the issue, especially by giving clearer pro-autonomy cues to the electorate (less so by giving the issue more salience). Whether the regionalist party competes on the left, right or in the centre of the political spectrum does not appear to make a difference.

This pattern appears to be more in line with the proximity model of party competition. The stronger the regionalist party, the more the centre of gravity in the system will move towards the regionalist pole of the dimension. We may assume that this will also have an effect on public opinion in the sense that the distribution will shift to the regionalist pole and the modal voter will become more autonomist. From a proximity point of view, it is logical that the statewide party, in the case of the PSOE, will follow suit and also shift to the autonomist pole. At the same time, the fact that the statewide parties never give much emphasis to the issue and thus avoid an intense position on the issue attests to the directional point of view that in a multiparty system the parties will not try to beat the regionalist parties on their own terrain, but instead attempt to prime their own core issues and make these more central to the voters' choice.

The findings with regard to the larger inter-regional variation of the PSOE dovetail with the results of other research, showing that the general salience profiles (the extent to which the various issues are emphasized in the manifestos) vary considerably more across the regional party manifestos of the PSOE than across those of the PP (Libbrecht et al., 2006). A straightforward explanation is that the PSOE is more decentralized than the PP (see Fabre and Mendez-Lago in this volume). In the PSOE, the regional party branches have more autonomy and are formally involved in the central organs and processes, in particular via the *Consejo Territorial*, established at the end of the 1990s to elaborate the party's position on the *Estado de las Autonomías*. In contrast, the PP adopted a very hierarchical and centralized party organization in 1989 and has been more reluctant to adapt its internal structure to the federalization process. Still, the autonomy of the regional branches somewhat increased at the start of the 1990s since the party came to accept the highly decentralized nature of the state and gained power in some regions (Méndez Lago, 2004; Fabre et al., 2005). Our results confirm the hypothesis that the less vertical integration in the party, and more particularly the greater the autonomy of the regional party branch to take the strategic decisions in regional elections, the greater are the odds that the regional position will deviate from the position of the statewide party as a whole (expressed in statewide elections).

An alternative explanation is that the PP was the governing party at the statewide level (with an absolute majority of seats), at the time of the 2001 and 2003 regional elections. It will arguably be more difficult for a statewide party to take a strong stance against the centre in a regional election in favour of more autonomy for the region when the party takes part in the federal government. Conversely, an opposition party at the statewide level may have more latitude to adopt a strong regionalist position (Filippov et al., 2004: 193–4).

11
Statewide Parties and Regional Party Competition: An Analysis of Party Manifestos in the United Kingdom

Elodie Fabre and Enric Martínez-Herrera

Introduction

In the UK, the arrival of devolution has compelled statewide parties to adapt their internal organization and campaign strategies to the presence of regional elections. The dynamics of party competition in which these regional elections are fought are noticeably distinct from the pattern of party competition which prevails in statewide elections. One of the main causes of such highly differentiated dynamics is the substantial presence of autonomist parties, the Scottish National Party (SNP) and Plaid Cymru, respectively in Scotland and Wales. Although these parties have existed for a very long time (Plaid Cymru was founded in 1925 and the SNP in 1934), they have rarely been significant players in the statewide political arena. Devolution represented for them a clear opportunity to weigh into the political debate. Within their regional party systems they have routinely collected 20 percent of the vote or more and gained significant numbers of seats in regional elections. Consequently, regional party competition has increased the pressure on statewide parties to diversify their regional campaign strategies and messages. However, too much diversification may undermine the cohesion of the statewide parties. This chapter explores, and seeks to explain, how the British statewide parties sought to balance these two conflicting goals (diversification versus cohesion) by analysing their party programmes for statewide and regional elections (Scotland and Wales) between 1997 and 2003.[1]

The chapter is structured in two parts. In the first part we develop a few hypotheses with regard to how British statewide parties may respond to the emergence of regional elections. We focus on three sets of independent variables: the distribution of competences in the state, party-specific factors such as incumbency, organization and ideology and the nature of the party system. In the second part of the chapter we consider how these variables help to explain (1) the overall issue profile of a statewide party, based on a comparison of the salience of *all issues* in its party programmes for statewide and regional elections; (2) for each party the *divergence* in issue profiles between statewide and regional elections; and (3) the profiles of the statewide party on the *regionalist* issue alone, based on the computation of salience, directional certainty and intensity (see the preceding chapter by Maddens and Libbrecht for a detailed analysis) and a complementary identity-rhetoric analysis.

Explaining issue salience and policy divergence between and within parties

Proximity theory argues that parties compete by taking diverging positions along a set of given issue dimensions. The closer a party's position (on any given issue) to the position of any given group of voters, the more likely these voters are to vote for the party. In contrast, directional theorists (Rabinowitz and MacDonald, 1989; MacDonald et al., 1991) take the view that a party's campaign strategy will reflect a combination of salience (some parties may want to be 'associated' with or to 'own' an issue by repeatedly emphasizing it) and position (for instance, with regard to 'regional autonomy', Maddens and Libbrecht assume that parties may opt for less autonomy, the status quo or more autonomy). High directional certainty is the product of high salience and a consistent position on an issue, whereas directional certainty will be reduced when (a) positions are consistent but salience is low, (b) salience is high but positions are not consistent, or (c) positions are not consistent and salience is low.

A salience analysis is the first component of a more comprehensive understanding of party programmes in line with directional theory. We provide such an analysis for *all* the issues that appear in the statewide and regional party programmes of three British statewide parties, the Scottish National Party and Plaid Cymru. Subsequently, we discuss the values of directional certainty on the 'regionalist issue' for the three statewide parties. In this chapter, we distinguish between *two components* of the regionalist issue: one component relates to *institutional* regionalism, the other component to *cultural-ideational* regionalism. For instance, where a party demands a stronger role for a region in social assistance policies, the issue is coded as an expression of 'institutional regionalism'; where the party appeals to more respect for the regional language or culture, the issue is interpreted as an expression of 'cultural regionalism'. The following hypotheses relate to expectations with regard to the salience profile of a party on all issues and/or its issue profile with regard to the regionalist issue. The hypotheses frequently derive from assumptions that were put forward in the Introduction or in subsequent chapters in this volume (in particular those by Fabre and Méndez-Lago, Bradbury and Hopkin).

Context of the federal framework and issue salience

The first hypothesis relates to the institutional context of the federal or decentralized state. It should affect each party in equal measure. Devolution entrusted Scotland and Wales with self-rule in a significant number of policy areas (see Government of Wales Act 1998 and Scotland Act 1998) under the form of either primary (Scotland) or secondary or 'executive' (Wales) legislation. With respect to their respective salience profiles, we expect issues which fall within the competence of the centre to prevail in manifestos for statewide elections, whereas we expect issues for which Scotland or Wales are responsible to dominate the manifestos for Scottish or Welsh regional elections. There is one important caveat here, which we should acknowledge from the beginning. In their manifestos for statewide elections, parties are also likely to address issues that have been devolved to Scotland or Wales, given that the UK parliament still addresses such issues to the full for England (which lacks a regional parliament and represents more than 80 per cent of the UK population).

Party ideology, incumbency and organization, and their expected effect on issue salience and levels of divergence

We cannot expect all statewide parties to diverge to the same extent between statewide and regional elections in the salience that they attribute to certain issues. On the basis of what has already been specified in previous chapters, ideology may be expected to make a mark in this respect (e.g., Fabre and Méndez-Lago). The expected divergence on issue salience should be highest for the Liberal Democrats and lowest for the Conservatives, with the Labour Party somehow occupying an intermediate position.

On the other hand, we also expect the incumbency status of a party (whether in central or in regional government) to wield an important influence. We expect salience profiles to diverge the least for parties in statewide and regional government, and the most for parties in opposition at the statewide level. Because their policy responsibility and visibility in the media are higher, parties in central executive office can be expected to strive for the highest level of consistency in the messages which they convey in statewide and regional elections. During the entire period under investigation, Labour was the sole party in central government and the lead party in Scotland and Wales. The central Labour Party should therefore try to enforce a high level of consistency between the manifestos. The Conservatives, on the other hand, were in opposition at the central and regional levels. Therefore, they should have rather distinctive issue profiles. Finally, the Liberal Democrats have been in opposition at the central level but served in coalition with Labour in Scotland (1999–2003) and Wales (2000–3). As a result, the Scottish and Welsh Liberal Democrats are likely to have a significant level of authority and autonomy to determine their own policies, and the divergence between the statewide and regional manifestos should be quite high.

Party organization, and more particularly the level of autonomy of the regional branches of the statewide parties, is likely to be an important factor. Regional branches with substantial autonomy are freer to adopt an electoral strategy to their own liking, thus potentially producing more divergent salience profiles. Hence, although a centralized party could decide to adopt distinct profiles for different sets of elections, policy divergence is more likely to occur in decentralized parties.

As the chapters by Bradbury, Fabre and Méndez-Lago have shown, the Labour Party is the party with the least autonomous regional branches. While the regional branches of Labour have some autonomy over policy-making for regional elections, the central party, via the National Executive Committee (NEC), can influence the making of regional party policy. Representatives of the NEC take part in the joint body in charge of making Scottish or Welsh election manifestos. Moreover, the Labour Party has paid a great deal of attention to the process of candidate selection (see the chapter by Bradbury in this volume). By influencing the selection of party leaders and candidates, the central party sought to produce a generation of Scottish and Welsh party leaders who shared its beliefs and policies and would therefore follow the party line established by the central party for general elections.

In contrast with Labour, the Liberal Democrats define themselves as a federal party with regional branches that are free to select their own political personnel and decide on the content of their manifestos. As a result of this federal conception of party organization, the central party does not intervene in the process of regional policy making. This freedom is not, of course, completely unchecked, in the sense that the regional branches try to retain a degree of congruence with the statewide party, so that their policies may be 'different but not dissimilar'.

Finally, the Conservative Party is positioned somewhat between Labour and the Liberal Democrats in terms of the autonomy of its regional branches. The party's Scottish and Welsh branches have been able to develop their manifestos relatively free from any central intervention. The policy-making process is mainly driven by the regional elites, in particular the regional leaders and their parliamentary parties. Unlike in the Labour Party, Conservative central office has shown little interest in the selection of its regional elites. These, however, are imbued with a strong sense of political loyalty towards the UK Conservatives. Overall, the regional branches follow the central party line for non-devolved matters but have been given considerable rein to develop their own policies over devolved areas (Seawright, 2004). On these grounds we would expect the Liberal Democrats to adopt the most distinctive salience profiles and the Labour Party the least distinctive. The Conservatives are expected to occupy an intermediary position.

The nature of the party system and the strategy of statewide parties with regard to the regionalist issue

The necessity to campaign in different sets of elections can have a strong impact on the strategy of the statewide parties across the different arenas of party competition. This is particularly the case if the regional party systems that emerge from regional elections are highly distinct from the statewide party system. Table 11.1 provides an overview of the electoral results for statewide and regional elections in the period covered by our investigation. The performance for statewide elections is based on how the relevant parties performed in the UK as a whole.

The table shows the highly distinctive nature of the Scottish and Welsh party systems compared with the statewide party system. In the regional party systems, autonomist parties easily absorb 20–30 percent of the vote, whereas they are largely absent from the statewide party system. Because of the strength of the autonomist parties in the Scottish or Welsh party systems, the statewide parties are less well represented there than in the statewide parliament. However, the discrepancy between the two levels is by far the highest for the Conservative Party (the party does about twice as well in UK elections than in Scottish or Welsh elections) and the lowest (at least in relative terms) for the Labour Party. If we consider the highly uneven performance of a party in statewide and regional elections as a predictor of a more diversified territorial strategy, then we should expect the salience

Table 11.1 Results of statewide and regional elections in Scotland and Wales, 1997–2003 (% of vote and number of seats)

		Conservative		Labour		Liberal Dem.		SNP/PC		Other	
		Votes	Seats	Votes	Seats	Votes	Seats	Votes	Seats	Votes	Seats
Scotland	1999	15.4	18 (0+18)	33.6	56 (53+3)	12.4	17 (12+5)	27.3	35 (7+28)	11.3	3 (1+2)
	2003	15.6	18 (3+15)	29.4	50 (46+4)	11.8	17 (13+4)	20.9	27 (9+18)	22.3	17 (2+15)
Wales	1999	16.5	9 (1+8)	35.4	28 (27+1)	12.5	6 (3+3)	30.5	17 (9+8)	5.1	0
	2003	19.2	11 (1+10)	36.6	30 (30+0)	12.7	6 (3+3)	19.7	12 (5+7)	8.4	1 (1+0)
UK	1997	30.7	165	43.2	418	16.8	46	2.5	10	6.8	20
	2001	31.7	166	40.7	412	18.3	52	2.5	9	6.9	20

Note: The share of the vote refers to the regional ballot. The figures between brackets are respectively for the number of constituency MSPs/AMs and regional (top-up) MSPs/AMs.
Source: House of Commons Library Research Paper 03/59 (2003) *UK Election Statistics: 1945–2003* http://www.parliament.uk/commons/lib/research/rp2003/rp03–059.pdf.

profiles of the Conservative Party to diverge the most between statewide and regional elections and those of the Labour Party to diverge the least.

The next step is to predict how parties will strategize differently in regional elections (compared with statewide elections) given the highly different nature of the party system in which they operate. In this respect we can rely on the insights of directional theory. Directional theory maps party strategies by considering the salience and position of an issue and combines both values to compute its directional intensity. Meguid (2005) has argued that parties can adopt three different attitudes with regard to any issue. A party can avoid or ignore an issue (a *dismissive* strategy, or what Maddens and Libbrecht called an 'evasive' strategy in their chapter); it can take a clear position on an issue and by doing so agree with the viewpoints of another party (an *accommodative* strategy); or it can take a clear position by explicitly opposing the viewpoints of the other party (an *adversarial* strategy).

We could argue that the strength of the UK autonomist parties may affect party competition in two ways. On the one hand, both autonomist parties are situated to the left of centre. Since they share this orientation with the Labour and Liberal Democrat parties, the Welsh and Scottish party systems are more left-wing than the UK statewide party system. In such a context, the Conservatives may wish to play safe, by emphasizing in regional elections the issues with which they are associated the most even more explicitly than in statewide elections (for example, crime, economic liberalism, law and order). However, the Conservatives could also opt for an adversarial strategy, by taking a position against the social welfare policies which the other parties propose.

The second way in which the presence of autonomist parties affects party competition follows immediately from their characterization as parties that perceive devolution as a step towards independence. In fact, the main *raison d'être* of these parties is to fight for more regional autonomy. Therefore, the regionalist issue is likely to feature as an issue of vital importance in regional elections, and in this regard party competition is structured along an autonomist–unionist axis in which all three statewide parties are positioned closer to the unionist end. After its initial rejection of devolution, the Conservative Party accepts the institutional status quo. The statewide party focuses mainly on the 'West Lothian question' and defends the existence of the union (Russel and Lodge, 2006: 68–76). The Labour Party also defends the institutional status quo and sees devolution as a way to save the union. The Liberal Democrats consider that devolution is a first step in the direction of a federal UK. The autonomist parties in turn will present themselves as the sole defenders of the regional interests while portraying the regional branches of statewide parties as merely serving the interests of the centre.

The location of the various parties on the left–right and centralist–autonomist axes of party competition affects how statewide parties will strategize. Since we cannot analyse the directional intensity for each issue in the party manifestos, we focus on the regionalist issue instead (as in the previous chapter). Given the choice, statewide parties would most likely opt for an elusive strategy with respect to this issue and emphasize their core issues instead. However, the relative strength of the autonomist parties denies statewide parties this option and forces them to explicitly address the regionalist issue. Given the 'unionist' ideology of all three statewide parties, an 'elusive strategy' remains the preferred option, but instead of giving the issue a low salience, elusiveness would result from issuing ambiguous statements. Yet not all statewide parties may be expected to adopt the same strategy; and we need to take their positions on the left–right axis into account to explain how and why they may react differently. The autonomist parties pose a stronger challenge to Labour and the Liberal Democrats than to the Conservatives because they are ideologically closer to Labour and the Liberal Democrats on the left–right scale (Webb, 2000: 19). Therefore, the Conservatives (as the only right-wing party) may wish to harm their largest statewide competitors by opting for an adversarial strategy on the regionalist issue instead. This way the Conservatives may wish to raise the importance of the regionalist issue in the campaign, and by doing so increase the salience of the regional-autonomist issue to divide the left-wing camp.

Analysis

The division of competences and issue salience

The first hypothesis asks whether the issue profiles of statewide parties reflect the division of competences between the centre and the regions. To this end we considered the salience given to specific issues in their party manifestos for statewide and regional elections (Robertson, 1976; Budge and Farlie, 1983b). We have categorized issues differently from the Comparative Manifesto Project categorization (Volkens, 2001) so as to make the analysis more suitable for a study of manifestos in the context of British regional elections (Pogorelis et al., 2005). The manifestos are divided into 18 categories (see Table 11.2).[2] As the previous chapter did, we calculated the total number of statements dedicated to each issue category as a percentage of the total number of quasi-sentences in the manifesto (Volkens, 2001). This enables us to compare party profiles on the basis of the relative salience of different issues in the manifestos of the three parties for the 1997 and 2001 general elections and for the 1999 and 2003 Scottish and Welsh elections. We include the 1997 general election in the analysis because it framed the electoral environment in which the first regional elections took place in 1999. We will observe whether each party adopts significantly different issue profiles in regional elections from those in the previous general election and how parties diverge from one another. Table 11.2 displays the salience profiles of the statewide parties. Each column lists the percentage of a party manifesto devoted to each of the 18 identified issue categories.

The data in Table 11.2 confirm that, overall, regional manifestos address issues in which the regions have gained competence more than issues which have remained under central control. This is particularly the case for issues such as education, health care and, to a lesser extent, housing, agriculture and language. The same observation applies to the issue of regional government.[3] Conversely, 'reserved matters', i.e., issues over which Westminster has retained legislative competence, are less prominent in regional election manifestos. This is most striking in foreign affairs, but this observation also applies to human rights, employment policy and taxation.

With regard to the composition of the manifestos for statewide elections, it may come as a surprise that the Labour Party did not particularly emphasize devolution in its 1997 manifesto, even though devolution was high on its agenda for constitutional reform. That statewide manifestos are not *more* distinctive in salience profiles from regional manifestos can be explained by reference to two factors. First, some issue categories contain responsibilities that are shared between the centre and the regions (in particular welfare and, in Scotland, law and order). This makes the relationship between issue salience and the type of election more difficult to evaluate. Second, and as indicated in the introductory paragraphs, statewide manifestos address issues that have been devolved to Scotland and Wales, yet remain a central competence for England. Since England represents 80 per cent of the population, such 'asymmetrically devolved' issues feature prominently in the statewide manifestos (a clear example is the high salience attributed to education in the Labour manifesto for the 1997 election, when the slogan 'education, education, education' featured prominently in the Labour campaign).

In terms of the issues that are emphasized by each party, Table 11.2 shows that Labour placed a strong emphasis on economic development and social issues (education, welfare and health care). The Conservatives have also focused on education and health care, but law and order, agriculture and rural affairs, all of which are 'traditional' Conservative concerns, occupy a greater share of the Conservative manifestos. Finally, the Liberal Democrats have put most of their emphasis on social themes such as education and health care, but have emphasized environmental issues more than the other parties. These inter-party differences appear in each and every election, irrespective of its type. They are consistent with the viewpoint that parties will want to 'own' certain issues, particularly those that are associated the most with the ideology they support.

Party ideology, incumbency and organization, and their effect on issue divergence

Perhaps the most interesting question from the viewpoint of analysing salience in a multilayered context is whether the salience profiles of the

Table 11.2 Issue salience in the manifestos of the British statewide parties, 1997–2003

Election	1997			1999						2001			2003						Average salience
Region/nation	UK			Scotland			Wales			UK			Scotland			Wales			
Party	Lab	Con	LD	Lab	Con	LD	Lab	Con	LD	Lab	Con	LD	Lab	Con	LD	Lab	Con	LD	
National gvt	6.4	5.8	3.8	0.0	0.0	0.0	0.0	0.0	0.0	1.9	7.0	4.0	0.0	0.0	0.0	0.0	0.0	0.0	1.61
Regional gvt	0.9	2.0	1.9	3.5	3.8	7.9	12.7	8.8	9.1	2.1	0.0	2.1	4.0	12.4	3.5	2.2	10.8	4.9	5.14
Local gvt	3.6	1.7	1.0	4.3	4.7	3.1	0.0	12.2	4.0	2.7	3.8	2.1	3.1	6.2	2.0	1.9	4.5	4.2	3.62
Econ. devt	9.3	14.3	9.6	10.2	3.8	10.1	6.3	7.3	6.2	6.7	3.4	6.6	10.0	8.9	3.5	10.4	8.8	6.6	7.88
Taxation	5.0	3.0	5.2	1.2	4.6	5.8	0.0	0.5	0.7	1.4	7.3	2.8	2.1	1.0	2.4	2.4	2.6	2.7	2.81
Education	12.3	11.9	11.4	14.1	13.2	18.2	13.7	7.8	14.7	10.7	6.4	11.1	15.5	14.6	13.3	16.1	11.5	10.5	12.62
Health care	6.5	5.1	9.3	12.9	12.9	10.3	10.3	9.8	10.6	7.7	8.7	8.3	11.3	13.9	17.9	14.1	13.6	10.6	10.77
Housing	3.1	2.8	3.7	4.3	3.3	3.6	2.3	1.0	5.0	1.3	1.7	1.7	1.9	0.8	4.4	3.5	1.0	4.9	2.79
Employment	7.4	3.4	1.8	4.0	2.9	0.9	3.3	0.0	0.5	6.9	1.9	2.8	1.4	0.0	0.4	5.7	0.4	0.0	2.44
Welfare	7.8	13.1	13.4	15.9	2.3	8.2	15.3	10.2	7.3	14.7	17.0	6.8	8.8	1.3	6.0	11.3	14.9	7.4	10.09
Law and order	5.9	12.2	4.9	4.8	18.9	6.3	0.3	0.0	3.0	9.5	9.1	9.5	9.4	15.8	14.1	6.3	4.4	5.2	7.77
Human rights	1.6	0.9	3.3	1.1	0.8	0.8	2.3	0.0	0.0	1.3	3.1	4.0	0.0	0.0	0.0	0.2	3.2	1.1	1.32
Environment	2.1	2.8	8.8	2.8	2.8	6.0	2.7	4.9	7.9	2.2	1.3	9.5	4.5	1.7	8.0	4.3	1.9	7.8	4.55
Leisure	2.6	2.9	2.4	4.8	3.3	2.9	4.7	5.4	10.5	3.7	5.3	3.7	4.1	2.5	4.8	5.0	8.3	7.8	4.72
Transport	3.5	3.2	2.1	2.7	2.6	3.9	2.7	3.9	6.6	4.0	2.8	7.8	5.2	3.8	6.7	6.7	4.4	7.0	4.42
Agriculture	1.9	3.2	3.1	5.5	16.6	5.6	3.7	9.3	8.0	2.3	7.0	2.1	3.8	10.6	7.4	2.8	5.5	8.5	5.93
Language	0.0	0.0	0.0	1.9	0.2	0.3	2.0	4.9	2.1	0.0	0.0	0.0	0.7	0.3	0.8	2.2	2.3	5.6	1.30
Foreign affairs	9.5	8.1	9.3	1.1	0.0	2.1	3.7	3.4	0.0	10.8	10.7	11.3	3.4	0.0	0.0	0.0	0.1	0.2	4.10
General	10.5	3.8	4.9	4.7	3.4	3.9	14.0	10.7	3.7	10.1	3.5	3.6	10.7	6.2	4.6	5.0	1.6	5.2	6.12
TOTAL	100	100	100	100	100	100	100	100	100	100	100	100	100	100	100	100	100	100	100

parties differ more between statewide and regional elections than between different sets of regional elections, and whether such differences can be related to differences in party ideology, party organizational culture or incumbency.

Taking a closer look at Table 11.2, we see that the salience profiles tend to vary the most between elections for the Conservative Party, particularly with regard to issues such as regional government (2001–2003), local government, education (2001–2003), healthcare (1997–1999) and agriculture. The degree of issue divergence between statewide and regional elections is much lower for the Liberal Democrats and the Labour Party. These data suggest that overall the degree of party organizational decentralization and the degree of divergence between manifestos for statewide and regional elections change together. Indeed, on that basis we would have expected issue divergence to be the most explicit for the Liberal Democrats, and the least for Labour (as the organizationally more centralized of the parties). The Conservatives would have occupied an intermediary position. Instead, the findings are consistent with the viewpoint that Labour as a party in central and regional office cannot tolerate issue divergence (in terms of salience) as much as the Conservatives (who as the statewide and regional opposition party are much less constrained to emphasize different issues in different sets of elections). On these grounds, the Liberal Democrats should occupy an intermediary position indeed.

For each party, we can measure changes in salience profile more systematically by computing a dissimilarity measure, calculated as the sum of the absolute differences between the issue percentages, divided by the number of issue categories. The higher the measure, the more distinctive are the two compared manifestos in terms of their salience. The formula for this measure is:

$$D = \frac{\sum \left(\left| S_{i1} - S_{i2} \right| + \ldots \left| S_{n1} - S_{n2} \right| \right)}{n},$$

with D the distinctiveness of the issue profile, S_{i1} the salience of the issue i for party 1, S_{i2} the salience of issue i for party 2, and n the number of issue categories. In this way, we can compare for each party (1) each statewide election manifesto with the successive regional election manifesto, and (2) the regional party manifestos in concurrent Scottish and Welsh elections (Table 11.3).

First, Table 11.3 confirms the observations that were inferred from Table 11.2. Overall, the Conservative Party systematically displays the highest degree of divergence, whereas divergence is lowest for the Labour Party. On average, the Liberal Democrat manifestos are slightly more distinctive than those of Labour, but not by much (only 0.04, a negligible difference). Furthermore, between 1997 and 1999 the Liberal Democrat manifestos were actually more alike than those of Labour in terms of issue salience, whereas

Table 11.3 Divergence of the parties' issue profiles between consecutive statewide and regional elections and between concurrent regional elections

	1997–Scotland 1999	1997–Wales 1999	Scotland–Wales 1999	Average 1997–1999	2001–Scotland 2003	2001–Wales 2003	Scotland–Wales 2003	Average 2001–2003	Total Average
Labour	3.18	3.68	2.36	3.07	2.33	2.90	1.74	2.32	2.70
Conservative	3.86	4.76	4.73	4.45	5.10	3.63	2.93	3.89	4.17
Liberal Democrats	2.48	3.76	2.12	2.79	3.03	3.00	2.07	2.70	2.74
Average	3.17	4.10	3.07	3.44	3.49	3.18	2.25	2.97	3.20

the opposite was true for the period between 2001 and 2003. However, these observations should be made against the backdrop of an overall very low divergence or distinctiveness of salience profiles in regional elections compared with statewide elections and of very small inter-regional differences in salience profile. Thus, one could make the case that even the Conservative profiles have remained relatively similar in spite of the scope for divergence being potentially much larger as a result of that party's opposition role at all levels. The fact that divergence remains limited suggests that the overall cohesion of the Conservative Party message may have remained a major consideration when the manifestos were drafted.

Second, Table 11.3 allows us to consider the development of divergence over time. We would have expected the distinctiveness of the issue profiles to increase over time, as the first regional elections (1999) were the formative elections for the Scottish Parliament and the Welsh Assembly. This is true only for two pairs of statewide–regional manifestos: the Scottish Conservatives and the Scottish Liberal Democrats. In Wales, however, the distinctiveness of the regional manifestos relative to the adjacent statewide manifestos decreased for all three parties. Moreover, while in 1999 the Welsh manifestos were systematically more different from the 1997 statewide manifestos than the Scottish ones, there is no clear trend in the 2003 election.

The strategy of the statewide parties with regard to the regionalist issue: A directional approach

As indicated above, directional theory assumes that party strategies will fluctuate with the nature of the party systems in which they compete. Due to the more left-wing orientation of the Scottish and Welsh party systems and the relative strength of the autonomist parties, we expected statewide parties to strategize very differently in Scottish or Welsh elections than in statewide elections. Thus far, the empirical evidence does not support this hypothesis: party strategies based on salience profiles alone do not display such a widely anticipated divergence. Furthermore, divergence can be attributed primarily to the fact that the devolved elections determine different sets of competences, and much less to the deliberate strategy of statewide parties to emphasize different issues.

However, the above analysis is entirely based on the mapping of salience profiles, and directional theory encourages us to take position (direction) into account as well. Although we cannot add positional information for each issue category, we focus on how statewide parties position themselves on the regionalist issue. The latter is a two-faceted concept: on the one hand, it refers to the debate about the structure of the state and the respective powers of the central and regional governments. This is the institutional dimension of the regionalist issue, which aims at redefining the institutional relations between the regions and the centre. On the other hand, the regionalist issue has a cultural-identitarian component that expresses or defends a distinct regional or cultural identity, separate from that of the centre or of the other regions (Keating and Loughlin, 1997: 2–3). The perception of a distinctive regional culture can be linked to the existence of a regional language. Therefore, references to linguistic policy and regional languages are included in this cultural dimension of regionalism. The two dimensions need not be mutually exclusive. On the contrary, the perception of a separate identity may lend support to claims of regional autonomy. However, it is also possible for a party to support regional identities and languages without requesting a strengthening of the regional institutions. Conversely, decentralization can be considered in purely functional terms alone, without reference to or support for cultural identity (as in France).

We have screened all the quasi-sentences in the party manifestos for the presence of 'the regionalist issue'. Whenever we believed that a statement expressed an opinion on the institutional or cultural dimension of regionalism, it was coded as a regionalist issue.[4] This directional coding enables us to go beyond the sole measure of salience and provides us with measures for the directional certainty and intensity of a party's position on the regionalist issue. The directional certainty measures the consistency of a party's position and ranges between 1 (all the sentences are in one direction) to minus 1 (all the sentences are in the opposite direction). For the calculation of directional certainty, the quasi-sentences coded 1 and minus 1 are given a weight of 0.5. The directional certainty is calculated by summing the number of clear statements in one direction and the number of hints in the same direction (weighted by half), deducting the sum of the clear statements in the other directions and the hints in that direction (weighted by half), and dividing the outcome by the total number of sentences on the issue.

$$DC = \frac{(s_2 + \frac{1}{2}s_1) - (s_{-2} + \frac{1}{2}s_{-1})}{s_r},$$

with s_2 the number of sentences with code 2, s_1 the number of sentences with code 1, etc., and s_r the total number of regionalist statements. A score of 0 indicates that the party has an equal number of sentences in each direction, meaning that it has no preference either way. Subsequently, directional intensity measures the strength of a party's position and is calculated by multiplying the directional certainty of an issue by its salience.

Table 11.4 presents the salience, directional certainty and directional intensity of the regionalism on both of its dimensions. The data for the Scottish National Party (SNP) and Plaid Cymru are included in order to compare the importance of the regionalist issues for autonomist and statewide parties.

A first observation is that, for each of the elections under consideration, the regionalist issue has not been very salient but also that in statewide and Scottish elections the institutional component of regionalism has been emphasized more consistently than the cultural component. In Wales,

Table 11.4   Party profiles on the regionalist issue, 1997–2003 (salience as a percentage of the whole manifesto)

	Conservative		Labour		Liberal Democrats		SNP		Plaid Cymru	
	Inst	Cult	Inst	Cult	Inst	Cult	Inst	Cult	Inst	Cult
Salience										
State 1997	1.50	0.47	2.47	0.26	0.55	0	16.56	2.51	12.71	3.79
Scotland 1999	2.45	0.82	5.38	3.10	4.42	0.94	10.57	1.90		
Wales 1999	4.39	11.22	5.33	2.67	1.46	3.41			7.11	4.60
State 2001	0.60	0	1.39	0.05	1.68	0.15	12.17	2.37	17.72	2.49
Scotland 2003	4.11	1.11	3.60	1.59	1.60	0.80	7.61	1.54		
Wales 2003	1.72	4.31	3.07	2.35	4.50	5.75			8.98	6.34
Directional Certainty										
State 1997	−0.37	0.33	0.69	0.17	1	0	0.98	0.63	0.99	0.74
Scotland 1999	−0.13	0.5	0.14	0.63	0.48	0.57	0.88	0.89		
Wales 1999	−0.50	−0.33	0.44	0.50	0.63	0.75			0.77	0.64
State 2001	−0.3	0	0.35	0.50	0.84	0.5	0.95	0.60	0.87	0.65
Scotland 2003	−0.04	0.36	0.46	0.67	0.63	0.63	0.94	0.83		
Wales 2003	0.33	0.53	0.32	0.58	0.91	0.76			0.95	0.86
Directional Intensity										
State 1997	−0.55	0.16	1.71	0.04	0.55	0	16.30	1.59	12.59	2.81
Scotland 1999	−0.33	0.41	0.74	1.95	2.14	0.54	9.35	1.70		
Wales 1999	−2.2	−3.66	2.33	1.33	0.91	2.56			5.47	2.95
State 2001	−0.18	0	0.49	0.03	1.41	0.08	11.52	1.43	15.44	1.61
Scotland 2003	−0.16	0.40	1.64	1.06	1.00	0.50	7.15	1.29		
Wales 2003	0.57	2.30	0.99	1.35	4.11	4.35			8.49	5.43

however, the Conservatives and Liberal Democrats ran against this trend by emphasizing regional culture and language more than the institutional dimension of regionalism. Even so, the institutional component of regionalism is not necessarily emphasized in Wales less than in Scotland or in statewide elections.

The relatively high salience of cultural and regional issues in 1999 among the Welsh Conservatives coincides with a period in which the Welsh Assembly was only nascent and the Conservatives portrayed it as a quasi non-governmental organization (quango); hence high salience coincides with negative position scores. This suggests that the Welsh Conservatives were trying to emphasize the issue by disparaging institutional regionalism. It appears that they behaved as if they sought to harm the Labour Party by drawing votes away from them to Plaid Cymru. In 2003, however, the Welsh Conservatives 'kept quiet', and the Liberal Democrats were more adamant in supporting full legislative powers for the Welsh Assembly and linked this with a positive evaluation of the Welsh identity. Hence, high salience combined with positive directional certainty led to high directional intensity values for the Liberal Democrats. This suggests that, while in 1999 the Welsh Conservatives may have believed that a clear but negative stance against regionalism could harm the electoral fortunes of Labour and the Liberal Democrats, they had retreated from this strategy by 2003. Taking such a clearly negative stance against Welsh devolution was perceived as a risk. The relatively strong stance against devolution might have harmed Labour in 1999, but it clearly did not draw votes to the Conservatives either, as the party performed poorly in the election. In 2003 the Conservatives preferred to de-emphasize the issue instead (institutional dimension) or to express more favourable statements with respect to Welsh identity (cultural dimension). Predictably, Table 11.4 also reveals that the autonomist parties devote considerably more attention to regionalism and position themselves consistently in favour of more regional autonomy or cultural regionalism.

A second observation which derives from Table 11.4 is that for each of the statewide parties the directional certainty of cultural-linguistic regionalism is generally higher than that of institutional regionalism. In a sense, this is predictable: the consequences of supporting Scottish or Welsh identity and culture are negligible, at least in the short term, whereas demands for more regional competences or a substantial reform of the devolution settlement generate direct policy repercussions. That said, the directional intensity of cultural-linguistic regionalism for the statewide parties remains rather lower than the intensity recorded for the autonomist parties.

Third, we can observe whether individual parties have strategized in the way predicted in our hypotheses. In the case of Labour, the lower directional intensity for institutional regionalism is more a consequence of satisfaction with the institutional status quo than of a lack of emphasis. In every election Labour emphasized institutions more than cultural-linguistic issues. Positional values close to 0 on the institutional dimension do not come as a surprise: after all, Labour shaped devolution from the top (parliamentary acts) and from the bottom (by dominating the composition of all regional governments). Therefore, it would be odd if the party were to propose drastic changes to the devolution settlement, so soon after devolution was established. Rather, with the competition from autonomist parties and a more proportional electoral system, the Labour Party seems to have chosen to become a little more regionalist in terms of supporting Scottish or Welsh identity (the directional certainty on this dimension is consistently superior at 0.5).

In line with our expectations, the Liberal Democrats are the statewide party with the highest directional intensity for the institutional dimension of regionalism. However, this is more a product of salience than of position. The 2003 Welsh manifesto has a higher directional intensity than that of any other statewide party. With regard to institutional change, the party remains committed to a federal United Kingdom and this is reflected in the party's scores. As indicated above, in the 2003 Welsh election the Liberal Democrats adopted their most intense position, on both institutional and cultural issues. Directional certainty values were higher than for any other statewide party in the regional elections (for Wales and Scotland).

As expected, the only party to have adopted a centralist position (negative score) on the institutional dimension is the Conservative Party. It did so in each and every election but the 2003 Welsh election. This position is consistent with the party's unionist creed and its initial opposition to devolution. At the same time, the intensity of the party's position is usually low. The most striking case of deviation from the central party is that of the Welsh Conservative Party. In 1999, the party was more intensely centralist on both dimensions of regionalism than in any other elections. In 2003, the Conservatives, however, adopted a rather regionalist position. They apparently decided to market themselves as a more 'Wales-friendly', party to reflect the growing acceptance of (or adaptation to) devolution within the party. In comparison, the Scottish Conservatives have been less reluctant to campaign against devolution throughout (negative score for directional certainty, but values for institutional regionalism are close to 0). However, save for the 1999 Welsh election, the Conservatives have shown a moderately favourable stance towards regional language and cultural matters.

A final observation is that all the statewide parties have been relatively consistent in their regionalist profiles. The regionalism is only slightly more prominent in regional than in statewide elections, in particular when one compares the salience of regionalism between statewide and autonomist parties. There is a tendency (albeit not consistent) for statewide parties to support cultural or linguistic regionalism (as, on the whole, directional intensity values are higher than for institutional regionalism) more than institutional regionalism. As indicated above, it is easier for statewide parties to accommodate regional sensitivities by promoting cultural regionalism than to advocate significant institutional change.

The strategy of the statewide parties with regard to the regionalist issue: a 'discourse analysis' approach

The previous subsection has shown that statewide parties have adopted a lower regionalist profile than their regionalist rivals. This is consistent with the predictions of directional theory, as regionalist themes are expected to be 'primed' by the autonomist parties. However, when examining and coding the manifesto statements we realised that the rhetoric of some statewide parties made ample use of substantives and adjectives referring to the name of the region. The words 'Scotland', 'Wales', 'Scottish', 'Scot' and 'Welsh' appeared very often in their regional manifestos, and we felt that some statewide parties even surpassed the autonomist parties in this respect. The use of these substantives or adjectives is not sufficient to categorize a quasi-sentence as a 'culturally' regionalist one. Nonetheless, statewide parties believe that such appeals to regional identity could help them assert their Scottish or Welsh roots.

Identity rhetoric is made up not only of references to a community's 'core values' (Smolicz, 1981 and 1988) that should be preserved and fostered. It is also made up of signs and indicators of the intensity of belonging, pride and commitment vis-à-vis the community of reference (Bollen and Hoyle, 1990; Bollen and Díez-Medrano, 1998; Martínez-Herrera, 2005). In this sense, the urge to mention national or regional denominations or to add adjectives alluding to the community of reference can be interpreted as such rhetorical signs of belonging and commitment. The possibility that the use of such denominations appeared as often or even more frequently in the manifestos of moderately regionalist statewide parties than in those of the autonomist parties seemed particularly telling. This suggests that they were concerned that their public image seemed less representative of and committed to Scotland or Wales than that of their autonomist rivals. Furthermore, statewide parties might seek to counterbalance a moderately or ambiguously regionalist profile with the assertion of a strong identification with the region as a whole. Thus, an additional analysis of party manifestos was performed in order to evaluate the extent to which statewide parties refer to the regions in which they compete. A word count revealing the frequency with which parties appeal to Britain provides a useful comparison in identity references.

Table 11.5 presents the word counts of regional references and of references to the British identity. A comparison of the two can show which identity statewide and autonomist parties tend to emphasize and how they deal with dual identities. A first observation is that manifestos for statewide elections mainly target an English electorate. As a result, it is not surprising to find such low levels of reference to Scotland and Wales. Second, in regional elections all three statewide parties make extensive use of references to the region, in particular in Wales, where the number of references to Wales even exceeded that made by Plaid Cymru. In Scotland, the Liberal Democrats and the Conservatives made as many references to the region as the SNP in the 2003 regional elections, and Labour even referred more frequently to the region than the SNP in both regional elections.

References to Great Britain ('Britain', 'British') could reflect the importance of the whole country and community for a party, while avoiding the term could imply an absence of allegiance (in particular in the case of autonomist parties) or, from the viewpoint of the statewide parties, a strategy to compete against the autonomist parties. References to Britain are particularly scarce in

Table 11.5   Word count of references to national identity (British, Scottish and Welsh) (figures in per thousand out of the total number of words in the manifesto)

	Conservative	Labour	Liberal Democrats	SNP	Plaid Cymru
Region (Wales/Welsh – Scotland/Scottish/Scot) name count					
General 1997	1.41	1.75	0.68	27.17	17.56
Scotland 1999	18.03	25.03	19.24	21.46	
Wales 1999	17.73	28.20	23.96		15.21
General 2001	1.11	0.98	1.51	22.43	13.57
Scotland 2003	15.53	18.95	15.38	15.90	
Wales 2003	28.26	23.78	31.87		18.19
'Brit-' count					
General 1997	6.48	5.54	6.40	0.44	0.43
Scotland 1999	0.55	1.13	0.35	0.00	
Wales 1999	4.43	0.00	0.29		0.17
General 2001	5.16	4.79	3.12	0.23	2.36
Scotland 2003	0.33	0.11	0.21	0.22	
Wales 2003	0.52	0.24	0.00		0.18

regional election manifestos. In 1999, the Welsh Conservatives made more frequently use of words starting with 'Brit-' than the other parties, but by 2003 the frequency was comparable to that of the other parties (less than 1 per thousand of the manifestos). This confirms the gradual trend in the party's issue profiles towards a regionalist position on cultural and linguistic issues.

Overall, this analysis confirms that statewide parties with a more ambiguous attitude to institutional regionalism and moderate support for cultural regionalism also make generous use of words that refer to the region in which they compete. This could be explained by the fact that they try to emphasize their loyalty and self-identification to the region and minimize their British identity as a statewide party in a context of electoral competition against autonomist parties. As a result, they seek to compensate a moderately or ambiguously regionalist profile with repeated references to the region. Again, it is much easier to refer to the identity of the region than to make pledges on institutional reform.

Conclusion

This chapter analysed the extent to which British statewide parties have adapted their campaign strategies to devolution. The empirical evidence is based on a salience analysis of all the issues in the party manifestos for statewide and regional elections between 1997 and 2003 and a directional analysis on the regionalist issue alone on the same set of manifestos.

The analysis confirms the hypothesis that statewide parties pay more attention to the issues in which the regions are competent during regional elections than during statewide elections. Overall, statewide parties display moderate levels of divergence in terms of their salience profiles between statewide and regional elections. To some extent, divergence is limited by the fact that even during statewide elections the parties cannot fail to address issues over which Scotland and Wales have gained competence because these issues have remained 'central' for all citizens living in England. Interestingly, the divergence in salience profiles between statewide and regional elections did not increase between 1999 and 2003.

The salience analysis does not confirm that more decentralized political parties adopt more divergent issue profiles, nor do they give credence to the assumption that party ideologies that are more favourable to decentralization coincide with more divergent campaigns. In fact, the Conservative Party has produced the most divergent salience profiles, whereas the profiles of the Labour Party are the most similar. The salience profiles of the Liberal Democrats, which on both accounts should be the most divergent, are hardly more divergent than those of Labour. However, these findings support the view that incumbent parties are under more pressure to produce congruent party platforms across the various levels in which they compete. As a party in statewide and regional opposition, the Conservatives are less constrained in this respect.

In the second part of the article we tested whether the observations based on a salience analysis could be confirmed by a directional analysis of the regionalist issue alone. Regionalism was chosen because it allows for a direct comparison with the previous chapter, and because it takes into account one of the most distinctive features of the Scottish and Welsh party systems: the presence of significant autonomist parties. Overall, the analysis confirmed that statewide parties emphasized regionalism a little more in regional than in statewide elections. Furthermore, the difference is somewhat larger for the cultural-linguistic component of the issue than for the institutional component. Ideology seems to have more predictive power with respect to regionalism: the Liberal Democrats displayed the highest values for directional intensity whereas directional intensity was much lower for Labour and the Conservatives. The Welsh Conservatives' strategy in 1999 was different from that in 2003. In 1999, they attempted an adversarial strategy and combined relatively high salience with negative positional values. However, as by 2003 opposition against Welsh devolution had waned, the party adopted a more elusive strategy.

The analysis of the regionalist issue has also shown that statewide parties, in particular Labour and the Conservatives, tend to focus on the cultural-linguistic dimension of regionalism rather than on proposals to alter the institutional status quo. This may be explained by the fact that both parties favour maintaining the institutional status quo. As a consequence, when competing against autonomist parties, they try to emphasize their allegiance to the regions by supporting their cultural heritage. This is a relatively easy and non-committal way to enhance their regional credentials. These findings were broadly confirmed by a comparison of their use of identity rhetoric. In regional manifestos statewide parties frequently use the name of the region, sometimes even more than the autonomist parties do. References to a region and its identity and culture provide the statewide parties with opportunities to show their attachment to that particular region without at the same time appearing to be disloyal towards the Union, the central party and its policies.

Our findings have implications for two rival theoretical models of voting: classical spatial theory and directional theory. When faced with a regionalist competitor, the British statewide parties have tended to adopt a dismissive or ambiguous profile on the institutional dimension of regionalism. Moreover, in the 1999 Welsh elections the Conservatives primed the issue by disparaging regionalism both in institutional and cultural-identitarian matters, which seems to aim both at drawing votes away from Labour towards the autonomist party, and at capitalizing on the scepticism towards devolution shared by a substantial section of the Welsh electorate. This lends further credence to directional theory. However, some exceptions to this pattern and the fact that statewide parties have often adopted a regionalist stance on the cultural dimension and on identitarian rhetoric support the spatial theory of voting. Evidence is mixed and neither theoretical model seems to fit the data better than the other. A further step (not pursued in this chapter) is to apply spatial and directional theory to issues which appeared to be much more salient in the campaign than the regional issue, for instance health or education. These issues have also proven to be more contentious, in particular for the governing party. They certainly account for a share of the divergences that Hopkin and Bradbury (2006) have observed in the 2003 election.

Concluding Observations

Wilfried Swenden and Bart Maddens

Having analysed the dynamics of territorial party politics in some significant West European countries, we wish now to consider to what extent our findings support the theoretically informed expectations that were formulated in the Introduction. We have formulated our concluding observations by linking them directly to the relevant hypotheses, and therefore they may not respect the order of the empirical chapters in this book.

The 'nationalization thesis' reconsidered and the relationship between the regionalization of the state and the denationalization of the multilevel party system

Testing 'nationalization'

In the Introduction we did not criticize the empirical evidence presented by the most significant studies of party system nationalization, but we raised two significant concerns. First, the 'nationalization thesis' is counter-intuitive, especially for countries such as Belgium, Spain, Italy (and, following unification, even Germany), which have decentralized their state structures in recent decades. Except for Belgium, these are all large and populous West European states. Hence, a longitudinal and detailed study of the extent to which the (multilevel) party systems of some of these states have (de)nationalized could shed a different light on the 'party system nationalization thesis' in Western Europe as a whole (Caramani, 2004). Second, we argued that such a test would benefit from studying party systems as 'multilevel' party systems and therefore also from taking into consideration the results for regional elections.

Two contributions to this volume address these concerns in some depth. The first contribution, by Kris Deschouwer, analysed developments in the *statewide* party systems of Belgium and Spain. The federalization or regionalization of these states since 1980 is indisputable, and in light thereof a denationalization of their statewide party systems could be anticipated. Yet Deschouwer does not find sufficient evidence to confirm this expectation.

In Belgium, the Dutch- and French-speaking statewide party systems, while noticeably different in the relative electoral strength of each party family member, have *not* grown much further apart since the early 1980s (the outcome of the federal election of 2007 notwithstanding). A similar pattern was observed in Spain: the results for Spanish general elections have not become more denationalized. In fact, compared with previous statewide elections, the results for the last election to be included in the analysis (March 2004) are the most distinctive in just two of the 17 autonomous communities.

Deschouwer's observations are based on an analysis of developments in the statewide party system alone. Hough and Koß pursue a comparable exercise for the German case but also incorporate regional election results. Their chapter serves two purposes: first, to test whether German voters have displayed increasing regional differences in the parties they vote for in statewide elections (to test the nationalization thesis); second, to analyse whether German voters increasingly display multilevel voting behaviour, and by doing so reduce the second orderness of German regional elections. With respect to the first objective, the authors find sufficient evidence of denationalization: unlike in Belgium and Spain, the German statewide party system has denationalized since 1990, although volatility patterns are much reduced if we consider movements within party blocs rather than between individual parties. With respect to the second objective, Hough and Koß find evidence of an increasing 'decoupling' between statewide and *Land* elections: how a party performs regionally in statewide elections has become a less reliable predictor of how it will perform in the nearest *Land* election. Their findings suggest that German regional elections no longer display all the characteristics of second-order elections: although there may be lower turnouts still and an stronger tendency to vote for smaller parties in regional elections than in statewide elections, regional voters may also become increasingly mobilized on regional issues.

The analysis of the German multilevel party system raises three important questions. First, to what extent is the 'denationalization' of the German statewide party system an isolated phenomenon that can be attributed to unification? Is unification an important 'critical juncture' that strengthened the territorial heterogeneity of Germany in socio-economic terms, triggered more regionally diversified voting patterns in statewide elections and increased the extent of multilevel voting? The data show that unification intensified electoral volatility and reduced the evenness of regional support for the large statewide German parties, especially as a result of the success for the PDS in Eastern Germany. Second, is this pattern set to continue or are we in fact witnessing a partial 'Easternization' of the West German party system, due to the electoral breakthrough of an all-German Left Party and the narrowing gap between East and West German voters in terms of volatility, at least in statewide elections? In this sense, could we be witnessing the stabilization or at least a partial 'renationalization' of the German statewide party system in the short term? Finally, is the rise of multilevel voting replicated across those West European states whose statewide party systems have not become more denationalized (such as Belgium and Spain)? Although the contributions to this volume do not consider this last question, in recent years several authors have analysed the scope of 'multilevel voting' in the UK and Spain (Trystan, Scully and Wyn Jones, 2003; Hough and Jeffery, 2006b; Pallarés and Keating, 2006). These studies demonstrate the presence of 'dual' and multilevel voting. However, in Spain the degree of multilevel voting varies considerably between the autonomous communities and does not seem to have *increased* since the early 1990s (see Hough and Jeffery, 2006b, Pallarés and Keating, 2006). If we combine the evidence presented in this volume, and the analysis of regional electoral behaviour mentioned above, it seems that a homogenization of electoral results in statewide elections does not frequently coincide with a heterogenization of electoral outcomes in regional elections. This statement remains to be tested among a much larger group of statewide and regional elections; but, if true, it would undermine a key assumption of our Introduction.

Developments in the party system and authority migration

The contributions by Deschouwer and Hough and Koß enable us to assess the relationship between the migration of authority (centralization or decentralization) within the state and the (de)nationalization of the party system. Chhibber and Kollman's work (2004) suggests that these two aspects are directly related. The evidence presented in these chapters does *not* bear this out. In fact, the gradual process in which Belgium and Spain have become *federalized* or *highly regionalized* states is not paralleled by an equally spectacular *denationalization* of their party systems. Arguably, in Belgium the denationalization of the party system was already complete when the country took its first steps towards federalizing the state. The break-up of the statewide parties removed the most crucial mechanism for aggregating votes from the regional to the statewide level. Yet, after they had split, both parties of the same family (e.g., Flemish and francophone Social Democrats, Flemish and francophone Christian Democrats, etc.) generally moved in similar directions while the state continued to decentralize. The 2007 elections may be a turning point insofar as the difference between the Dutch-speaking and the francophone party systems is increasing. This could be a consequence of the uncoupling of statewide and regional elections since 2003, and especially the asymmetries in the party political composition of the federal and regional governments. Similarly, in Spain major shifts in the migration of authority to the regional levels occurred in the 1990s, although the Spanish statewide party system did not become particularly more denationalized in that decade. Conversely, the denationalization of the German party system did not immediately generate a more decentralized federation, at least not in formal terms. Significant constitutional change did not take place until the formation of a federal 'Grand Coalition' (CDU/CSU-SPD) government in 2005.

Overall, these findings suggest three important conclusions. First, there is no straightforward correlation between authority migration and party system nationalization: state decentralization can coincide with a stabilization or even relative nationalization of the (statewide) party system. Conversely, a denationalizing party system does not necessarily coincide with a decentralizing state, at least not in formal or constitutional terms. For instance, while Detterbeck and Jeffery suggest that recent and pending constitutional reforms shift German federalism into a more decentralizing direction, not all parties that have contributed to denationalizing the party system (in particular the PDS) support, let alone stand to benefit from, a more denationalized federation. Furthermore, constitutional reforms take more time to register than shifts in electoral behaviour, especially in a federation like Germany where the *Länder* can exercise a collective veto right in the centre through the Bundesrat, and the federal majority parties do not necessarily hold a majority of seats in the second chamber.

Second, the findings do not lend support to the assumed *direction* of the relationship between authority migration and the (de)nationalization of the party system. Changes in the structure of the state do not necessarily trigger changes in the party system, as Chhibber and Kollman have argued (Chhibber and Kollman, 2004). In Belgium, the parties had almost entirely split *before* the state embarked upon a process of federalization, and in Spain, too, the formative elections of the late 1970s and early 1980s immediately demonstrated the success of autonomist parties. Therefore, in Belgium an increasing regional divergence of electoral results and swings seems to have *caused* institutional regionalization and not the other way around. At least until 2007, institutional regionalization may have contained the further denationalization of voting in statewide elections. In Spain, too, some of the autonomist parties have played an influential role in decentralizing the state, especially when the political opportunity structure to weigh into national politics was there, i.e., when a national minority government relied on their support. Progressive steps to further strengthen the powers of the Spanish regions may have prevented a further increase in their support or in the extent to which votes for statewide parties are spread heterogeneously across the regions of the state and thereby *contained* rather than increased a denationalization of voting.

Finally, the findings suggest that changes in the (de)centralization of the state or the (de)nationalization of the party system are often linked to broader societal developments which restructure the nature or change the relative importance of territorial cleavages. For instance, as Verleden illustrates in his chapter on Belgium, the decreasing salience of the ideological divide between Catholics and non-believers after the Second World War, coupled with a reversal of economic fortunes (now benefiting the Dutch-speaking Flemish population), gave a different meaning to long-standing Flemish demands for more cultural autonomy. The language divide became a more 'attractive' cleavage on which to mobilize support. The rise of new political agents (autonomist parties) prompted a (radical) response from the statewide parties. In turn, their break-up along linguistic lines and thereby also the break-up of the statewide party system as a whole paved the way for institutional reform, that is, the institutions were adapted to the disintegration of the party system, which in turn was caused by structural changes in society. Deschouwer's data nicely support this link between party systemic and state systemic developments: an increase in the regional divergence of electoral results and swings disintegrates the statewide party system. Yet, after adopting regional and eventually federal institutional devices, centrifugal tendencies in the statewide party system are again contained (notwithstanding a more recent upsurge of electoral heterogeneity). Unification has had a similar heterogenizing effect on the German party system (though the state systemic repercussions are still bearing fruit) since it generated a much more territorially heterogeneous society in which the East–West divide trumped an already present (but much less salient) divide between the rich *Länder* of the South, and some relatively poor *Länder* of the North (again, a reversal of fortunes, compared with the immediate post-war period). However, we should also warn against overemphasizing the impact of changes in the importance of (domestic) territorial cleavages alone. For instance, in Italy the North–South cleavage has been present throughout, yet remained without much political salience until the beginning of the 1990s. This has changed drastically since then, although Italian society as whole had not become territorially more heterogeneous. The end of the Cold War, and the scandals surrounding the long-governing Christian Democrats and Social Democrats that triggered the implosion of the old party system, opened up a window of opportunity for the mobilization of electoral support along the territorial cleavage. The *Lega Nord* quickly filled this void.

Statewide parties and the challenge of multilevel politics: Party organization and policy

Statewide parties provide by far the most important element of linkage between the statewide and the regional party systems. Therefore, the more successful these parties are in garnering electoral support across the regions of the state in statewide and regional elections, the stronger is the integration of the party system.

In this section we focus on two important questions. First, to what extent are the organization, strategies and policies of the statewide parties related to the processes of state (de)centralization and party system (de)nationalization? Second, insofar as there is a causal link between each of these processes (party organizational adaptation, party system nationalization and state decentralization) in what direction does it run? Before we discuss some findings in more detail, we summarize the overall tendencies that were found for our cases.

First, if we focus on the relationship between the statewide party organization and state (de)centralization alone, we have good reasons to expect a relatively decentralized state structure to coincide with a relatively decentralized statewide party organization. For instance, statewide parties which operate in a federal context not only organize for regional elections, but also vie for a position in regional office. Regional office in federal or regionalized states comes with potential access to important policy or expenditure resources, and generally requires a class of highly professionalized politicians. Each of these properties (even if the regional party branch of the statewide party is not likely to be elected into regional office) should strengthen the autonomy of regional party branches and their influence in the statewide party branch. Or to paraphrase van Houten's 'principal–agent' paradigm, the higher the levels of territorial autonomy, the stronger the expected position of the 'regional' agent vis-à-vis the 'statewide' principal.

Overall, the support that we find for these assumptions is very mixed at best. On the one hand, it is perfectly possible to have a relatively decentralized state in which the statewide parties have maintained a more centralized character. Spain illustrates this trend. The decentralization of the state has been orchestrated by two rather centralized parties, the Conservatives (PP) in particular. Although regional party leaders gradually built up capacity at home and in the statewide party branch, the level of regional branch autonomy still falls short of what could be expected based on the importance of autonomous communities within the state. On the other hand, Belgium and the UK illustrate the opposite trend, that is, a relatively centralized state may coincide with decentralized parties. As Verleden demonstrates in his contribution, the Belgian statewide parties had already started to disintegrate well before the regionalization of the Belgian state. Similarly, until the 1950s the Scottish Conservatives operated as an almost quasi-autonomous branch within the Conservative Party, despite the rather centralized character of the UK state.

With regard to the second question, we observed that statewide parties not only *respond to* but also play an active role in shaping the territorial structure of the state. Indeed, statewide parties not only actively mould such reforms through processes of constitutional change, but they even hold their own organizational charter as a template against which to structure the territorial organization of the state. In this respect, Verleden's analysis provides an intriguing account. He shows how the formerly statewide Belgian parties exported 'consociational mechanisms' which served to bridge differences of opinion between the Dutch- and French-speaking party members on the institutional structure of the Belgian state. After the parties had split, these mechanisms lived on in structures that were devised to pacify relations between the Dutch-speakers and francophones within the Belgian state (Swenden and Jans, 2006; Deschouwer, 2006b). Hence, paradoxically, at the time when consociationalism was 'cut and pasted' onto the overall state structure, the statewide party system had almost completely broken down and the consociational model had ostensibly failed as an instrument for accommodating intra-party territorial conflicts. In similar vein, one may wonder whether one day the *Consejo Territorial* which advises the PSOE national president and party executive could serve as a useful template against which to model a reformed and, from the viewpoint of territorial representation, more significant Spanish Senate.

In the following section, we will elaborate in further detail on the relationship between the territorial organization of the state, the organization of statewide parties and especially the strength of regional party branches therein. We discuss not only the organizational properties of statewide parties, but also how they campaign and make policy.

The territorial structure of the state and how statewide parties organize and campaign

The contributors to this volume were asked to consider whether the territorial organization of statewide parties reflects three distinct dimensions of how a state is structured territorially; first, the functional or jurisdictional method of distributing competencies in the state (where we expect the regional party branches to be more involved in statewide party matters but also to be more constrained in regional party matters the more competencies are distributed in a functional way); second, variations in the scope of regional self-rule (where we expect the autonomy of the regional party branches to increase with the scope of regional autonomy); and, finally, the presence of constitutional asymmetry (where we expect the autonomy of the regional branches to be greater and/or their participation in the statewide party to be stronger for those regions that have a higher degree of self-rule). The collected empirical evidence supports a relationship between each of these factors and the territorial organization of the statewide parties, but not always as strong as predicted. We consider each of these three hypotheses in turn.

A jurisdictional or functional design

For instance, with regard to the relationship between a functional/jurisdictional federal design and the territorial structure of statewide parties, we notice that, under Germany's joint-decision or integrated federal system, regional executive leaders acquired an unusually strong input in the governance of the centre through the collective veto power of the Bundesrat, the federal second chamber. In parallel, regional party leaders obtained a high degree of influence in statewide party matters, a pattern that is replicated across each of the statewide parties. Although not as 'functional' as the German model, the method of distributing competencies between the centre and the regions in Spain also requires a considerable amount of cooperation between both levels. Likewise, devolution to Wales assumes a very high level of cooperation. Yet in their comparative analysis Fabre and Méndez-Lago note a lack of 'shared rule' provisions in the case of most Spanish and UK statewide parties. This lack of systematically integrating regional party branches in statewide party decisions parallels a failure to incorporate regional elites in the functioning of the central state, either through highly institutionalized channels of intergovernmental relations or through an effective and powerful second chamber (Bolleyer, 2006; Roller, 2002). One could make a case that the decision of the Spanish Socialists to create an (advisory) *Consejo Territorial* in which regional party leaders advise the party president on matters of regional importance strengthens the shared-rule dimension somewhat. The regional branches of the UK parties are even less involved in statewide party matters than the Spanish regional party branches. Arguably, the weight of Scotland and Wales in the union is so small, that a strong involvement in the central party executive or strategic policy committees cannot be realistically expected. On the other hand, the lack of primary legislative powers for Wales requires strong channels of intra-party coordination, for instance (at the time of writing) between Welsh Labour and the UK Labour Party. Such channels exist, but only informally. Finally, Hopkin shows how in Italy regional branches, and especially regional party leaders in executive office (governors), increased their capacity to influence statewide party policy. This happened despite decentralizing reforms that seemed to have disentangled somewhat – at least formally – the statewide and regional layers of policy-making by entrusting the latter with 'exclusive' autonomy in a larger area of competencies (except for their financing). However, the greater role of regional policy leaders in the centre is attributed less to the rise in regional autonomy than to the direct election of the governors and their capacity to play an important 'brokerage' role in the clientelistic networks connecting party elites at the central and local levels.

The comparative contributions also demonstrate that regional branch participation in a statewide party does not preclude a considerable level of regional party branch autonomy. Indeed, the substantial autonomy of the regional party branches in Germany contradicts our initial hypothesis that a highly cooperative or joint decision-making design implies a lesser degree of autonomy for the regional branches. The contribution by Detterbeck and Jeffery has shown that the degree of autonomy of the German regional party branches in selecting candidates, devising a party programme for regional elections and determining regional coalition partners of their choice following regional elections is high notwithstanding their relatively strong participatory rights in the centre. Furthermore, the growing autonomy of regional party branches in recent years is – at least for the time being – not offset by a parallel decrease of influence in the statewide party. Similarly, Ştefuriuc shows that German regional party leaders have not refrained from purposefully building or sustaining incongruent coalitions (i.e., coalitions that are different in composition from the coalition at the centre) when this was seen as benefiting the party in terms of policy or votes. For instance, in North-Rhine Westphalia the CDU-FDP coalition remained in place, despite a federal coalition swap after the 2005 federal elections. In particular, the NRW CDU perceived incongruence as an advantage that would shield the NRW coalition from unpopular federal decisions.[1] A similar capacity of German regional party branches to withstand federal party pressure is also shown by van Houten in his analysis of the negotiations on the federal Solidarity Pact (1993). He shows how *Länder* governments with very different party political compositions utilized the Bundesrat to join forces and 'defeat' the CDU-led federal government.

In comparison, the Spanish example illustrates that weaker 'shared-rule' provisions frequently coincide with lower levels of regional party branch autonomy. Overall, Spanish statewide party branches keep a closer eye on the process of candidate selection; they impose 'a framework programme' ('*programa marco*') for regional elections and constrain regional party branches in their freedom to form the coalition governments of their choice. As a result, Spanish regional party branches find it harder to stand up against the statewide party line, even if they operate in a context where the need to do so is arguably greater, due to the lack of institutionalized intergovernmental coordination mechanisms that effectively channel territorial interests into the centre (as specified above). It follows that in Spain regional party branches or regional parties attach more importance to forming coalitions that are congruent with the central government. For instance, Ştefuriuc shows how the regionalists of the Canaries (CC) always preferred a coalition with the governing party in Madrid, due to their dependence on bilateral cooperation with the centre on regionally important policies such as health, fiscal matters, water policy, regional development (EU Structural Funds) or asylum policy. Therefore, the CC decided to expel the PP from the regional government of the Canary Islands shortly after the PSOE had entered the central government in 2004.

The scope of decentralization

With regard to the second aspect of state decentralization, we can confidently state that, by and large, the greater the scope of regional competencies, the greater is the autonomy of the regional party branches. We can observe this pattern by considering the development of regional party branch autonomy over time, or by comparing regional party branch autonomy between states with different levels of regional autonomy. The chapters discussing regional party branch autonomy in the UK, Spain, Germany and Italy demonstrate that the *increase* of regional autonomy within each of these states was never paralleled by a significant *decrease* in regional party branch autonomy. More likely, decentralization increased the profile and resources of regional party leaders and thus gave them additional capital to fight against statewide party interference. However, what these contributions also show is that the effect of decentralization does not play out uniformly across all statewide party organizations and may not manifest itself immediately. It can take considerable time before changes in how the state is governed transform long-standing party practices and rules. For example, notwithstanding the presence of a 'federal' tradition in Germany which pre-dates the Weimar republic, Detterbeck and Jeffery show that it took the Social Democrats a considerable time to come to terms with a federal state structure. In fact, it was not until the party reformed its internal party structures in the late 1950s or early 1960s that its party organization came to reflect the German federal state structure in which the party operates. Conversely, the CDU 'travelled' in the opposite direction: the statewide party branch was weaker initially, but, reflecting the role of the CDU as the dominant party in federal government until 1966, it gradually increased its leverage. This centralizing 'trajectory' more or less made the CDU and the SPD look alike in terms of the relative strength of their regional party branches. A similar time-lag effect can be observed in Bradbury's analysis of candidate selection for devolved elections in the UK. Prior to the first devolved elections in 1999, the statewide Labour Party intervened heavily in the process of candidate selection as candidates were tested on the extent to which they showed loyalty to 'New Labour' party principles. Some of these practices backfired electorally (especially in Wales). In light of this the party was inclined to give regional party branches a freer rein in preselecting candidates for subsequent devolved elections, although it could also more easily take a 'hands off' approach, due to the long-lasting effects of its gunboat interventions in 1999. A comparable 'institutional learning' effect has been observed for the UK Conservatives which even adapted a 'confederal' constitution in 2003 for streamlining UK–Scottish relations. In Spain, too, the statewide party branches of the PSOE and the PP 'recognized' the territorial organization of the state only in recent years, especially by setting up Territorial Councils (PSOE) or Autonomous Councils (PP) with an advisory capacity.

Asymmetry

Our contributions provide partial evidence to support the expected link between constitutional asymmetry and asymmetry in how statewide parties organize campaign or make policy. The evidence is most consistent for the UK, and especially for the Conservative Party. As Fabre and Mendéz-Lago demonstrate, the Scottish Conservatives are responsible for drafting 'devolved' parts of general election manifestos, whereas the British party devises matters in which Wales has obtained executive devolution giving the Welsh party autonomy to adapt the details of these policies to the Welsh context. The autonomy of the Scottish Conservatives in drafting manifestos for devolved elections is also greater than that of the Welsh branch. Similar asymmetries were noted in the process of candidate selection, and again especially within the Conservative Party. In Wales the process of candidate selection for general elections is still supervised by a statewide election committee, while in Scotland a Scottish Candidate's Board appointed by the Scottish Conservatives assumes this role. There is some evidence of asymmetry in the organization of the Spanish statewide parties as well, most notably in the peculiar position of the Catalan PSC and the Navarrese UPN, both of which are semi-autonomous members respectively of the Spanish Socialist and Conservative families. However, apart from the PSC and the UPN, the other regional party branches are more or less treated in the same way, at least formally, even if some of them may appear under a different label in regional elections. Hence, the special status of the Basque Country or Galicia (as historic communities) does not find special recognition in the structures of the leading statewide parties. Similarly, the asymmetric process of decentralization, especially during the first 15 years of Spanish regionalism and again after 2005, did not produce more widespread asymmetry within the statewide party organizations. Likewise, in his contribution on the Italian statewide parties Hopkin does not make reference to higher levels of autonomy for those regional party branches which operate in regions with a special status. Sometimes, the de facto autonomy of a regional party branch can be enhanced as a result of specific circumstances, for instance, the presence of a regional leader with high moral standing in the party (see below). Conversely, as van Houten has demonstrated, the Spanish PSOE managed to turn the peculiar position of the Catalan PSC to its own benefit in order to secure statewide parliamentary approval for the highly contentious reform of the Catalan autonomy statute. The Catalan government and parliament, including the PSC, had 'set the agenda' by proposing a radical revision of the regional statute, but the status of the PSC as a formally distinct party enabled the governing PSOE to distance itself somewhat from this draft statute. Eventually, the central government successfully managed to water it down and threatened to cooperate with the CiU instead. In this case at least, where more autonomy for the regional branch means quasi-independence, it has not been paralleled by a stronger say in the politics of the statewide party. Even so, it is assumed that Spanish Prime Minister Zapatero was instrumental in the 'unseating' in 2006 of Pasqual Maragall as President of the Catalan government. Such intrusive behaviour of the PSOE in PSC matters runs against the common assumption of PSC autonomy.

Finally, the effects of institutional asymmetry can also be felt in the campaign messages of statewide parties in devolved elections. The issue of whether Scottish, Welsh or Northern Irish autonomy should be extended concerns only a relatively small part of the electorate (even if it requires a decision of the Westminster parliament) whereas in Spain the issue of regional autonomy affects the entire electorate. Therefore, in the UK statewide parties tend to give more attention to the issue of institutional regionalism and regional culture ('the regionalist issue') in regional elections than in statewide elections, whereas in Spain statewide parties emphasize the regionalist issue more in statewide than in regional elections.

In sum, we can conclude that how statewide parties organize territorially reflects how the state is organized, but only partially so. Not all statewide parties which operate in the same territorial context may adjust their organizational structure or campaign strategies in the same way. Or, as Hopkin puts it, parties have their own internal organizational inertias. Furthermore, how they respond may derive from a set of unrelated variables: the broader dynamics of party competition, other institutional variables (for instance, a change in electoral rules) or the legacy of party ideology, variables to which we now turn.

Explaining variations in the territorial organization or strategy of statewide parties: Party ideology and party development

So far, the analysis has made clear that not all statewide parties adapt themselves in identical ways to the multilevelled nature of party competition. In the Introduction we focused on three potential explanatory variables which remain relatively stable across the lifespan of a party: ideology, party development and party type. We briefly discuss the effect of the first two of these variables on the territorial organization and strategies of statewide parties.[2]

Party ideology

We first assumed that party ideology serves as an important factor to explain the extent to which statewide parties are willing to embrace a federal type of party organization or vary their campaign content. In states which have decentralized in recent decades, the internal organization of a party can sometimes be considered as a prefiguration of a *desired* state structure, instead of as a reflection of the actual state structure. The 'federal' party structures of the British Liberal Democrats and the Spanish IU clearly illustrate this. Similarly, the internal structure of the Spanish PSOE bears more resemblance to a federal institutional design than does the more centralized structure of the PP, reflecting the PSOE's stance in favour of a 'federal' Spain. On the whole, so we hypothesized in the Introduction, Conservative and Labour ideologies are the least accommodative of territorial differentiation within the state, while Liberal and Christian Democratic ideologies are more favourable to territorial autonomy. The evidence only partially supports this assumption.

We take a look at the Conservative parties (of which there are two in our sample: the Conservatives in Britain and the Partido Popular (PP) in Spain) first. Fabre and Méndez-Lago show that, while the British Conservatives were the least supportive of devolution at the time of the devolution referendums in 1997, they are certainly not the most centrally organized of the British statewide parties. For instance, the chairman or deputy chairman of the Scottish and Welsh Conservative branches are members of the statewide party executive; the regional branches have more than a consultative input in drafting the general election manifestos and they are entirely free to choose their own leaders. Regional branches in the Labour Party are comparatively weaker. In his contribution Bradbury demonstrates that the statewide Conservative Party seems to have interfered less in the process of candidate selection for general and devolved elections than the Labour Party. This somewhat higher level of regional autonomy is paralleled by the territorially more divergent campaign messages issued by the Conservatives compared with Labour and even the Liberal Democrats. For instance, on the occasion of the 1999 Welsh Assembly elections, the Welsh Conservatives strongly supported the Union, with regard to institutions and culture. However, in 2003 the Welsh Conservatives adopted a fairly intense regionalist position, marketing themselves as a more 'Wales-friendly' party. This U-turn – which was not imposed by the statewide party – was most conspicuous with regard to promoting the Welsh cultural identity, but it also involved a more favourable stance with respect to regional autonomy, notwithstanding the more sceptical position of the Conservatives in both the 1997 and 2001 general elections. In comparison, in Spain the Partido Popular is clearly the most centralized of the large statewide parties. Unlike in the PSOE, the PP national President can prevent regional party leaders from occupying prominent positions within the national executive. Compared with the PSOE, the Consejo Autonómico is a more recent and also less relevant body for injecting territorial concerns into the statewide party. The PP statewide branch is more likely to intervene informally in the drafting of provincial candidate lists, in the forming of regional coalitions and in safeguarding the 'internal cohesion' of PP party politics within the autonomous communities. However, as for the Conservatives in Britain, we find some inconsistency in the content of their campaign messages with regard to the regionalist issue in statewide and regional elections. In statewide elections, the PP adopts a low-intensity profile in favour of a strong centre, but in regional elections the PP takes a somewhat more regionalist position, though always with a large dose of ambiguity and without giving the issue much salience. Perhaps, as for the Welsh Conservatives, we may ascribe the inconsistency of the Spanish Conservative Party to the nature of regional party competition, which forces them into a more accommodative position with regard to the regionalist issue. Furthermore, while the regional PP branches may tend to cross over to the regionalist side in regional elections, they also maintain a very low intensity – in line with their more centralist creed – and almost never surpass the PSOE, which is ideologically more inclined towards decentralization. Overall, the PP regional manifestos diverge less from each other than the PSOE manifestos, which may be due to a larger degree of central coordination or oversight by the PP statewide party branch.

Similarly, where Labour parties compete against Christian Democrats (as in Germany or Italy), the more 'centralized' nature of the former cannot always be taken as given. As discussed before, Detterbeck and Jeffery have shown that the German SPD was the least decentralized of the statewide parties in 1949, yet by 2007 its party organizational structures looked similar to those of the CDU. On the other hand, we find more evidence for the less centralized nature of the Christian Democrats in Italy and Belgium. For instance, Hopkin, in his comparative treatment of the Italian statewide parties, illustrates the greater dependence of the DCI (Christian Democrats) from regional and especially local support. In contrast, the national executive of the Socialist PSI was less dependent on similar support networks for intra-party decision-making. Indeed, the PSI is perhaps the only example of a statewide party which centralized (under Craxi's leadership between 1970 and 1990), while the Italian state moved into a more decentralizing direction. The Belgian case provides some indirect support for our hypothesis, insofar as the Belgian Socialist Party was the last of the three formerly statewide parties to split along linguistic lines, about a decade after the Christian Democrats, the first party to break up.

Finally, we observe a similarly inconsistent pattern when comparing the two Liberal and both of the Communist or far-left wing parties among our sample. The strong support for a federal Britain is also fully reflected in the internal organization of the British Liberal Democrats. The regional branches of the Liberal Democrats are the best-represented branches in the statewide party and on paper they have the highest level of autonomy in candidate selection or policy-making. On the other hand, the German FDP is not more decentralized than the German Social Democrats or Christian Democrats. Similarly, although we expected Communist or far-left parties to adopt a centralized organizational structure, only the Italian Communists (PCI) fulfil this expectation. This is so notwithstanding the limited degree of decentralization since the late 1980s and especially 1990s (when the party transformed into the PDS). Yet the contrast with the Spanish IU (United Left) is strong. The IU has defined itself as a 'federal' party and has entrusted its regional branches with the highest degree of autonomy of the Spanish statewide parties in candidate selection and in developing regional party policy. On the other hand, as Ştefuriuc has shown, the IU sanctions regional branches that sign coalition deals without the prior consent of the statewide party. In this respect the IU is as centralized as the PP.

On the basis of these brief comparative reflections on the link between ideology and party organizational decentralization, we can conclude that party ideology cannot easily predict how parties organize internally, let alone how they diversify their campaign messages across the regions. Liberal parties are not necessarily the most decentralized, Socialist parties are not necessarily more centralized than Christian Democratic parties, and so on. However, the absence of a clear link is primarily due to the weakness of 'ideology' as a solid *cross-national* predictor of a party's preference with regard to how the state should be organized. There is in fact less contradiction between a party's preferences with respect to the territorial organization of the state and the territorial organization of the party. For instance, Social Democrats in Britain (who support devolution but not federalism) organize themselves in a devolved rather than federal way, whereas Social Democrats in Germany (who are supportive of the German federal state) organize themselves in a federal way. Or, to cite another example, the Italian Communists were, at least in the first years after the Second World War, opposed to devolution or decentralization and adopted a very centralized party organization, while their Spanish counterparts supported a decentralized state from the start and reflected this by organizing themselves in some respects as the most decentralized of all Spanish statewide parties. Admittedly, the Italian Communists became more supportive of devolution as early as the 1950s, when their exclusion from governance at the centre became obvious but they developed some regional strongholds instead. The more important question then is: why is UK Labour less favourable to federalism than the German SPD, or why does the Spanish Left support a federal Spain while the Italian Communists, at least in the first years after the Second World War, took issue with a devolved Italy?

Party development and ideology as a compass

One possible explanation for the divergent preferences of ideologically related parties with regard to the territorial structure of the state lies in the positions they took on this issue when the contours of modern party development and competition were set. Hence, the pro-federal attitude of the UK Liberal Democrats could build upon a tradition of long-term Liberal support for Home Rule (Ireland), which made it natural for the Liberals to capture this ideological space after the Second World War. For similar reasons, the pro-federal attitude of the Spanish United Left should not come as a surprise. The party was not formed until 1986, in a context when the (at that point somewhat centralizing) PSOE and the highly centralized Popular Alliance (later PP) defended a strong centre. The IU filled this void and simultaneously built upon a tradition of 'resistance' from below inherited from more than 40 years of dictatorship. Furthermore, unlike in Italy, meaningful regional parliaments or governments already existed when the IU was established. These regional institutions provided a useful opportunity structure from which to build up electoral support and statewide recognition.

If ideology cannot predict the extent to which statewide parties decentralize – at least not cross-nationally – statewide party ideology nonetheless functions as an anchor that prevents regional branches from drifting too far from the statewide positions on regionalism. For instance, the comparative manifesto analysis demonstrated that in Spain 'regionalism' features more prominently in general than in regional elections, but it is also dealt with in a more ambiguous way. In regional elections the Spanish statewide parties, and particularly the PSOE, are more explicit in their policy choices, mostly in an autonomist direction. Since they may face strong competition from autonomist parties that exclusively address the electorate of the region, they reduce the level of ambiguity with regard to the institutional and identity components of regionalism. However, the difference from statewide elections is most substantial with regard to identity politics. A similar tendency was found in the UK, although the regionalist issue received clearly more attention in devolved than in UK elections. The manifestos for devolved elections particularly emphasized regional identity matters more than institutional matters. The more restrained attitude of statewide parties in supporting more regional autonomy than regional identity matters was also confirmed by a separate discourse analysis of the UK manifestos, which showed that references to Britain are particularly scarce in the regional manifestos of statewide parties. In sum, statewide parties counterbalance a moderately or ambiguously regionalist profile on the institutional dimension with the assertion of a strong identification with the region: a logical outcome since the political consequences of supporting regional identity and culture for the statewide party are small, whereas demands for more regional autonomy generate immediate political implications and are more likely to contradict the ideology and policies of the central party.

Explaining variations in the territorial organization or strategy of statewide parties: Incumbency, leadership and institutional reform

Ideological change and the institutional development of parties are long-term processes, not events. Although they can have a profound impact on how parties organize, they take time to unfold. In this sense, they are different from relatively short-term shifts in the territorial allocation of power within a party that come (or go) with more 'sudden' events such as the election of a party leader (though of course some leaders may remain in place for a decade or even longer and may push through organizational reforms with long-lasting legacies) or a party's position in government or in opposition. Such events can affect the territorial organization of statewide parties, if only on a temporary basis. We should also emphasize that shifts in the balance of power between statewide and regional party branches that are linked to incumbency are not normally accompanied by statutory or party constitutional changes. Instead they could lead to a situation in which, for instance, statewide party leaders upon assuming central office revert to statutory (disciplinary) mechanisms that may have lain dormant when the party was in statewide opposition. More often, pressure or influence is conveyed through *informal* channels. For instance, the 'clientelistic' networks in Spain and Italy provide opportunities to reward loyal regional party behaviour by pledging certain types of regional distributive aid to supportive regional party leaders, an instrument that can be used (if at all) much less effectively when the party is in opposition. Conversely, media exposure, access to resources and the ability to make and implement public policy that come with regional office strengthen the authority (and therefore also likely the influence) of regional party leaders in the party as a whole.

Incumbency

Several authors stress the (temporary) impact of incumbency on recalibrating power between the statewide and the regional party branches. In the Introduction we assumed that holding office at the centre (combined with a position of regional opposition) is most conducive to statewide party influence on regional matters, while a position of regional incumbency (combined with statewide opposition) is likely to generate the largest degree of regional party branch autonomy and influence in the statewide party. Although we have not collected systematic evidence to test this hypothesis for all statewide parties in each of the five West European states, several authors provide supporting evidence for these assumptions.

For instance, in their comparative analysis of the Spanish and British statewide parties, Fabre and Méndez-Lago argue that the statewide party branch of the Spanish Social Democrats kept a close eye on its regional party branches when the party was in power at the central level during much of the 1980s and the first half of the 1990s. This was the case notwithstanding the influence of regional party barons in the statewide party. These authors (and Bradbury) also attribute some of the more interfering tendencies of the British Labour Party to its uninterrupted control of Westminster since 1997. The interference of Labour in the process of candidate selection, especially on the occasion of the first devolved elections in 1999, illustrate the party's concern to uphold a 'uniform' party message across the country as a whole. Earlier, we suggested that the bad results for Labour in these elections, especially in Wales, could be attributed to such 'meddling' in regional party matters. However, these 'founding' elections took place without a regional incumbent in place. The role of Labour as a party in office at the regional level thereafter strengthened the capacity and legitimacy of its regional party branches to fight or prevent similar displays of interventionism when selecting candidates for devolved elections in 2003. Furthermore, we assume that, if Labour had been in central opposition, it would have been less inclined to supervise regional party matters.

The role of incumbency can also serve as an alternative explanation for the more limited divergence in campaign profiles for Labour in comparison with the other British statewide parties or for the PP in comparison with the PSOE. We initially assumed that statewide parties that are more centralized are less likely to tolerate territorially divergent campaign strategies than statewide parties with a more decentralized party organization. We found some evidence to support this assumption, but only in the Spanish case. The PSOE is ostensibly more decentralized than the PP and, perhaps as a result, its profiles on the regionalist issue are more territorially divergent. However, a similarly consistent pattern was not found for the UK. For instance, the divergence between the issue profiles of the manifestos of the Liberal Democrats proved to be smaller than the divergence for the Conservative Party, notwithstanding the more decentralized party organization of the Liberal Democrats. These findings could be explained by the incumbency status of Labour. The larger strategic leeway which the PSOE branches appear to have enjoyed may well have been due to that party's role in central opposition at the time of the 2001 and 2003 regional elections. This is consistent with the UK findings, where Labour – as a party in central office – appeared to have tolerated less divergence in its issue profiles than the Conservatives, who were in opposition at both levels, while the Liberal Democrats (who were in office at the regional level alone) occupied an intermediate position.

In their chapter, Detterbeck and Jeffery clearly show how *regional* incumbency, especially when it is combined with a role in central opposition, strengthens the influence of regional party leaders in the statewide party executive. This applies especially to the Social Democrats and the Christian Democrats who (unlike the smaller coalition partners) can frequently lay claim to the most coveted post in *Land* politics: that of the Minister-President. Minister-Presidents are nearly always members *ex officio* of the federal party executive and through their prominent role in the Bundesrat, or possibly even the bicameral Concertation Committee, they are bound to develop a strong 'federal' profile. Particularly after long periods in federal opposition, statewide party branches, such as that of the SPD in 1998, tend to recruit from several of their (formerly) regional party leaders to fill ministerial posts in the federal cabinet. As a result the contingent of regional party leaders in the statewide party presidium (i.e., the 'decision-making core' of the statewide party executive) usually shrinks substantially shortly after a party assumes central office (Lehmbruch, 2000; Swenden, 2004). The same tendency has been observed in the CDU after it was elected to federal power in 1982.

Leadership

As argued above, statewide and/or regional leadership affects the relative strength of the statewide and regional party branches. For instance, the identification of *Forza Italia* with Silvio Berlusconi has been a strong centralizing force. The status of Helmut Kohl in the German CDU or of Felipe Gonzalez in the Spanish PSOE, at least during the first terms of their reign in central office, may also have had a temporary centralizing effect. Conversely, the presence of regional barons within the Spanish Social Democrats, or the personal authority of Donald Dewar in the Labour Party or of Manuel Fraga in the Spanish Conservative party (PP), entrusted these regional leaders with a disproportionate level of influence in the statewide party. In the case of Dewar and Fraga, their personal history as influential ministers at the statewide level (in Fraga's case even as a founding member of the Popular Party) helped to maintain significant channels of influence at that level when they became respectively First Minister of Scotland and President of the Galician government.

Extra- and intra-party institutional reform

Lastly, the relative strength of the central and regional party levels can be affected by institutional changes that have little or nothing to do with (de)centralization. Such changes can take place within the state or within the party. For instance, in their contributions Hopkin and Bradbury discuss the effect of changes to the electoral system on party (de)centralization, especially in the process of candidate selection. In 1993 the Italian electoral system was transformed from a largely proportional to a largely majoritarian one. However, the creation of single-member electoral districts did not decentralize power within the statewide parties. On the contrary, the continued fragmentation of the party system compelled parties to form pre-electoral alliances to support each others' candidates in single-member contests. 'This enhanced the role of parties' national leadership in candidate selection, since reciprocal arrangements of *désistement'* require coordination at a higher level than the electoral district' (Hopkin, this volume: 97). Or, as Bradbury shows, the parallel existence of constituency and list candidates raised new challenges for British parties in selecting candidates for Scottish and Welsh devolved elections, even if in this case the level of statewide party interference remained more or less identical for selecting both sets of candidates. Another institutional measure that has been raised in this volume is the direct election of regional presidents in Italy since 1995. This increased the legitimacy and profile of regional executive leaders and thereby strengthened their influence in the statewide party, even in highly centralized parties such as *Forza Italia* (as the influence of Lombardian regional President Formigoni attests).

Shifts in the relative influence of the regional party branches can also emerge as an (unintended) side effect of changing decision-making rules *within* a party. For instance, as Fabre and Méndez demonstrate, the introduction of individual secret ballots for the election of the party executive and secretary general of the PSOE reduced the capacity of regional party leaders to lobby for their preferred candidates. This was the case in 2000, when regional party leader José Bono lost the election for PSOE secretary general to Rodríguez Zapatero, notwithstanding the support for the former among a majority of the regional party leaders.

Territorial party politics in Western Europe: Concluding impressions and which way from here?

This volume has brought together a number of contributions that focus on the territorial integration of the multilevel party system and the organization and strategies of statewide parties with respect to campaigning, policy-making or coalition building at the central and regional levels. What, in a nutshell, are the main conclusions that can be drawn from this research, and where do we go from here?

Readers who were hoping to find unambiguous correlations or causal relations between the integration of the multilevel party system and the territorial organization and strategies of statewide parties may feel somewhat disappointed. In fact, the contributions show that there is no grand theory to explain the organizational or campaign strategies of statewide parties which operate in a multilevel electoral context. Statewide parties do not react in uniform ways to territorial party competition or shifts in authority migration within the state. Indeed, the assumption that we can simply measure 'federalism by measuring parties', as Riker once claimed, is as straightforward as it is wrong (Riker, 1975: 137). Not all statewide parties within a state adapt to territorial politics in similar ways. Some statewide parties may wish to maintain a tight grip on the regional party branches even if this prevents them from adjusting campaign messages to specific regional desires. A statewide party that leaves its regional branches with too much autonomy risks becoming a bifurcated party, as has been the case with of several Canadian parties (Dyck, 1997). Conversely a statewide party that has too tight a grip on its regionalist branches risks falling into oblivion or sparking the breakaway of a regional party branch. Statewide parties do not provide uniform answers to this strategic paradox. However, there are some generalizations (arguably of lower theoretical ambition) that are worth reiterating.

First, we found a correlation between the domestic preferences of statewide parties with regard to what the state structure should look like and their own organizational templates. Cross-nationally, this works as a better predictor than party ideology, since not all Social Democrats, Conservatives or Communists oppose decentralization and not all Liberals or Christian Democrats favour it. Where parties stand often depends on where they stood on these issues when parties institutionalized and the party system was 'locked in'. On the other hand, parties can drift on the 'centre–periphery' axis of competition as much as they have on the left–right axis.

Second, where the territorial design of the state enables regional party leaders to exert a strong influence on the politics of the centre, regional party branches also tend to play a significant role in statewide party politics and retain a considerable level of regional autonomy. On the other hand, where the territorial design of the state does not provide the same mechanisms of 'intra-state federalism' (Smiley and Watts, 1985), the position of the regional branches in the centre tends to be weaker as well. Where cooperation between the two levels is nonetheless required, for instance due to a large amount of central framework laws as in Spain, regional party branches will be more inclined to follow a congruent logic in regional coalition-building or policy-making if this could help to strengthen their access and influence at the statewide level. In such a context, to opt for a confrontational strategy is the more risky alternative.

Third, perhaps the most consistent centralizing logic within statewide parties stems from incumbency, especially when the party is in government at the central level. In this regard our findings entirely support the assumed hypotheses.

Finally, irrespective of where they stand on the left–right scale or how strong the regionalist competitors may be, the dominant strategy of statewide parties in regional elections is to evade the issue of regional autonomy and to adopt a more regionalist profile by playing the regional identity card instead. Only the case of the Welsh Conservatives provides some (tempo-rary) evidence of a statewide party adopting a centralist adversarial strategy in order to harm the success of Labour Party against its most significant (and equally left-wing) competitor, Plaid Cymru.

Notwithstanding these findings, it is obvious that our work has only just begun and that many questions require further elaboration, for which we hope we have whetted the appetite of many political scientists.

For instance, we have (re)considered the hypothesis of the nationalization of the party system with respect to Belgium, Spain and Germany. This analy-sis could be extended to include most of the other West European states. A comprehensive database should incorporate the 'multilevel party systems' for all West European federal or regionalized states, that is, include develop-ments in regional party systems and their interaction with the statewide party system. Similarly, we have questioned the direction of Chhibber and Kollman's (2004) assumed causal relationship between the (de)centraliza-tion of the state and the (de)nationalization of the statewide party system on the basis of the Belgian, German and Spanish examples. Here, too, there is scope to test this relationship among a greater number of states. For instance, since early 2008 the scholarly community has had access to a data-base which systematically measures patterns of authority migration for 42 democracies since 1950 (Hooghe, Marks and Schakel, 2008). The 'regional authority index' that is introduced in this study captures variations in the degree of shared rule and self-rule for each of these 42 democracies. As such it is a more refined and arguably more accurate measurement of regional institutional power than indices that have relied solely on levels of regional expenditure decentralization (Rodden, 2004). The regional authority indices (longitudinally and cross-nationally) could be linked to indices which cap-ture the (de)nationalization of the multilevel party system, enabling a more rigorous testing of the relationship between authority migration and the integration of the multilevel party system. Yet our research agenda would be advanced not only by providing more large N statistical analyses of the type described above: testing for the effect of ideology, incumbency, and the institutional environment in which the party was formed and developed on party strategy also requires delving into the complex network of intra-party relations and dynamics. Such studies require extensive elite interviewing and documental research, ideally on as many cases as possible.

To conclude, the study of territorial party politics in Western Europe and beyond has only just begun. We have set the framework and the various contributions have provided preliminary answers based on some of the most significant federal or regionalized states in Western Europe. The questions raised here show how the territorial dimension of party politics can be analysed through a comparative framework and why scholars of party politics should not overlook the importance of this regional dimension, even if their scholarly interest remains with developments at the statewide level or even the supra-national level alone.

Notes

1 Towards a Regionalization of Statewide Electoral Trends in Decentralized States? The Cases of Belgium and Spain

1. The heavy losses of the Walloon Socialists in 1995 can be explained by a corruption scandal that hit them especially hard. The Flemish party president was clearly not involved and focused his campaign heavily on social security.
2. http://argos.mir.es/MIR/jsp/resultados

2 Territory and Electoral Politics in Germany

1. Berlin is excluded from consideration to simplify the analysis.
2. And there is indeed good reason to include the Left Party in Western Germany as it defines itself as an all-German party. Furthermore, it is represented in the Bundestag and contests elections throughout the country.
3. In this chapter, we slightly modify a simple model that has recently been used to analyse the relationship between federal and *Land* election results in Germany as well as in similar elections in other countries (Dinkel, 1977; Jeffery and Hough, 2001; Hough and Jeffery, 2006b). The original model, propagated by Rainer Dinkel, (consciously) focuses just on the performance of those parties which happen to be in federal government during a particular legislative period. It has a number of significant weaknesses (see Jeffery and Hough, 2001) and also lacks predictive power, but its effectiveness in showing basic trends none the less makes it a useful tool. In this model, Dinkel introduced the notion of 'expected vote share' for *Land* elections. This was a simple average of party vote shares in a *Land* at two successive federal Land. If the federal government parties scored, say, 50 per cent in a *Land* in one federal election and 46 per cent in the next, then its 'expected vote' for any Land *election* in the intervening period in that *Land* would be 48 per cent (see Jeffery and Hough, 2001). The result of the federal election *after* any round of *Land* elections is needed in order to calculate the trend in support for each of the parties. Despite a number of limitations, the model has a genuine heuristic value and it is one of the few attempts to systematically model the relationship between party performance in state and substate elections. It therefore provides a useful base from which to explore developments in party vote share both pre- and post-unification, and also to tease out some of the differences in nuance that exist between West and East.

3 Rediscovering the Region: Territorial Politics and Party Organizations in Germany

1. Even in times of divided majorities, the Bundesrat has vetoed only a small portion of federal laws. The peak level of obstruction was reached between 1976 and 1980, when the Bundesrat declined to endorse 15 federal laws, that is, just 5.7 per cent of the legislative output of the Bundestag (Sturm and Zimmermann-Steinhart, 2005: 57).

2. In his classic study on the subject, Lehmbruch (1976) identified a structural 'inconsistency' between a structure of party competition based on ideologically opposing party camps and the need for federal accommodation. In times of divergent majorities in Bundestag and Bundesrat, either partisan disagreement would lead to gridlock or an informal 'Grand Coalition' would delegitimize party competition in the electoral arena. With some nuances, Lehmbruch maintained his position in later editions of the book (1998, 2000). For a critical discussion, see Sturm (1999) and Renzsch (2000).

3. The one partial exception is the CSU, which contests (federal and *Länder*) elections only in Bavaria. But while the CSU decided not to join the federal CDU in 1950, the two parties have cooperated closely since then and form a common party caucus in the Bundestag. The CDU does not contest elections in Bavaria.

4. http://www.bundesfinanzministerium.de/lang_de/DE/Finanz__und__ Wirtschaftspolitik/Foederale__Finanzbeziehungen/Laenderfinanzausgleich/Vorl_C3_ A4ufige_20Abrechnung_202004,templateId=raw,property=publicationFile.pdf.

5. Interestingly enough, the German Party Law provides federal parties with the right to disown *Land* organizations and to deselect *Land* party executives which have defected from the common cause (see Poguntke, 1994: 207). Although this provision is rarely used in practice, the federal executive of the WASG (Labour and Social Justice – The Electoral Alternative, a left-wing offshoot of the SPD and the trade union movement) deselected the *Land* executives of Berlin and Mecklenburg-Western Pomerania, both of which rejected a proposed merger with the PDS. However, in the Berlin case, a civil court declared the deselection void. The judges argued that competing with the PDS in a *Land* election would not violate the statutes of the WASG.

6. A similar party reform, involving similar internal conflicts between the *Land* party leadership and the three party districts, was carried by the SPD in Rhineland-Palatinate in 2002. In Lower Saxony, there still is staunch opposition to modifying the position of the four traditional party districts within the SPD *Land* organization.

7. Therefore, in legal terms the CDU consists of 17 *Land* branches. There is one *Land* party organization in each of the 16 *Länder*, except Bavaria (none) and Lower Saxony (three).

8. Own calculations, based on the data compiled by Niedermayer (2007). East Germany accounts for some 16 per cent of the German population.

9. There is an ongoing debate in the literature on whether federal developments – that is, growing electoral volatility and dissatisfaction with federal governments – or the growing autonomy of regional patterns of voting behaviour are the main factor explaining the degree of diversity of regional election results. See Detterbeck (2006: 15–24).

10. In the 1990s German parties introduced the option of using membership-wide meetings for selecting constituency candidates. In addition, some CDU *Land* parties allowed for postal ballots (Beil and Lepzy, 1995: 18–24; Scarrow, 1999: 348–9). While such intra-party plebiscites have been used to some extent, they have rarely challenged the capacity of local party elites to preselect candidates.

11. The *Land* party executives are strongly interlocked with the substate party in public office. The majority of their members are either *Land* government ministers and legislators or representatives of the subregional party branches, as in the case of the CDU Baden-Württemberg with its strong subunits. There are only a few active federal politicians at the *Land* party level (see Detterbeck, 2004: 23–5).

12. At the federal level, the single example has been the consultation of SPD members during the crisis of the party leadership race in 1993. At the *Land* level, electoral motives (for example, the oppositional SPD Baden-Württemberg in 2000) or internal disputes (for example, the oppositional CDU Rhineland-Palatinate in 2004 and the governing CDU Baden-Württemberg in 2006) led to intra-party plebiscites on party leaders and top candidates.
13. According to the Party Law, *Land* parties, which have won at least 1 per cent in the latest *Land* election, are eligible for €0.50 per vote (§ 19a, 6 Party Law). The remainder – €0.70 per vote in European, national and *Land* elections, as well as matching funds for member fees and small donations – is directed towards the federal parties (§ 18 Party Law). However, some of the money is subsequently channelled back to the substate and local branches in the form of organizational services and campaign assistance provided by the federal party headquarters (see Ebbighausen et al., 1996).
14. Political donations are the most important source of revenue for the FDP (some 40 per cent of total party income). The federal-level FDP experienced severe financial crises in the 1970s and 1980s (see Vorländer, 2007: 286). Both the Greens and the Left Party are financed primarily by their members (for detailed reports on both parties, see Ebbighausen et al., 1996: 325–402). For all three smaller parties, public subsidies, paid mainly to the federal party level, are the second most important contribution to their budgets.
15. See the annual reports (*Rechenschaftsberichte der Parteien*) published by the Bundestag on www.bundestag.de [for the most recent reports, see *Bundestag Drucksachen* 14/2508; 15/2800; 15/5550; 16/1270; 16/5090].
16. An example of the former is the trend towards the left in SPD *Land* parties, which coincided with the passing of unpopular labour market and social policies by the Schröder federal government in 2002–3. An example of the latter is the move of the Baden-Württemberg Greens in 2006 towards economic policy preferences close to positions of the governing CDU, creating a basis for a potential new coalition (Debus, 2007).
17. Most significantly, SPD-FDP *Land* coalitions which had been formed as congruent coalitions in the 1970s ended with the change in federal government (CDU, CSU, FDP) in 1982. They were replaced in the early 1980s by either single-party governments or now congruent bourgeois coalitions (Detterbeck and Renzsch, 2003, 260–1). On the other hand, the *Land* level has sometimes served as a kind of laboratory for new federal coalition patterns. This applies to the SPD-FDP coalition in North Rhine-Westphalia (1966–80), the CDU-FDP coalition in the Saarland (1977–85) or the SPD-Green Party coalitions in Hesse (1985–7 and 1991–9) and other *Länder*, which pre-dated later government formations at the federal level.
18. 'Abstention clauses' have become a regular feature of coalition agreements at the *Land* level. The coalition partners agree to abstain in Bundesrat votes whenever they prove unable to agree on a common policy position.
19. At the time of writing (October 2007), there are six single-party governments (three CDU, one CSU, one SPD), four congruent Grand Coalitions (CDU-CSU and SPD) and six incongruent coalitions – five of them CDU-FDP governments and one a SPD-Green Party cabinet – in the *Länder*.
20. For example, the SPD in Saxony-Anhalt decided to rely on the external support of the PDS for its red–green coalition in 1994 and its single-party government in 1998. In both instances, the federal SPD leadership facing a Bundestag election

favoured a Grand Coalition for Saxony-Anhalt but failed to convince the *Land* party leadership.

21. Both have been particularly pronounced in cases where SPD *Land* parties cooperated with the PDS, i.e., in Saxony-Anhalt (1994–2002), Mecklenburg-Western Pomerania (1998–2006) and Berlin (since 2002). As of this writing, the federal party leader Beck favours a policy of not entering coalitions with the Left Party in the Western *Landtage*; however, *Land* party leaders have made clear that this is a decision to be taken by the individual *Land* parties. In other cases, SPD *Land* parties were internally split over favouring the Green Party or a bourgeois party as coalition partner (e.g., Bremen 1995, Schleswig-Holstein 1996, North Rhine-Westphalia 1995–2005).

22. Although there are no systematic data, estimates suggest that the federal headquarters of both the CDU and the SPD employ roughly as many people as all of their *Land* counterparts combined (Schmid, 1990: 146; Poguntke and Boll, 1992: 338–40). Both federal parties significantly expanded their party headquarters during the 1970s with staffing at around 200, though this fell back to around 150 during the 1990s (Detterbeck, 2002: 216–8).

23. The development of the CDU is particularly telling. In 1977–8, the substate party units held nearly half of the seats in the federal party executive, led by Helmut Kohl, Prime Minister of Rhineland-Palatinate. During the Kohl Chancellorship (1982–98) the trend was reversed. In 1992–3, national MPs and cabinet ministers held more than three quarters of the seats in the federal CDU executive committee. The *Land* party level was no longer strong enough to retain control of the federal party. After the loss of federal power in 1998, however, the representation of substate party elites rose again (see Detterbeck, 2002: 61–8).

24. Indeed, since 1991 only one out of seven SPD party chairmen has never been a *Land* prime minister, namely, Franz Müntefering, who served as SPD general secretary before leading the party from February 2004 to November 2005.

4 Decentralization and Party Organizational Change: The Case of Italy

* Thanks go to Gianfranco Baldini, Robert Leonardi, Raffaella Nanetti and Salvatore Vassallo for helpful comments and suggestions for this paper. The author acknowledges the support of the Economic and Social Research Council's Devolution and Constitutional Change Programme (grant number L219252105).

1. Although it is worth pointing out that, with the exception of some Alpine areas, the languages and dialects spoken in Italy were all Latinate and therefore closely related to the Tuscan dialect that became established as 'Italian'.

2. To give an idea of the discontinuity, the turnover of parliamentary personnel in the Italian lower chamber was an astonishing 71 per cent (Ignazi, 2002).

5 Decentralization and Party Organizational Change: The British and Spanish Statewide Parties Compared

1. Although *Izquierda Unida* was created as a coalition of different political parties (see Ramiro, 2003), it now describes itself as a 'sociopolitical movement' that brings together parties and individual people. See www.izquierda-unida.es

2. 'If United Left defends a federal and republican model for Spain, it must also do so in its own organization' (Statutes IU, VII Asamblea, art. 10, 2004).
3. Although the MPs of the PSC and those of the PSOE have formed a single parliamentary group in the Congress of Deputies since 1982, the PSC has threatened to form its own parliamentary group during periods of tensions between the two organizations.
4. The other part of the Federal Political Council is chosen directly by the regional federations, and when the whole Council has been elected it ratifies the election of the General Coordinator.
5. See Méndez Lago (2007: 93) for an analysis of the evolution of the presence of regional leaders in the PSOE's Federal Executive Committee.
6. Party statutes approved at the 36th congress (2004), art. 48.
7. Provincial sections are relevant because provinces are the electoral districts in general elections.
8. Membership ballots have been used in United Left and in the PSOE for the selection of candidates to the presidency of Autonomous Communities and the mayoralty of large cities.
9. The most recent one is the resignation of Josep Piqué, head of the Catalan PP, after denouncing repeated interference by the PP's central authorities in this regional branch (*El Pais*, 20 July 2007).
10. Roller and van Houten (2003: 18–9) argue that over time, and in particular when the PSOE was in the opposition to the PP in central office and under the leadership of Maragall, the PSC has increasingly affirmed its Catalan interests and adapted its strategy to the regional circumstances. This has sometimes created difficulties at the statewide level, particularly in relation to the reform of the Statute of Autonomy of Catalonia. One could interpret the end of Maragall's political career as a result of this assertiveness, which cost him the support of the PSOE, although there are also other factors internal to the PSC that could also help explain it.
11. The most recent example is the decision of the PSOE's Federal Executive Commission not to allow the Socialists in Navarre to form a coalition with the nationalist *Nafarroa Bai*, against the wishes of the regional branch, which had already committed to do so.

6 Devolution and Party Organization in the UK: Statewide Parties and Statewide–Regional Branch Relations over Candidate Selection in Scotland and Wales

1. The use of the term 'statewide' is used advisedly in a UK context, as in Northern Ireland the Conservative, Labour and Liberal Democrat parties organize either not at all or certainly not on the same basis as elsewhere in the UK. Equally though, it should be noted that Northern Ireland represents less than 5 per cent of UK population.
2. The author acknowledges research conducted in the project 'Party Candidate Procedures and Characteristics at the 1999 Scottish Parliament and Welsh Assembly Elections' with the assistance of ESRC grant number L3227253004. The project was led by Professor David Denver and the co-researchers were Professor James Mitchell and Dr Lynn Bennie.

8 Authority in Multilevel Parties: A Principal–Agent Framework and Cases from Germany and Spain

1. It should be noted that there is evidence that the subnational level became somewhat stronger again in these parties from the late 1980s on (Jeffery, 1999a; Sturm, 2001; Benz, 2003).
2. This account is based on Sally and Webber (1994), Czada (1995), Renzsch (1998), Wachendorfer-Schmidt (2003) and especially Altemeier (1998).
3. Party considerations may have played some (limited) role in the negotiations. Waigel, the federal finance minister and main negotiator for the government, was the President of CSU, the party controlling the Bavarian government. He may have wanted to reach an agreement once he faced a common regional front led by Bavaria, in order to avoid a confrontation with his own party (Altemeier, 1998: 223–4; Sally and Webber, 1994: 27).
4. This draft is available at www.parlament.cat/porteso/estatut/estatut_english.pdf.
5. The new Catalan autonomy statute is available at www.gencat.cat/generalitat/eng/estatut/index.htm.
6. The PSC and the ERC both lost some seats in these elections, while the CiU recaptured its position as the largest party in the Catalan parliament. Coalition negotiations eventually returned the same coalition as before to power, but with a reduced majority.
7. Another electoral consideration for the PSC was probably the fact that appearing to be extreme (by opposing the revised draft) might alienate the non-nationalist part of its electorate. Balancing nationalist and non-nationalist parts of its electorate has been a challenge for the PSC throughout its existence (Roller and van Houten, 2003).

9 Governing Strategies in Multilevel Settings: Coordination, Innovation or Territorialization?

1. Congruence is highly significant, as the general rule that regional coalitions observe in voting in the Bundesrat is to abstain when they do not all agree on the direction of the vote. An abstention technically counts as a vote against. Parties who are in opposition in the Bundestag and in government at the regional level thus have at their disposal a powerful tool with which to attempt to defeat federal government bills in the second chamber.
2. Notorious examples are the increases in fiscal allocations for Catalonia that were obtained by the CiU twice in succession from the PSOE and the PP at times when these two parties had formed a minority government and needed the legislative support of the CiU (Aja, 2003). These allocations were later extended to the other regions, but the example shows that government policy can be influenced by single territorial actors acting in the interest of their own region only.
3. This is now changing as the Linke attempted to pass the electoral threshold in three Western *Länder*. The first breakthrough occurred in the 2007 Bremen election, when the Linke gained parliamentary representation for the first time in a Western region, by winning 6 out of 151 seats (and 2 more than the FDP). This was followed by the 2008 Hessen, Lower Saxony and Hamburg elections.

4. Results are aggregated at regional level. The exact formula used for computing the index of dissimilarity is:

$$Dissimilarity\ index = \Sigma\ (|Vi_{reg} - Vi_{nat}| + \ldots + |Vn_{reg} - Vn_{nat}|)$$

where Vi_{reg} = Percentage of votes that Party i received in regional elections
Vi_{nat} = Percentage of votes that Party i received in the previous most recent national elections
N = Number of parties winning votes.

5. A recent example is that of the Navarre Social Democratic Federation, which was strictly forbidden to enter a coalition agreement with the United Left (IU) and with the Basque nationalist parties in Navarre after the 2007 regional elections, although this meant keeping the party altogether out of government.
6. Although Méndez-Lago and Fabre (this volume) show that the IU is the most decentralized of the Spanish statewide parties, the fact that the central leadership still formally retains the power to veto regional coalitions with which it does not agree underscores the argument that parties are much willing to let regional branches decide when participation in executive power is at stake.
7. In recent years, the arrival of illegal immigrants in the harbours of the Canary Islands has intensified. Cooperation with the central government and the urgency of elaborating a joint immigration plan intensified accordingly.
8. The EA was born as a splinter from the PNV in 1995. Both parties define themselves as nationalist. The two big differences between them are: (1) the EA is more in favour of Basque independence while the PNV is the proponent of a special relationship of the Basque Country with Spain, to be defined through the people's right to self-determination; (2) the EA is more to the left while the PNV is a centre-right political party (Llera-Ramo, 2000).
9. Generally the territorial units are federated to the IU. The Basque EB used to be federated to the IU, but it changed its status in 2004 when it became a separate organization associated with the federal IU.
10. Previous research on Spain shows that the value of congruence also consistently varies depending on the type of party considered (SWP or NSWP) in combination with the weight it has at different levels of government (Ştefuriuc, 2009). As the SWP/NSWP classification is not valid across all multilevel settings (Germany being one case where it does not apply), this argument is not explored here.

10 How Statewide Parties Cope with the Regionalist Issue: The Case of Spain; A Directional Approach

1. The authors wish to thank Wilfried Swenden, Elodie Fabre and Enric Martínez-Herrera for their useful comments on an earlier draft. The usual disclaimer applies.
2. In contrast to directional and issue ownership theory, however, Meguid (2005: 349) argues that an accommodative strategy may challenge the exclusivity of a niche party and undermine its issue ownership and thus its electoral support. Her empirical findings (regarding the environmentalist and radical right parties) indicate that an accommodative strategy has a weak negative effect on the electoral success of the niche party, while an adversarial strategy has a much stronger positive effect. This model is based on a categorical distinction between the three

strategies and does not take into account the intensity of an accommodative or an adversarial stance.

3. Manifestos are a primary data source; most electoral debates in secondary sources, such as the mass media, would concentrate on policy pledges contained in the manifestos (Ashworth, 1999). Budge et al. (2001) refers to political texts as 'the major source of evidence . . . for how democracy functions'. Moreover, manifestos are major statements in which parties aim to present comprehensive accounts of their positions; they are issued by the whole party and not by one particular faction. Ashworth (1999) adds that party manifestos are publicly available and easily accessible, and they can be easily re-analysed. Moreover, in contrast with interview data, party programmes are suitable for quantitative content analysis.

4. Apart from this broad distinction between regionalist and non-regionalist statements we also applied a more fine-grained coding scheme, based on the Eurovoc Thesaurus, which reflects the specific policy fields allocated to the competence of either the regional or the national government. These data are not used in this chapter.

11 Statewide Parties and Regional Party Competition: An Analysis of Party Manifestos in the United Kingdom

1. The elections to the Greater London Assembly and the Northern Ireland Assembly will not be studied because of the nature of the former as a city assembly and its more limited range of powers, and because of the different party system and the long interruptions in the functioning of the latter.

2. For a more detailed explanation of the coding scheme that was developed and why it departs from the traditional issue categorization of the CMP project, see the contribution by Maddens et al. in this volume and Pogorelis et al. (2005).

3. 'Regional government' is defined here as statements specifically referring to 'structures, principles, powers and autonomy'. Statements in a (statewide) manifesto like 'social security policies should take into account the specific social interests of Scotland' are considered as 'social security issues' when the overall salience profile of a party is analysed. In this sense 'regional government' is conceptualized differently from the 'regionalist issue' discussed below, where such a statement would be interpreted as an expression of a 'regionalist issue – institutional dimension' (alongside other issues which may express the cultural or identity component of regionalism).

4. The coding scheme is available upon request from Elodie Fabre.

Concluding Observations

1. That said, the assessment of incongruence varies with the size of the (prospective) coalition party in a regional government: for senior parties incongruence offers the (strategically beneficial) opportunity to 'distance itself' from the statewide party and junior regional coalition partner. For junior parties, such as the NRW FDP, the disadvantages outweigh the benefits. A 'supportive' role outside the government may be preferable as a vote-seeking strategy.

2. The effect of the third variable (party type) has not been analysed in systematic detail for its effect on statewide party organizational decentralization. The rather centralized character of parties that revolve around a particular leader or 'brand' of

the party (such as Silvio Berlusconi for *Forza Italia*), or of parties that put a strong emphasis on ideological purity (such as the Italian Communists), speaks for itself. Yet most parties referred to here have acquired the features of catch-all parties, although they have been going through a process of 'cartelization' in recent years (Katz and Mair, 1995; Detterbeck, 2005, for a critique on the extent to which cartelization applies across most parties in Western Europe). Cartelization is said to strengthen the party-in-office vis-à-vis the extra-parliamentary party (party bureaucracy). However, this 'horizontal' shift in powers is not necessarily accompanied by a vertical shift (i.e., the parliamentary party at the statewide level does not necessarily have to develop into the hub of all party activities). Cartel parties operate in an electorally volatile environment and, compared with catch-all parties, they are increasingly dependent on state funding. These funds in turn hinge on their electoral performance at the statewide *and* regional levels. A 'stratarchical' organization is better suited to the task of translating regional electoral preferences into a coherent programme for regional elections. Yet, as Bradbury demonstrates in his coverage of candidate selection for UK devolved elections, statewide parties may seek to balance regional autonomy with vertical hierarchy by giving regional branches the right to select candidates, but only within centrally set parameters (for instance, with respect to ideology, gender and minority representation as well as the methods of candidate selection, often requiring a stronger influence of the local or regional rank and file). Furthermore, the explanatory power of cartelization is limited: if we assume that cartelization has affected the largest statewide parties within each of the countries in roughly equal measure, it cannot explain why the UK Liberal Democrats have a more decentralized organization than Labour or the Conservatives, or why the Spanish Conservatives are more centralized than the Spanish Social Democrats.

Bibliography

Abromeit, H. (1992), *Der Verkappte Einheitsstaat* (Opladen: Leske + Budrich).

Agranoff, R., ed., (1999), *Accommodating Diversity: Asymmetry in Federal States* (Baden-Baden: Nomos).

Aja, E. (2003), *El Estado Autonómico: Federalismo y Hechos Diferenciales* (Madrid: Alianza, 2nd edition).

Aja, E. (2004), 'Spain: Nations, Nationalities and Regions', in J. Loughlin, ed., *Subnational Democracy in the European Union* (Oxford: Oxford University Press), 229–53.

Alesina, A. and Spolaore, E. (2003), *The Size of Nations* (Cambridge, MA: MIT Press).

Allum, P. (1973), *Italy: Republic Without Government?* (London: W. W. Norton).

Altemeier, J. (1998), *Föderale Finanzbeziehungen unter Anpassungsdruck: Verteilungskonflikte in der Verhandlungsdemokratie* (Frankfurt: Campus).

Arzheimer, K. (2002), 'Ist der Osten wirklich rot? Das Wahlverhalten bei der Bundestagswahl 2002 in Ost-West-Perspektive', *Aus Politik und Zeitgeschichte*, 49–50, 27–35.

Arzheimer, K. (2005), 'Das Wahlverhalten. Besonderheiten in Ostdeutschland als Modell künftiger gesamtdeutscher Entwicklungen', in H. Bahrmann and C. Links, eds, *Am Ziel vorbei: Die Deutsche Einheit – eine Zwischenbilanz* (Berlin: Ch. Links Verlag), 60–74.

Ashworth, R. (1999), 'Political Priorities: A Content Analysis of Welsh Local Election Pledges', paper presented at the Annual Conference of the British Political Studies Association. http://www.pas.ac.uk/cps/19999/asworth.pdf

Astudillo, J. and García-Guereta, E. (2005), 'La distribución territorial del poder en los partidos políticos: el caso del Partido Popular', paper presented at the VII Congreso, Asociación Española de Ciencia Política y de la Administración.

Astudillo, J. and García-Guereta, E. (2006), 'If it isn't broken, don't fix it: The Spanish Popular Party in power', *Southern European Society and Politics*, 11, 3–4.

Baccetti, C. (1997), *Il Pds* (Bologna: Il Mulino).

Badriotti, A. (2007), 'To what extent do Central governments erode states jurisdiction using fiscal arrangements? A perspective from Italy', paper presented at 4th International Conference on Federalism, Salzburg, 13–14 October.

Baldi, B. and Baldini, G. (forthcoming), 'Italia', in S. Ventura, ed., *Da Unitario a Federale* (Bologna: Il Mulino).

Baldini, G. (1998), 'The failed renewal: The DC from 1982 to 1994', in P. Ignazi and C. Ysmal, eds, *The Organization of Political Parties in Southern Europe* (London: Praeger), 110–33.

Baldini, G. and Legnante, G. (2000), *Città al Voto: I Sindaci e le Elezioni Comunali (1993–1998)* (Bologna: Il Mulino).

Baldini, G. and Vassallo, S. (2001), 'The regions in search of a new institutional identity', in M. Caciagli and A. Zuckerman, eds, *Italian Politics: Emerging Themes and Institutional Responses* (Oxford: Berghahn), 85–102.

Balfour, S. (2005), 'The reinvention of Spanish conservatism: The Popular Party since 1989', in S. Balfour, ed., *The Politics of Contemporary Spain* (London: Routledge), 146–68.

Bardi, L. and Morlino, L. (1994), 'Italy: Tracing the roots of the great transformation', in R. S. Katz and P. Mair, eds, *How Parties Organize: Change and Adaptation in Party Organizations in Western Democracies* (London: Sage), 242–77.

Bartolini, S. (2004), 'Old and new peripheries in the process of European integration', in C. K. Ansell and G. Di Palma, eds, *Restructuring Territoriality: Europe and the United States Compared* (Cambridge: Cambridge University Press).

Beil, S. and Lepzy, N. (1995), *Die Reformdiskussion in den Volksparteien* (Sankt Augustin: Konrad-Adenauer-Stiftung).

Beke, W. (2005), *De Ziel van een Zuil: De Christelijke Volkspartij 1945–1968* (Leuven: Universitaire Pers Leuven).

Bendor, J., Glazer, A. and Hammond, T. (2001), 'Theories of delegation', *Annual Review of Political Science*, 4, 235–69.

Benz, A. (2003), 'Reformpromotoren oder Reformblockierer? Die Rolle der Parteien im Bundesstaat', *Aus Politik und Zeitgeschichte*, 29–30/2003, 32–8.

Benz, A. (2006), 'Kein Ausweg aus der Politikverflechtung? Warum die Bundesstaatskommission scheiterte, aber nicht scheitern musste', *Politische Vierteljahresschrift*, 46, 2, 195–214.

Best, H. and Jahr, S. (2006), 'Politik als prekäres Beschäftigungsverhältnis: Mythos und Realität der Sozialfigur des Berufspolitikers im wiedervereinten Deutschland', *Zeitschrift für Parlamentsfragen*, 37, 63–79.

Biehl, H. (2005), *Parteimitglieder im Wandel: Partizipation und Repräsentation* (Wiesbaden: VS Verlag für Sozialwissenschaften).

Bille, L. (2001), 'Democratizing a democratic procedure: Myth or reality? Candidate selection in Western European parties, 1960–1990', *Party Politics*, 7, 3, 363–80.

Billiet, J., Maddens, B. and Frognier, A. P. (2006), 'Does Belgium (still) exist? Differences in political culture between Flemings and Walloons', *West European Politics*, 2006, 5, 912–32.

Biorcio, R. (1997), *La Padania Promessa* (Milan: Il Saggiatore).

Boeynaems, M. (1972), 'De lijstensamenstelling in de PVV', *Res Publica*, 14, 2, 251–78.

Bollen, K. and Díez-Medrano, J. (1998), 'Who are the Spaniards? The effect of ethnic origin, economic development, economic specialization, and cognitive skills on attachment to the nation-state in the Spanish context', *Social Forces*, 77, 2, 587–621.

Bollen, K. A. and Hoyle, R. H. (1990), 'Perceived cohesion: A conceptual and empirical examination', *Social Forces*, 69, 2, 479–504.

Bolleyer, N. (2006), 'Intergovernmental arrangements in Spanish and Swiss federalism: The impact of power-concentrating and power-sharing executives on intergovernmental institutionalization', *Regional and Federal Studies*, 16, 4, 385–408.

Bomberg, E. and Peterson, P. (1999), *Decision-making in the European Union* (Basingstoke: Palgrave Macmillan).

Borchert, J. (2001), 'Movement and linkage: Individual ambition and institutional repercussions in a multi-level setting', paper presented at the ECPR Joint Sessions, Grenoble, April 2001.

Borchert, J. and Golsch, L. (2003), 'Germany: From "guilds of notables" to political class', in J. Borchert and J. Zeiss, eds, *The Political Class in Advanced Democracies* (Oxford: Oxford University Press), 142–63.

Borchert, J. and Stolz, K. (2003), 'Die Bekämpfung der Unsicherheit: Politikerkarrieren und Karrierepolitik in der Bundesrepublik Deutschland', *Politische Vierteljahresschrift*, 44, 148–73.

Borchert, J. and Stolz, K. (2004), 'Political careers in Germany: The view from the states', paper presented at the Workshop on 'Political careers in multi-level systems', Kloster Seeon/Bavaria, July 2004.

Bösch, F. (2005), 'Oppositionszeiten als Motor der Parteireform? Die CDU nach 1969 und 1998 im Vergleich', in J. Schmid and U. Zolleis, eds, *Zwischen Anarchie und Strategie: Der Erfolg von Parteiorganisationen* (Wiesbaden: VS Verlag für Sozialwissenschaften), 172–85.

Bösch, F. (2007), 'Christlich Demokratische Union Deutschlands (CDU)', in F. Decker and V. Neu, eds, *Handbuch der deutschen Parteien* (Wiesbaden: VS Verlag für Sozialwissen-schaften), 201–19.

Bradbury, J. (2006), 'British political parties and devolution: Adapting to multilevel politics in Scotland and Wales', in D. Hough and C. Jeffery, eds, *Devolution and Electoral Politics* (Manchester: Manchester University Press), 214–47.

Bradbury, J., Denver, D., Mitchell, J. and Bennie, L. (2000a), 'Devolution and party change: Candidate selection for the 1999 Scottish Parliament and Welsh Assembly elections', *Journal of Legislative Studies*, 6, 3, 51–72.

Bradbury, J., Denver, D., Mitchell, J. and Bennie, L. (2000b), 'Candidate selection, devolution and modernisation: The selection of Labour Party candidates for the 1999 Scottish Parliament and Welsh Assembly Elections', *British Elections and Parties Review*, 10, 151–72.

Bradbury, J., Denver, D., Mitchell, J. and Bennie, L. (2000c), 'Devolution, parties and new politics: Candidate selection for the 1999 National Assembly elections', *Contemporary Wales*, 13, 159–81.

Braun, D., Bullinger, A. B. and Walti, S. (2002), 'The influence of federalism on fiscal policy making', *European Journal of Political Research*, 41, 115–45.

Brepoels, J. (1981), *Wat zoudt gij zonder 't werkvolk zijn? Anderhalve eeuw arbeidersstrijd in België* (Leuven: Kritak).

Bromley, C. (2006), 'Devolution and electoral politics in Scotland', in D. Hough and C. Jeffery, eds, *Devolution and Electoral Politics* (Manchester: Manchester University Press), 192–213.

Brown, A., McCrone, D. and Paterson, L. (1998), *Politics and Society in Scotland* (Basingstoke: Macmillan, 2nd edition).

Budge, I. and Farlie, D. J. (1983a), *Explaining and predicting Elections: Issue-Effects and Party Strategies in Twenty-three Democracies* (London: Allen and Unwin).

Budge, I. and Farlie, D. (1983b) 'Party competition – Selective emphasis or direct confrontation? An alternative view with data', in H. Daalder and P. Mair, eds, *Western European Party Systems: Continuity and Change* (London: Sage), 267–306.

Budge, I., Klingemann, H. D., Volkens, A., Bara, J. and Tanenbaum, E. (2001), *Mapping Policy Preferences: Estimates for Parties, Electors, and Governments 1945–1998* (Oxford: Oxford University Press).

Budge, I., Robertson, D. and Hearl, D., eds, (1987), *Ideology, Strategy and Party Choice: Spatial Analyses of Post-war Election Programmes in 19 Democracies* (Cambridge: Cambridge University Press).

Buelens, J. and Van Dyck, R. (1998), 'Regionalist parties in French-speaking Belgium: The *Rassemblement Wallon* and the *Front Démocratique des Francophones*', in L. De Winter and H. Türsan, eds, *Regionalist parties in Western Europe* (London: Routledge), 51–69.

Bufacchi, V. and Burgess, S. (2001), *Italy Since 1989: Events and Interpretations* (Basingstoke: Macmillan, 2nd edition).

Bull, A. (1994), 'Regionalism in Italy', *Europa*, 1, 2/3, 69–83.

Bulpitt, J. (1983), *Territory and Power in the United Kingdom, an Interpretation* (Manchester: Manchester University Press).

Burgess, M. (2006), *Comparative Federalism: Theory and Practice* (New York, Routledge).

Burkhart, S. (2004), 'Parteipolitikverflechtung: Der Einfluss der Bundespolitik auf Landtagswahlentscheidungen von 1976 bis 2002', *Max-Planck-Institut für Gesellschaftsforschung*, Discussion Paper 04/1.

Bürklin, W. and Jung, C. (2001), 'Deutschland im Wandel: Ergebniss einer repräsentativen Meinungsumfrage', in K. Korte and W. Weidenfeld, eds, *Deutschland-Trendbuch* (Bonn: Bundeszentrale für politische Bildung).

Bürklin, W. and Klein, M. (1998), *Wahlen und Wählerverhalten – Eine Einführung* (Opladen: Leske und Budrich).

Buznego, O. R. (1998), 'Elecciones autonómicas, sistema de partidos y gobiernos en Asturias', in M. Alcántara and A. Martínez, eds, *Las elecciones autonómicas en España 1980–1997* (Madrid: CIS), 81–97.

Cammelli, M. (2003), 'Un grande caos chiamato *devolution*', *Il Mulino*, 52, 405, 87–99.

Caramani, D. (1996), 'The nationalisation of electoral politics: A conceptual reconstruction and review of the literature', *West European Politics*, 19, 2, 205–24.

Caramani, D. (2000), *The Societies of Europe: Elections in Western Europe since 1815: Electoral Results by Constituencies* (Basingstoke: Palgrave Macmillan).

Caramani, D. (2004), *The Nationalization of Politics: The Formation of National Electorates and Party Systems in Western Europe* (Cambridge: Cambridge University Press).

Carty, R. (2004), 'Parties as franchise systems: The stratarchical organisational imperative', *Party Politics*, 10, 1, 5–24.

Cazzola, F. and Motta, R. (1984), 'Dalle assemblee regionali al parlamento nazionale', *Le Regioni*, 12, 4, 621–32.

CEPESS (1977), *De Belgische staatshervorming van 1974 tot het Gemeenschapspact* (Brussel: CEPESS).

Ceuleers, J. (1977), 'De regering Tindemans, de partijen en het overleg onder de gemeenschappen', *Res Publica*, 19, 2, 165–78.

Ceuleers, J. (1980), 'De splitsing van de Belgische Socialistische Partij: Een B te veel', *Res Publica*, 22, 3, 373–82.

Chandler, W. (1987), 'Federalism and political parties' in H. Bakvis and W. Chandler, eds, *Federalism and the Role of the State* (Toronto: University of Toronto Press), 149–70.

Chhibber, P. K. and Kollman, K. (2004), *The Formation of National Party Systems: Federalism and Party Competition in Canada, Great Britain and the United States* (Princeton, NJ: Princeton University Press).

Chubb, J. (1982), *Patronage, Power and Poverty in Southern Italy: A Tale of Two Cities* (Cambridge: Cambridge University Press).

Claeys-Van Haegendoren, M. (1967), *25 jaar Belgisch socialisme: Evolutie van de verhouding van de Belgische Werkliedenpartij tot de parlementaire democratie in België van 1914 tot 1940* (Antwerp: Standaard Wetenschappelijke Uitgeverij).

Colino, C. (2008), 'Deepening or transforming Spanish federalism? The new round of reform and the challenges for the Autonomic State', in Europäisches Zentrum für Föderalismus-Forschung, ed., *Jahrbuch des Föderalismus* (Nomos: Baden-Baden).

Conradt, D. P. (2005), *The German Polity* (New York: Pearson Longman Education).

CRISP (1970), *L'évolution récente des structures du CVP-PSC* (Courrier Hebdomadaire 484). (Brussels: CRISP).

Curtice, J. (1988), 'Great Britain – Social liberalism reborn?', in E. J. Kirchner, ed., *Liberal Parties in Western Europe* (Cambridge: Cambridge University Press), 93–123.

Czada, R. (1995), 'Der Kampf um die Finanzierung der deutschen Einheit', in G. Lehmbruch, ed., *Einigung und Zerfall: Deutschland und Europa nach dem Ende des Ost-West-Konflikts* (Opladen: Leske + Budrich), 73–102.

Dachs, H. (2003), 'Politische Parteien in Österreichs Bundesländern – Zwischen regionalen Kalkülen und bundespolitischen Loyalitäten', in H. Dachs, ed., *Der Bund und die Länder: Über Dominanz, Kooperation und Konflikte im österreichischen Bundesstaat* (Vienna: Signum Verlag), 69–138.

Davies, A. (1998), 'Creating the new politics', *Agenda: Journal of the Institute of Welsh Affairs*, summer, 14–16.

Debus, M. (2006), 'Party competition and coalition formation in the German federal states: Different party strategies, but similar coalition game outcomes?', paper presented at the ECPR Graduate Conference, September 2006, Essex.

Debus, M. (2007), 'Die programmatische Entwicklung der deutschen Parteien auf Bundes- und Landesebene zwischen den Bundestagswahlen 1998 und 2005', in F. Brettschneider, O. Niedermayer and B. Weßels, eds, *Die Bundestagswahl 2005: Analysen des Wahlkampfes und der Wahlergebnisse* (Wiesbaden: VS Verlag für Sozialwissenschaften), 43–63.

Decker, F. and von Blumenthal, J. (2002), 'Die bundespolitische Durchdringung von Landtagswahlen: Eine empirische Analyse von 1970 bis 2001', *Zeitschrift für Parlamentsfragen*, 33, 144–65.

Della Porta, D. (1992), *Lo Scambio Occulto* (Bologna: Il Mulino).

Della Porta, D. and Vannucci, A. (1994), *Corruzione Politica e Pubblica Amministrazione* (Bologna: Il Mulino).

Della Porta, D. and Pizzorno, A. (1996), 'The business politicians: Reflections from a study of political corruption', in M. Levi and D. Nelken, eds, *The Corruption of Politics and the Politics of Corruption* (Oxford: Blackwell), 73–94.

Delwit, P. and Pilet, J.-B. (2004), 'Fédéralisme, institutions et vie politique: Stabilité, instabilité et retour', in M.-T. Coenen, ed., *L'Etat de la Belgique 1989–2004: Quinze années à la charnière du siècle* (Brussels: De Boeck), 43–79.

Dente, B. (1997), 'The sub-national governments in the long Italian transition', *West European Politics*, 20, 1, 176–93.

Denver, D. (1988), 'Britain: Centralised parties with decentralised selection' in M. Gallagher and M. Marsh, eds, *Candidate Selection in Comparative Perspective: The Secret Garden of Politics* (London: Sage), 50–7.

De Ridder, H. (1989), *Sire, geef me 100 dagen* (Leuven: Davidsfonds).

Deschouwer, K. (1999), 'From consociation to federation: How the Belgian parties won', in K. R. Luther and K. Deschouwer, eds, *Party Elites in Divided Societies: Political Parties in Consociational Democracy* (London: Routledge), 74–107.

Deschouwer, K. (2003), 'Political Parties in Multi-Layered Systems', *European Urban and Regional Studies*, 10, 3, 213–26.

Deschouwer, K. (2005), 'Kingdom of Belgium', in J. Kincaid and A. Tarr, eds, *Constitutional Origins, Structure, and Change in Federal Countries* (Montreal: McGill-Queen's University Press), 49–75.

Deschouwer, K. (2006a), 'Political Parties as multi-level organizations', in R. S. Katz and W. Crotty, eds, *Handbook of Party Politics* (London: Sage), 291–300.

Deschouwer, K. (2006b), 'And the Peace goes On? Consociational Democracy and Belgian Politics in the Twenty-First Century', *West European Politics*, 29, 5, 895–911.

Detterbeck, K. (2002), *Der Wandel Politischer Parteien in Westeuropa* (Opladen: Leske + Budrich).

Detterbeck, K. (2004), 'Party careers in federal systems: A comparison between Austria, Germany, Canada and Australia', paper presented at the Workshop on 'Political careers in multi-level systems', Kloster Seeon/Bavaria, July 2004.

Detterbeck, K. (2005), 'Cartel Parties in Western Europe?', *Party Politics*, 11, 2, 173–91.

Detterbeck, K. (2006), 'Zusammenlegung von Bundes- und Landtagswahlen? Die Terminierung von Wahlen und ihre Konsequenzen im europäischen Vergleich', *Bertelsmann Stiftung*, Zukunft Regieren. Beiträge für eine gestaltungsfähige Politik, 1/2006.

Detterbeck, K., and Renzsch, W. (2003), 'Multi-level electoral competition: The German case', *European Urban and Regional Studies*, 10, 257–69.

De Winter, L. (2006) 'In memoriam the Volksunie 1954–2001: Death by overdose of success', in L. De Winter, M. Gómez-Reino and P. Lynch, eds, *Autonomist Parties in Europe: Identity Politics and the Revival of the Territorial Cleavage* (vol. II) (Barcelona: Institut de Ciènces Polítiques I Socials, 2006), 13–45.

De Winter, L. and Dumont, P. (2006), 'Regeringsformatie', in E. Witte and A. Meynen, eds, *De geschiedenis van België na 1945* (Antwerpen: Standaard Uitgeverij), 289–329.

De Winter, L. and Türsan, H., eds, (1998), *Regionalist Parties in Western Europe* (London: Routledge).

De Winter, L., Gómez-Reino, M. and Lynch, P., eds, (2006), *Autonomist Parties in Europe: Identity Politics and the Revival of the Territorial Cleavage* (Barcelona, ICPS 2006, vols. I, II).

D'Hoore, M. (1989), 'De liberale partij als organisatie van 1914 tot 1961', in A. Verhulst and H. Hasquin, eds, *Het liberalisme in België: Tweehonderd jaar geschiedenis* (Brussels: Delta), 83–90.

D'Hoore, M. (1997), *Du PLP-PVV au PRL-FDF. I. 1961–1992 (CH 1554)* (Brussels: CRISP).

Diamanti, I. (1993), *La Lega: Geografia, Storia e Sociologia di un Soggetto Politico* (Rome: Donzelli).

Diamanti, I. (1996), *Il Male del Nord: Lega, Localismo, Secessione* (Rome: Donzelli).

Diamanti, I. (2003), *Bianco, Rosso, Verde . . . e Azzurro: Mappe e Colori dell'Italia Politica* (Bologna: Il Mulino).

Díez-Medrano, J. (1995), *Divided Nations: Class, Politics and Nationalism in the Basque Country and Catalonia* (Ithaca, NY: Cornell University Press).

Dinkel, R. (1977), Der Zusammenhang zwischen Bundes- und Landeswahlergebnissen', *Politische Vierteljahrschrift*, 18, 348–60.

Downs, A. (1957), *An Economic Theory of Democracy* (New York: Harper and Row).

Downs, W. M. (1998), *Coalition Government, Subnational Style: Multiparty Politics in Europe's Regional Parliaments* (Columbus: Ohio State University Press).

Dyck, R. (1996), 'Relations between federal and provincial parties', in A. B. Tanguay and A. G. Gagnon, eds, *Canadian Parties in Transition* (Scarborough, Ontario: Nelson Canada), 160–89.

Dyck, R. (1997) 'Federalism and Canadian political parties,' in M. Westmacott and H. Mellon, eds, *Challenges to Canadian Federalism* (Scarborough, Ontario: Prentice-Hall) 55–62.

Ebbighausen, R., Düpjohann, C., Prokein, D., Raupach, J., Renner, M., Schotes, R. and Schröter, S. (1996), *Die Kosten der Parteiendemokratie: Studien und Materialien zu einer Bilanz staatlicher Parteienfinanzierung in der Bundesrepublik Deutschland* (Opladen: Westdeutscher Verlag).

Elazar, D. J. (1987), *Exploring Federalism* (Tuscaloosa, AL: The University of Alabama Press).

Eldersveld, S. (1964), *Political Parties* (Chicago: Rand McNally).

Enelow, J. M. and Hinich, M. J. (1984), *The Spatial Theory of Voting: An Introduction* (Cambridge: Cambridge University Press).

Epstein, L. (1980), *Political Parties in Western Democracies* (New Brunswick: Transaction Books).

Erikson, R. (1988), 'The puzzle of mid-term loss', *Journal of Politics*, 50, 4, 1011–29.

Erk, J. (2008), *Explaining Federalism: State, society and congruence in Austria, Belgium, Canada, Germany and Switzerland* (London: Routledge Series in Federalism).

Esposito, M. (2003), *Chi Paga la Devolution?* (Bari: Laterza).

Fabre, E. (2008) 'Party organisation in a multi-level setting: Spain and the UK', PhD dissertation (Leuven: Katholieke Universiteit Leuven).

Fabre, E., Swenden, W., Maddens, B. and Libbrecht, L. (2005), 'Party organisation in decentralised countries: The cases of Spain and the United Kingdom', paper prepared for the workshop 'Democracy and Political Parties', ECPR Joint Sessions, Granada.

Falony, R. (2006), *Le parti socialiste: Un demi-siècle de bouleversements De Max Buset à Elio di Rupo* (Brussels: Luc Pire).

Fedele, M. (1990), 'I processi politico-istituzionali nei sistema regionali', Dossier N.416, Parliamentary Committee for Regional Questions (Rome: Camera dei Deputati).

Fernández Ferrero, M. A. (1997), *Procesos Electorales: Elecciones Autonómicas en La Rioja 1979–1995* (Logroño: Universidad de La Rioja).

Fiers, S., Gerard E. and Van Uytven, A. (2006), 'De uitverkorenen: De federale en Vlaamse parlementsleden (1946–2004)', in S. Fiers and H. Reynaert, eds, *Wie zetelt? De gekozen politieke elite in Vlaanderen doorgelicht* (Leuven: Lannoo Campus), 87–111.

Filippov, M, Ordeshook, P. C. and Shvetsova, O. (2004), *Designing Federalism: A Theory of Self-Sustainable Federal Institutions* (Cambridge: Cambridge University Press).

Flora, P., Kuhnle, S. and Urwin, D., eds, (1999), *State Formation, Nation-building and Mass Politics in Europe: The Theory of Stein Rokkan* (Oxford: Oxford University Press).

Flynn, P. (1999), *Dragons Led by Poodles, The Inside Story of a New Labour Stitch Up* (London: Politics).

Font, J. and Rico, G. (2003), 'Spanish multilevel turnout: Learning to vote?', Working Paper, Democratic Participation and Political Communication in Systems of Multi-Level Governance (Fifth Framework Research Programme).

Gabriel, O. W. (1989), 'Federalism and party democracy in West Germany', *Publius*, 19, 65–80.

Gallagher, M. (1988a), 'Introduction', in M. Gallagher and M. Marsh, eds, *Candidate Selection in Comparative perspective: The Secret Garden of Politics* (London: Sage), 1–19.

Gallagher, M. (1988b), 'Conclusion', in M. Gallagher and M. Marsh, eds, *Candidate Selection in Comparative perspective: The Secret Garden of Politics* (London: Sage), 236–83.

Gallagher, M. and Marsh, M., eds, (1988), *Candidate Selection in Comparative perspective: The Secret Garden of Politics* (London: Sage).

Geldolf, W. (2006) *Een Stuk Oude Politieke Cultuur achteraf Bekeken* (Antwerp: De Vries-Brouwers).

Gerard, E. (1985), *De Katholieke Partij in Crisis: Partijpolitiek Leven in België 1918–1940* (Leuven: Kritak).

Gerard, E. (1999), 'De Senaat, 1918–1970', in V. Laureys and M. Van den Wijngaert, eds, *De Geschiedenis van de Belgische Senaat 1831–1995* (Tielt: Lannoo), 140–212.

Gibson, E. and Suarez-Cao, J. (2007), 'Federalized party systems: Patterns of competition and hegemony', paper presented at APSA Annual Conference, Chicago, 30 August–2 September 2007.

Gold, T. W. (2003), *The Lega Nord and Contemporary Politics in Italy* (Basingstoke: Palgrave Macmillan).

Govaert, S. (1995) *Du PLP-PVV au VLD. I. 1971–1995 (CH 1501–1502)* (Brussels: CRISP).

Grabow, K. (2001), 'The re-emergence of the cadre party? Organizational patterns of Christian and Social democrats in unified Germany', *Party Politics*, 7, 23–43.

Grande, E. (2002) 'Parteiensystem und Föderalismus – Institutionelle Strukturmuster und politische Dynamiken im internationalen Vergleich', in A. Benz, and G. Lehmbruch, eds, *Föderalismus: Analysen in entwicklungsgeschichtlicher und vergleichender Perspektive* (Wiesbaden: Westdeutscher Verlag), 179–212.

Greer, S., ed., (2006), *Territory, Democracy and Justice* (Basingstoke: Palgrave Macmillan).

Greer, S. (2007), *Nationalism and Self-Government: The Politics of Autonomy in Scotland and Catalonia* (Albany, NY: SUNY Press).

Greß, F. and Huth, R. (1998), *Die Landesparlamente: Gesetzgebungsorgane in den deutschen Ländern* (Heidelberg: Hüthig).

Grotz, C. (2004), 'Die CDU', in M. Eilfort, ed., *Parteien in Baden-Württemberg* (Stuttgart: Kohlhammer), 37–74.

Grube, N. (2004), 'Unverzichtbares Korrektiv oder ineffektive Reformbremse? Wahrnehmungen föderaler Strukturen und Institutionen in Deutschland', *Jahrbuch des Föderalismus 2004* (Baden-Baden: Nomos), 163–75.

Guadagnini, M. (1984), 'Il personale politico dalla "periferia" al "centro": riflessioni su alcuni dati di una ricerca', *Le Regioni*, 12, 4, 589–620.

Gundle, S. and Parker, S., eds, (1996), *The New Italian Republic: From the Fall of the Berlin Wall to Berlusconi* (London: Routledge).

Gunlicks, A. B. (2003), *The Länder and German Federalism* (Manchester, Manchester University Press).

Gunther, R., Montero, J. R. and Botella, J. (2004), *Democracy in Modern Spain* (New Haven: Yale University Press).

Hadley, C., Morass, M. and Reiner, N. (1989), 'Federalism and party-interaction in West Germany, Switzerland and Austria', *Publius*, 19, 4, 81–97.

Harvie, C. (1994), *The Rise of Regional Europe* (London: Routledge).

Hassan, G. and Warhurst, C. (2001), 'New Scotland? Policy, parties and institutions', *Political Quarterly*, 72, 2, 213–26.

Hazell, R., ed., (2000), *The State and the Nations: The First Year of Devolution in the UK* (Thorverton: Imprint Academic).

Heath, A., McLean, I., Taylor, B. and Curtice, J. (1999), 'Between first and second order: A comparison of voting behaviour in European and local elections in Britain', *European Journal of Political Research*, 35, 389–414.

Hepburn, E. (2008), 'The Rise and Fall of a Europe of the Regions: The Territorial Strategies of Regional Political Parties 1969–2006', *Regional and Federal Studies*.

Hernández-Bravo, J. (1998), 'La construcción electoral de Canarias en la autonomía: una questión no resuelta', in M. Alcántara and A. Martínez, eds, *Las elecciones autonómicas en España 1980–1997* (Madrid: CIS), 119–49.

Herzog, D. (1997), 'Die Führungsgremien der Parteien: Funktionswandel und Strukturentwicklungen', in O. W. Gabriel, O. Niedermayer and R. Stöss, eds, *Parteiendemokratie in Deutschland* (Bonn: Bundeszentrale für politische Bildung), 301–22.

Hine, D. (1989), 'The Italian Socialist Party' in T. Gallagher and A. Williams, eds, *Southern European Socialism* (Manchester: Manchester University Press), 109–30.

Höbelt, L. (2002), 'Die FPÖ und die Konflikte in ihren Landesorganisationen', in A. Khol, G. Ofner, G. Burkert-Dottolo and S. Karner, eds, *Österreichisches Jahrbuch für Politik 2002* (Vienna/Munich: Verlag für Geschichte und Politik/Oldenbourg).

Holtschneider, R. and Schön, W. (2007), *Die Reform des Bundesstaates* (Baden-Baden: Nomos).

Hooghe, L. and Marks, G. (2001), *Multi-Level Governance and European Integration* (Lanham: Rowman & Littlefield).

Hooghe, L., Marks, G. and Schakel, A. (2008), 'Regional authority in 42 democracies, 1950–2006: A measure and five hypotheses', Special Issue of *Regional & Federal Studies*, 18, 2–3.

Hopkin, J. (1999), *Party Formation and Democratic Transition in Spain: The Creation and Collapse of the Union of the Democratic Centre* (Basingstoke: Macmillan).

Hopkin, J. (2003), 'Political decentralization, electoral change and party organizational adaptation: A framework for analysis', *European Urban and Regional Studies*, 10, 227–38.

Hopkin, J. (2005), 'Forza Italia Ten years on', in C. Guarnieri and J. Newell, eds, *Italian Politics 2005* (Oxford: Berghahn), 102–27.

Hopkin, J. and Bradbury, J. (2006), 'British Statewide Parties and Multilevel Politics', *Publius: The Journal of Federalism*, 36, 1, 135–62.

Hopper, J. (2001), 'Research Note – Old Parties in the New Germany: The CDU, FDP and Eastern Germany, 1989–1994', *Party Politics*, 7, 5, 621–42.

Hough, D. (2002), *The Fall and Rise of the PDS in Eastern Germany* (Birmingham: Birmingham University Press).

Hough, D. and Jeffery, C. (2006a), 'An introduction to multi-level electoral competition', in D. Hough and C. Jeffery, eds, *Devolution and Electoral Politics* (Manchester: Manchester University Press), 2–13.

Hough, D. and Jeffery, C. (2006b), 'Germany: An erosion of federal-Länder linkages?' in D. Hough and C. Jeffery, eds, *Devolution and Electoral Politics* (Manchester: Manchester University Press), 119–39.

Hough, D. and Jeffery, C., eds, (2006c), *Devolution and Electoral Politics* (Manchester: Manchester University Press).

Hough, D., Koß, M. and Olsen, J. (2007), *The Left Party in Contemporary German Politics* (Basingstoke: Palgrave Macmillan).

Hunin, J. (1999), *Camille Huysmans: Het enfant terrible* (Leuven: Kritak).

Ignazi, P. (1992), *Dal PCI al PDS* (Bologna: Il Mulino).

Iglesias, M. (2003), *La Sucesión: La Historia de Cómo Aznar Eligió a Mariano Rajoy* (Madrid: Temas de Hoy).

Ingle, S. (1996), 'Party organisation', in D. MacIver, ed., *The Liberal Democrats* (Hemel Hempstead: Prentice-Hall), 113–33.

Jeffery, C. (1995), 'The non-reform of the German federal system after unification', *West European Politics*, 18, 2, 252–72.

Jeffery, C. (1999a), 'Party politics and territorial representation in the Federal Republic of Germany', in J. B. Brzinski, T. D. Lancaster and C. Tuschhoff, eds, *Compounded Representation in West European Federations* (London: Frank Cass), 130–66.

Jeffery, C. (1999b), 'From cooperative federalism to a "Sinatra doctrine" of the Länder?', in C. Jeffery, ed., *Recasting German Federalism: The Legacies of Unification* (London: Pinter), 329–42.

Jeffery, C. (2003), 'Cycles of conflict: Fiscal equalisation in Germany', *Regional and Federal Studies*, 13, 4, 22–40.

Jeffery, C. (2005), 'Federalism: The new territorialism', in S. Green and W. Paterson, eds, *Governance in Contemporary Germany: The Semi-Sovereign State Revisited* (Cambridge: Cambridge University Press), 78–93.

Jeffery, C. and Hough, D. (2001), 'The electoral cycle and multi-level voting in Germany', *German Politics*, 10, 2, 73–98.

Jeffery, C. and Hough, D. (2003), 'Regional elections in multi-level systems', *European Urban and Regional Studies*, 10, 199–212.

Jeffery, C. and Hough, D. (2009), 'Understanding elections in Scotland and Wales after devolution', *Party Politics*, 15, 1.

Jones, M. P. and Mainwaring, S. (2003), 'The nationalization of parties and party systems: An empirical measure and an application to the Americas', *Party Politics*, 9, 2, 139–66.

Jun, U. (1994), *Koalitionsbildungen in den deutschen Bundesländern: Theoretische Betrachtungen, Dokumentation und Analyse* (Opladen: Leske + Budrich).

Katz, R. S. (2001), 'The problem of candidate selection and the models of party democracy', *Party Politics*, 7, 3, 277–96.

Katz, R. S. and Mair, P. (1992), 'Introduction: The cross-national study of party organizations', in R. S. Katz and P. Mair, eds, *Party Organizations: A Data Handbook* (London: Sage), 1–20.

Katz, R. S. and Mair, P. (1993), 'The evolution of party organizations in Europe: The three faces of party organization', *American Review of Politics*, 14, 593–617.

Katz R. S. and Mair, P. (1995), 'Changing models of party organization and party democracy: The emergence of the cartel party', *Party Politics*, 1, 1, 5–28.

Keating, M. (1998), *The New Regionalism in Western Europe: Territorial Restructuring and Political Change* (Aldershot: Edward Elgar).

Keating, M. (2001a), *Plurinational Democracy: Stateless Nations in a Post-Sovereignty Era* (Oxford: Oxford University Press).

Keating, M. (2001b), *Nations against the State: The New Politics of Nationalism in Quebec, Catalonia and Scotland* (London: Palgrave, 2nd edition).

Keating, M. and Loughlin, J. (1997), 'Introduction', in M. Keating and J. Loughlin, eds, *The Political Economy of Regionalism* (London: Frank Cass), 1–13.

Keating, M., Loughlin, J. and Deschouwer, K. (2003), *Culture, Institutions and Economic Development: A study of Eight European Regions* (Cheltenham: Edward Elgar).

Kelemen, R. S. (2004), *The Rules of Federalism: Institutions and Regulatory Politics in the EU and Beyond* (Cambridge, MA: Harvard University Press).

Kelly, R. (2001), 'Farewell Conference, Hello Forum: The Making of Labour and Tory Policy', *The Political Quarterly*, 72, 3, 329–34.

Kiewiet, D. R. and McCubbins, M. D. (1991), *The Logic of Delegation: Congressional Parties and the Appropriations Process* (Chicago: University of Chicago Press).

Kircheimer, O. (1966), 'The transformation of the Western European party Systems', in J. Lapalombara and M. Weiner, eds, *Political Parties and Political Development* (Princeton, NJ: Princeton University Press), 177–200.

Klingemann, H. D., Volkens, A., Bara, J., McDonald, M. and Budge, I. (2006), *Mapping Policy Preferences II: Estimates for Parties, Electors and Governments: Eastern Europe, EU and OECD 1990–2003* (Oxford: Oxford University Press).

Kogan, Norman (1975). 'Impact of the new Italian regional governments on the structure of power within the parties', *Comparative Politics*, 7, 3, 383–406.

Koß, M. (2006), 'Federalism and intraparty integration: Vagueness, loose coupling, hypocrisy and fragmentation within the German Left Party and the Greens', paper presented at the ECPR Graduate Conference, September 2006, Essex.

Koß, M. and Hough, D. (2006), 'Landesparteien in vergleichender Perspektive: Die Linkspartei.PDS zwischen Regierungsverantwortung und Opposition', *Zeitschrift für Parlamentsfragen*, 37, 312–33.

König, T., Blume, T. and Luig, B. (2003), 'Policy change without government change? German gridlock after the 2002 election', *German Politics*, 12, 2, 86–146.

Kropp, S. and Sturm, R. (1999), 'Politische Willensbildung im Föderalismus: Parteienwettbewerb, Regierungsbildungen und Bundesratsverhalten in den Ländern', *Aus Politik und Zeitgeschichte*, B 13/1999, 37–46.

Krouwel, A. (2006), 'Party models', in R. S. Katz and W. Crotty, eds, *Handbook of Party Politics* (London: Sage), 249–69.

Laffin, M. and Shaw, E. (2007), 'British devolution and the Labour Party: How a national party adapts to devolution', *British Journal of Politics and International Relations*, 9, 1, 55–72.

Laffin, M., Shaw, E. and Taylor, G. (2007), 'The new sub-national politics of the British Labour Party', *Party Politics*, 13, 1, 88–108.

Lancaster, T. D. (1999), 'Complex self-identification and compounded representation in federal systems', in J. Brzinski, T. D. Lancaster and C. Tuschhoff, eds, *Compounded Representation in Western European Federations* (London: Frank Cass), 59–89.

Lees, C. (2000), *The Red-Green Coalition in Germany* (Manchester: MUP).

Legnante, G. (2005), 'The elections in the cities: Yet another defeat for the centre-right', in C. Guarnieri and J. Newell, eds, *Italian Politics: Quo Vadis?* (Oxford: Berghahn), 65–82.

Lehmbruch, G. (1976), *Parteienwettbewerb im Bundesstaat* (Opladen: Westdeutscher Verlag).

Lehmbruch, G. (2000), *Parteienwettbewerb im Bundesstaat: Regelsysteme und Spannungslagen im politischen System der Bundesrepublik Deutschland* (Wiesbaden: Westdeutscher Verlag, 3rd edition).

Leonardi, R. and Wertman, D. (1989), *Italian Christian Democracy: The Politics of Dominance* (London: Macmillan).

Leonardy, U. (2002), 'Parteien im Föderalismus der Bundesrepublik Deutschland: Scharniere zwischen Staat und Politik', *Zeitschrift für Parlamentsfragen*, 33, 180–95.

Leonardy, U. (2004), 'Federalism and parties in Germany: Organizational hinges between constitutional and political structures', in R. Hrbek, ed., *Political Parties and Federalism* (Baden-Baden: Nomos), 183–202.

Leton, A. and Miroir, A. (1999), *Les conflits Communautaires en Belgique* (Paris: Presses Universitaires de France).

Leunig, S. (2003), 'Öl' oder "Sand" im Getriebe?: Der Einfluss der Parteipolitik auf den Bundesrat als Veto-spieler im Gesetzgebungsprozess', *Zeitschrift für Parlamentsfragen*, 34, 778–91.

Libbrecht, L., Maddens, B., Fabre, E. and Swenden, W. (2006), 'Issue salience and regional party competition in Spain', paper presented at the ECPR Graduate Conference, panel 'Electoral and Governing Strategies in Multi-level Systems', University of Essex, 7–9 September 2006.

Lipset, S. M. and Rokkan, S., eds, (1967), *Party Systems and Voter Alignments* (New York: Free Press).

Llamazares, I. and Reinares, F. (1998), 'Elecciones autonómicas y sistema de partidos en La Rioja (1983–1995)', in M. Alcántara and A. Martínez, eds, *Las elecciones autonómicas en España 1980–1997* (Madrid: CIS), 309–24.

Llera Ramo, F. (1998), 'Pluralismo y gobernabilidad en Euskadi (1980–1994)', in M. Alcántara and A. Martínez, eds, *Las elecciones autonómicas en España 1980–1997* (Madrid: CIS), 413–43.

Lösche, P. (1994), *Kleine Geschichte der deutschen Parteien* (Stuttgart: Kohlhammer, 2nd edition).

Lösche, P. (1998), 'Kanzlerwahlverein? Zur Organisationskultur der CDU', in T. Dürr and R. Soldt, eds, *Die CDU nach Kohl* (Frankfurt: Fischer), 68–84.

Lösche, P. and Walter, F. (1992), *Die SPD: Klassenpartei – Volkspartei – Quotenpartei* (Darmstadt: Wissenschaftliche Buchgesellschaft).

Loughlin, J., ed., (2001), *Subnational Democracy in the European Union: Challenges and Opportunities* (Oxford: Oxford University Press).

López Alba, G. (2003), *El Relevo: Crónica Viva del Camino hacia el II Suresnes del PSOE* (Madrid: Taurus).

López Pintor, R. and Gratschew, M., eds, (2002), *Voter Turnout since 1945: A Global Report*, International Institute for Democracy and Electoral Assistance (IDEA).

Lundell, K. (2004), 'Determinants of candidate selection: The degree of centralization in comparative perspective', *Party Politics*, 10, 25–47.

Lupia, A. and McCubbins, M. D. (2000), 'Representation or abdication? How citizens use institutions to help delegation succeed', *European Journal of Political Research*, 37, 291–307.

Lutz Kern, H. and Hainmüller, J. (2006), 'Electoral balancing, divided government and 'midterm' loss in German elections', *Journal of Legislative Studies*, 12, 2, 127–49.

Lynch, P. (2004), 'Saving the Union: Conservatives and the "Celtic fringe"', *Political Quarterly*, 75, 4, 386–91.

Lynch, P. and Birrell, S. (2004), 'The autonomy and organisation of Scottish Labour', in G. Hassan, ed., *The Scottish Labour Party: History, Institutions and Ideas* (Edinburgh: Edinburgh University Press), 176–95.

Macdonald, S. E., Listhaug, O. and Rabinowitz, G. (1991), 'Issues and party support in multiparty systems', *American Political Science Review*, 85, 1107–31.

Macdonald, S. E. and Rabinowitz, G.(1993), 'Direction and uncertainty in a model of issue voting', *Journal of Theoretical Politics*, 5, 1, 61–87.

Mackay, F. (2003), 'Women and the 2003 elections: keeping up the momentum', *Scottish Affairs*, 44, 74–90.

Mackenstein, H. and Jeffery, C. (1999), 'Financial equalisation in the 1990s: On the road back to Karlsruhe?', in C. Jeffery, ed., *Recasting German Federalism: The Legacies of Unification* (London: Pinter), 155–76.

Maddens, B. (1994), 'Kiesgedrag en partijstrategie: De samenhang tussen de beleidsmatige profilering van de partijen en het kiesgedrag van de Vlamingen op 24 november 1991', PhD dissertation (Leuven: Afdeling Politologie Katholieke Universiteit Leuven).

Mainwaring, S. and Scully, T. (1995), *Building Democratic Institutions: Party Systems in Latin America* (Cambridge: Cambridge University Press).

Mair, P. (1997), *Party System Change* (Oxford: Oxford University Press).

Mannheimer, R. (1991), *La Lega Lombarda* (Milan: Feltrinelli).

Manow, P. and Burkhart, S. (2006), 'Kompromiss und Konflikt im parteipolitisierten Föderalismus der Bundesrepublik Deutschland', *Zeitschrift für Politikwissenschaft*, 11, 807–24.

Mares, A. (2006), 'Communautaire spanningen in een "moeilijk" kiesarrondissement: De wordingsgeschiedenis van de Rode Leeuwen of de Vlaamse BSP-federatie Brussel-Halle-Vilvoorde', *Brood en Rozen*, 2, 63–71.

Martens, W. (2006), *De Memoires:Luctor et Emergo* (Tielt: Lannoo).

Martín, E. (2003), 'Asturias', in O. Bartolomeus, ed., *La Competencia Política en la España de las Autonomías: El Eje Izquierda-Derecha en las Comunidades Autónomas* (Barcelona: ICPS), 79–93.

Martínez-Herrera, E. (2005), 'The effects of political decentralisation on support for political communities: A multivariate longitudinal and cross-sectional comparison of the Basque Country, Catalonia, Galicia, Quebec and Scotland', PhD dissertation (Florence: European University Institute).

Meguid, B. M. (2004), 'The critical role of non-proximal parties in electoral competition: Evidence from France', paper prepared at the 2004 Conference of Europeanists, Chicago.

Meguid, B. M. (2005), 'Competition between unequals: The role of mainstream party strategy in niche party success', *American Political Science Review*, 99, 3, 347–59.

Méndez Lago, M. (2000), *La Estrategia Organizativa del Partido Socialista Obrero Español (1975–1996)* (Madrid: Centro de Investigaciones Sociológicas).

Méndez-Lago, M. (2004), *Federalismo y Partidos Políticos: Los Casos de Canadá y España*, ICPS working paper nr.232 (Barcelona: ICPS).

Méndez Lago, M. (2005), 'The Socialist Party in government and in opposition', in S. Balfour, ed., *The Politics of Contemporary Spain* (London: Routledge), 169–97.

Méndez Lago, M. (2006), 'Turning the page: Crisis and transformation of the Spanish Socialist Party', *South European Society and Politics*, 11, 419–37.

Méndez Lago, M. (2007), *Turning the Page: Crisis and Transformation of the Spanish Socialist Party* (London: Routledge).

Mitchell, J. and Bradbury, J. (2004), 'Political recruitment and the 2003 Scottish and Welsh elections: Candidate selection, positive discrimination and party adaptation', *Representation*, 40, 289–302.

Molina, M. (2003), 'Cantabria', in O. Bartolomeus, ed., *La Competencia Política en la España de las Autonomías: El Eje Izquierda-Derecha en las Comunidades Autónomas* (Barcelona: ICPS), 129–42.

Montero, A. P. (2005), 'The politics of decentralization in a centralized party system', *Comparative Politics*, 38, 1, 63–82.

Mora, H. (2003), 'La Rioja', in O. Bartolomeus, ed., *La Competencia Política en la España de las Autonomías: El Eje Izquierda-Derecha en las Comunidades Autónomas* (Barcelona: ICPS), 315–32.

Moreno, L. (2001), *The Federalization of Spain* (London: Frank Cass).

Morlino, Leonardo (1996), 'Crisis of parties and change of the party system in Italy', *Party Politics*, 2, 5–30.

Müller, W. C. (2000), 'Political parties in parliamentary democracies: Making delegation and accountability work', *European Journal of Political Research*, 37, 309–33.

Nagel, K. (2006), 'North Rine Westphalia: The land election that dismissed a federal government', *Regional and Federal Studies*, 16, 3, 347–54.

Nassmacher, K. (1989), 'Structure and impact of public subsidies to political parties in Europe: The examples of Austria, Italy, Sweden and West Germany', in H. Alexander, ed., *Comparative Political Finance in the 1980s* (Cambridge: Cambridge University Press), 236–67.

Neu, V. (2007), 'Partei des demokratischen Sozialismus/Die Linke (PDS/Linke)', in F. Decker and V. Neu, eds, *Handbuch der deutschen Parteien* (Wiesbaden: VS Verlag für Sozialwissenschaften), 231–41.

Newell, James (2000), *Parties and Democracy in Italy* (Aldershot: Ashgate).

Niedermayer, O. (1998), 'German unification and party system change', in P. Pennings and J.-E. Lane, eds, *Comparing Party System Change* (London, Routledge), 127–50.

Niedermayer, O. (2001), 'Beweggründe des Engagements in politischen Parteien', in O. W. Gabriel, O. Niedermayer and R. Stöss, eds, *Parteiendemokratie in Deutschland* (Bonn: Bundeszentrale für politische Bildung, 2nd edition), 297–311.

Niedermayer, O. (2007), 'Parteimitgliedschaften im Jahre 2006', *Zeitschrift für Parlamentsfragen*, 38, 368–75.

Niklauß, K. (1998), *Der Weg zum Grundgesetz: Demokratiegründung in Westdeutschland 1945–1949* (Paderborn: Schönig).

Norris, P. and Lovenduski, J. (1995), *Political Recruitment* (Cambridge: Cambridge University Press).

Nothomb, C.-F. (1987), *De Waarheid mag gezegd worden* (Brussels: Elsevier).

Oberndörfer, D. and Schmitt, K., eds, (1991), *Parteien und regionale politische Traditionen in Deutschland* (Berlin: Duncker & Humblot).

Ocaña, F. A. and Oñate, P. (2000), 'Las elecciones autonómicas de 1999 y las Españas electorales', *Revista Española de Investigaciones Sociológicas*, 90, 183–228.

Ohmae, K. (1995), *The End of the Nation State: The Rise of Regional Economies* (New York: Free Press).

Orte, A. (2006), 'Sobre la autonomía federal del PSC', *La Vanguardia*, 25 September 2006.

Orte, A. and Wilson, A. (2008), 'Reforming the Spanish "State of Autonomies": Coalition politics and the multi-level dynamics of institutional change', paper presented at the PSA British and Comparative Territorial Politics Conference, Edinburgh, 10–11 January 2008.

Padgett, S. (1994), 'The German Social Democratic Party: Between old and new left', in D. S. Bell and E. Shaw, eds, *Conflict and Cohesion in Western European Social Democratic Parties* (London: Sage), 10–30.

Palermo, F. (2005), 'Italy's long devolutionary path towards federalism', in S. Ortino, M. agar and V. Mastny, eds, *The Changing Faces of Federalism: Institutional Reconfiguration in Europe from East to West* (Manchester: Manchester University Press), 182–201.

Pallarés, F. (1994), 'Las elecciones autonómicas en España : 1980–1992', in P. del Castillo, ed., *Comportamiento político y electoral* (Madrid: CIS), 151–220.

Pallarés, F. and Keating, M. (2003), 'Multi-Level electoral competition: Regional elections and party systems in Spain', *European Urban and Regional Studies*, 10, 3, 239–55.

Pallarés, F. and Keating, M. (2006), 'Multi-level electoral competition: Sub-state elections and party systems in Spain', in D. Hough and C. Jeffery, eds, *Devolution and Electoral Politics* (Manchester: Manchester University Press).

Pallarés, F., Montero, J. R. and Llera, F. J. (1997), 'Non statewide parties in Spain: An attitudinal study of nationalism and regionalism', *Publius: The Journal of Federalism*, 27, 4, 135–69.

Panebianco, A. (1984), 'I partiti', in ISAP, *Le Relazioni Centro-Perifera* (Milan: Giuffrè), 109–36.

Panebianco, A. (1988), *Political Parties: Organization and Power* (Cambridge: Cambridge University Press).

Pappalardo, A. (2001), 'Il sistem partitico italiano fra bipolarismo e destrutturazione', *Rivista Italiana di Scienza Politica*, 31, 561–600.

Pappi, F., Becker, A. and Herzog, A. (2005), 'Regierungsbildung in Mehrebenensystemen: Zur Erklärung der Koalitionsbildung in den deutschen Bundesländern', *Politische Vierteljahresschrift*, 432–58.

Parti Ouvrier Belge (1926), *Rapports présentés au XXXVIIe congrès annuel* (Brussels: l'Eglantine).

Pasquino, G. (1986), 'Modernity and reform: The PSI between political entrepreneurs and gamblers', *West European Politics*, 6, 118–41.

Pedersen, M. (1979), 'The dynamics of European party systems: Changing patterns of electoral volatility', *European Journal of Political Research*, 7, 1, 1–26.

Peele, G. (1998), 'Towards new Conservatives? Organisational reform and the Conservative Party', *Political Quarterly*, 69, 141–7.

Perrigo, S (1996), 'Women and change in the Labour Party', in J. Lovenduski and P. Norris, eds, *Women in Politics* (Oxford: Oxford University Press), 116–29.

Peters, B. G. and Pierre, J. (2005), *Governing Complex Societies: Trajectories and Scenarios* (Basingstoke: Palgrave Macmillan).

Petrocik, J. (1990), '*The theory of issue ownership: Issues, agendas, and electoral coalitions in the 1988 election*', unpublished paper (University of California, Los Angeles).

Petrocik, J. (1996), 'Issue ownership in presidential elections, with a 1980 case study', *American Journal of Political Science*, 40, 825–40.

Pierre, J., Svåsand, L. and Widfeldt, A. (2000), 'State subsidies to political parties: Confronting rhetoric with reality', *West European Politics*, 23, 1–24.

Pierson, P. (2004), *History, Institutions, and Social Analysis* (Princeton/Oxford: Princeton University Press).

Platel, M. (1979), *De prinsen van Stuyvenberg: Historische beslissing of vergissing?* (Leuven: Davidsfonds).

Poggi, G., ed., (1968), *L'organizzazione Partitica del PCI e la DC* (Bologna: Il Mulino).

Pogorelis, R., Maddens, B., Swenden, W. and Fabre, E. (2005), 'Issue salience in regional and national party manifestos in the UK', *West European Politics*, 28, 5, 992–1014.

Poguntke, T. (1994), 'Parties in a legalistic culture: The case of Germany', in R. S. Katz and P. Mair, eds, *How Parties Organize: Change and Adaptation in Party Organizations in Western Democracies* (London: Sage), 185–215.

Poguntke, T. (2001), 'Parteiorganisationen in der Bundesrepublik Deutschland: Einheit in der Vielfalt', in O. W. Gabriel, O. Niedermayer and R. Stöss, eds, *Parteiendemokratie in Deutschland* (Bonn: Bundeszentrale für politische Bildung, 2nd edition), 253–67.

Poguntke, T. and Boll, B. (1992), 'Germany', in R. S. Katz and P. Mair, eds, *Party Organizations: A Data Handbook on Party Organizations in Western Democracies, 1960–90* (London: Sage), 317–88.

Porter, M. E. (1998), *The Competitive Advantage of Nations* (New York: The Free Press, 2nd edition).

Prevenier, W. (1989), 'De taalkundige splitsing (1968–1979)', in A. Verhulst and H. Hasquin, eds, *Het liberalisme in België: Tweehonderd jaar geschiedenis* (Brussels: Delta), pp. 341–52.

Prevenier, W. and Pareyn, L. (1989), 'De oprichting van de PVV/PLP en haar gevolgen (1958–1969)', in A. Verhulst and H. Hasquin, eds, *Het liberalisme in België. Tweehonderd jaar geschiedenis* (Brussels: Delta), pp. 331–40.

Probst, L. (2007), 'Bündnis 90/Die Grünen (Grüne)', in F. Decker and V. Neu, eds, *Handbuch der deutschen Parteien* (Wiesbaden: VS Verlag für Sozialwissenschaften), 173–88.

Putnam, R. (1993), *Making Democracy Work: Civic Traditions in Modern Italy* (Princeton: Princeton University Press).

Rabinowitz, G. and Macdonald, S. E. (1989), 'A directional theory of issue voting', *American Political Science Review*, 83, 1, 93–121.

Rahat, G. and Hazan, R. (2001), 'Candidate Selection Methods: An Analytical Framework', *Party Politics*, 7, 3, 297–322.

Ramiro, L. (2003), *Cambio y Adaptación en la Izquierda: La Evolución del Partido Comunista de España y de Izquierda Unida (1986–2000)* (Madrid: Centro de Investigaciones Sociológicas).

Ramiro, L. and Pérez Nievas, S. (2005), 'El impacto de los procesos de descentralización territorial en la organización de los partidos políticos: el caso del Izquierda Unida', paper presented at the VII Congreso, Asociación Española de Ciencia Política y de la Administración, Barcelona.

Ramos-Rollón, L. (1998), 'Análisis de las elecciones autonómicas en Cantabria: el difícil proceso de creación de una autonomía', in M. Alcántara and A. Martínez, eds, *Las Eelecciones Aautonómicas en España 1980–1997* (Madrid: CIS), 151–77.

Rawnsley, A. (2000), *Servants of the People* (London: Hamish Hamilton).

Reif, K. (1984), 'National electoral cycles and European elections', *Electoral Studies*, 3, 3, 244–55.

Reif, K. and Schmitt, H. (1980), 'Nine Second-Order National Elections: A Conceptual Framework for the Analysis of European Election Results', *European Journal of Political Research*, 8, 3–44.

Reniu, J. M. (2002), 'What are they looking for? Why Spanish political parties do not coalition at national level (1977–1996)', paper presented at the ECPR Joint Sessions, Torino.

Renzsch, W. (1991), *Finanzverfassung und Finanzausgleich* (Bonn: Dietz).

Renzsch, W. (1998), 'Parteien im Bundesstaat: Sand oder Öl im Getriebe?', in U. Männle, ed., *Föderalismus zwischen Konsens und Konkurrenz* (Baden-Baden: Nomos), 93–100.

Renzsch, W. (1999), 'Party competition in the German federal state: Variations on an old theme', *Regional and Federal Studies*, 9, 3, 180–92.

Renzsch, W. (2000), 'Bundesstaat oder Parteienstaat: Überlegungen zu Entscheidungsprozessen im Spannungsfeld von föderaler Konsensbildung und parlamentarischem Wettbewerb', in E. Holtmann and H. Voelzkow, eds, *Zwischen Wettbewerbs- und Verhandlungsdemokratie: Analysen zum Regierungssystem der Bundesrepublik Deutschland* (Wiesbaden: Westdeutscher Verlag), 53–78.

Renzsch, W. (2004), 'Bifurcated and integrated parties in parliamentary federations: The Canadian and German cases', in R. Hrbek, ed., *Political Parties and Federalism* (Baden-Baden: Nomos), 11–38.

Reutter, W. (2006), 'The transfer of power hypothesis and the German Länder: In need of modification', *Publius: The Journal of Federalism*, 36, 2, 277–301.

Riker, W. H. (1975), 'Federalism', in F. I. Greenstein and N. W. Polsby, eds, *Handbook of Political Science, Volume 5: Governmental Institutions and Processes* (Reading, MA: Addison-Wesley), 93–173.

Roberts, G. K. (1989), 'Party system change in West Germany: Land-federal linkages', *West European Politics*, 13, 4, 98–113.

Roberts, G. (2006), *German Electoral Politics* (Manchester: Manchester University Press).

Robertson, D. (1976), *A Theory of Party Competition* (New York: Wiley).

Rodden, J. (2004), 'Comparative federalism and decentralization: On meaning and measurement', *Comparative Politics*, 36, 4, 481–500.

Roller, E. (2002), 'Reforming the Spanish Senate: Mission Impossible?', *West European Politics*, 25, 4, 69–93.

Roller, E. and van Houten, P. (2003), 'A national party in a regional party system: The PSC-PSOE in Catalonia', *Regional and Federal Studies*, 13, 3, 1–21.

Rose, R. and Urwin, D. (1975), *Regional Differentiation and Political Unity in Western Nations* (London: Sage).

Russel, M. and Lodge, G. (2006), 'The Government of England by Westminster', in R. Hazell, ed., *The English Question* (Manchester: Manchester University Press), 64–95.

Saalfeld, T. (2003), 'The German party system – Continuity and change', *German Politics*, 1, 99–130.

Sally, R. and Webber, D. (1994), 'The German Solidarity Pact: A case study in the politics of the unified Germany', *German Politics* 3, 1, 18–46.

Sarcinelli, U. and Schatz, H., eds, (2000), *Mediendemokratie im Medienland – Inszenierungen und Themensetzungsstratgien im Spannungsfeld von Medien und Parteieliten am Beispiel der nordrhein-westfälischen Landtagswahl 2000* (Opladen: Leske + Burdrich).

Sartori, G. (1976), *Parties and Party Systems: A Framework for Analysis. Vol. 1* (Cambridge: Cambridge University Press).

Sartori, G. (2005), *Parties and Party Systems: A Framework for Analysis* (Colchester: ECPR Press).

Sawer, G. (1976), *Modern Federalism* (Sydney, NSW: Pitnam Australia, 2nd edition).

Scarrow, S. E. (1999), 'Parties and the expansion of direct democracy: Who benefits?', *Party Politics*, 5, 341–62.

Scarrow, S. E. (2002), 'Party decline in the parties state? The changing environment of German politics', in P. Webb, D. Farrell and I. Holliday, eds, *Political Parties in Advanced Industrial Democracies* (Oxford: Oxford University Press), 77–106.

Scarrow, S., Webb, P. and Farrell, D. (2000), 'From social integration to electoral contestation', in R. Dalton and M. Wattenberg, eds, *Parties Without Partisans* (Oxford: Oxford University Press), 129–53.

Scharpf, F. (1995), 'Federal arrangements and multi-party systems', *Australian Journal of Political Science*, 30, 27–39.

Scharpf, F. W. (2005), 'No exit from the joint decision trap? Can German federalism reform itself? *EUI Working Papers* 24.

Scharpf, F. W., Reissert, B. and Schnabel, F. (1976), *Politikverflechtung: Theorie und Empirie des kooperativen Föderalismus in der Bundesrepublik* (Kronberg: Scriptor).

Schmid, J. (1990), *Die CDU: Organisationsstrukturen, Politiken und Funktionsweisen einer Partei im Föderalismus* (Opladen: Leske + Budrich).

Schmidt, M. G. (1985), 'Allerweltsparteien in Westeuropa? Ein Beitrag zu Kirchheimers These vom Wandel des westeuropäischen Parteiensystems', *Leviathan*, 13, 376–97.

Schmidt, M. G. (2001), 'Parteien und Staatstätigkeit', in O. W. Gabriel, O. Niedermayer and R. Stöss, eds, *Parteiendemokratie in Deutschland* (Bonn: Bundeszentrale für politische Bildung, 2nd edition), 537–58.

Schmidt, M. G. (2002), 'Germany: The Grand Coalition state', in J. M. Colomer, ed., *Political Institutions in Europe* (London: Routledge, 2nd edition), 57–93.

Schmitt, H. and Wüst, A. M. (2006), 'The extraordinary Bundestag election of 2005: The interplay of long-term trends and short-term factors', in E. Langenbacher ed. *Launching the Grand Coalition: The 2005 Bundestag Elections and the Future of German Politics* (New York, Oxford: Berghahn Books), 29–48.

Schneider, H. (2001), 'Parteien in der Landespolitik', in O. W. Gabriel, O. Niedermayer and R. Stöss, eds, *Parteiendemokratie in Deutschland* (Bonn: Bundeszentrale für politische Bildung, 2nd edition), 385–405.

Schönbohm, W. (1985), *Die CDU wird moderne Volkspartei: Selbstverständnis, Mitglieder, Organisation und Apparat 1950–1980* (Stuttgart: Kohlhammer).

Schüttemeyer, S. (1999), 'Fraktionen und ihre Parteien in der Bundesrepublik Deutschland: Veränderte Beziehungen im Zeichen professioneller Politik', in L. Helms, ed., *Parteien und Fraktionen: Ein internationaler Vergleich* (Opladen: Leske + Budrich), 39–66.

Schultze, R.-O. (1999), 'Föderalismusreform in Deutschland: Widersprüche, Ansätze, Hoffnungen', *Zeitschrift für Politik*, 46, 173–94.

Schweiger, C. (2007), 'Intrinsic instability in the semi-sovereign state: The lessons from the Merkel grand coalition government', paper presented at the PSA Annual Conference.

Seawright, D. (2004), '"The Scottish Conservative and Unionist Party: The lesser spotted Tory?"', *POLIS Working Paper No.13*, School of Politics and International Studies, University of Leeds.

Seyd, P. (1999), 'New parties/new politics? A case-study of the British Labour Party', *Party Politics*, 5, 3, 383–405.

Seyd, P. and Whiteley, P. (2001), 'New Labour and the party: Members and organization', in S. Ludlam and M. J. Smith, eds, *New Labour in Government* (Basingstoke: Macmillan), 73–91.

Shaw, E. (1996), *The Labour Party Since 1945* (Oxford: Blackwell).

Shaw, E. (2001), 'New Labour: New pathways to Parliament', *Parliamentary Affairs*, 54, 35–53.

Smiley, D. V. and Watts, R. L. (1985), *Intra-State Federalism in Canada* (Toronto: University of Toronto Press).

Smolicz, J. J. (1981), 'Core values and cultural identity', *Ethnic and Racial Studies*, 4, 1, 75–90.

Smolicz, J. J. (1988), 'Tradition, core values and intercultural development in plural societies', *Ethnic and Racial Studies*, 11, 387–410.

Soler Llebaria, J. (1998), 'Las elecciones autonómicas en Cataluña (1980–1995)', M. Alcántara and A. Martínez, eds, *Las Elecciones Autonómicas en España 1980–1997* (Madrid: CIS), 225–56.

Soriano, E. (2003), 'Canarias', in O. Bartolomeus, ed., *La Competencia Política en la España de las Autonomías: El Eje Izquierda-Derecha en las Comunidades Autónomas* (Barcelona: ICPS), 111–28.

Soyke, C. (2006), *Professionelle Personen-Kampagnen als moderne Wahlkampfstrategie: Eine empirische Untersuchung der SPD-Landtagswahl-Kampagnen in Brandenburg 2004 und Nordrhein-Westfalen 2005* (Siegen: Schriftenreihe des Faches Politikwissenschaft der Universität Siegen).

Stanyer, J. (2001), *The Creation of Political News: Television and British Party Conferences* (Brighton: Sussex Academic Press).

Ştefuriuc, I. (2009), 'Government formation in multi-level settings: Spanish regional coalitions and the quest for vertical congruence', *Party Politics*, 15, 1.

Stolz, K. (2003), 'Moving up, moving down: Political careers across territorial levels', *European Journal of Political Research*, 42, 223–48.

Strohmeier, G. (2004), 'Der Bundesrat: Vertretung der Länder oder Instrument der Parteien?', *Zeitschrift für Parlamentsfragen* 35: 717–31.

Strøm, K. (1990), 'A behavioral theory of competitive political parties', *American Journal of Political Science*, 34, 565–98.

Sturm, R. (1999), 'Party competition and the federal system: The Lehmbruch hypothesis revisited', in C. Jeffery, ed., *Recasting German Federalism: The Legacies of Unification* (London: Pinter), 197–216.

Sturm, R. (2001), *Föderalismus in Deutschland* (Opladen: Leske + Budrich).

Sturm, R. and Zimmermann-Steinhart, P. (2005), *Föderalismus: Eine Einführung* (Baden-Baden: Nomos).

Swenden, W. (2002), 'Asymmetric federalism and coalition-making in Belgium', *Publius: The Journal of Federalism*, 32, 2, 67–87.

Swenden, W. (2004), *Federalism and Second Chambers: Regional Representation in Parliamentary Federations* (Brussels: Peter Lang).

Swenden, W. (2006), *Federalism and Regionalism in Western Europe: A Comparative and Thematic Analysis* (Basingstoke: Palgrave Macmillan).

Swenden, W. and Jans, M. T. (2006), 'Will it stay or will it go? Federalism and the sustainability of Belgium', *West European Politics*, 5, 877–94.

Ştefuriuc, I. and Deschouwer, K. (2007), 'Political representation in culture-based federations: Containing and reinforcing regional identities in Belgium and Spain', paper presented at the ECPR Joint Sessions of Workshops, Helsinki.

Tarrow, S. (1977), *Between Center and Periphery: Grassroots Politicians in Italy and France* (New Haven: Yale University Press).

Thorlakson, L. (2001), 'Federalism and party organisational adaptation: A cross-national comparison', paper prepared for ECPR Joint Sessions of Workshops, Grenoble, 6–11 April 2001.

Thorlakson, L. (2006), 'Party systems in multi-level contexts', in D. Hough and C. Jeffery, eds, *Devolution and Electoral Politics* (Manchester: Manchester University Press), 37–52.

Thorlakson, L. (2007), 'An Institutional Explanation of Party System Congruence: Evidence from Six Federations', *European Journal of Political Research*, 46, 1, 69–95.

Thorlakson, L. (2009), 'Patterns of party integration, influence and autonomy in seven federations', *Party Politics*, 5, 1.

Trench, A., ed., (2004), *The State of the Nations: Has Devolution Made a Difference?* (London: Imprint Academic).

Trystan, D., Scully, R. and Wyn Jones, R. (2003), 'Explaining the "quiet earthquake": Voting behaviour in the first election to the National Assembly for Wales', *Electoral Studies*, 22, 635–50.

Tufte, E. R. (1975), 'Determinants of the outcomes of midterm congressional elections', *American Political Science Review*, 69, 3, 812–26.

Urwin, D. (1982), 'The United Kingdom', in S. Rokkan and D. Urwin, eds, *The Politics of Territorial Identity* (London: Sage).

van Biezen, I. (2003), *Political Parties in New Democracies: Party Organization in Southern and East-Central Europe* (London: Palgrave Macmillan).

van Biezen, I. and Hopkin, J. (2006), 'Party organization in multi-level contexts', in D. Hough, and C. Jeffery, eds, *Devolution and Electoral Politics* (Manchester: Manchester University Press), 14–36.

van der Eijk, C., Franklin M. and Marsh M. (1996), 'What voters tell us about Europe-wide Elections; What Europe-wide Elections teach us about voters', *Electoral Studies*, 15, 2, 149–66.

van Houten, P. (2009), 'Multi-level relations in political parties: A delegation approach', *Party Politics*, 15, 1.

Vandelli, L. (2002), *Devolution e Altre Storie* (Bologna: Il Mulino).

Vassallo, S. (2005), 'Electoral linkage, party discipline, coalitions' range, and policy stability in Italian regions: A preliminary exercise in measurement', paper presented to ECPR Joint Sessions, Granada.

Vintró, J. and Padrós, X. (2007), *El Estatuto de Autonomía de Cataluña de 2006: Rasgos Generales* (Barcelona: Instituto de Derecho Publico).

Volkens, A. (1992), 'Content analysis of party programmes in comparative perspective: Handbook of coding instructions' (Berlin: WZB).

Volkens, A. (2001), 'Manifesto research since 1979: From reliability to validity', in M. Laver, ed., *Estimating Policy Positions of Political Actors* (London: Routledge), 33–49.

von Beyme, K. (2000), *Parteien im Wandel: Von den Volksparteien zu den professionalisierten Wählerparteien* (Wiesbaden: Westdeutscher Verlag).

Vorländer, H. (2007), 'Freie Demokratische Partei (FDP)', in F. Decker and V. Neu, eds, *Handbuch der deutschen Parteien* (Wiesbaden: VS Verlag für Sozialwissenschaften), 276–88.

Wachendorfer-Schmidt, U. (2003), *Politikverflechtung im vereinigten Deutschland* (Wiesbaden: Westdeutscher Verlag).

Ware, A. (1996), *Political Parties and Party Systems* (Oxford: Oxford University Press).

Watts, R. L. (1999), *Comparing Federal Systems in the 1990s* (Montreal: McGill-Queen's University Press).

Wauters, B. (2005), 'Divisions within an ethno-regional party: The *Volksunie* in Belgium', *Regional and Federal Studies*, 15, 3, 329–52.

Webb, P. (2000), *The Modern British Party System* (London: Sage).

Weekers, K., Maddens, B., Vanlangenakker, I. and Fiers, S. (2007), 'Het Profiel van de Kandidaten op de Lijsten voor de Federale Verkiezingen van 10 juni 2007' (Leuven, unpublished research paper).

Weßels, B. (2000) 'Gruppenbindungen und Wahlverhalten: 50 Jahre Wahlen in der Bundesrepublik', in M. Klein, W. Jagodzinski, E. Mochmann and D. Ohr, eds, *50 Jahre Empirische Wahlforschung in Deutschland* (Opladen: Westdeutscher Verlag), 129–55.

Wiesendahl, E. (2001), 'Die Zukunft der Parteien', in O. W. Gabriel, O. Niedermayer and R. Stöss, eds, *Parteiendemokratie in Deutschland* (Bonn: Bundeszentrale für politische Bildung, 2nd edition), 592–619.

Witte, E., Craeybeckx, J. and Meynen, A. (2000), *Political History of Belgium from 1830 onwards* (Brussels: VUB University Press).

Witte, E. and Van Velthoven, H. (1998), *Taal en Politiek: De Belgische Casus in een Historisch Perspectief* (Brussels: VUB Press).

Wyn Jones, R. and Scully, R. (2006), 'Devolution and electoral politics in Wales', in D. Hough and C. Jeffery, eds, *Devolution and Electoral Politics* (Manchester: Manchester University Press), 176–91.

Ziblatt, D. (2006), *Structuring the State: The Formation of Italy and Germany and the Puzzle of Federalism* (Princeton: Princeton University Press).

Zohlnhöfer, R. (2003), 'Partisan politics, party competition and veto players: German economic policy in the Kohl era', *Journal of Public Policy*, 23, 2, 123–56.

Zuckerman, A. (1979), *The Politics of Faction: Christian Democratic Rule in Italy* (New Haven: Yale University Press).

Party Documents or Speeches

Canavan, D. (1999), Speech at Lesser Town Hall, Falkirk, 22/1/1999.

Labour Party (2001), *Procedures for Selection of Members of the Scottish Parliament and National Assembly for Wales*, National Executive Committee, Organisation Committee Paper, DO/03/1101, 27/11/2001.

Scottish Conservatives (1998), *Made in Scotland*, Edinburgh: Scottish Conservatives.

Scottish Liberal Democrats (1995), *The Final Steps: Towards the Completion of the Scottish Constitutional Convention's scheme for a Scottish Parliament*.

Wales Labour Party (2002), *Ensuring the level of women's representation for Labour in the National Assembly for Wales*, Cardiff, Labour Party Executive.

Party Statutes of Partido Popular.

Newspaper sources

El País, 23/01/2006.

El País, 20/07/2007.

The Herald (1998) 21/12/1998.

The Herald (1999) 26/1/1999.

No author – *L'évolution récente des structures du CVP-PSC*. (CH 484). (Brussels: CRISP, 1970).

Web-sources

Forschungsgruppe Wahlen http://www.forschungsgruppe.de/Studien/Wahlanalysen/

UK Electoral Commission http://www.electoralcommission.org.uk/

Index